Mastering Clip Studio Paint

Discover advanced CSP techniques to create breathtaking
illustrations quickly and easily

Bruna Belfort

‹packt›

Mastering Clip Studio Paint

Portfolio Director: Pavan Ramchandani
Relationship Lead: Tejashwini R
Project Manager: Divij Kotian
Content Engineer: Nathanya Dias
Technical Editor: Vidhisha Patidar
Copy Editor: Safis Editing
Proofreader: Nathanya Dias
Indexer: Tejal Soni
Production Designer: Ponraj Dhandapani
Growth Lead: Nivedita Singh

First published: May 2025

Production reference: 3051125

Published by Packt Publishing Ltd.
Grosvenor House
11 St Paul's Square
Birmingham
B3 1RB, UK.

ISBN 978-1-80512-403-0

www.packtpub.com

To my mother, Mary Anne, and to the memory of my father, Aliomar. Thank you for your love, your sacrifices, and the quiet strength that taught me to keep going.

– Bruna Belfort

Contributors

About the author

Bruna Belfort is a digital artist who specializes in character-focused and story-driven illustrations, with over 15 years of experience in digital media. Since 2021, she has worked with book publishers, comic editors, and independent writers to make covers, interior pages, character design, and character spotlight art. Bruna focuses on the use of light and color to tell stories, change the mood of a scene, and touch the audience's heart. Her art can be found on Instagram at *@brunabelfortartist*.

Writing this book turned out to be one of the most fulfilling challenges I've ever taken on. It was far from easy, but the growth, discovery, and support I experienced made it all worthwhile. I couldn't have done it without the incredible people who stood by me.

I'm thankful to my mom, Mary Anne, and my sister, Deborah, for supporting me in my artistic journey and frequently asking "How's the book going?". I know an art career doesn't always make sense to you, and that makes me even more grateful for your support.

To my partner, Hugo. I can't fully express how grateful I am for your constant love and encouragement. You believe in me more than I do and there's nothing in the world I would trade for that.

To Juli, my best friend. Thank you for dealing with my insanity for over two decades! Our conversations always help me see the world from a new perspective.

Thank you to my dear friends who helped me laugh even when things were tough. I can't name everyone here (what if I forget someone?), but when you read this, you know it's you!

I would also like to express my appreciation to the entire team at Packt Publishing—especially my editor, Nathanya—for their guidance, patience, and dedication. This book would not exist without your assistance.

And finally, to you, dear reader—thank you for picking up this book and bringing it to life with your curiosity and creativity. I'm so glad you're here!

About the reviewer

Shauna Hadinger is a 35-year-old full-time forgery investigator who spends her free time as an online hobby artist posting under the name *@postingmyartxo* on Instagram. She has been working on her art for several years and has read many art enhancement training books. This was her first-ever book review.

Table of Contents

Preface   xv

Free Benefits with Your Book   xix

Part 1: Workflow Optimization

1

Customizing Your Workspace for Efficiency   3

Understanding the basics of workspace configuration	3	Layer-related palettes	11
		Other palettes	12
Main canvas area	4	Configuring the Command Bar	12
Tool-related palettes	5	Tailoring the Tool Property palette	15
Color-related palettes	7	Configuring my workspace	18
Command Bar	8	Summary	23
Navigator and other reference palettes	9		

2

Streamlining Your Workflow with Shortcuts and Actions   25

Creating personalized shortcuts	25	Using and modifying auto actions	33
Changing a tool temporarily with modifier keys	28	Creating your own auto actions	35
		Downloading pre-made auto actions	37
Getting the most out of auto actions	31	Summary	37

3

Setting Up Materials for Consistency and Speed   39

Navigating the Material palette	40	Setting up templates	55
Creating Image materials	43	Registering other types of materials	57
Making your own patterns	47	Downloading and uploading materials in CLIP STUDIO ASSETS	58
Creating seamless patterns	48		
Applying patterns efficiently	52	Summary	60

4

Organizing Your Projects Effectively   61

Organizing your layers efficiently	61	Streamlining your workflow with best practices	69
Naming your layers	62		
Color-coding your layers	63	Maintain a consistent file structure	69
Grouping layers	64	Use clear naming conventions for files	70
		Save and back up your work	70
Non-destructive editing for a stress-free process	66	Review and reflect on your workflow	72
		Summary	73

Part 2: Fine-Tuning Your Drawings

5

Unlocking the Full Potential of Brush Settings   77

Understanding brush dynamics	77	Mastering brush properties for complete customization	86
Pen pressure	78		
Tilt	81	Brush Size	87
Velocity	82	Ink	88
Random	82	Color Jitter	92
Angle Dynamics	83	Anti-aliasing	94
Direction of particle Dynamics	84	Brush shape	95
		Dual brush (2 - Brush shape)	103
		Watercolor edge	107

Erase   108

Correction   109

Starting and ending   111

Anti-overflow   113

Creating custom brushes   **115**

Summary   **119**

6

Enhancing Your Lines with Vector Layers   121

**Understanding what vector layers are
and how to create them**   **121**

Creating vector layers from scratch   122

Importing SVG files from other software   123

Converting raster layers into vector   124

Editing and transforming vector lines 125

Transforming vector lines with the Object sub
tool   126

Editing vector lines with the Correct line tool   129

Erasing vector lines   **136**

Summary   **138**

7

Utilizing Rulers and Guides for Precision   139

Understanding guides in CSP   **139**

The Ruler bar   140

Guide lines   142

The Grid tool   142

The Ruler tool   144

Using Linear, Curve, and Figure rulers 147

The Linear ruler   147

The Curve ruler   148

The Figure ruler   150

**Making the most out of the Ruler pen
and the Special ruler**   **152**

The Ruler pen   152

The Special ruler   153

**Applying a Perspective ruler for
dynamic images**   **155**

Using the Perspective ruler for 1-, 2-, and
3-point perspectives   157

Understanding the parts of a Perspective ruler   158

Using the Perspective ruler in practice   162

**Optimizing your use of the
Symmetrical ruler**   **164**

Summary   **165**

Part 3: Time-Saving Painting Techniques

8

Maximizing Efficiency and Organization with Layers   169

Navigating the Layer palette	**170**	Layer color	189
The Layer palette's menu	171	Expression color	190
The Layer palette's property bar	172	Display decrease color	191
The Layer palette's command bar	175	Mask expression	192
The layer list	177	Tool navigation	192
		Overlay texture	193
Customizing your layers with the Layer Property palette	**179**	Color mode	193
Border effect	181	**Optimizing your layers with pro techniques**	**194**
Extract lines (EX only)	183	**Summary**	**196**
Tone	186		

9

Mastering Layer Blending Modes for Stunning Colors   197

Understanding blending modes	**198**	Add (Glow)	211
Enhancing shadows	**201**	Divide	212
Darken	202	Lighter color	213
Multiply	203	**Refining contrast, hue, saturation, and color**	**215**
Color burn	204		
Linear burn	204	Overlay	215
Subtract	205	Soft light	216
Darker color	206	Hard light	216
		Difference	217
Illuminating your artwork	**208**	Vivid light	218
Lighten	208	Linear light	219
Screen	208	Pin light	220
Color dodge	209	Hard mix	221
Glow dodge	210	Exclusion	222
Add	211		

Hue	223	Applying blending modes to a real painting	227
Saturation	224	Summary	233
Color	224		
Brightness	225		

10

Perfecting Your Selections   235

Using the Selection area tool like a pro	235	Using Quick Masks and Selection Layers	247
The Rectangle and Ellipse sub tools	236	Quick Mask	248
The Lasso sub tool	238	Selection Layer	249
The Magnetic lasso sub tool	240		
The Polyline sub tool	241	Optimizing your use of the selection tools	252
The Selection pen and the Erase selection sub tools	242	Practical uses of selections	255
The Shrink selection sub tool	243		
Mastering the Auto select tool	244	Summary	256

11

Applying Color Quickly with Pro Techniques   257

Using the Lasso fill sub tool for quick color blocks	258	Color Match	266
		Gradient maps	270
Mastering the Fill tool for fast painting	260	Saving color sets for quick access to frequently used colors	273
Applying Color Match and Gradient Maps for quick experimentation	266	Summary	276

12

Enhancing Your Art with Post-Processing Adjustments   277

Utilizing correction layers for final touches	278	Posterization	282
		Reverse Gradient	283
Brightness/Contrast	279	Level Correction	284
Hue/Saturation/Luminosity	280	Tone Curve	286

Color balance   288
Binarization   291
Gradient map   292

**Exploring filters for creative
enhancements   292**
Blur filters   292
Correction filters   296
Distort filters   297
Effect filters   299

The Render filter   302
Sharpen filters   302

**Maximizing the Liquify and
the Puppet warp tools for quick
structural changes   303**
Liquify   303
Puppet warp transformation   307

Summary   308

Part 4: Leveraging 3D Models and Materials

13

Manipulating 3D Objects on the Canvas   313

**Introducing 3D materials onto your
canvas   313**
**Mastering 3D manipulators for
precise adjustments   321**
Movement Manipulator   321
Object Launcher   326

Root Manipulator   329

**Modifying the camera angle of a 3D
scene   334**
**Maximizing the 3D material
hierarchy for easier manipulation   339**
Summary   342

14

Altering and Posing 3D Figures   343

**Changing the proportions of your 3D
figure   343**
Altering the 3D body shape   344
Modifying a 3D head   350

Posing your 3D figure   356
Importing 3D poses into CSP   357
Setting up poses with Posemaniacs   357

Using Pose Scanner   359
Modifying 3D character poses   361

Posing 3D hands   370
Summary   374

15

Illuminating Your Artwork with 3D Lighting and Shading Assist   375

Setting up light in 3D space   375
Changing the main light source of a 3D scene   376
Adding ambient light and a secondary light source   379

Using Shading Assist for quick light experiments   382
Summary   389

16

Creating 3D Backgrounds   391

Crafting background representations with primitive shapes   391
Modifying a 3D Primitive's shape   392
Altering the color and texture of a 3D Primitive   394
The Billboard primitive   397

Making complex backgrounds with multiple 3D objects   399
Using 3D Panorama materials for 360-degree backgrounds   404
Editing and creating 3D Panoramas   406
Summary   411

17

Unlock Your Exclusive Benefits   413

Index   417

Other Books You May Enjoy   426

Preface

Digital art has come a long way in recent years, and **Clip Studio Paint** (**CSP**) has emerged as one of the most versatile and powerful tools available to illustrators, comic artists, and character designers. With its vast array of brushes, intuitive interface, and growing library of features—including advanced 3D tools and customizable automation—CSP has become a cornerstone of digital workflows around the world.

This book was created to help you take full advantage of what CSP has to offer. Whether you're already familiar with the software or just beginning to explore its capabilities, this guide is designed to walk you through the tools, functions, and strategies that can make your process faster, smoother, and more enjoyable. You'll learn not just *what* each tool does, but *how* and *why* to use it in your creative workflow.

This book will help you to utilize the technical possibilities of CSP while maintaining the personal style you want to express through your art.

> **Important note**
> Clip Studio Paint and Clip Studio are the trademark or registered trademark of Celsys.

Who this book is for

This guide is for intermediate to advanced digital artists, illustrators, character designers, environment and prop designers, and comic artists familiar with CSP. You'll be able to build on your foundation in digital media and CSP to fully personalize your experience with the software.

What this book covers

Chapter 1, *Customizing Your Workspace for Efficiency*, will teach you how to tailor CSP's interface to your needs so that you can work faster and stay focused on your art.

Chapter 2, *Streamlining Your Workflow with Shortcuts and Actions*, is where you will discover how to automate repetitive tasks and speed up your process using keyboard shortcuts and auto-actions.

Chapter 3, *Setting Up Materials for Consistency and Speed*, will show you how to save time and maintain consistency across projects by creating custom templates and tool presets.

Chapter 4, *Organizing Your Projects Effectively*, will help you to master file and layer organization techniques to keep complex illustrations clear, manageable, and easy to update.

Chapter 5, Unlocking the Full Potential of Brush Settings, will dive into brush customization to gain more control over your lines, textures, and painting techniques.

Chapter 6, Enhancing Your Lines with Vector Layers, will explore the power of vector layers to create clean, editable linework that's easy to adjust without compromising on quality.

Chapter 7, Utilizing Rulers and Guides for Precision, will show you how to use CSP's ruler and guide tools to create accurate shapes, patterns, and perspectives with ease.

Chapter 8, Maximizing Efficiency and Organization with Layers, will help you master the Layer and Layer Property palettes to streamline your workflow using features such as reference layers, masks, and layer color for better control and clarity.

Chapter 9, Mastering Layer Blending Modes for Stunning Colors, will show you how to unlock the creative potential of blending modes to add depth, lighting, and dynamic effects to your artwork.

Chapter 10, Perfecting Your Selections, will help you get precise with your edits and color placement by mastering selection tools and advanced selection techniques.

Chapter 11, Applying Color Quickly with Pro Techniques, will enable you to discover efficient methods to apply colors using smart tools and layer techniques that speed up your coloring process.

Chapter 12, Enhancing Your Art with Post-Processing Adjustments, will teach you how to elevate your final image using tonal corrections, Liquify, and other finishing touches to refine composition and impact.

Chapter 13, Manipulating 3D Objects on the Canvas, is where you will get hands-on with 3D objects as you learn how to move, scale, and rotate them for accurate perspective and quick scene building.

Chapter 14, Altering and Posing 3D Figures, will explore how to pose, customize, and adjust 3D figures to match your vision, whether for reference or final artwork.

Chapter 15, Illuminating Your Artwork with 3D Lighting and Shading Assist, uses 3D lighting tools and the Shading Assist feature to simulate realistic light and shadow directly on your characters and scenes.

Chapter 16, Creating 3D Backgrounds, will show you how to build environments using 3D primitives, objects, and panoramic materials to add depth and immersion to your illustrations.

To get the most out of this book

You will need a version of CSP installed on your computer—version 4.0 or above, if possible. All painting examples have been tested using CSP 4.0 on Windows. However, they should work with future version releases too.

Software/hardware covered in the book	Operating system requirements
Clip Studio Paint 4.0 or above	Windows, macOS, iPadOS, iOS, Android, or ChromeOS

You can see all the system requirements by going to `https://www.clipstudio.net/en/dl/system/`.

You will need the EX version to extract lines from images and 3D models (*Chapter 8, Maximizing Efficiency and Organization with Layers*) and use the **All sides view** palette (*Chapter 13, Manipulating 3D Objects on the Canvas*). All other features covered in this book are available in the PRO version.

Conventions used

There are a number of text conventions used throughout this book.

Bold: Indicates a new term, an important word, or words that you see onscreen. For instance, words in menus or dialog boxes appear in **bold**. Here is an example: "Inside the **Sub Tool Detail** palette, navigate to **Ink** and set **Blending mode** to **Erase**."

> Tips or important notes
> Appear like this.

Get in touch

Feedback from our readers is always welcome.

General feedback: If you have questions about any aspect of this book, email us at `customercare@packtpub.com` and mention the book title in the subject of your message.

Errata: Although we have taken every care to ensure the accuracy of our content, mistakes do happen. If you have found a mistake in this book, we would be grateful if you would report this to us. Please visit `www.packtpub.com/support/errata` and fill in the form.

Piracy: If you come across any illegal copies of our works in any form on the internet, we would be grateful if you would provide us with the location address or website name. Please contact us at `copyright@packt.com` with a link to the material.

If you are interested in becoming an author: If there is a topic that you have expertise in and you are interested in either writing or contributing to a book, please visit `authors.packtpub.com`.

Share Your Thoughts

Once you've read *Mastering Clip Studio Paint*, we'd love to hear your thoughts! Scan the QR code below to go straight to the Amazon review page for this book and share your feedback.

https://packt.link/r/1-805-12403-X

Your review is important to us and the tech community and will help us make sure we're delivering excellent quality content.

Free Benefits with Your Book

This book comes with free benefits to support your learning. Activate them now for instant access (see the "*How to Unlock*" section for instructions).

Here's a quick overview of what you can instantly unlock with your purchase:

PDF and ePub Copies

Next-Gen Web-Based Reader

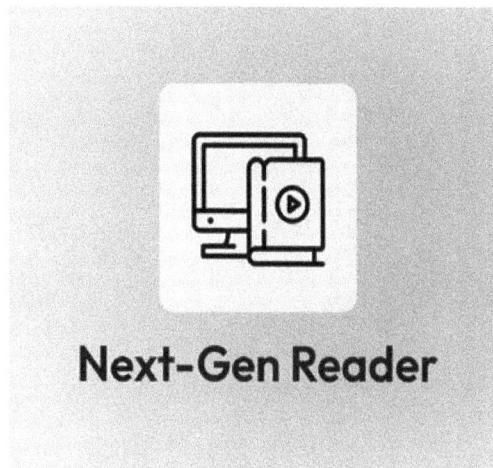

Access a DRM-free PDF copy of this book to read anywhere, on any device.

Use a DRM-free ePub version with your favorite e-reader.

Multi-device progress sync: Pick up where you left off, on any device.

Highlighting and notetaking: Capture ideas and turn reading into lasting knowledge.

Bookmarking: Save and revisit key sections whenever you need them.

Dark mode: Reduce eye strain by switching to dark or sepia themes

How to Unlock

UNLOCK NOW

Scan the QR code (or go to `packtpub.com/unlock`). Search for this book by name, confirm the edition, and then follow the steps on the page.

Note: Keep your invoice handly. Purchase made directly from packt don't require one.

Part 1: Workflow Optimization

Before diving into the creative aspects of digital art, it's essential to build a strong foundation that supports a smooth and efficient workflow. This part of the book focuses on optimizing your workspace and habits in Clip Studio Paint to help you save time, stay organized, and maintain consistency in your work. You'll learn how to customize your workspace, set up shortcuts and actions, create useful templates and presets, and keep your projects neatly structured. With these tools and strategies in place, your creation process will become smoother and quicker, helping you get the most out of the software.

This part has the following chapters:

- *Chapter 1, Customizing Your Workspace for Efficiency*
- *Chapter 2, Streamlining Your Workflow with Shortcuts and Actions*
- *Chapter 3, Setting Up Materials for Consistency and Speed*
- *Chapter 4, Organizing Your Projects Effectively*

1

Customizing Your Workspace for Efficiency

In the dynamic world of digital art, having a well-organized and personalized workspace is crucial for maximizing your efficiency and creativity. **Clip Studio Paint** (**CSP**) offers a highly customizable interface that allows you to tailor your workspace to suit your specific needs and workflow preferences. This chapter will guide you through the process of customizing your workspace, helping you create an environment that enhances productivity and minimizes distractions.

In this chapter, we're going to cover the following main topics:

- Understanding the basics of workspace configuration
- Configuring the Command Bar
- Tailoring the Tool Property palette
- Configuring my workspace

By the end of this chapter, you will know how to manipulate each panel and bar in the workspace, as well as understand how to use the Command Bar and the Tool Property palette for a smoother workflow.

CSP's workspace is completely customizable according to your own preferences, and it's important that you change it to fit *your* workflow. So, let's get started!

Understanding the basics of workspace configuration

Workspace configuration in CSP is fundamental to creating an efficient and personalized environment for your digital art. By understanding how to customize and organize your workspace, you can enhance your productivity, streamline your workflow, and ensure that your most-used tools and panels are always within easy reach. In this section, we will cover the essential steps to set up and optimize your workspace for maximum efficiency.

When you first open CSP, this is what you see:

Figure 1.1 – CSP's default workspace

This may seem daunting at first, but we'll break it down so it's easy to understand what each area represents. First, it's important that you know what CSP's *palettes* are—this is CSP's name for each panel within your workspace. So, you have the Sub Tool palette, the Brush Size palette, the Auto Action palette, and so on. You can find all palettes in the **Window** drop-down menu.

Now that you know what a palette is, let's explore the key components and customization options available in CSP's interface.

Main canvas area

The main canvas area is the central workspace where your artwork is displayed. In the preceding screenshot, it's the largest central area, surrounded by all the palettes. Its size is adjustable to fit your preferred screen size and resolution, and it offers options for zooming, panning, and rotating the canvas.

Now, let's see the palettes on the left side of the default workspace:

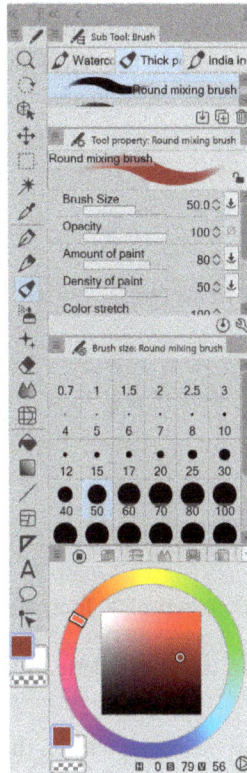

Figure 1.2 – The left side of the default workspace

We will cover each of these palettes, starting with the one related to tools.

Tool-related palettes

There are three palettes applicable to all tools. They are as follows:

- The **Tool** palette (the vertical bar with tool icons on the extreme left of *Figure 1.2*) contains all essential drawing and editing tools. On this palette, you'll find your tools, such as Brush, Eraser, and Auto Select. Each icon represents one tool, and you can see the tool's name in the Sub Tool palette, which we'll cover in the next topic.

  - The Tool palette is fully customizable and you can add, remove, and rearrange tools based on your needs—just drag and drop them. It also supports the creation of custom tool sets for quick access to frequently used tools. To create a custom tool set, click on a sub tool and drag it to your desired position within the Tool palette. A new tool will be created. Any sub tools you drag and drop into this new tool will become part of its sub tools.

- The **Sub Tool** palette is where you'll find the name of your currently selected tool and all the sub tools that belong to it. A tool is a category, and the sub tools are specific instruments you can use in each category. For example, within the Pencil tool, it'll show all pencil groups and individual pencils you have, and within the Selection area tool, it'll show different options for selection:

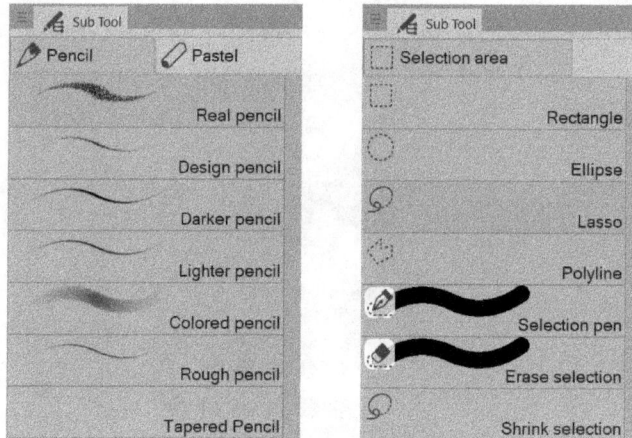

Figure 1.3 – Different options in the Sub Tool palette, according to the selected tool

To use a tool, first select it in the **Tool** palette. A list of sub tools will appear in the **Sub Tool** palette for you to pick.

In *Figure 1.4*, you can see some examples. On the left, the tool is **Brush** and the sub tool is **Round watercolor brush**, and on the right, the tool is **Blend** and the sub tool is **Blend**.

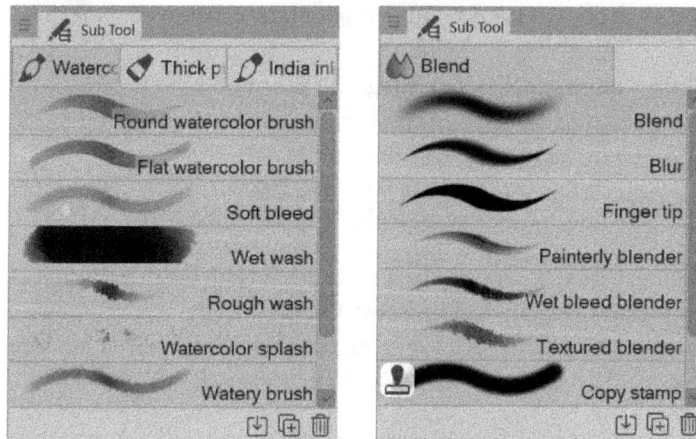

Figure 1.4 – Options of sub tools to choose according to the tool selected

- The **Tool Property** palette shows more detailed settings for each tool. This is highly customizable, and we'll see how to use it for each tool in the next few chapters.

Figure 1.5 – The Tool Property palette

Besides these, there are specific palettes for some tools. One of these is the **Brush Size** palette, which is below **Tool Property** on the default workspace. It displays different brush sizes you can quickly pick. Now that you've optimized the palettes that control how you use your tools, let's move on to the ones that control how you color with them—your color-related palettes.

Color-related palettes

There are seven color-related palettes. The one visible in the default workspace is **Color Wheel**. On top of it, you can see five tabs with different icons: each one of them represents a different color-related palette.

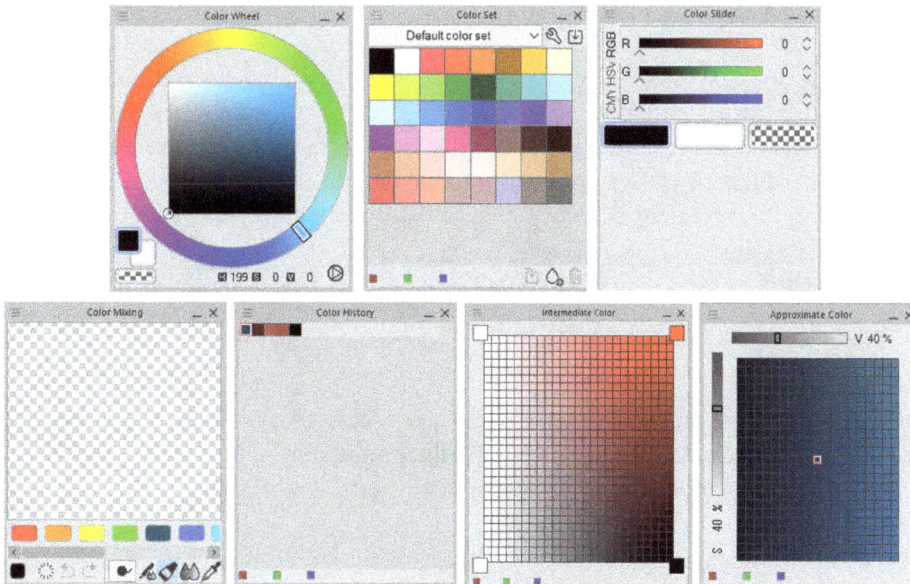

Figure 1.6 – Different color palettes

Each of them has its own role:

- **Color Wheel** (*Figure 1.6, top left*): Shows a hue ring and value-saturation area, so you can pick whichever color you want. This is my preferred color palette since it lets me pick any colors intuitively.

- **Color set** (*Figure 1.6, top center*): You can create color sets, which are useful for frequently used colors and for when you have a specific color palette to follow.

- **Color slider** (*Figure 1.6, top right*): This lets you pick a specific color using the RGB, HSV, or CMYK slider. This is great for picking specific colors and making very small changes to it or changing only one of its elements—for example, desaturating it a little bit by moving the saturation slider in the HSV mode.

- **Color mixing** (*Figure 1.6, bottom left*): Like a real-life palette, you can add colors and mix them.

- **Color history** (*Figure 1.6, bottom, second from left to right*): This shows your history of colors, so you can go back to a previous one if you want.

- **Intermediate color** (*Figure 1.6, bottom, third from left to right*): This lets you pick intermediate colors considering the reference colors configured in each of the four corners.

- **Approximate color** (*Figure 1.6, bottom right*): Displays a grid of colors that closely resemble your current selection, arranged along two adjustable axes such as Hue/Saturation/Value or Red/Green/Blue.

Now that we have seen what's on the left side of the default workspace, let's see the top part, which is the Command Bar.

Command Bar

The Command Bar is a customizable toolbar that provides quick access to your most frequently used commands and functions. By organizing essential tools in one convenient location, the Command Bar enhances your workflow efficiency and helps streamline your creative process:

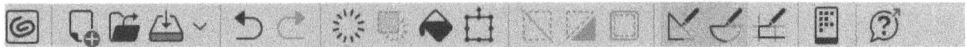

Figure 1.7 – The Command Bar

Located at the top of the interface, it provides quick access to commonly used commands. You can add or delete command icons as you wish. We'll see more about it later in this chapter.

Navigator and other reference palettes

Let's see next what's on the right side of the default workspace:

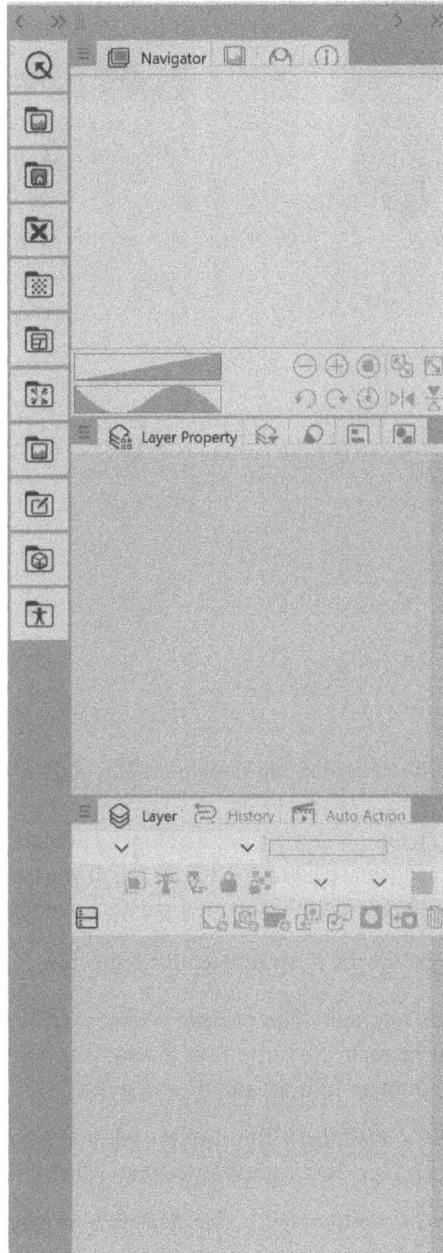

Figure 1.8 – The right side of the default workspace

The first group, on top, is made of some palettes related to your current artwork or reference images.

Figure 1.9 – The Navigator, Sub View, Item bank, and Information palettes

The first one is **Navigator** (*Figure 1.9, top left*), which shows a miniature of your artwork. This is great for quickly seeing whether your image looks good from afar. If you zoom in too much, you might lose sight of your overall composition, and the Navigator palette is wonderful in that scenario.

Then, on that same palette group, the other tabs are the following:

- **Sub View** (*Figure 1.9, top right*): You can add reference images to it. In *Figure 1.9*, I added a photo of a road as an example. It's convenient to have your reference next to your canvas since it makes it easier to compare your art and the reference.

- **Item bank** (*Figure 1.9, bottom left*): This displays selected items for use in an artwork, such as 3D models and .clip files. This is great for comics, which can frequently use repeated items.

- **Information** (*Figure 1.9, bottom right*): This displays information related to coordinates, time spent, and the workload of the system memory.

Layer-related palettes

There are three layer palettes. On the default workspace, they are on the middle-right side (**Layer Property** and **Search Layer**) and bottom-right side (**Layer**):

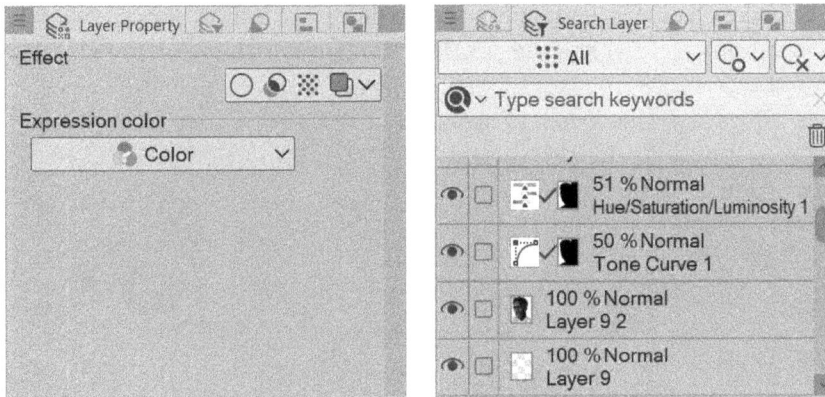

Figure 1.10 – Layer Property and Search Layer palettes

Layer Property allows you to choose and change effects and colors on a specific layer. The **Search Layer** palette, on the other hand, is useful for finding layers with shared qualities, such as type.

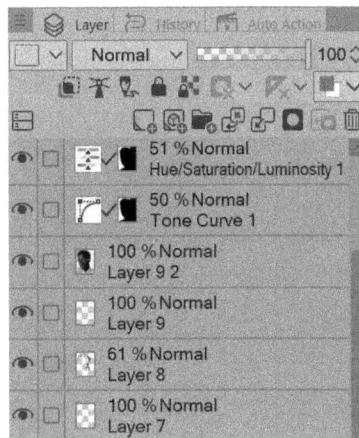

Figure 1.11 – The Layer palette

The **Layer** palette is one of the most useful palettes while operating on CSP. It displays all layers in your document, including their hierarchy and properties. It's customizable for managing layer visibility, opacity, blending modes, and grouping, and it includes options for creating, deleting, and organizing layers. You can make it as large or as small as you need.

We'll see these palettes in detail in *Chapter 8, Maximizing Efficiency and Organization with Layers*.

Other palettes

There are many other palettes, including some specific for animation and auto-actions. What matters the most is that each of them can be opened and closed at any time and moved within the workspace to whichever position you prefer. To choose which palettes are visible and which are not, navigate to the **Window** menu and see the list of palettes. The ones with a checkmark next to them are visible, while the ones with an empty space are invisible. You can leave palettes as floating windows, like the **Color Wheel** here:

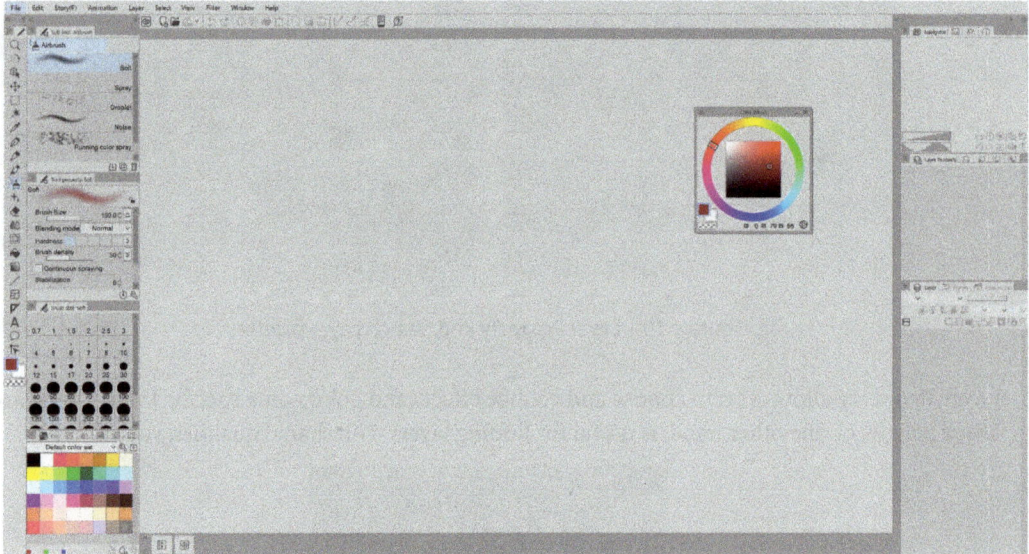

Figure 1.12 – An example of a floating palette

Floating palettes can be docked and undocked as you wish with a simple drag and drop. You can experiment with their positions and analyze which ones you use the most and what placement will make you spend the least time to reach them.

Once your workspace is set up to support your process, drawing becomes much more fun—and far less frustrating. Now, let's take it a step further by customizing the Command Bar so your most-used tools are always just a click away.

Configuring the Command Bar

The Command Bar is one of the most useful and underrated parts of CSP. If you learn to use it to your advantage, it'll make your workflow much smoother.

You can have single functions or groups of functions on the Command Bar. With a single function, once you click it, it'll select that function. When in a group, when you click the group, it'll open a menu so you can click the function. Here's an example of a group:

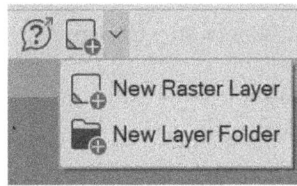

Figure 1.13 – Example of a group within the Command Bar

You can add and remove commands easily. First, open **Command Bar Settings**. You can do so by clicking on **File | Command Bar Settings**, or right-clicking on the Command Bar and selecting **Command Bar Settings**. The following panel will open:

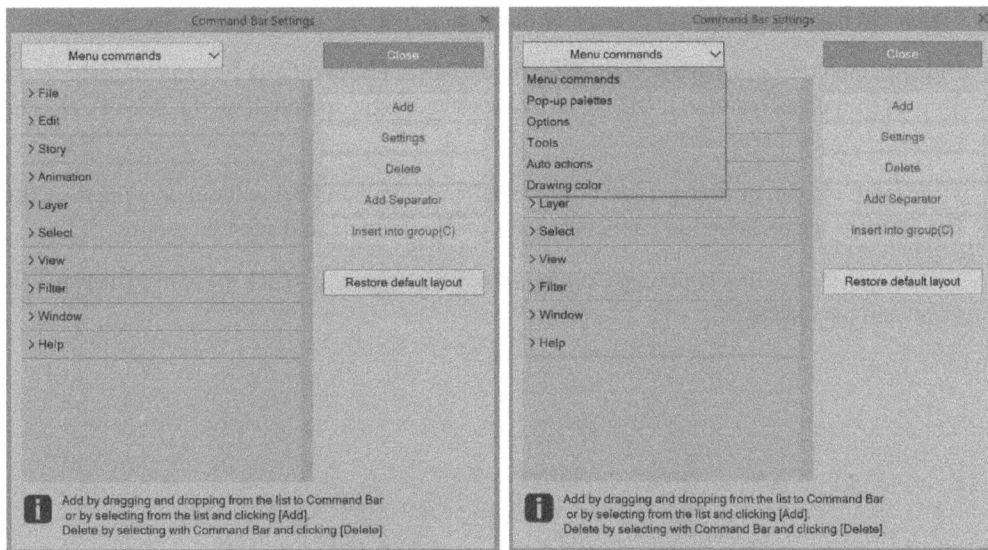

Figure 1.14 – Command Bar Settings

On the first menu on the left side, you can choose a category, such as **Menu commands** or **Pop-up palettes**, as you can see in *Figure 1.14 (right side)*. Once you pick it, there will be a list of functions related to that category. To add or delete any of them, use the buttons on the right. Besides adding and deleting, there are buttons for the following:

- **Close**: Closes **Command Bar Settings**. Click this once you've finished configuring, and it'll save all changes.

- **Settings**: Modifies settings related to the Command Bar, such as the icon or name of the function.

- **Add Separator**: Can be used to create sections of similar functions.

- **Insert into group(C)**: Used for grouping icons.

To group icons, follow these instructions step by step:

1. Open **Command Bar Settings**.
2. Click on the desired icon that is already on the Command Bar.
3. Click on the function you want to group with it. The **Insert into group** option will become available.
4. Click on **Insert intro group** and press **Close**.
5. Now, the first icon you selected and the new function will be grouped together.

Once you have modified which functions show up on the Command Bar, you can always drag and drop them to reorganize them as you wish, *as long as you press Ctrl or command as you do it* or *have Command Bar Settings opened*. If none of these apply, you will not be able to drag and drop.

Dragging and dropping icons on the Command Bar can have different effects on separators. If you drop an icon on a separator, it will create a new category. If you drop it on the side of a separator, the icon will become part of that section.

Some functions can be dragged and dropped *into* the Command Bar without opening the **Command Bar Settings** menu: Selection Launcher icons, tools, sub tools, and sub tool groups.

To delete an icon without opening **Command Bar Settings**, right-click the icon to display its context menu and tap **Delete**.

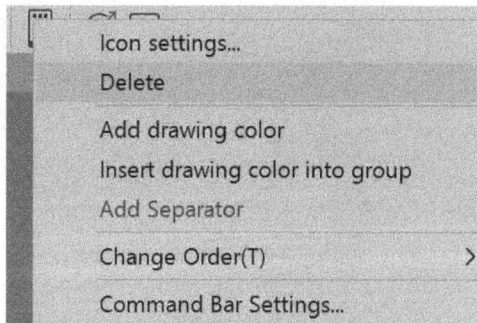

Figure 1.15 – How to delete an icon without opening Command Bar Settings

A cool feature you should experiment with is changing the color of icons on the Command Bar. That makes it very quick and easy for you to pick your desired function while painting. To change its color, follow these instructions step by step:

1. Go to **Command Bar Settings**.
2. Click on the icon you want to change on the Command Bar.
3. The **Settings** button will become available. Click on it.

4. **Icon settings** will open up. Click on the **Background color of icon** box and choose your desired color.

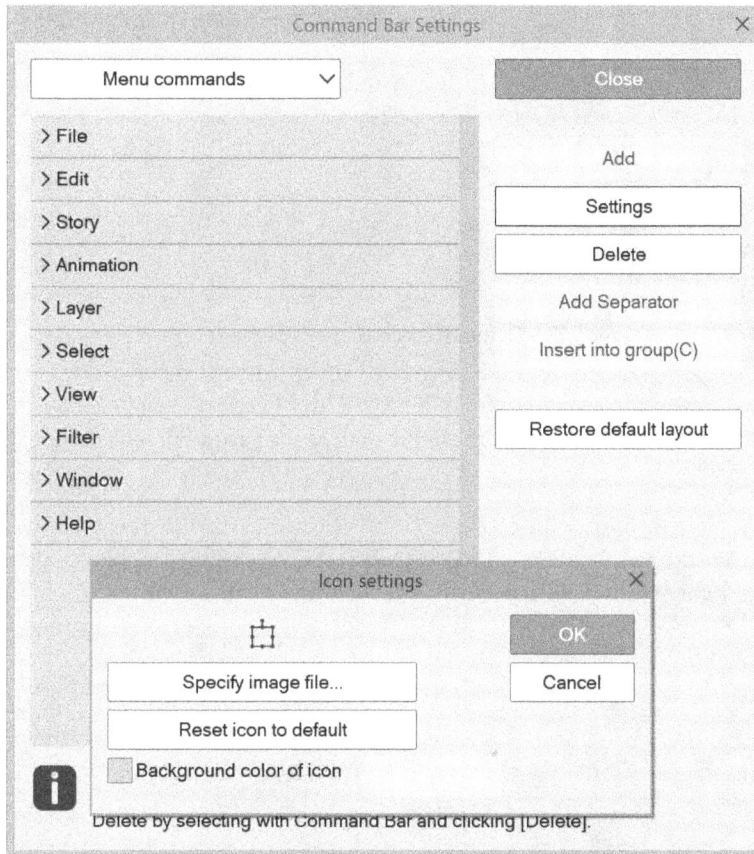

Figure 1.16 – How to add color to an icon on the Command Bar

You can also add a personalized image icon if you click on **Specify Image File…**. This way, you can fully customize any icons inside the Command Bar.

In the next section, we'll dive into tailoring the Tool Property palette, ensuring that your tools are precisely configured to suit your unique artistic needs and preferences.

Tailoring the Tool Property palette

The Tool Property palette is a powerful feature that allows artists to fine-tune their tools and brushes for maximum efficiency and effectiveness. Customizing this palette can significantly enhance your workflow, making it easier to access and adjust the settings you use most frequently with each tool.

Each tool will show different settings on the **Tool Property** palette. Below are some examples:

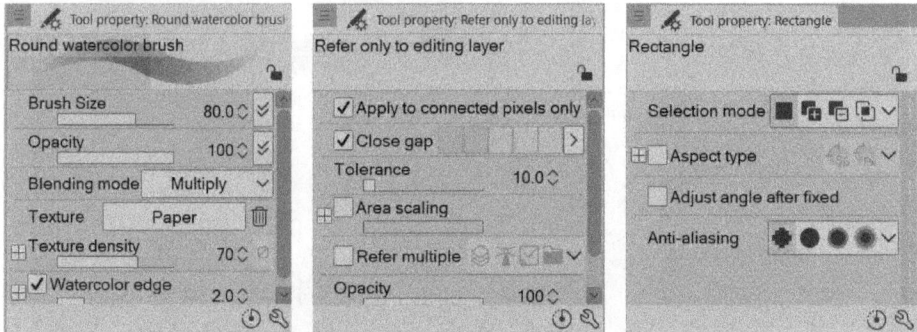

Figure 1.17 – Different configurations of the Tool Property palette

In *Figure 1.17*, you can see examples of how the **Tool Property** palette changes depending on the tool. On the left side, we have a Brush; in the middle, we have a Fill tool; and on the right, we have a Selection tool.

Sometimes, there are more settings that are not visible within the Tool Property. You can see all possible settings inside the **Sub Tool Detail** palette, which can be opened by clicking on the wrench icon at the bottom right of the **Tool Property** palette. Below you can see the Sub Tool Detail palette (right):

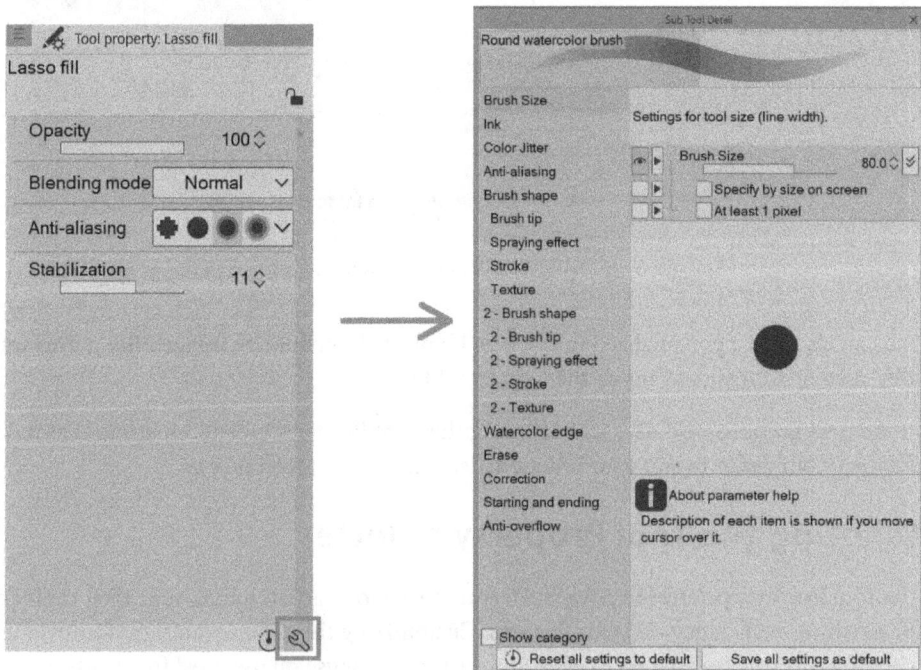

Figure 1.18 – How to open the Sub Tool Detail palette

Inside **Sub Tool Detail**, there are several other settings. You can choose which settings will be visible on the **Tool Property** palette by clicking on the square box by the side of each setting. If there's an eye icon within it, this setting is visible in the **Tool Property** palette, and if it's just an empty box, this setting is invisible. For instance, in the following figure, **Brush Size** is visible, while **Specify by size on screen** and **At least 1 pixel** are not:

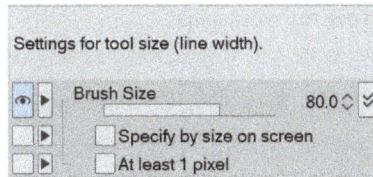

Figure 1.19 – The eye on the left side shows visibility

It is possible to lock the settings of a tool—just click on the padlock icon located near the stroke preview inside the **Tool Property** palette. Another option is going to **Tool Property | Lock**:

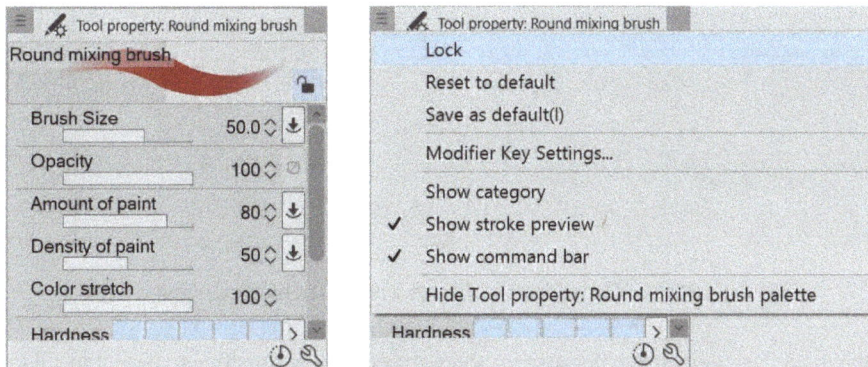

Figure 1.20 – Different ways to lock settings of a sub tool

When the settings are locked, *you can still change the settings of the sub tool*. However, the next time you select that tool, it'll return to its locked settings.

Lastly, let's talk about adjusting the palette layout for optimal workflow. The layout of the Tool Property palette can be customized to fit your needs—you can resize the panel and hide properties you don't use frequently.

Additionally, you can dock the Tool Property palette in a convenient location within your workspace, ensuring that it is always within easy reach—it's what I usually do. This level of customization helps create a more intuitive and efficient working environment.

Next, we'll explore how to configure your entire workspace for maximum productivity, sharing practical tips and examples to help you create an optimal environment for your creative process.

Configuring my workspace

Now that you know all about CSP's workspace, I suggest you experiment with different workspace configurations until you find one you feel comfortable with. I'll share with you my workspace and the reasons behind it, so you understand my thought process and try to apply it to your own workflow.

In the next screenshot, you can see my workspace:

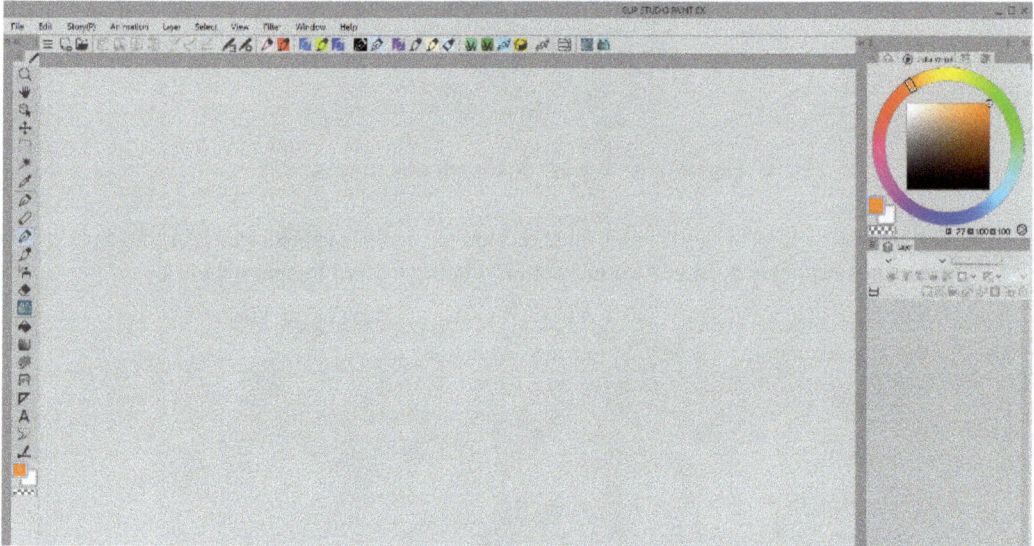

Figure 1.21 – My workspace. There's a reason behind everything here!

I like having a dark workspace because my eyes are extremely sensitive to light, but I'll keep it light in the screenshots for the sake of readability.

> **Important note**
>
> Although I prefer the dark theme, I don't leave it at the darkest tone possible; having a workspace that is too dark or too light will change your perception of values and colors. I suggest you experiment with different tones until you find one that you're comfortable with and that will not affect your value perception too much.

You can adjust how light or dark your workspace is by going to **File** | **Preferences** | **Interface**. Under **Color**, go to **Interface Color** and choose whether you want dark or light, and how dense it is:

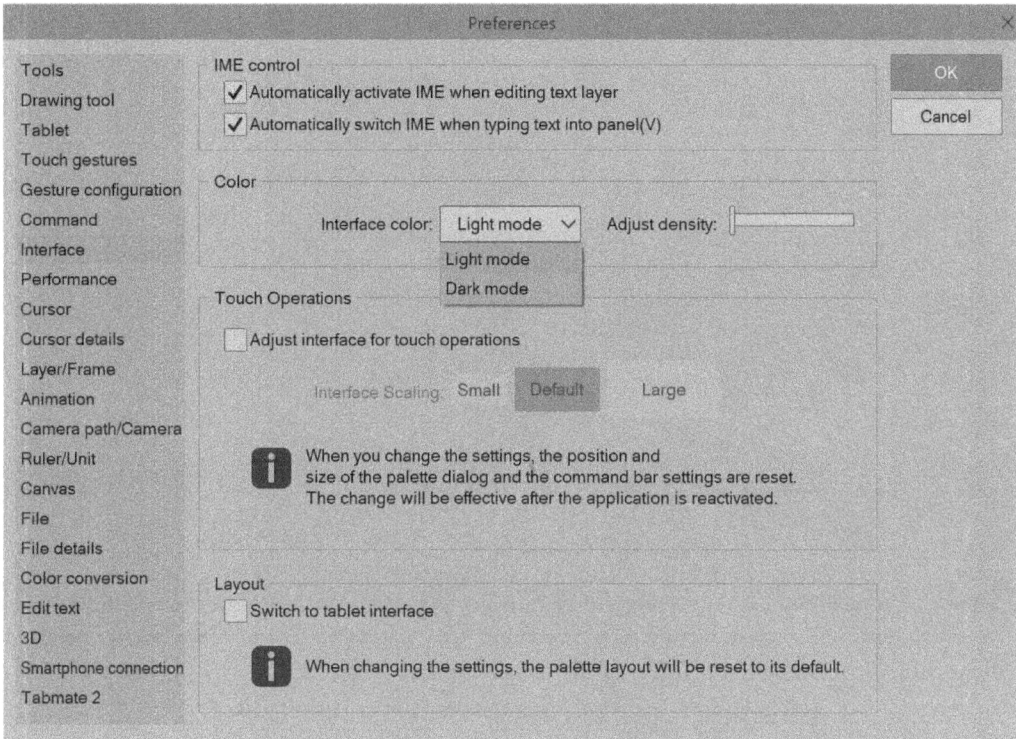

Figure 1.22 – How to change the tone of the workspace

On the left side of my workspace, I only leave the Tool palette open. If you look closely, you can see that on its left side, there's a very thin strip, which is closed because of the double arrow at the top of it. In *Figure 1.23*, I zoomed in so you can see it more clearly:

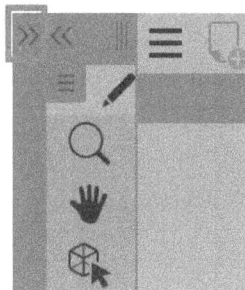

Figure 1.23 – This arrow shows there are hidden palettes here

When I click on this double arrow, it opens the Sub Tool palette and the Tool Property palette:

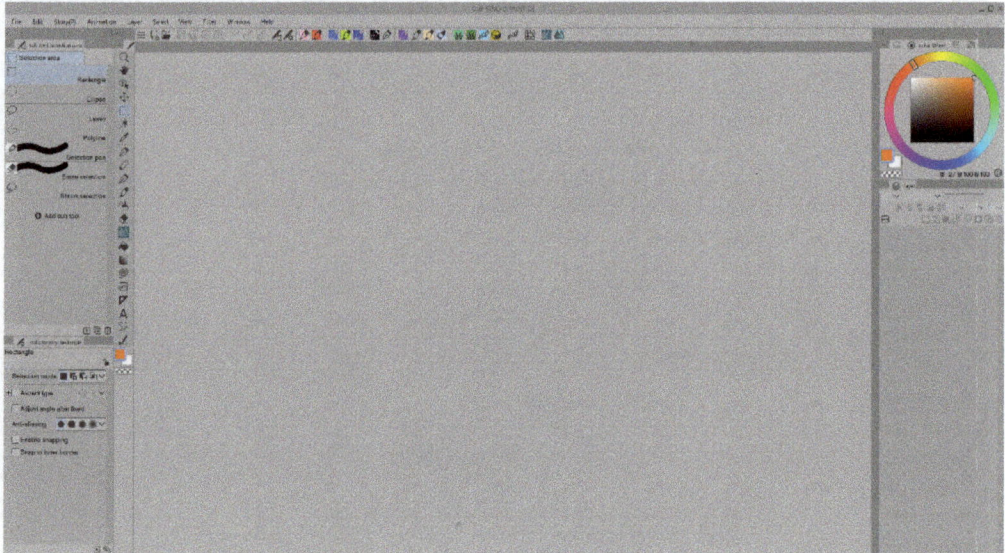

Figure 1.24 – How the workspace looks when those hidden palettes are visible

I leave it closed because I like having a large drawing area available, and these are palettes I don't use very frequently. If I need it opened for a moment, I just click on the arrows, do whatever needs to be done, and then close it again. This way, I have more space for the canvas.

As for my Command Bar, this is what I have:

Figure 1.25 – My Command Bar

It may seem crowded, but it's easy to navigate because they're color-coded and separated by function:

1. **File-related icons**: I've added **Create new from clipboard** and **Open** for quick file management.

2. **Tonal Correction** layers: I've placed the Tonal Correction layers I use the most, which are **Tone curve**, **Level correction**, **Color balance**, and **Hue/saturation/luminosity**.

3. **Snap**: These icons are for snapping properties, so we have **Snap to Ruler**, **Snap to Special Ruler**, and **Snap to Grid**.

4. **Sub Tool** and **Tool Property palettes**: I like keeping these palettes here so if I need anything quick from them, such as changing brush stabilization, I just click on the icon, change it, and it closes again, keeping my space clean. I only use those fixed palettes on the far left when it's something that will take me a while to figure out and I want more space in the process, such as when I'm searching for a brush on the Sub Tool palette.

5. **Hard brushes**: I keep my sketch pencil and cel shading brush here.

6. **Soft paint brushes**: Here I keep my favorite brushes that have soft edges.

7. **Ink brushes**: My favorite brushes with an ink-like nature, such as G-Pen, are kept here.

8. **Textured paint brushes**: Here I keep my favorite brushes with texture.

9. **Decorative brushes for natural elements**: These decorative brushes can be used to draw elements such as grass, bushes, clouds, and rocks.

10. **Particle brush**: I use this brush a lot for finishing touches.

11. **Liquify**: I use this for quick fixes in the proportion and structure. We'll dive deeper into it in *Chapter 12, Enhancing Your Art with Post-Processing Adjustments*.

12. **Blending sub tools**: This is used for smoother rendering.

Almost all my brushes are color-coded because this way, I know where each one is at a glance. I don't have to look closely at the icon to know which is which.

For me, configuring it in this way was very instinctive, and I suggest you do the same. Just start adding your most-used tools and functions for which you don't have a keyboard shortcut. Then, group them by similarities.

Now, on the right side of my workspace, I have **Color Wheel** and the **Layer** palette:

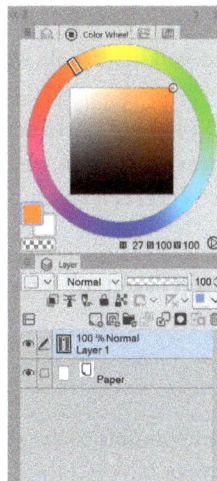

Figure 1.26 – The right side of my workspace has Color Wheel and the Layer palette

I like having the Color Wheel quite large so I can pick colors more precisely, and I also like having a lot of space for my layers, so the Layer palette is very tall. On the same panel as the Color Wheel, in different tabs, I leave the Layer Property panel and the color slider panel, which I don't use very frequently.

Notice there's a thin strip with double arrows near Color Wheel as well. These arrows open the Material palette, which you can use to find materials like 3D models, brushes, and patterns. We'll cover the Material palette in detail in *Chapter 3, Setting Up Materials for Consistency and Speed*. You can see how it looks when I open it below:

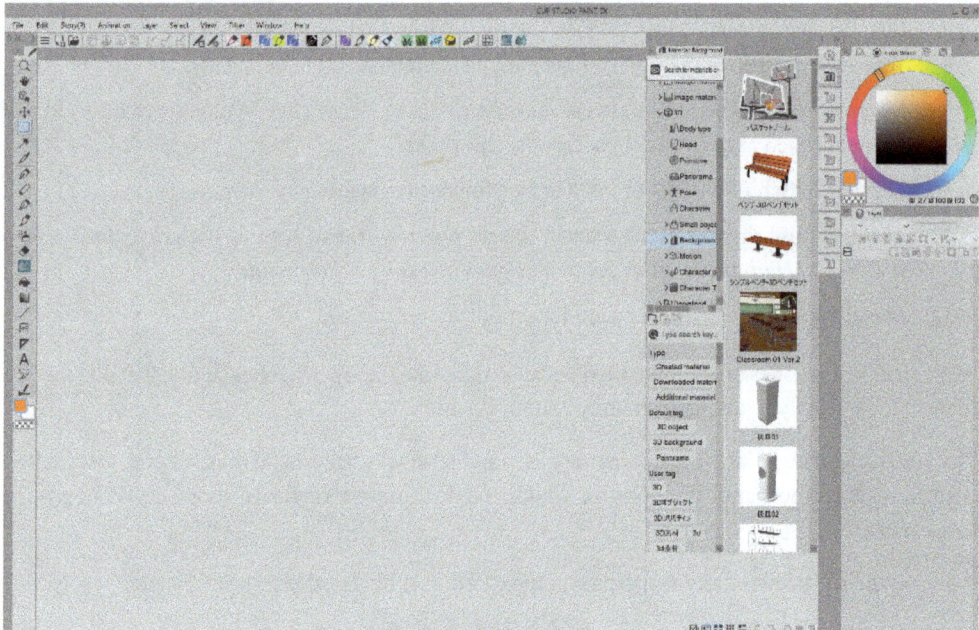

Figure 1.27 – This is how the workspace looks when I open the Materials palette

When I'm working on a painting and I know I'll frequently choose different colors, I remove the Color Wheel from the right side and leave it close to where my hand is while painting, as shown in the screenshot with the floating Color Wheel (*Figure 1.12*). This way, I make minimal movement to choose colors quickly.

Once you've configured a workspace you like, don't forget to save it. Go to **Window** | **Workspace** | **Register Workspace**.

Important note

Whatever changes you make will be applicable to the saved workspace as well, so save different versions of it if you want to experiment.

And that's it! These are the most important things you need to know about your workspace. Experiment a little bit, see how other artists organize theirs, and try to rationalize how *you* work and how you could reduce time spent choosing tools, picking actions, and so on. This way, you'll be able to work more smoothly and naturally, without as much friction.

Summary

In this chapter, we explored the importance of a well-organized and personalized workspace in CSP to enhance productivity and creativity.

We began by learning how to customize the layout of the workspace, as well as what the palettes are and how they work. We've covered how to personalize the Command Bar and the Tool Property palette, ensuring frequently used tools and commands are easily accessible. Additionally, we looked at how I configured my own workspace and how you can apply this type of thinking to your own.

Now that you have finished this chapter, you have the skills to create an efficient and intuitive workspace that supports your unique workflow, ultimately enhancing your overall CSP experience.

In the next chapter, we'll delve into streamlining your workflow with shortcuts and auto actions. These powerful features will help you further increase your efficiency by enabling quick access to essential functions and automating repetitive tasks, allowing you to maintain your creative momentum seamlessly.

2

Streamlining Your Workflow with Shortcuts and Actions

In the realm of digital art, efficiency and speed are crucial to maintaining a productive and creative workflow. **Clip Studio Paint** (**CSP**) offers powerful tools to help you achieve this by using shortcuts, modifier keys, and auto actions. This chapter is dedicated to teaching you how to set up and use these features to their full potential, making your artistic process smoother and more intuitive.

In this chapter, we'll cover the following topics:

- Creating personalized shortcuts
- Changing a tool temporarily with modifier keys
- Getting the most out of auto actions

These lessons are invaluable for any digital artist looking to optimize their work process. By mastering shortcuts and actions, you'll be able to work more quickly and efficiently, allowing you to dedicate more time and energy to your creative vision.

> **Important note**
> In this chapter, any reference to the *Ctrl* key is equivalent to the *command* key on a Mac.

Creating personalized shortcuts

Keyboard shortcuts are customized key combinations that allow you to quickly access tools, commands, and functions without having to navigate through menus or toolbars. These shortcuts are designed to streamline your workflow, making it faster and more efficient to perform common tasks and actions.

Shortcuts can be used for a wide range of functions, such as selecting a specific tool (such as the **Brush** or **Eraser** tools), performing actions (such as undoing a mistake or saving your work), and navigating the canvas (such as zooming in or out).

CSP comes with a variety of predefined shortcuts. Here's a list of some of the most useful predefined shortcuts:

Tool/Operation	Predefined Shortcut
Move (Hand)	H
Move (Rotate)	R
Selection	M
Auto select	W
Brush	B
Eraser	E
Blend	J
Fill	G
Switch main color and sub color	X
Switch main color and transparent color	C
Tonal correction – Hue/Saturation/Luminosity	Ctrl + U
Free transform	Ctrl + Shift + T
New Raster Layer	Ctrl + Shift + N
Create folder and insert layer	Ctrl + G
Clip to layer below	Ctrl + Alt + G
Merge with layer below	Ctrl + E
Select all	Ctrl + A
Deselect	Ctrl + D
Show/Hide all palettes	Tab
Increase brush size	[
Reduce brush size	]
Create selection from layer	Ctrl + left-click layer thumbnail

Table 2.1 – Some of the most useful predefined shortcuts

There are many other shortcuts. These are the ones I find most useful in my workflow. You can find all the predefined shortcuts under **File | Shortcut Settings**.

I suggest you try to learn two to three at a time. Don't try to memorize all of them at once—it's a lot. Once a few of those shortcuts become completely automatic for you, try to incorporate new ones. The more shortcuts you use, the quicker your workflow.

Now, there may be tools and functions you want to use that don't come with a predefined shortcut, or maybe you've been using a different software before and want to keep using the shortcuts you're already used to. For that, you can easily change any shortcut to your liking.

To create personalized shortcuts, navigate to the **File** menu and select **Shortcut Settings**. Here, you can assign custom key combinations to virtually any function within the software. For example, if you frequently use the **Advanced Fill** setting, you can set a specific key combination to activate it instantly, reducing the time spent navigating through menus.

Here's how to set up your shortcuts:

1. Open **Shortcut Settings**.
2. Select the category of the function you want to customize (for example, **Tools**, **Commands**, and so on).
3. Find the specific command or tool.
4. Click on the **Current shortcut** field and press the desired key combination.
5. Press **OK** to save your changes.

By thoughtfully setting up shortcuts, you can streamline your workflow and make your creative process more fluid and responsive.

As an example, here are some of my customized shortcuts:

Tool/Operation	My customized shortcuts
Zoom	*Z*
Blend	*K*
Liquify	*J*
Airbrush	*V*
Decoration	*D*
Reset rotation	*Shift + R*
Flip horizontal (canvas)	*Ctrl + H*
Flip horizontal (selection)	*Ctrl + Shift + H*
Change layer name	*F2*
Duplicate layer	*Ctrl + J*

Tool/Operation	My customized shortcuts
Hide/show selection border	*Ctrl + Q*
Outline selection	*Shift + G*
Save duplicate (.jpg)	*Ctrl + Alt + S*
Close file	*Ctrl + Alt + W*

Table 2.2 – Some of my customized shortcuts

Some predefined shortcuts include more than one tool, such as *B* for **Brush**, **Airbrush**, and **Decoration**, so I also changed them. When it comes to defining shortcuts, I have two rules:

1. I only assign shortcuts to operations and tools I use frequently.
2. Each shortcut is assigned to a single function.

Because of the rules I created, and also because I was already used to my previous software's shortcuts, I have changed many of the original shortcuts to fit my workflow, as you can see in the preceding table.

> **Important note**
> When painting, pay attention to which functions and tools you use the most. Find out their shortcuts or create new ones for them. That'll speed up your process a considerable amount!

Now that you've learned how to create personalized shortcuts to access your most-used tools and commands quickly, let's explore another powerful technique: changing tools temporarily with modifier keys. This method allows you to switch between tools seamlessly, maintaining your workflow efficiency and enhancing your creative process.

Changing a tool temporarily with modifier keys

Modifier keys allow you to switch between tools on the fly without permanently changing your current settings, enabling quick adjustments and seamless transitions between tasks. This feature is invaluable for tasks that require frequent toggling between tools, such as refining details or making quick corrections.

You can assign operations to the *Ctrl*, *Alt*, *Shift*, and *Space* keys, as well as the *mouse wheel*, *right-click*, *tail switch*, and *touch gestures*. With these, you can temporarily switch tools and change brush sizes.

For example: for the **Eyedropper** tool, I don't use the original keyboard shortcut, which is the letter *I* on your keyboard. I prefer a modifier key, which is *Alt*. If I have a tool that uses color (**Brush**, **Fill**, and so on) and press *Alt*, it'll automatically temporarily switch to the **Eyedropper** tool. Once I stop pressing *Alt*, it goes back to the coloring tool.

CSP comes with *Alt* as a predefined modifier key for all color-related tools, so don't worry about having to make this change manually.

Here's how to customize which keys serve as modifiers:

1. Navigate to **File | Modifier Key Settings**. The following dialog will appear:

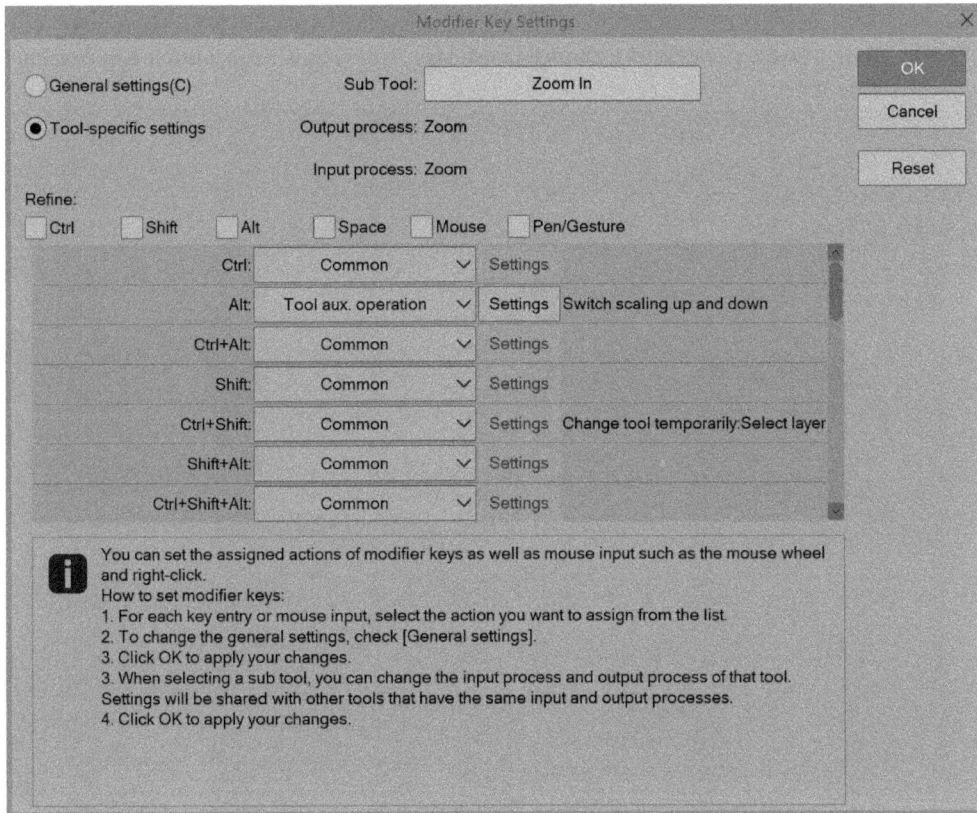

Figure 2.1 – Modifier Key Settings

2. On the top-left side, you can decide whether to change modifier keys for general settings or specific tools. **General settings** applies to your workflow no matter what tool you have selected.

3. If **Tool-specific settings** is chosen, new options will appear on the top right side. Click on the box next to **Sub Tool** – which shows **Zoom In** in *Figure 2.1* – to choose which sub tool will be affected.

4. Use **Refine** to specify which modifier keys are shown.

5. Select a modifier key and what action it will take: **Show Menu**, **Change brush size**, or **Change tool temporarily**.

Here's an example. Let's say I want the middle click of the mouse to change the size of **Soft Airbrush**. This is how I would proceed:

1. Select **Tool-specific settings**.

2. On **Sub Tool**, select **Airbrush | Soft**.

3. Select **Refine | Mouse**.

4. Go to **Middle click** | select **Change brush size**. This is how the **Modifier Key Settings** screen looks now:

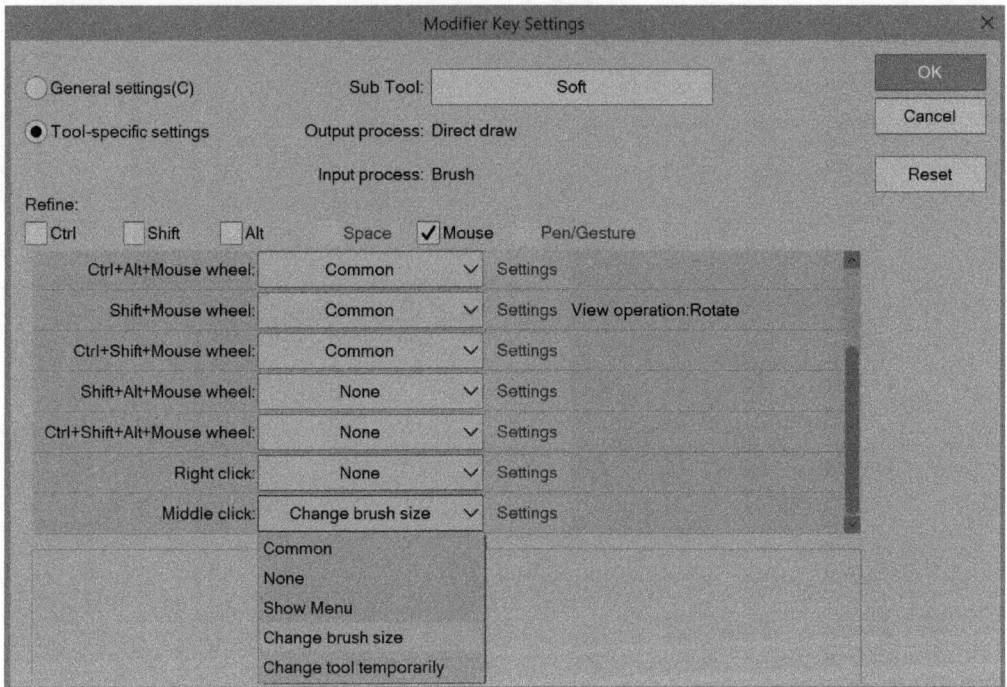

Figure 2.2 – This is how you assign Change brush size to the middle click of the mouse

And it's done! You can apply this step by step to whichever modifier key you want to assign a function.

After mastering the technique of temporarily changing tools with modifier keys for seamless transitions, it's time to optimize your workflow further by taking advantage of auto actions. This powerful feature will help you automate repetitive tasks, enhancing your efficiency and consistency.

Getting the most out of auto actions

Auto actions are recorded sets of processes within the software that you can repeat any time you need *those specific functions* in *that specific order*. They are extremely useful for saving time. *Figure 2.3* shows examples of how auto actions can affect your image:

Figure 2.3 – Examples of auto actions

At the top of *Figure 2.4*, the auto-action added a soft red overlay on the image. On the bottom, the auto-action added a golden glitter pattern on top of the stars, which had been previously selected.

Let's say you'd like to add a certain pink tone to all your images. You do so by using **Color balance layer**, adding a **New Raster Layer** instance in **Soft Light** mode with a specific color, and then using a **Level Correction layer** to make the image brighter. You could do this long process every single time.

Or, instead of having to perform these actions and select individual settings every time, you could create an auto action of it and just press the **Start to play auto action** button:

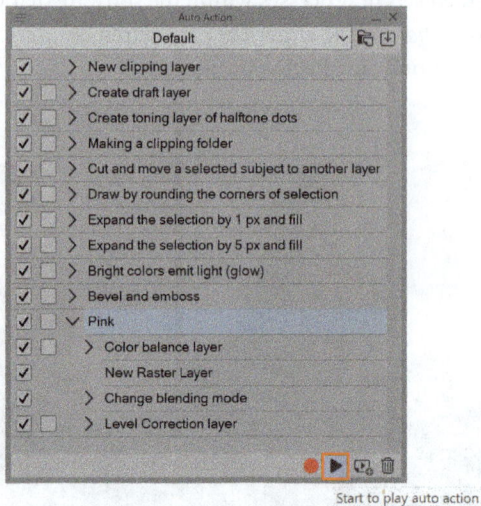

Figure 2.4 – The Start to play auto action button

And CSP would perform all these operations automatically for you. Pretty neat, right? Let's dive into how this works!

To open the **Auto Action** palette, go to **Window | Auto action**. Below you can see how it looks:

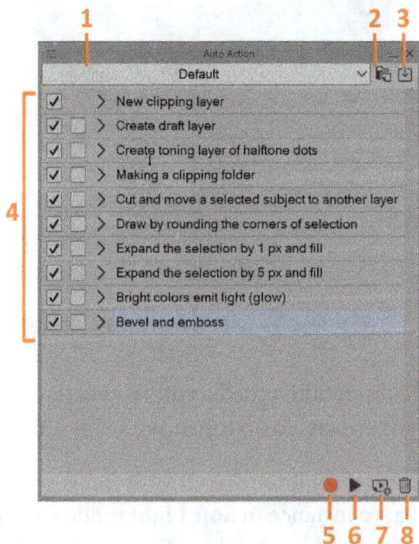

Figure 2.5 – The Auto Action palette

Each of these buttons on the palette has a purpose within the auto actions:

1. **Switch action set to use**: You can separate auto actions into sets, and this drop-down menu allows you to switch which auto action set is currently visible.

2. **Create new auto action set**: You can create as many sets as you wish.

3. **Add auto action set**: This allows you to import sets downloaded from the *CLIP STUDIO ASSETS* website, which we'll talk more about later in this chapter.

4. List of auto actions: You can choose which auto action you want to use.

5. **Start to record auto action**: Use this to record operations into auto actions. This button appears after you have tapped the **Add new auto action to current auto action** button.

6. **Start to play auto action**: Runs all the operations within an auto action.

7. **Add new auto action to current auto action**: Creates a new auto action. After pressing this button, the **Start to record auto action** button will become available..

8. **Delete selected auto action**: Select an auto action and press this button to delete it.

This is the basic structure of the **Auto Action** palette. Next, let's see how to use and modify auto actions.

Using and modifying auto actions

Whenever you want to use an auto action, select it on the list and press the **Start to play auto action** button or double-tap the auto action. The operations of the auto action will run, and that's it! No need for any extra work.

You don't always need to run the entire auto action, though. On the list of auto actions, each auto action has an arrow on its left side. If you press this arrow, it'll show or hide all operations of that auto action:

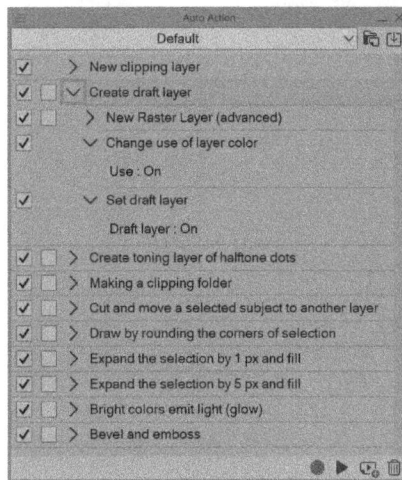

Figure 2.6 – Tap the arrow on the left side of an auto action name to see its operations

When the arrow is pointing to the right side, it means the operations are collapsed, as seen next to **New Raster Layer (advanced)**. When it's pointing down, it shows all operations, as seen next to **Change use of layer color** and **Set draft layer**.

If you click on any of these operations and then press the **Start to play auto action**, it'll run the auto action only from that step onward and ignore all previous steps. Not only that: if you uncheck the checkmark on the left side of an operation, it'll play all the other operations and ignore the unchecked ones. That way, they become even more customizable!

It's also possible to change the order of operations within an auto action and even move one operation to another auto action. You just need to drag and drop them within the **Auto Action** palette. If you press *Ctrl* or *Shift*, more than one operation can be moved; however, *multiple operations can only be moved within the same auto action*.

If you right-click on an auto action, a menu shows up:

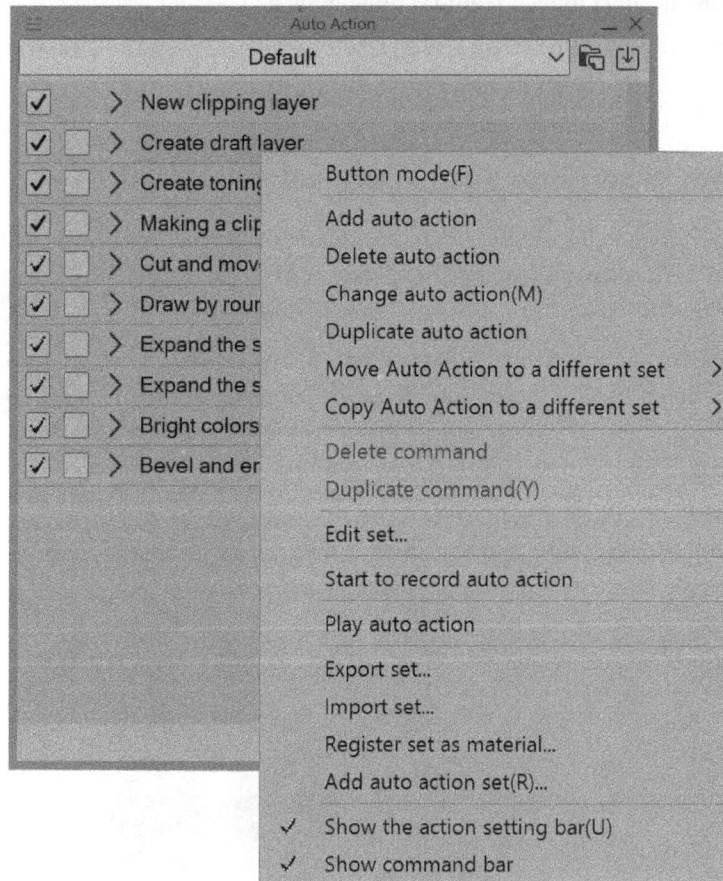

Figure 2.7 – The Auto Action menu

Notice this menu allows you to duplicate auto actions, move auto actions to another set, and more! Most of these are intuitive, but I want to explain **Button mode**. When you select it, the **Auto Action** palette changes and looks like this:

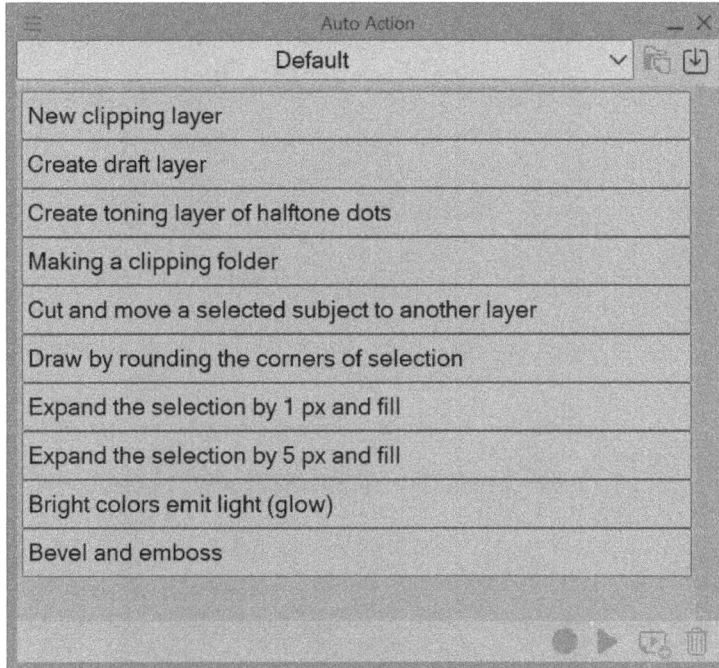

Figure 2.8 – Auto Action palette in Button mode

Each of these auto actions has now become a button, and when you click its name, it will run automatically.

To go back to the previous layout, navigate to the top-left icon on the **Auto Action** palette and click it. A drop-down menu will show, then you click on **Button mode** and it will return to normal.

Now that you know how to use auto actions, let's see how to create your own!

Creating your own auto actions

When you have processes you frequently repeat, creating auto actions will surely save you a lot of time. It's very easy to create an auto action:

1. On the **Auto Action** palette, press the **Add new auto action to current auto action** button.

2. Press the **Start to record auto action** button (red circle).

3. Make the operations you wish to record.

4. Press the **Stop to record auto action** button (red square).

This is how it looks before and after recording:

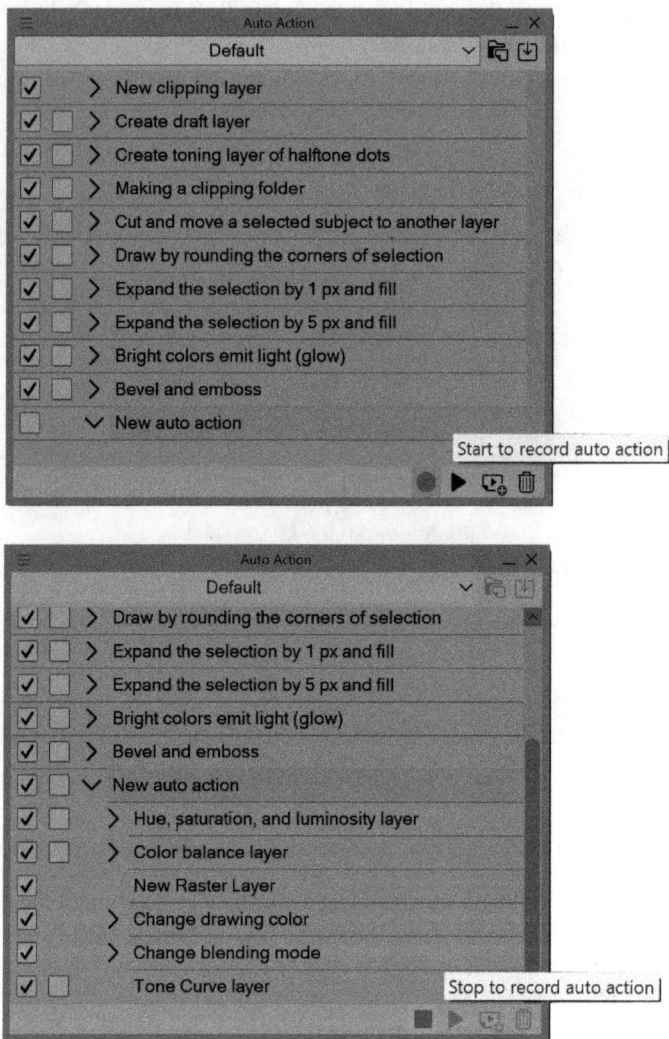

Figure 2.9 – Before and after recording an auto action

And voilà! Your auto action is ready to go. All the operations you performed are now under the new auto action's name, as you can see at the bottom of *Figure 2.9*. Whenever you want to perform these same operations again, just press the **Start to play auto action** button.

Now you know how to create any auto actions to fit your process. However, you might prefer finding auto actions created by other artists instead of making your own—or better yet, combining both! So, what should you do? That's easy as well; let's learn about it next!

Downloading pre-made auto actions

Downloading pre-made actions can save you a lot of time and help you explore creative alternatives to your processes.

To download them, you can go to *CLIP STUDIO ASSETS* and find thousands of auto actions. *CLIP STUDIO ASSETS* is an invaluable catalog for all sorts of CSP assets, including brushes, templates, 3D models, and much more!

To visit it, go to `https://assets.clip-studio.com/`. Then, on the website's search bar, you can type `auto action` or go to the right side of the search bar, click on **Filter** | **Auto action**, and you'll find all the options available.

Incredible artists have shared all sorts of auto actions over there, including things such as the **Watercolor marker** auto action, which turns your painting into a watercolor-like image, and the **Auto line color** auto action, which automatically colors the lines considering the colors you've painted.

There are many auto actions for things you've probably never even thought of before! So, have fun exploring them in *CLIP STUDIO ASSETS*.

Once you've decided on an auto action, just log on to the website with your Clip Studio username and download the auto action, and it'll show under your **Materials** tab on CSP. If you don't know where to find it, go to **Window** | **Materials** and look for **Downloads**.

Summary

And that's it for this chapter! By mastering shortcuts and actions in CSP, you've taken significant steps toward enhancing your digital art workflow.

Personalized shortcuts allow you to access tools and commands instantly, maintaining your creative momentum. Temporarily changing tools with modifier keys adds flexibility and fluidity to your process, enabling seamless transitions between tasks. Leveraging auto actions helps you automate repetitive tasks, ensuring consistency and saving valuable time.

These techniques collectively streamline your workflow, making your creative process more efficient and enjoyable. As you continue to explore and refine these features, you'll find your productivity and artistic output reach new heights, empowering you to focus more on your creative vision and less on navigating the software!

In the next chapter, we'll explore setting up templates and presets to further boost your efficiency and maintain consistency across your projects. This will enable you to work faster and more effectively, ensuring a streamlined creative process from start to finish.

Get This Book's PDF Version and Exclusive Extras

UNLOCK NOW

Scan the QR code (or go to packtpub.com/unlock). Search for this book by name, confirm the edition, and then follow the steps on the page.

Note: Keep your invoice handly. Purchase made directly from packt don't require one.

3

Setting Up Materials for Consistency and Speed

Materials are premade assets and resources that you can use in your artwork to save time and boost your creativity. These materials can include a wide range of elements, such as textures, patterns, brushes, 3D models, and even illustrations. By integrating materials into your projects, you can speed up your creative process and ensure consistent quality across your work. This chapter will guide you through the process of creating and utilizing materials to streamline your workflow and ensure uniformity across your projects.

We're going to cover the following main topics:

- Navigating the Material palette
- Creating Image materials
- Making your own patterns
- Setting up templates
- Registering other types of materials
- Downloading and uploading materials inside CLIP STUDIO ASSETS

By the end of this chapter, you will have the skills to create and implement presets that significantly boost your productivity and ensure consistency across your work. You'll learn how to effectively set up and manage materials in **Clip Studio Paint** (**CSP**) to enhance your workflow and maintain consistency in your projects. You'll discover how to utilize the **Material** palette, register new materials, and organize your resources for quick access and efficient use.

Mastering these functions is essential for artists who want to streamline their workflow, maintain a high level of quality in their work, and save time on project setup and execution.

Navigating the Material palette

The **Material palette** in CSP is a versatile tool that provides access to a wide range of resources designed to enhance your digital artwork. From textures and patterns to custom brushes and 3D models, the Material palette serves as a centralized hub for managing and integrating various elements into your creative projects.

To open it, go to **Window | Material | Material: All Materials**. If you select a different option, such as **Material: Downloads**, the Material palette will open directly to the **Downloads** folder. Regardless of the initial command you choose from the list, you can always navigate to other sections within the Material palette afterward.

In *Figure 3.1*, you can see how the Material palette looks:

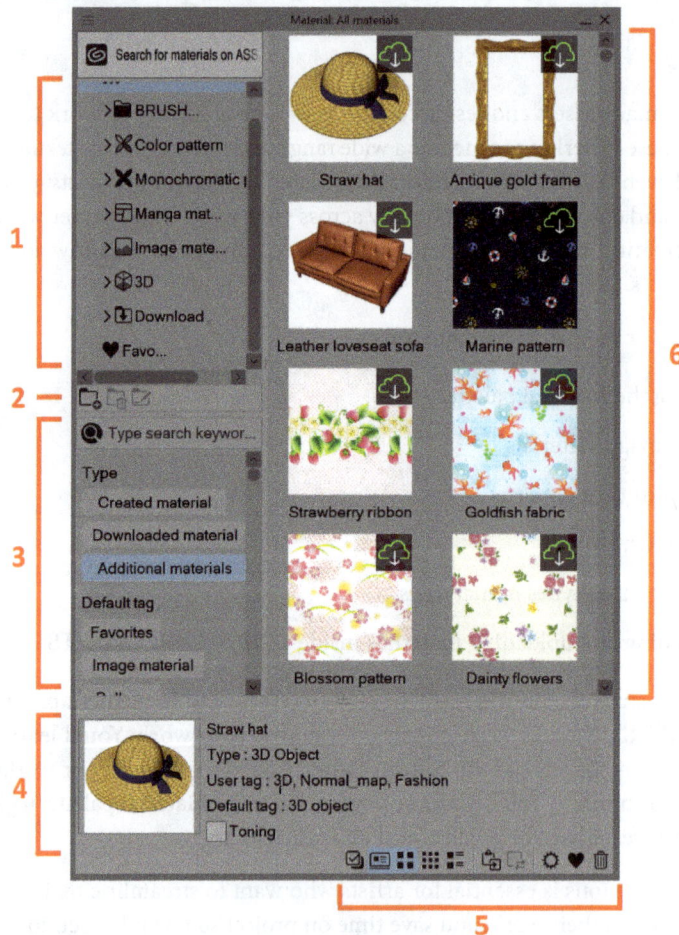

Figure 3.1 – The Material palette

The following settings are available inside the Material palette:

1. **Material Folders**: These are used for navigating premade and personalized categories of materials.

2. **Command bar for material folders**: This set of icons includes buttons for creating, deleting, and renaming folders. Premade folders cannot be deleted or renamed.

> **Important note**
> When you delete a folder, the materials inside it will also be deleted.

3. Search bar and filters: Use these functions to find materials. You can filter materials by **Type**, **Default Tag**, and **User Tag**.

4. **Material Details**: This area displays details on a selected material, such as name, type and tags.

5. **Command bar**: Use this row of icons to show or hide item checkboxes and material details, change the thumbnail size, and paste the material on canvas. When you hover on top of each icon, a description of its function appears. The functions are as follows, from left to right:

   - **Switch show and hide of the item check box**: When you tap on this icon, it shows or hides a checkbox next to each material in the Material palette. When you want to modify multiple materials, use this feature to select them.

   - **Switch show and hide of the detail information of material**: Hides or shows the **Material Details** tab.

   - **Switch thumbnail of the material to large**: Tap this icon to make the thumbnails large on the **Material** palette.

   - **Switch thumbnail of the material to small**: Tap this icon to make the thumbnails small on the **Material** palette.

   - **Switch thumbnail of the material to detail**: Tap this icon to make the thumbnails large and show details on the **Material** palette.

   - **Paste selected material to canvas**: Tap this icon to paste the selected material on the canvas. The material will be placed at the center of the canvas.

   - **Replace editing layer with selected material**: Replaces the editing layer with the selected material.

   - **Show property window of selected materials**: Opens the **Material property** palette, where you can edit the material's details.

   - **Add to/Remove from Favorites**: Use this icon to favorite a material. Then, you can go to the **Material Folders** and select **Favorite** to see all of your favorites.

   - **Delete selected materials**: Tap this icon to delete a material. This action cannot be undone.

6. **List of materials**: Materials of the selected folder will show up in this area. Some of them will have a cloud symbol in the top-right corner; it means the material is available but has not been downloaded yet.

At the bottom part of the **Material Details** area, shown in *Figure 3.1* (4), there's a checkbox for **Toning**. If you check it, the material will be used as a black-and-white screentone, and the **Simple tone settings** dialog appears:

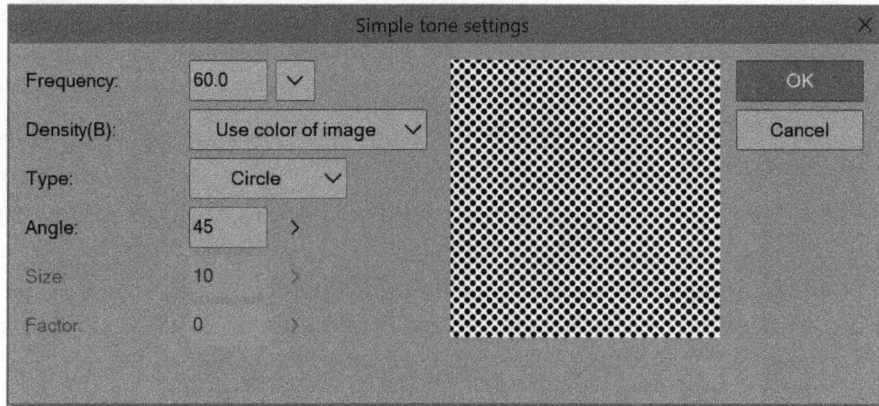

Figure 3.2 – Simple tone settings

With these settings, you can determine the frequency of dots, density, type of tone, and angle.

After seeing all the possible settings within the Material palette, you might ask yourself how to actually use materials. There is more than one way to include materials in your artwork, and it's very simple. One method is to click on the **Paste selected material to the canvas** icon on the command bar of the Material palette, which is applicable to all types of materials.

Some material types have specific methods. If you want to paste an **Image**, **3D**, **Workspace**, or **Animation** material to your artwork, you can drag and drop it onto the canvas.

Important note

If you drag and drop an image or 3D material onto the canvas, it will be placed exactly at the mouse location. To paste the asset at the center of the canvas, use the **Paste selected material to the canvas** icon on the command bar of the Material palette.

Brush materials can be dragged and dropped onto the **Sub Tool** palette, and color set materials, onto the **Color Set** palette.

Now that you understand how the Material palette works and how to paste materials onto a canvas, let's explore creating your own image materials to further personalize and streamline your workflow.

Creating Image materials

Creating Image materials enables you to personalize your resource library, enabling greater customization and efficiency in your digital art projects.

You can register not only one layer as a material but also multiple layers as a single material. However, if you save them as image material, they will all be saved as a *single layer*. If you wish to save multiple layers as such, then you must register them as a template, as we will cover later in this chapter, under the section *Setting up templates*.

When creating an Image material, all layers will be saved as one, so you must be thoughtful during the creative process and plan ahead. How will you use this material? Do you need to register only lines, or include flat colors? What about shading? Make sure you have this planned before saving the material.

To register one or more layers as a material, follow these steps:

1. Select the desired layers you wish to register as material.

2. Go to **Edit | Register Image as Material…**.

3. The **Material property** dialog will appear:

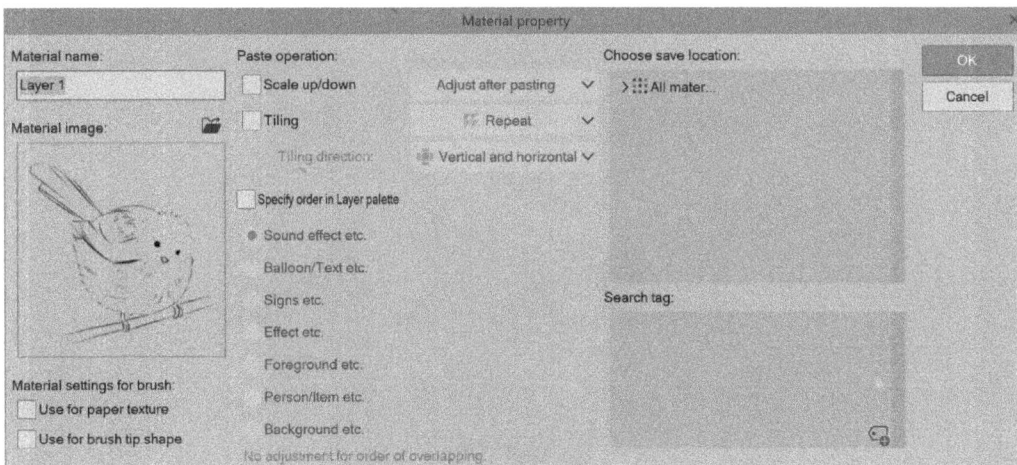

Figure 3.3 – The Material property dialog

> **Important note**
>
> If you wish to register only part of one or more layers as a material, make a selection and proceed to register the material. If no selection is made, the entire layer will be registered.

4. You can name the material on the top left side of the **Material property** dialog, under **Material name**. Use a descriptive name so it's easier for you to know what it is, and also easier for you to find using the search box of the Material palette.

5. Below **Material image**, there's a preview of the material. Check this thumbnail every time to ensure the material looks exactly how you want.

6. On the bottom left side, there are two checkboxes for **Material settings for brush**. If it's a single layer, you can set it to be used for paper texture and brush tip shape. We'll see more about brush materials in *Chapter 5, Unlocking the Full Potential of Brush Settings*.

7. In the middle section of the **Material property** dialog (*Figure 3.3*), you can see settings for **Paste operation**: **Scale up/down** and **Tiling**.

   Tiling is especially useful for patterns, which we'll cover in the next section.

8. If you select **Scale up/down**, the material will be pasted onto the canvas with a transformation box around it. When setting up this feature, you can determine how the transformation will occur. Below are the five different operation options, each illustrated with an example image.

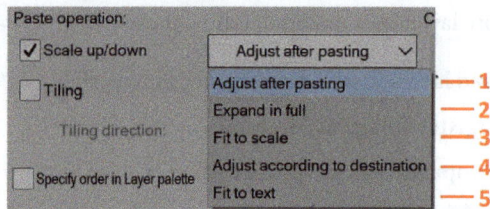

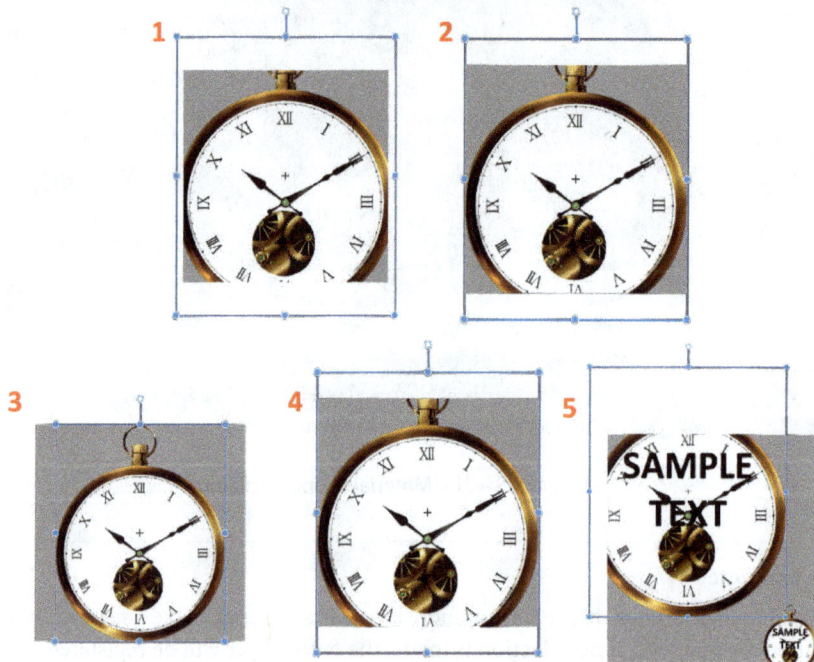

Figure 3.4 – Options for scaling the material up or down

Let's understand the explanations of each numbered element from *Figure 3.4* in depth:

- **Adjust after pasting**: The material will be pasted with the transformation box around it, but no automatic changes will be made. The material's size will match the dimensions of the layers at the time they were registered.

- **Expand in full**: The material will be pasted and scaled to cover the entire canvas, even if some of its edges extend beyond the canvas boundaries.

- **Fit to scale**: The material will be scaled up or down to fit the canvas, and no part of it will go outside of the canvas.

- **Adjust according to destination**: The material will be scaled up or down in accordance with the size of the destination.

- **Fit to text**: The material will be sized to completely encompass a text layer. This function is most useful for balloon materials. When pasting a material with this setting, its effect will change depending on how you paste it:

  - If you drag and drop, the material will be placed over the text where you drop it.

  - If you use **Paste operation**, the material will *not* be placed on top of any text. It will be pasted just like the **Adjust after pasting** setting.

If you have a selection and paste an image, the selection will become a layer mask (*Figure 3.5*):

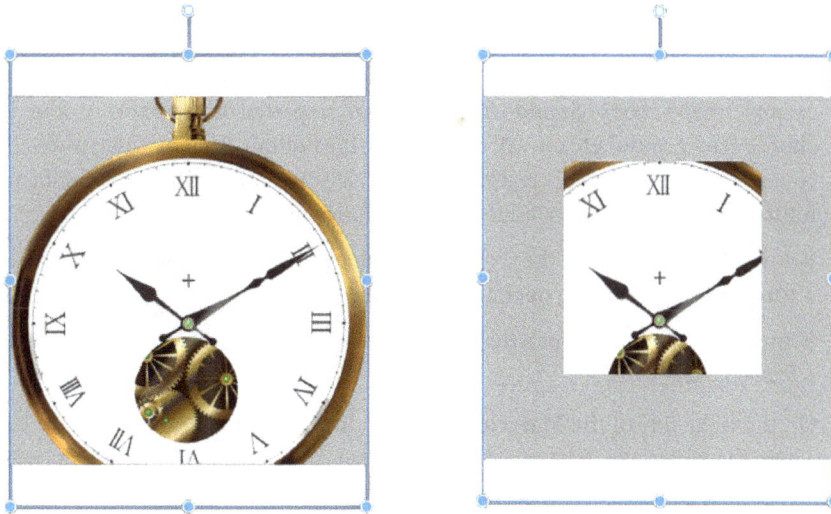

Figure 3.5 – Expand in full (left side: without selection; right side: with selection)

9. On the **Material property** dialog (*Figure 3.3*), you can also select **Specify order in Layer palette**, as seen in *Figure 3.6*:

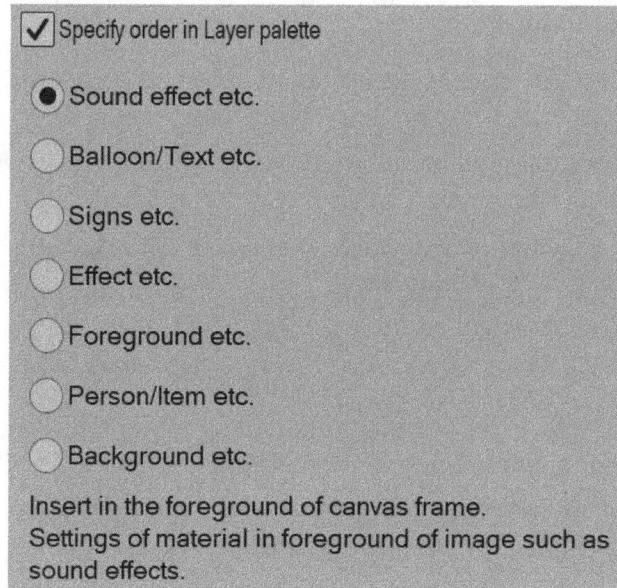

Figure 3.6 – Specify order in Layer palette

That means the material will be pasted in a specific position within the layers of the file. For example, if you choose **Sound effect etc.**, it will be pasted on top of every other layer, but if you choose **Background etc.**, it will be pasted at the bottom. That can always be changed later, of course. However, if you're creating an asset that you know will serve a specific function within future images, it can be useful to set this beforehand.

Below all of the options, there's a short explanation of what each one does, so if you're ever unsure how each of them operates, check that explanation.

If **Specify order in Layer palette** is not checked, the image will be pasted on top of the currently selected layer.

10. On the right side of the **Material property** dialog (*Figure 3.3*), you must select the location where the material will be saved and add a tag if you wish. I always add a custom tag so that it's easier to find my own materials later.

11. Press **OK**, and it's done!

If you wish for a quicker process, you can drag and drop the layer you want to register onto the material list in the Material palette. All those properties can be changed afterward by double-tapping the thumbnail of the material in the material list.

Having explored the creation of image materials and how to use them, we now turn our attention to another powerful tool in CSP: creating patterns.

Making your own patterns

Patterns can add intricate details and textures to your work, providing depth and visual interest. It can add a nice touch of detail and believability to your art since we find so many patterns around us in real life. Let's delve into the process of designing and applying patterns to elevate your digital art even further.

After you have drawn the image you'll use as a pattern, go to **Edit** | **Register Material** | **Image…**. On the **Material property** window, select **Tiling**, and a few options will appear:

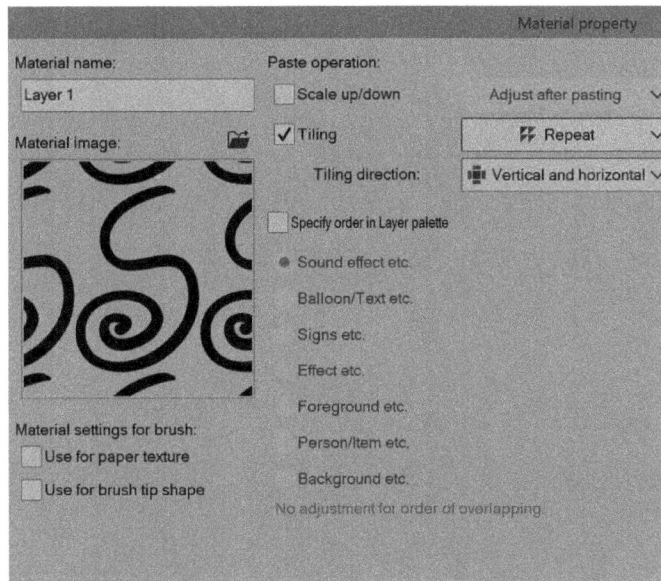

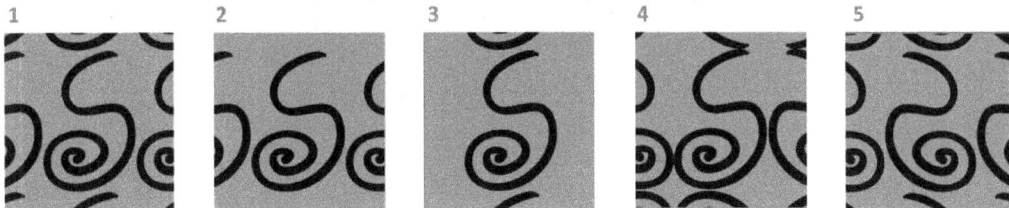

Figure 3.7 – Tiling options

Below are the **Tiling** options:

1. **Repeat | Vertical and horizontal**: The image will be repeated in both directions.

2. **Repeat | Only horizontal**: The image will be repeated only horizontally.

3. **Repeat | Only vertical**: The image will be repeated only vertically.

4. **Reverse**: Each row will be horizontally reversed compared to the ones next to it. So, it will be one row turned to the left, then one row to the right, and so on.

5. **Flip**: All rows will be horizontally flipped.

Notice that when you set the image to repeat vertically and horizontally, gaps in the original image can alter the final effect:

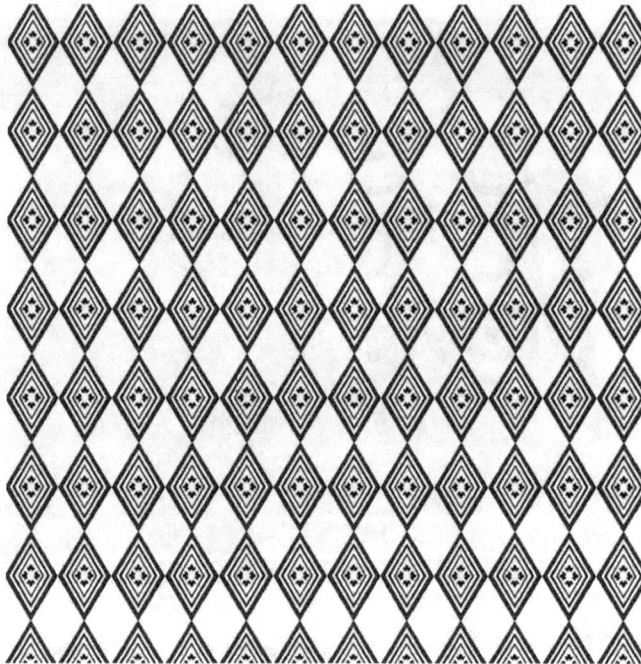

Figure 3.8 – Gaps inside a pattern

This may be intentional, but sometimes, it's not our desired result. Let's see how to create a seamless pattern without any gaps next.

Creating seamless patterns

For the pattern in *Figure 3.8*, I want all the shapes to connect with each other, leaving no gaps in between. That means I need to ensure that the image connects on all sides of the canvas: the right edge must connect to the left edge, and the top edge must connect to the bottom edge.

I will explain step by step how to achieve this:

1. Start by placing your shape on the canvas:

Figure 3.9 – Place your shape on the canvas

If you want the design to fill the pattern completely, with no empty areas, then you want to ensure there are no gaps around the design. If you're unsure how to start, placing a simple rectangle in another layer can help you visualize which areas need to be filled. This rectangle isn't necessarily the one we'll use for the final pattern, so be sure to fill a little more than just this area.

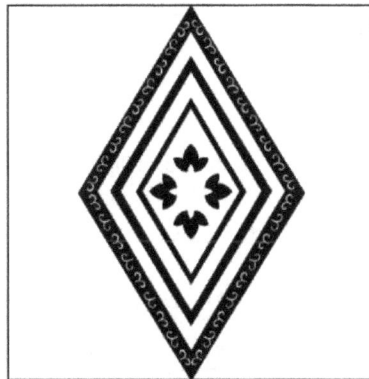

Figure 3.10 – This black frame can help visualize what needs to be filled

2. Now, copy and paste the original shape to the right side. I filled the top-right side completely by using two shapes – depending on your original shape, it might take more or fewer shapes.

Figure 3.11 – Copy and paste the shape until it fills one side

3. Next, duplicate it and flip it horizontally by going to **Edit | Transform | Flip horizontal…**. Using the transform tool (*Ctrl* or *command + T*), drag it until the opposite side is filled.

Figure 3.12 – Copy, paste it, and flip it to fill the opposite side

4. Duplicate it again and fill the bottom area.

Figure 3.13 – Fill the entire area with no gaps

5. This is enough for now since I can find a rectangle that encompasses the whole original structure, as well as the corners of the duplicated ones:

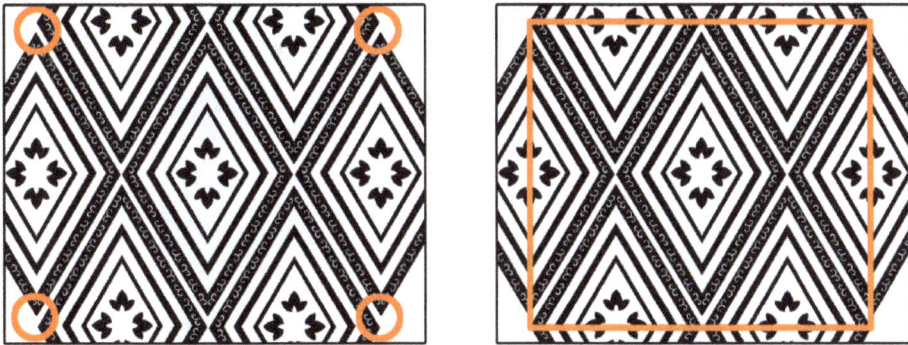

Figure 3.14 – Find the corners that crop each shape in half
vertically (sides) or horizontally (top and bottom)

Notice that to identify this rectangular area, I aligned the corners so that the shape on the far right is vertically divided in half, the shape on the far left is also vertically divided in half, and the shapes at the top and bottom are horizontally divided in half. This is what results in a seamless pattern with no gaps:

Figure 3.15 – Finished pattern with no gaps

After seeing how to make patterns, you need to know how to use them effectively in your images.

Applying patterns efficiently

Let's see now how to apply patterns efficiently We'll use the following image as our base:

Figure 3.16 – This is our base, and we'll add a pattern to her shirt

1. The first thing we'll do is paste a pattern to the image and resize it. At first, it's completely flat and covers the whole scene:

Figure 3.17 – The pattern as soon as applied is flat and spills outside of the shirt

How do we fix this? It's quite easy. We'll begin by adjusting the pattern so it conforms to the surface of her shirt. Once the pattern follows the contours of the surface, we'll erase any areas that extend beyond the shirt. Following this order is important because wrapping the pattern around the shirt can bring into the shirt some areas that were previously outside of it.

2. To make this change, we will duplicate the pattern layer and rasterize it, so it becomes editable. Right-click the layer on the **Layer** palette, then go to **Rasterize**.

3. After rasterizing the pattern, you can now edit it. We'll use the **Liquify** tool to mold the pattern in a way that pushes and pulls it according to the fabric. We'll cover the Liquify tool in detail in *Chapter 12, Enhancing Your Art With Post Processing Adjustments. Figure 3.18* shows one flower after being liquified.

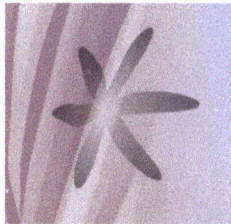

Figure 3.18 – Part of the pattern after being liquified

4. Next, do this to the entire pattern that covers the shirt:

Figure 3.19 – After liquifying the entire pattern

5. At this point, we can erase everything outside of the shirt. We'll use a layer mask (more about those in *Chapter 8, Maximizing Efficiency and Organization with Layers*) to avoid destructive editing. Simply erase everything that is not part of the shirt:

Figure 3.20 – Limiting the pattern to the shirt

6. To finish it, we'll change the color of the pattern, and it's done:

Figure 3.21 – Finished painting with pattern applied

Now that you've mastered the art of pattern creation, let's move on to setting up templates. Templates will help you maintain consistency and speed across your projects by providing predefined settings and structures tailored to your specific needs.

Setting up templates

Templates are multiple layers and/or layer folders that you can save and use in future artworks. Setting up templates in CSP is a powerful way to maintain consistency and speed in your projects.

Registering a template is very similar to registering an image material:

1. First, create the layer structure you wish to save.
2. Then, go to **Edit** | **Register material...** | **Template**.
3. The **Material Property** dialog will appear.
4. Just like registering an image material, you name it, select a save location, add tags, and then press **OK**.

> **Important note**
>
> All the layers in the project – except the paper layer – will be registered, so make sure to delete any layers you do not wish to include in the template.
>
> If you're dealing with a complex image and only wish to register part of it, I suggest you copy (*Ctrl* or *command* + *C*) the desired layers, go to **File** | **Create New from Clipboard**, and then register it.

Although the processes for registering images and templates are very similar, there are two important differences between them.

The first one is that you can't set **Material settings for brush** and **Paste operation** when it comes to templates, as shown on the bottom left part of the following figure:

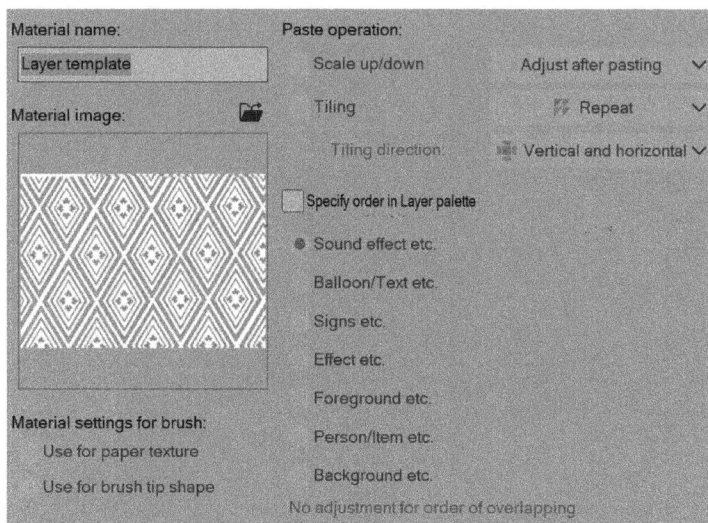

Figure 3.22 – Material settings for brush and Paste operation are unavailable for templates

That's because templates are multi-layered structures, so they can't be used for brushes and patterns.

Another interesting difference is that when you choose to register as a template, it will only consider what's on the canvas, as seen in *Figure 3.22*, while if you register as an image, it will consider everything on the layer – even if the canvas has been cropped, as you can see in *Figure 3.23*:

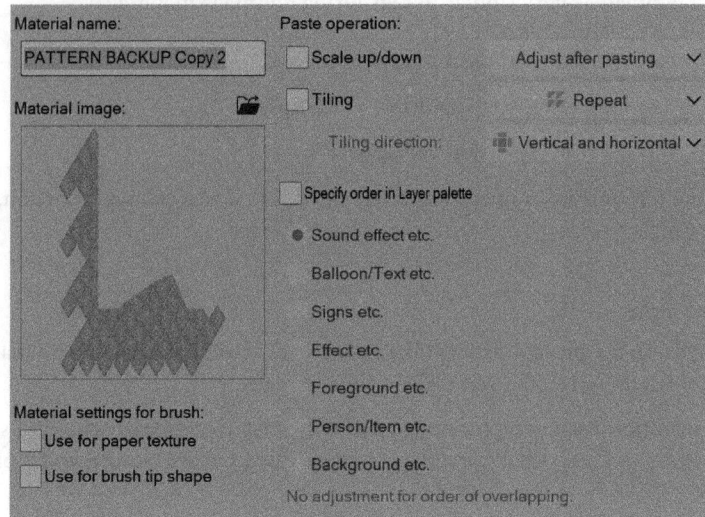

Figure 3.23 – Registering an image considers the whole layer, even what's outside of the canvas

Templates are more flexible than image materials because you can turn parts of them on and off, use layer masks on specific sections, and customize individual layers without altering the entire template. That means you can register a material with color and shading, and easily change that color and shading for a specific artwork later. So, if you plan on changing parts of a material later, it's best to register it as a template.

If your project contains a frame folder, it will be registered as a frame template material, which can be applied from the moment you create a new file by selecting the **Template** checkbox in the **New** dialog, as shown in *Figure 3.24*:

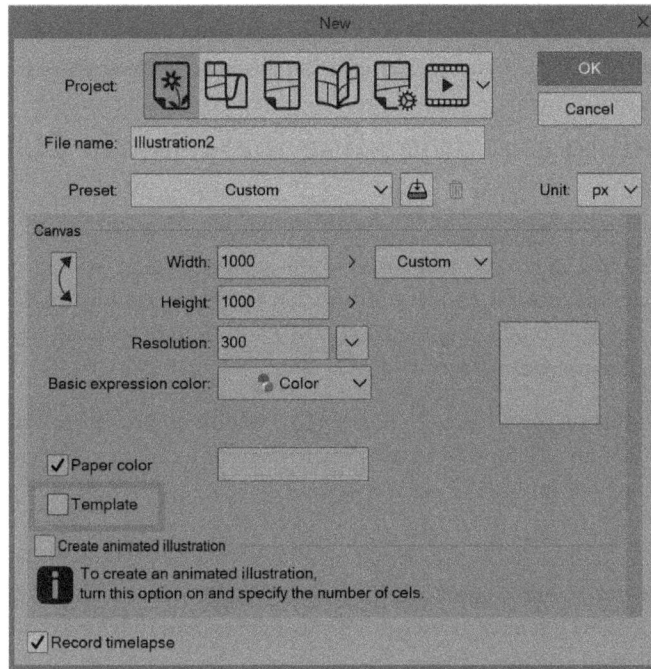

Figure 3.24 – Create a new file with a template

Up to this point, we've covered how to create image, pattern, and template materials. There are still many other types of materials you can register, which we'll see in the next section.

Registering other types of materials

There are specific steps you must take to register workspaces, sub-tools, animations, auto actions, and color sets:

1. **Workspace**: Navigate to **Window** | **Workspace** | **Register Workspace as Material**.

2. **Sub Tool**: In the **Sub Tool** palette, navigate to the **Sub Tool** palette menu | **Register Sub Tool as material…**.

3. **Color Set**: In the **Color Set** palette, navigate to the **Color Set** palette menu | **Register color set as material…**.

4. **Auto Action**: In the **Auto Action** palette, navigate to the **Auto Action** palette menu | **Register set as material…**.

5. **Animation**: On a canvas with the timeline enabled, select a track or clip from the **Timeline** palette. Then, navigate to **Edit** | **Register material…** | **Animation**.

3D materials have their own specifications, which we'll cover in *Chapter 14, Altering and Posing 3D Figures*, and *Chapter 16, Creating 3D Backgrounds*.

Now that we've covered all you must know about creating materials, let's explore CLIP STUDIO ASSETS, which you can use to find materials other artists have created and share your own materials.

Downloading and uploading materials in CLIP STUDIO ASSETS

CLIP STUDIO ASSETS is a comprehensive online resource where artists can download a vast array of materials, including brushes, textures, 3D models, and more, to enhance their projects. This section will guide you through navigating the *CLIP STUDIO ASSETS* website, finding and downloading resources, as well as uploading your own.

Accessing and utilizing the *CLIP STUDIO ASSETS* website is straightforward once you understand its layout and functionality. Start by visiting the website. You can go to `https://assets.clip-studio.com` in your browser or open it from CSP:

1. To open it from CSP, navigate to **File | Open CLIP STUDIO...**.

2. Once the new window opens, click on the top-right corner of the **CLIP STUDIO** window, on the grid icon with nine squares. Click on **Search for materials**, and the **CLIP STUDIO ASSETS** page will open on your browser.

3. Another option is on the home page of **CLIP STUDIO**, which already shows some materials. Navigate to the right-side of the heading **Top Free Materials** and click on the link named **Assets**. The **CLIP STUDIO ASSETS** page will open on your browser.

The main page offers various categories, such as brushes, patterns, and 3D models, making it easy to browse and find what you need. Use the search function and filters to narrow down your options based on specific criteria, such as **Type**, **Software**, **Uploaded by**, **Price**, and **Monthly/annual plan bonus materials**.

There are paid and free assets. If you wish to buy an asset, you need to first add Clippy Coins or GOLD, which are the currencies used on the website, to your wallet. You can buy those by logging in, then clicking on your profile image and tapping either **GOLD Wallet** or **Clippy Wallet**. From either of those pages, click on the overview to see both wallets. You can buy GOLD points with your credit card, while Clippy points can be acquired in two ways:

- By uploading free materials to CLIP STUDIO ASSETS.

- By becoming a GOLD member, which is a monthly membership you pay with your GOLD points.

You can find in-depth explanations about Clippy points at the following link: `https://accounts.clip-studio.com/help#clippy`.

Once you're familiar with navigating the site, you can start exploring the different categories of assets available. Each asset comes with a description and a preview image or video to help you decide if it suits your needs.

> **Important note**
>
> All materials inside *CLIP STUDIO ASSETS* can be used for commercial purposes. However, there are licensed materials, which have specific conditions of use. You can recognize licensed materials by the phrase *limited license* in their thumbnail image.
>
> Always check the terms of use of licensed materials.

To download an asset, simply click on the download button, and it will be directly imported into CSP. Then, navigate to the **Material** palette | **Download**, and locate your recently downloaded asset. To keep your materials organized, I suggest you remove downloaded materials from the **Download** folder and place them in their respective folders.

CLIP STUDIO ASSETS is not just a place to download resources; it's also a platform where you can contribute with your own materials. Creating and uploading your own brushes, textures, or models can enrich the community and showcase your unique style.

To share your resources, you must use CSP as well as your web browser. Here's a step-by-step guide:

1. In your web browser, click on your profile picture. Select **New Post** | **Materials for CLIP STUDIO software**.

2. **CLIP STUDIO** will launch on the **Manage Materials** screen. Double-click the material you'd like to publish. A new dialog will open.

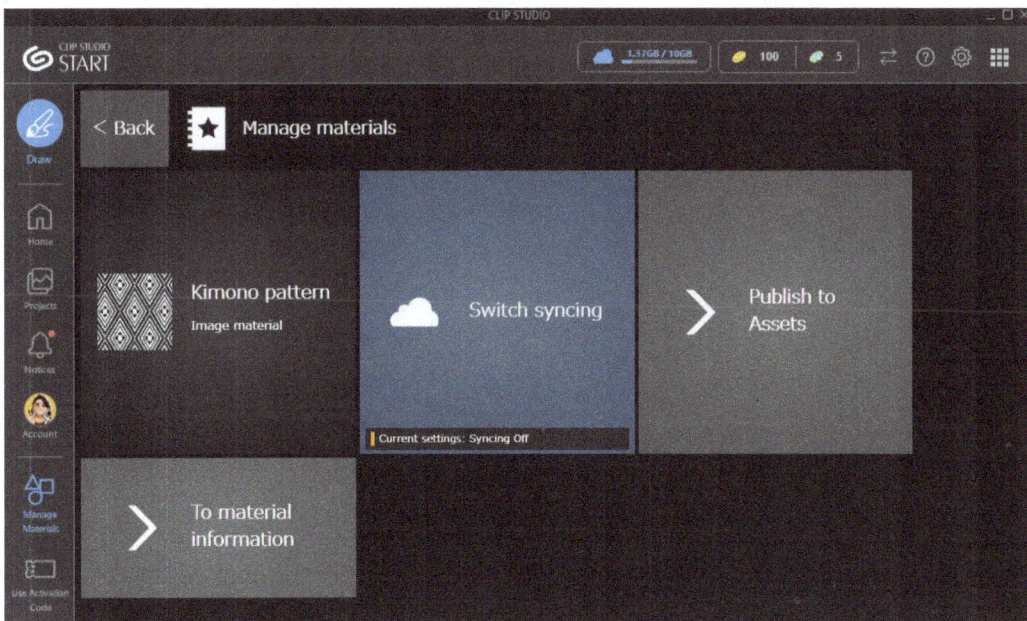

Figure 3.25 – Select Publish to Assets to upload the material

3.   Select **Publish to Assets**. This will start uploading the material.

4.   After uploading it, publish it from the **Uploads** screen.

With this, we've covered the most essential information you must know about CLIP STUDIO ASSETS.

Summary

In this chapter, we've explored essential techniques for setting up materials to ensure consistency and speed in your digital art projects. Mastering the setup and utilization of CSP materials is a pivotal step in enhancing both the consistency and efficiency of your digital art projects.

On top of knowing how to manipulate assets with the Material palette, you can now create image materials, templates, and patterns, transforming your artwork into reusable assets. This process allows you to build a personal library of materials that can be easily applied across multiple projects. If you don't want to create assets or if you want to share yours, you're ready to download and upload materials inside CLIP STUDIO ASSETS and access a vast online repository of resources.

By organizing your materials, customizing resources to fit your style, and leveraging the power of CSP's extensive material library, you can maintain a high standard of quality across your work. As you continue to explore and refine your use of these materials, you'll find that your creative process becomes smoother and more intuitive.

In the next chapter, we will delve into organizing projects effectively. You will learn techniques and strategies to keep your projects well-structured and manageable, ensuring that you can easily navigate and maintain your creative work with confidence and ease.

4

Organizing Your Projects Effectively

Efficient project management is a game-changer for digital artists, enabling them to streamline their workflow and maximize productivity. This chapter provides invaluable insights and skills that every digital artist can benefit from, making project management less of a chore and more of a strategic advantage. Sometimes, out of distraction, artists will create obstacles for their own work without realizing it, so this chapter is about taking these out of the way and improving your workflow on **Clip Studio Paint** (CSP).

Many will skip this chapter, thinking they don't need it. Don't be one of them! This knowledge is foundational to crafting your most efficient art process.

Here's what we'll learn in this chapter:

- Organizing your layers efficiently
- Non-destructive editing for a stress-free process
- Streamlining your workflow with best practices

By the end of this chapter, you will be able to maintain a clutter-free workspace, keep your projects organized from start to finish, and enhance your overall efficiency. This will free up more time for you to focus on your creative process, ultimately leading to higher-quality artwork and a more satisfying artistic journey.

Organizing your layers efficiently

When working on a complex piece with several layers, you must organize them well so you don't spend precious minutes trying to find a layer. After all, layers should simplify your life, not complicate it.

Before we begin, I want to emphasize that you should *use as few layers as possible*. The more layers you have, the more cluttered and difficult your image will be to edit!

For example, I've seen many beginner artists create several layers just for the line art. Sure, if you feel the need to use multiple layers, do it. But once you're satisfied with them, you should merge them to make them easier to handle. You can keep a backup of the original layers if you want, which we'll learn more about later in this chapter, in the *Streamlining your workflow with best practices* section.

We'll start with a foundational step: naming your layers, which will save you time and make your process smoother.

Naming your layers

The first practice we'll approach is naming layers. Many artists are repelled by this idea, but it's so quick and makes our lives much easier. That's why you must make sure to automate this into your workflow.

When creating a new layer, press *F2*, name it, and then press *Enter*. It's really that simple.

Here's an example of what my layers look like in an actual painting:

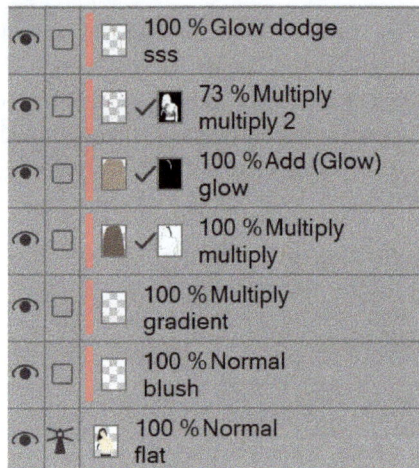

Figure 4.1 – Example of how I name my layers

Imagine if I had dozens of layers named Layer 1, Layer 2, … Layer 54. What a nightmare!

There are moments when you can let go of naming, but you must decide on particular conditions for that so you always follow the same process intuitively. In my case, I don't name layers if either of the following apply:

- There's only one layer in the file
- It's an adjustment layer

You might decide on a different set of rules depending on your process. Just make sure you follow them.

In my process, I name all layers at first – sketch, line art, flat colors, shading, and so on –but I stop when I merge them into a single layer.

However, if you still find yourself unsure of which layer a specific part is on, even with named layers, there's a solution for that!

Press *Ctrl/command + Shift* and click on the exact point you want to locate. CSP will automatically select its layer for you.

Layer organization involves more than just naming, though. Another great way to organize layers is by color-coding.

Color-coding your layers

Assigning different colors to layers based on their function (e.g., sketches, line art, colors, or effects) or part of the image (e.g., character skin, character hair, or background trees) can be very convenient. This visual organization method helps you navigate complex projects with ease.

To color-code a layer, navigate to the **Layer** palette, then select **Change palette color** (the square box at the top left), and select a color:

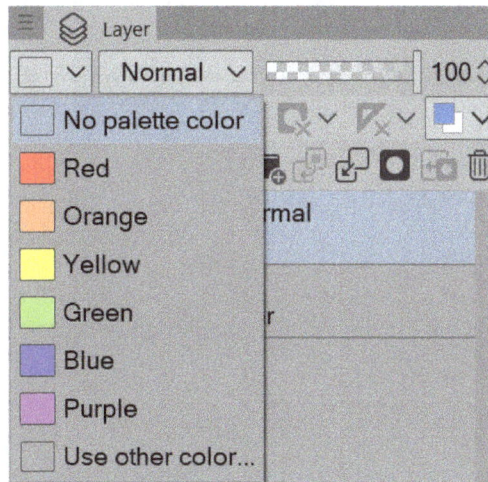

Figure 4.2 – Changing the color of a layer

You can choose between some predefined colors, or you can click on **Use other color...** and hand-pick exactly what color you wish to use.

I usually color-code layers when creating different light setups for a painting – I want to separate the layers of each setup so it's easy to switch them on and off:

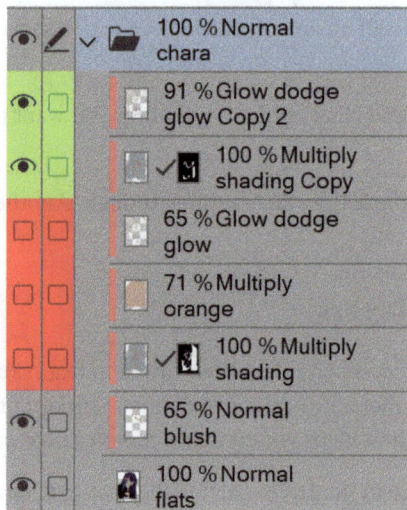

Figure 4.3 – How I color-code layers for different lighting setups

I don't usually name the second lighting setup since I already differentiate it by color, and I'll erase one of the setups later anyway.

Sometimes, I also use it to separate characters from backgrounds or lines from colors. There are many ways you can use this feature!

Grouping layers

Layer folders are essential for keeping everything neat and uncluttering your **Layer** palette. I use them all the time!

There are a few different ways to group layers:

- Go to **Layer | New Layer Folder**. An empty folder will be created. Then, you can drag and drop layers inside the folder.

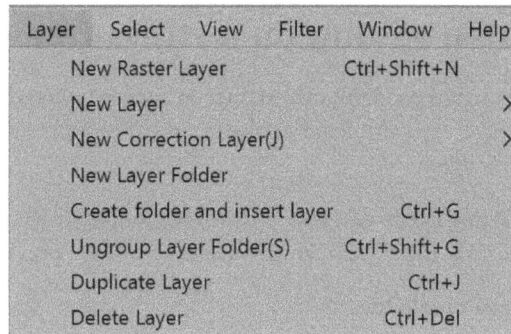

Figure 4.4 – Grouping layers with the Layer menu

- Another option is to select the layers you wish to group, then navigate to **Layer** | **Create folder and insert layer**. The selected layers will be grouped.

- Alternatively, you can select the layers you wish to group and press *Ctrl/command* + *G*. Those layers will be grouped.

Important note

If you don't select a specific layer and press *Ctrl/command* + *G*, your currently active layer or folder will be moved to a new folder.

I usually group my layers for two reasons:

- The first reason is to separate elements of the image. So, I'll group background layers in one folder and character layers in another. Then, within the background folder, I might make one group for trees, another for the sky, and so on.

- The other reason is to back up previous versions of my work. We'll talk more about this in the next section, which is about non-destructive editing. For now, I just want you to know that this possibility exists.

When working with layers, there are three main ways to organize them: naming, color-coding, and grouping. Use all three simultaneously and you'll never waste time looking for a layer again!

Next, you'll learn about non-destructive editing, which will save you from the suffering of making a significant change and then deciding it was better before… only to discover you cannot change it back.

Non-destructive editing for a stress-free process

We've all been there: you make a significant change in your artwork, decide it was better before, and when you try to go back… you can't. Panic settles in, and after some internal struggle, you accept that you must redo it all over again.

Well, not anymore! It is possible to edit your artwork without destroying what you created previously; this way, if you change your mind, you can go back to one of the previous versions.

There are three ways you can do this.

- The first one is to simply save a new file with a new name and make the changes you wish to make. I don't prefer this method because it clutters my computer with files, and I sometimes get confused by all the versions. But it's still a possibility, especially if you wish to delete layers to reduce the file size.

- The second method is to group layers, duplicate them, and then make changes to the new group of layers. That is my preferred method because it doesn't clutter my computer while still saving previous versions.

  Its downside is that your file might become huge (I have artwork files that take up several GB of space). Another downside is that too many folders can clutter your **Layer** palette. My solution for this is just to group even further by selecting all backup layers and grouping them in a new folder named backup.

- The third way to make backup versions is very new and was only created for CSP version 3.0: the use of layer comps.

Layer comps are a function available on **Clip Studio Paint EX** that lets you save different versions of artwork within the same file, keeping the different layer visibility of each version separate. You can then toggle them on and off. They provide an efficient way to manage and organize complex projects, particularly when working on multi-layered illustrations, comics, or animations.

Layer comps allow you to save different combinations of layer visibility without the need to manually toggle layers on or off each time you want to see a different version of your work. This feature is especially useful when you need to show multiple stages or versions of a project, such as alternate color schemes, background variations, or different lighting setups, without duplicating files or layers.

> **Important note**
> Layer comps only record the visibility of your layers. If you change the layer order or delete any of the layers, they will disappear from all comps.

Using layer comps, you can quickly create multiple views of your work and switch between them with a single click. For example, if you're working on a character with multiple outfit variations or a comic page with different dialogue options, you can set up each variation as a separate layer comp. This helps streamline your workflow, making it easy to present different options to clients or adjust various stages of your project without the risk of losing previous settings.

You can find them by going to **Window | Layer Comps (2).** When you select it, the following palette will open:

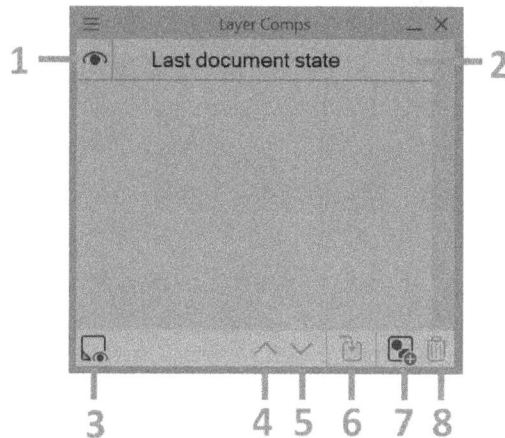

Figure 4.5 – The Layer Comps palette

The numbers in *Figure 4.5* represent the following settings:

1. Toggles visibility on/off.
2. Displays the name of the layer comp.
3. **Added layers are visible on all layer comps**: If toggled on, when you add a new layer after saving a layer comp, the new layer will be visible on all of them. It's best to keep this turned off, or it can mess up your saved comps.
4. **Apply previous layer comp**: Quickly switch to the previous layer comp (above).
5. **Apply next layer comp**: Quickly switch to the next layer comp (below).
6. **Save layer comp**: Saves any changes made to the currently selected layer comp.
7. **Add layer comp**: Create a new layer comp.
8. **Delete layer comp**: Deletes the selected layer comp.

When you create a layer comp, all the layer visibility is saved as a version you can refer to. For example, let's say I have one painting and want to create two versions of it, with and without a background.

Figure 4.6 – Example of a layer comp

Figure 4.6 shows the image with a background, which I saved as a new comp called **Yellow bg**.

After toggling the background layer visibility off and saving it as a new layer comp (**No bg**), this is how it looks:

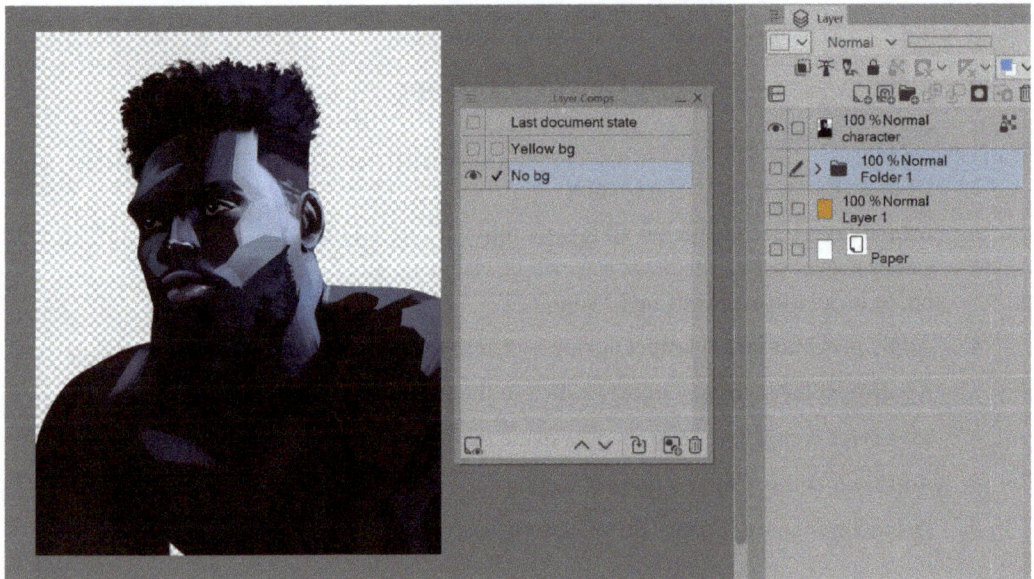

Figure 4.7 – Example of another layer comp within the same image

Notice that the visibility of the layers on the right side is different in *Figure 4.7*. If I click to toggle **Yellow bg** on, it'll go back to *Figure 4.6*.

After you create a new layer comp, any changes you make to the file will not be saved to this layer comp. You must press the **Save layer comp** button in the **Layer Comps** palette if you wish to apply changes to a layer comp. Alternatively, you can right-click the layer comp's name and select **Save layer comp**. The following dialog will open:

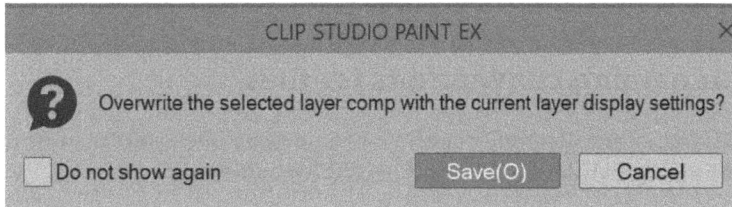

Figure 4.8 – Overwriting a layer comp

If you're certain you wish to overwrite the layer comp, press **Save(O)**, and it will be done.

Now that you've learned how to edit non-destructively, it's time to learn some best practices to streamline your workflow.

Streamlining your workflow with best practices

Streamlining your workflow with best practices is essential for enhancing productivity and ensuring the quality of your digital artwork. In this section and its subsections, we'll explore critical techniques and strategies that will help you work more efficiently, from maintaining a consistent file structure to regularly backing up your work.

By applying these best practices, you'll speed up your process and produce higher-quality work in less time. Let's dive into these proven methods that will transform your digital art workflow.

Maintain a consistent file structure

Maintaining a consistent file structure is crucial for keeping your projects organized and easily accessible. Establishing a clear and logical hierarchy will save time and reduce frustration when locating specific layers.

Establish a layer folder hierarchy that makes sense for your workflow and stick to it. Create separate folders for different parts of the project, and within each folder, try sticking to the same process. This consistent organization will save you time when finding specific layers quickly.

As an example, my file structure usually goes as follows.

I start with a sketch layer; then, I'll create a folder for the background below it. Between the two, I'll add character layers in a specific order: flat colors, blush, shading (two layers for it), subsurface scattering, reflective light, and glow.

Having this specific process makes it a no-brainer for me to take a painting from start to finish and find any layers within the image. Of course, you'll create your own organization that makes sense to you. For that, I suggest you consider what is the best layer structure – what should be placed on top and what should be placed below – and notice your own artistic process.

Use clear naming conventions for files

By adopting a logical and descriptive system for naming your files, you can easily track different stages of your work and quickly locate them within your computer.

Adopt a clear naming system for your files. Include dates, version numbers, and descriptive keywords in your filenames.

For example, I use a date-name approach, making sure the name is descriptive enough, such as `20240627 figure study.clip`, instead of a generic name such as `Sketch1.clip`. Notice that I write the date using the *yyyymmdd* format so that my files are organized chronologically within my PC folders.

You can also add a version description at the end, such as `20240830 short hair girl - dark background.clip`. This practice makes it easier to track different stages of the work and quickly locate specific files. You can also use layer comps, as mentioned earlier in this chapter, and you won't need to create different files for different versions.

Save and back up your work

Regularly saving and backing up your work is vital to prevent data loss and ensure your progress is secure. By developing a habit of frequent saves and maintaining backups on external drives or cloud storage, you protect your projects from unexpected issues. This practice provides peace of mind and allows you to focus on your creative endeavors without fear of losing valuable work. Below are some techniques you can adopt to save and back up your work frequently:

- Develop the habit of saving your work frequently. Just press *Ctrl/command + S* every few minutes, and your file will be safe from any issues. It will become automatic and instinctive with time – nowadays, I don't even think about it; I do it on autopilot.

  But just in case you forget to do it, it's good to have CSP's auto-recovery feature on.

- Adjust CSP's auto-recovery feature by navigating to **File | Preferences | File | Auto-Recovery**. Just check the checkbox and decide on a time frame to auto-recovery:

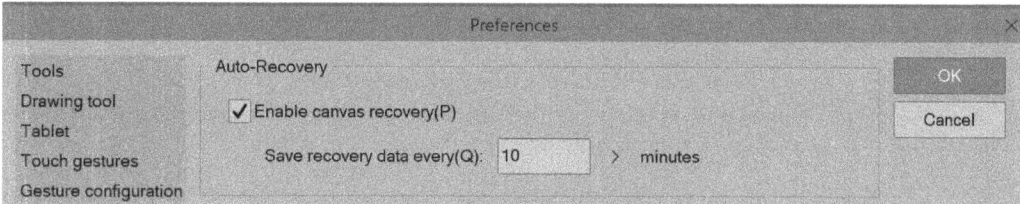

Figure 4.9 – The Auto-Recovery function

While CSP is auto-saving, you cannot work on your piece, and the larger the file, the longer it will take. That's why I set its frequency to **10** minutes: it's frequent enough that I won't lose much progress but sparse enough that it doesn't hinder my process significantly. Consider setting it between 10 and 15 minutes.

If CSP or your computer crashes, CSP will open to the last saved auto-recovery data so that you won't lose as much!

To find local backup files on your device, follow these steps:

I.   Navigate to **File | Open CLIP STUDIO…**.

II.   Then, click on the top-right gear to open **Settings | Maintenance Menu**.

III.   From this menu, scroll down until you find **Open folder with Clip Studio Paint backup data**:

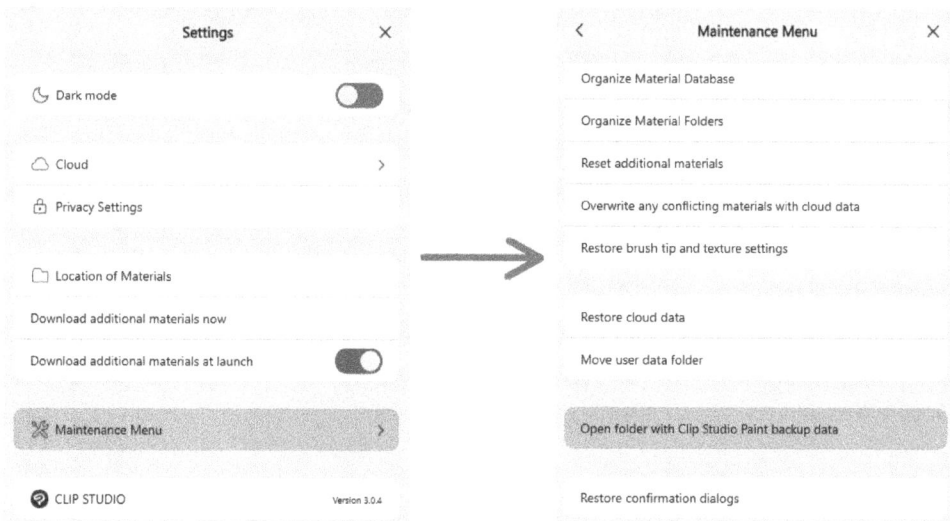

Figure 4.10 – Open folder with backup data

- Additionally, back up your projects regularly to external drives or cloud storage. I save all my files in an external cloud storage service, but CSP also has its own cloud service. You can sync several types of assets and your drawings! To see details of which assets you can sync, go to `https://www.clipstudio.net/guide/en/cloud`.

To sync your projects onto Clip Studio's cloud:

1. Go to **File | Open CLIP STUDIO…**. Then, in the new window, navigate to the left-side menu, and click on **Projects | This device**.

2. Check the checkboxes of works you wish to synchronize and tap the **ON** toggle next to **Switch syncing status**:

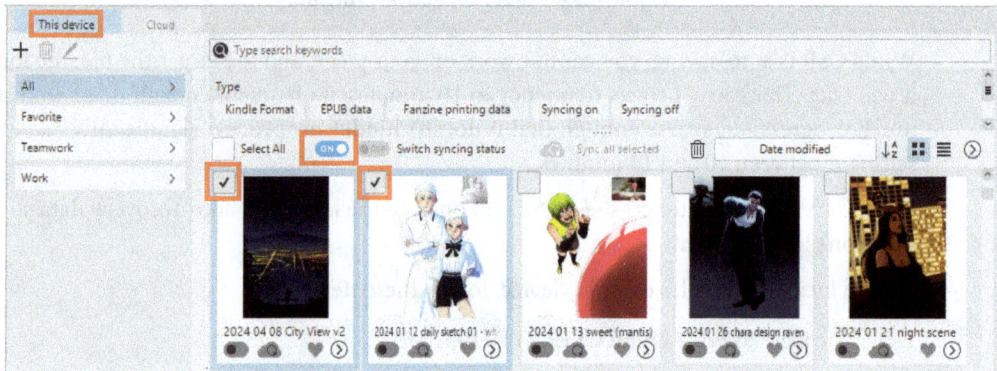

Figure 4.11 – Cloud synchronization

Now, your files will be saved on Clip Studio's cloud! Such precautions protect your work from unexpected data loss and allow you to recover files easily if something goes wrong. You can also use it to sync files within different devices, which can come in handy.

Review and reflect on your workflow

Reviewing and reflecting on your workflow is essential for continuous improvement. By periodically assessing your processes and identifying areas for enhancement, you can refine your techniques and increase efficiency. This practice ensures that your creative workflow remains effective and evolves to meet your changing needs.

Periodically review your workflow and organizational methods to identify areas for improvement. Reflect on what works well and what could be more efficient. Adjust your strategies accordingly to optimize your project management approach continuously.

Summary

Mastering project organization is crucial for any digital artist aiming to streamline their workflow and maximize creative output. Throughout this chapter, we've delved into essential skills such as efficiently naming and grouping layers, creating and managing folders, and utilizing color coding to keep track of different elements within your projects. By implementing these practices, you can ensure a more structured and less cluttered workspace, which not only saves time but also reduces stress when navigating complex compositions.

By implementing these practical tips and best practices, you'll maintain a well-organized, efficient workflow in CSP, allowing you to focus more on your creative vision and less on administrative tasks.

As we move forward, in the next chapter, we'll dive into the advanced techniques for optimizing your use of brushes, a fundamental skill for any digital artist looking to refine their craft.

Get This Book's PDF Version and Exclusive Extras

UNLOCK NOW

Scan the QR code (or go to packtpub.com/unlock). Search for this book by name, confirm the edition, and then follow the steps on the page.

Note: Keep your invoice handly. Purchase made directly from packt don't require one.

Part 2: Fine-Tuning Your Drawings

Once your workflow is optimized, the next step is refining your drawing tools and techniques. This part focuses on helping you gain more control and precision in your linework and sketches. You'll explore how to unlock the full potential of brush settings, make the most of vector layers to enhance and edit your lines with ease, and use rulers and guides to achieve clean, accurate results. These chapters will empower you to create polished, professional-quality drawings with confidence.

This part has the following chapters:

- *Chapter 5, Unlocking the Full Potential of Brush Settings*
- *Chapter 6, Enhancing Your Lines with Vector Layers*
- *Chapter 7, Utilizing Rulers and Guides for Precision*

5

Unlocking the Full Potential of Brush Settings

Customizing brush settings is a fundamental skill for any digital artist. In this chapter, you'll discover the tools and techniques that will elevate the quality of your lines, making them an essential addition to your portfolio and ensuring your art stands out. Whether you're preparing pieces for a client, building a portfolio, or simply striving to improve your projects, mastering brush settings is crucial – and **Clip Studio Paint** (**CSP**) has incredible tools to aid you.

CSP has different drawing and painting tools, such as **Pen**, **Brush**, and **Pencil**. I'll refer to all of them as *brushes* throughout this chapter since they all follow the same rules within CSP, and it's standard procedure in digital art to call them as such.

In this chapter, we're going to cover the following main topics:

- Understanding brush dynamics
- Mastering brush properties for complete customization
- Creating custom brushes

By the end of this chapter, you'll have gained a comprehensive understanding of how to manipulate various brush properties, optimize pen pressure, and use line stabilization effectively. You'll also be proficient in creating your own brushes, a skill that will save you time and enhance your creative workflow. With these techniques, you'll be able to produce professional-looking brushstrokes that will impress clients and elevate your artistic projects.

Understanding brush dynamics

Mastering brush dynamics is essential for creating expressive lines in CSP. This section will guide you through the various dynamic settings and adjustments that can transform your brushstrokes, making them more versatile and effective.

Brush dynamics determine how your brush behaves based on various inputs, such as pen pressure, tilt, speed, and direction. Understanding and utilizing these settings effectively can transform your digital artwork, allowing you to achieve a level of precision and expressiveness that rivals – traditional media.

Let's start by learning how to locate brush dynamics. Many settings, such as **Brush Size**, have a button on the right-hand side with either a downward-pointing arrow (when dynamics are toggled on) or a box with a diagonal line (when dynamics are toggled off):

Figure 5.1 – The button that opens the Dynamics dialog

This button opens the **Dynamics** dialog.

> **Important note**
> You can apply brush dynamics to several different brush settings, not only **Brush Size**. Whenever you see the **Dynamics** button next to a setting, brush dynamics are available.

There are eight brush dynamics: **Pen pressure, Tilt, Velocity, Random, Direction of pen, Direction of line, Direction of whole spray**, and **Spray toward center**. Let's start by covering **Pen pressure**.

Pen pressure

Pen pressure dynamics change the brushstroke according to how much pressure you apply to your stylus. For example, let's say I turn pen pressure brush dynamics on for **Brush Size**. That means the line I make will differ depending on how strongly I press on the tablet.

Figure 5.2 shows an example of how pen pressure can affect brush output:

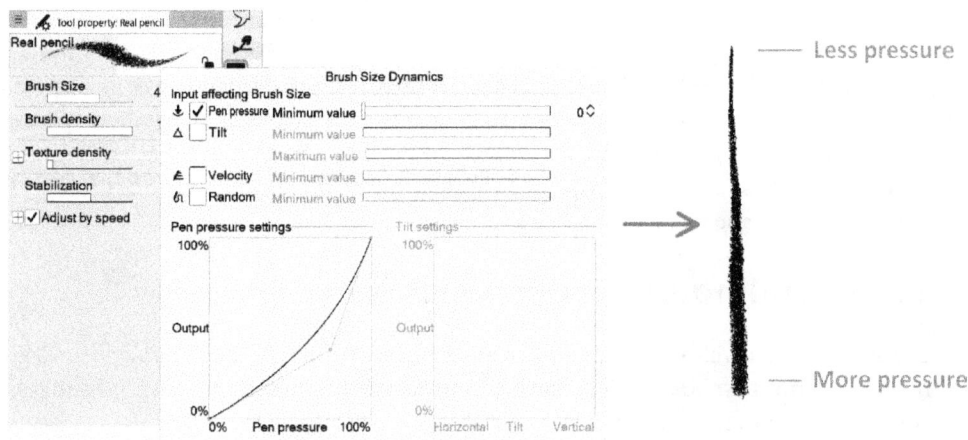

Figure 5.2 – How pen pressure can affect the brushstroke

To access **Brush Size Dynamics**, click on the right-hand side of the **Brush Size** slider; the **Brush Size Dynamics** popup will open:

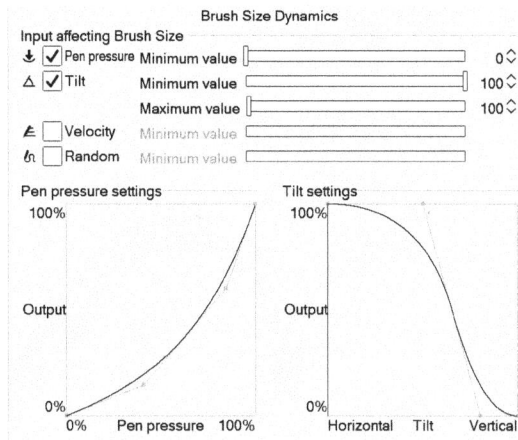

Figure 5.3 – Brush Size Dynamics

In the **Brush Size Dynamics** window, you'll see the **Pen pressure** curve, which represents the relationship between input pressure and output pressure. The default curve is typically linear, meaning the output increases proportionally with the pressure that's applied. However, you can customize this curve to suit your drawing style and preferences better.

The vertical axis of the **Pen pressure** curve represents the brush size: the higher the curve in the graph, the thicker the brush. The horizontal axis goes from **0%** pen pressure, on the left-hand side, to **100%** pen pressure, on the right-hand side.

Adjusting the points on this curve modifies the brush sensitivity to pressure:

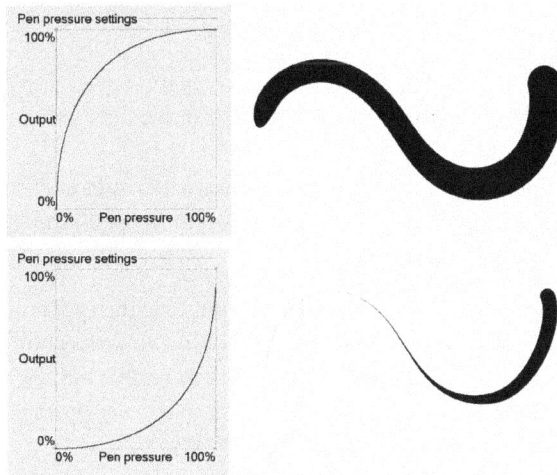

Figure 5.4 – Different pen pressure curves create different responses

A concave curve (*Figure 5.4*, top) makes the brush more responsive to light pressure, which is ideal for bold lines. Conversely, a convex curve (*Figure 5.4*, bottom) requires more pressure for the same output, providing better control for thin lines.

You can also set a minimum and maximum value, either by using the value scale or changing the curve's starting or ending point:

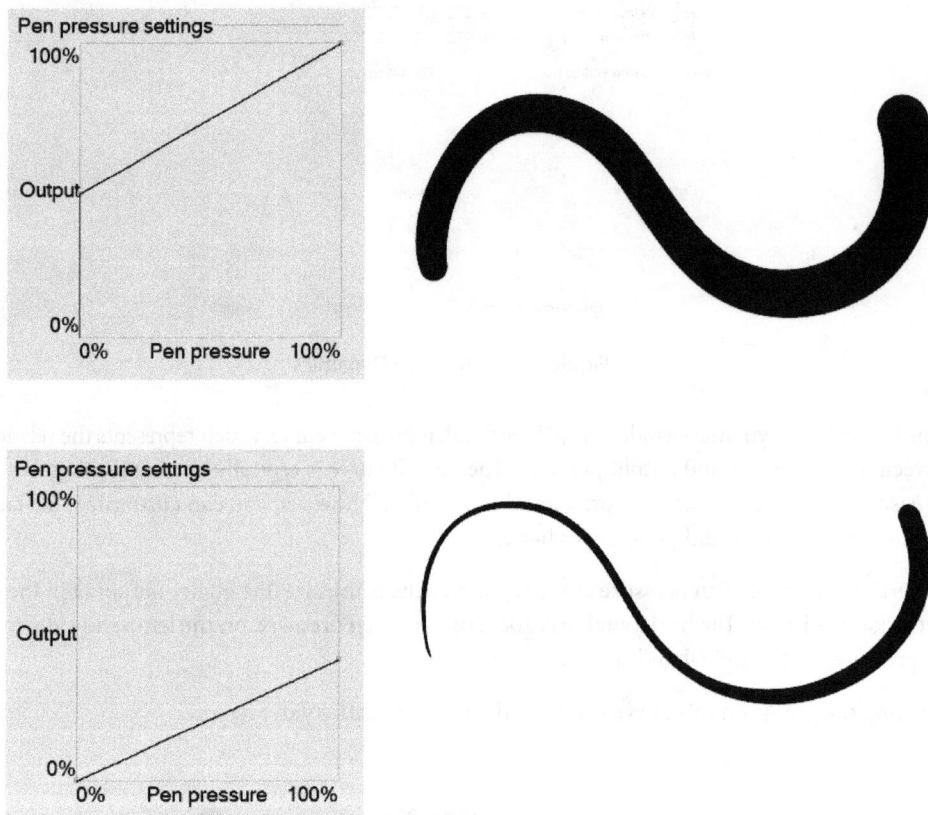

Figure 5.5 – Setting a minimum (top) and maximum (bottom) brush size

When the curve's starting point is high, as seen in the top-left corner of *Figure 5.5*, the minimum brush size is larger. When the curve's ending point is low, as seen in the bottom left-hand side of *Figure 5.5*, the maximum brush size is smaller.

Understanding pen pressure settings can drastically improve the expressiveness and control of your brushstrokes, allowing for a more nuanced and dynamic range in your digital artwork. Now that we've covered pen pressure, let's explore how pen tilt can further enhance brush dynamics and add even more versatility to strokes.

Tilt

In traditional art, when you tilt your pencil or brush, the strokes will become thicker because the surface area in contact with the paper increases. This effect can be replicated in digital art by using **Tilt** features in CSP. By adjusting the pen tilt settings, you can control the angle sensitivity of your digital brush, thereby mimicking the natural variations and broad strokes found in traditional media.

The **Tilt** setting reflects the capability of your drawing tablet to detect the angle at which you hold your stylus and to translate this into your brushstrokes. More advanced tablets will include this feature, and CSP lets you make the most of it.

Figure 5.6 shows the **Tilt settings** graph:

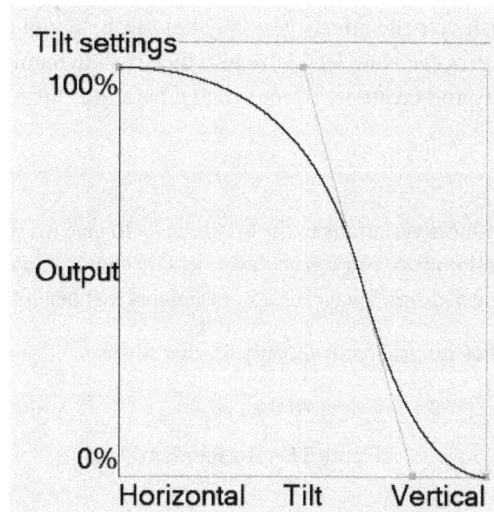

Figure 5.6 – The Tilt settings graph

The vertical axis represents the brush size: the higher the curve in the graph, the thicker the brush, up to **100%**. The horizontal axis goes from horizontal tilt, on the left-hand side, to vertical tilt, on the right-hand side.

To simulate a real pencil, your brush must become thicker the more horizontal your stylus is, and thinner the more vertical it is to the tablet's surface. Therefore, the curve must be higher on the left-hand side – pairing **100%** thickness with horizontal tilt – and lower on the right-hand side – pairing **0%** thickness with vertical angle. *Figure 5.6* shows an example of such a graph.

Mastering **Tilt** settings allows you to create more varied and natural brushstrokes, simulating traditional media techniques and adding depth to your digital artwork. Next, let's explore how **Velocity** settings can impact your strokes, adding another layer of control and fluidity to your digital art.

Velocity

The **Velocity** setting adjusts the brush's behavior based on the speed of your stroke. When you move the stylus quickly, the brushstroke can become thinner or more transparent, and when you move it slowly, the stroke can become thicker or more opaque. This dynamic setting helps to create more natural and expressive lines, mimicking the effects of traditional media where the speed of your hand influences the appearance of the stroke. There's no pressure curve to it because it's related to speed, so you can vary the effect by changing the value on the slider:

Figure 5.7 – The Velocity slider

Understanding how brush velocity affects your strokes can help you achieve a more realistic and dynamic flow in your art process. Now, let's delve into the brush dynamics of randomness so that you can enhance the versatility and creativity of your digital paintings further.

Random

The **Random** setting introduces variations in the brushstroke to give it a more organic and less uniform appearance. By adding randomness, you can achieve a less mechanical look, which is particularly useful for creating natural-looking textures, foliage, or other elements that benefit from a bit of unpredictability.

Like **Velocity**, **Random** has no graph curve, only a value slider:

Figure 5.8 – The Random slider

Figure 5.9 shows two different types of randomness. Above, a cel-shading brush has **Random** applied to **Brush Size Dynamics**. Below, the same brush has **Color Jitter | Change brush tip color** toggled on, and within it, the **Hue Dynamics** settings have been randomized:

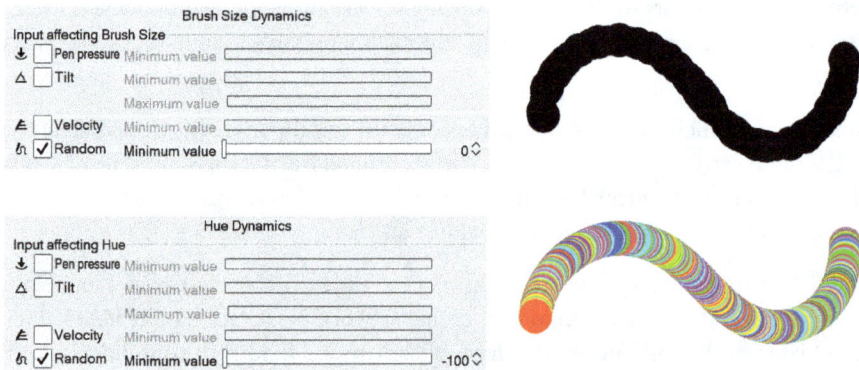

Figure 5.9 – Brush Size Dynamics and Hue Dynamics

Figure 5.9 shows how toggling **Random** on can create an unusual and organic feel for the brushstroke. Mastering the **Random** setting allows for more varied brushstrokes, adding a touch of spontaneity to your work. Next, we'll explore brush dynamics related to angle, which will help you control the orientation of your strokes for even greater precision and creativity.

Angle Dynamics

Pen angle dynamics allow artists to manipulate the direction and orientation of their brushstrokes based on the angle of their pen or stylus. This feature provides greater control and versatility, enhancing their ability to create more natural and expressive lines. The following figure shows the settings that are available for **Angle Dynamics**:

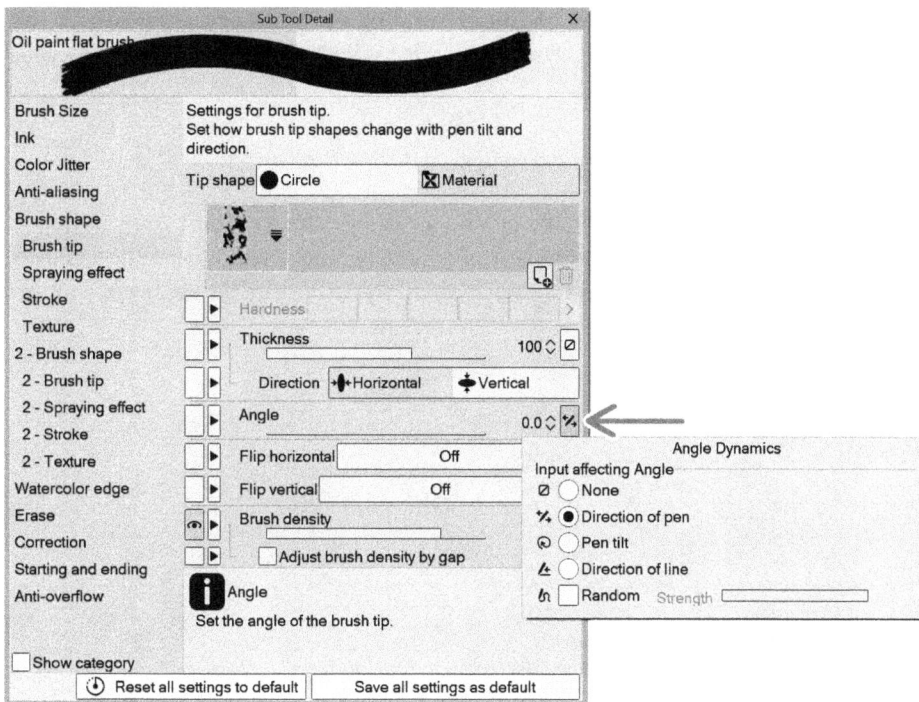

Figure 5.10 – Angle Dynamics

To find brush **Angle Dynamics**, follow these steps:

1. In the **Sub Tool Detail** palette, navigate to **Brush tip**.

2. You'll find a list of settings related to the brush tip. Find **Angle** and click on the right-hand side box (the orange arrow points to it in *Figure 5.10*).

3. The **Angle Dynamics** dialog will open.

Inside **Angle Dynamics**, there will be three new options – **None**, **Direction of pen**, and **Direction of line**:

- **None**: No dynamics are applied.

- **Direction of pen**: This option changes the brush tip's angle according to the tilt of your pen. As you tilt your pen in different directions, the brush tip will rotate accordingly.

- **Direction of line**: This option adjusts the brush tip's angle based on the direction of your brushstrokes. With this setting, the brush tip will automatically rotate to align with the movement of your hand.

By mastering pen angle dynamics, artists can achieve higher precision and control in their digital artwork, replicating the nuances of traditional drawing and painting techniques. Moving forward, we'll look at **Direction of particle Dynamics**, which will allow you to manage particle behavior for intricate and dynamic brush effects.

Direction of particle Dynamics

In CSP, the **Direction of particle Dynamics** feature gives artists robust controls for shaping how particles are distributed along their brushstrokes. This setting is critical for creating intricate textures and effects, and understanding how to use it effectively can elevate the quality of your artwork. The following figure shows its settings:

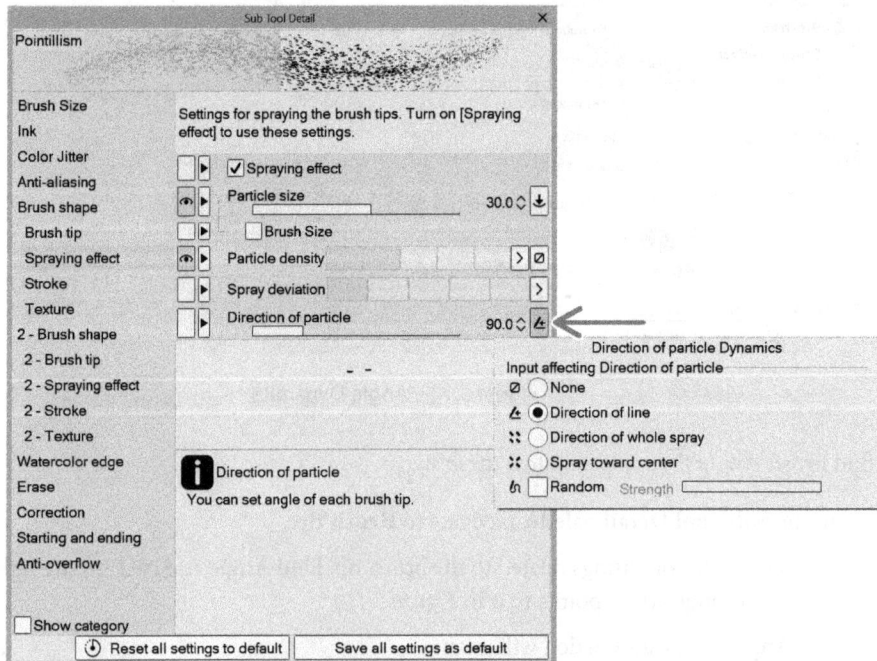

Figure 5.11 – Direction of particle Dynamics

To locate **Direction of particle Dynamics**, follow these steps:

1. In the **Sub Tool Detail** palette, navigate to **Spraying effect**.
2. Toggle **Spraying effect** on by tapping the left-hand side box. We'll cover Spraying effect in detail in the next section, Mastering brush properties for complete customization.
3. Go to **Direction of particle** and click on the right-hand side box (the orange arrow points to it in *Figure 5.11*).
4. The **Direction of particle Dynamics** dialog will open.

Inside **Direction of particle Dynamics**, there are three new options – **Direction of whole spray**, **Direction of line**, and **Spray toward center**.

Direction of whole spray differs from **Direction of line** because it considers all of the spray. We'll cover Spraying effect in detail in the next section, Mastering brush properties for complete customization. You can see the difference in *Figure 5.12*:

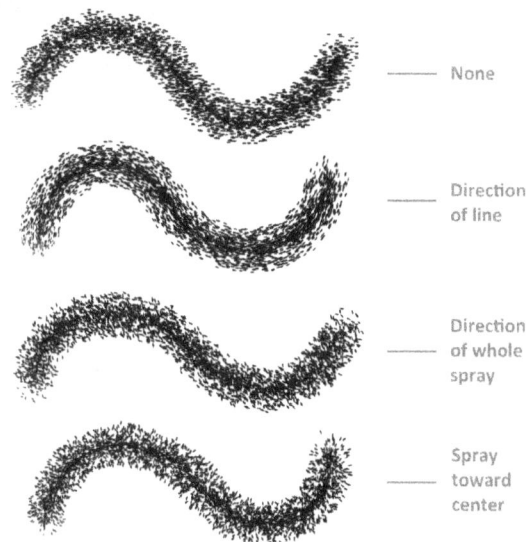

Figure 5.12 – Direction of particle Dynamics

Spray toward center directs particles so that they move toward the center of your brushstroke. This setting can be used to create effects where particles converge at a central point, such as the explosion of fireworks or a swirling vortex.

Having explored the various brush dynamics settings, you now have a solid foundation for understanding how different aspects such as pressure, tilt, and velocity can influence your brushwork. With this knowledge, we can move on to other brush properties in the **Sub Tool Detail** palette, where you'll find a comprehensive array of tools and settings designed to refine and customize your brushes even further. This palette is where you'll put your understanding of brush dynamics into practice, allowing you to adjust properties such as brush size, opacity, and texture to achieve the exact effects you envision for your art.

Mastering brush properties for complete customization

Unlocking the full potential of your digital brushes requires a deep dive into the **Sub Tool Detail** palette. This powerful tool allows you to fine-tune every aspect of your brushes, from size and shape to texture and dynamics. Understanding each part of this palette will enable you to harness the full potential of your brushes and improve your digital painting process.

Figure 5.13 shows the groups of settings available on the left-hand side of the **Sub Tool Detail** palette:

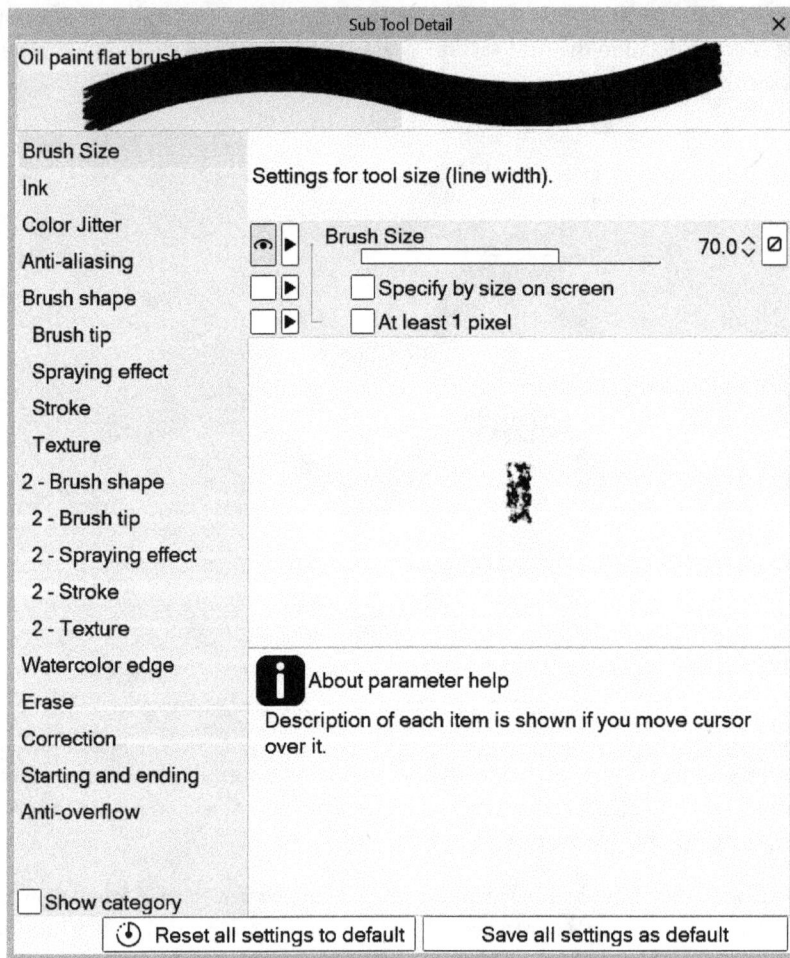

Figure 5.13 – The Sub Tool Detail palette

Each of the settings inside the **Sub Tool Detail** palette can become visible in the **Tool property** palette. Just toggle on the left-most box next to each setting's name; an eye icon will appear when the setting is visible in the **Tool** property. In *Figure 5.13*, out of the **Brush Size** group of settings, only **Brush Size** is visible, while **Specify by size on screen** and **At least one pixel** are not visible in the **Tool** property palette.

You can set custom shortcuts for most of these settings. Just navigate to **File | Shortcut Settings… | Category: Options | Tool property palette** and explore which shortcuts you want to set.

Let's analyze the available settings, starting with **Brush Size**.

Brush Size

The **Brush Size** setting is one of the fundamental aspects of customizing your brush in CSP. It determines the diameter of your brushstrokes, allowing you to control the width of the lines and marks you make. Adjusting the brush size can drastically change the look and feel of your artwork, making it an essential tool for both detailed and broad strokes.

The **Brush Size** settings are shown in *Figure 5.13*. Let's take a closer look at them:

- **Brush Size**: Determines the overall width of your brushstrokes. You can make your brush larger or smaller, depending on the level of detail you need for your artwork. There are several ways to adjust it:

  - **Slider**: Use the slider to increase or decrease the brush size. This is a quick and intuitive way to find the perfect size for your needs.

  - **Numerical input**: Enter a specific numerical value to control the brush size precisely. This is useful when you need an exact size for consistency across your artwork.

  - **Keyboard shortcuts**: Use the [key to decrease the brush size and the] key to increase it, enabling seamless transitions between different brush sizes as you work. The brush size will increase or decrease constantly for as long as you press these keyboard shortcuts.

  In addition to setting a static size, you can customize **Brush Size Dynamics** to make it responsive to various inputs, as we covered in the previous section.

- **Specify by size on screen**: This option allows you to set the brush size based on its appearance on your screen rather than in real-world units. This is useful for changing the brush size according to how much you zoom in.

- **At least 1 pixel**: When this option is enabled, the brush size won't go below 1 pixel, ensuring that even the smallest strokes are visible and distinct.

- **Brush preview**: This option shows a real-time display of how your brushstroke will look based on the current settings. This helps you visualize the effects of your adjustments before you start drawing, making it easier to achieve the desired results.

Choosing the right brush size is crucial for achieving the desired effects in your artwork. Larger brushes are great for broad strokes, filling in large areas, and creating background elements, whereas smaller brushes are ideal for fine details, line work, and intricate patterns. By mastering the **Brush Size** settings, you can enhance the precision and quality of your digital art, ensuring that every stroke contributes to your piece's overall composition and style.

Now that you understand how to adjust **Brush Size**, let's explore the **Ink** settings, which you can use to control opacity and color blending.

Ink

The **Ink** section of the **Sub Tool Detail** palette allows you to control the flow and opacity of your brushstrokes, mimicking the behavior of genuine ink or paint. Here, you can fine-tune how your brush interacts with the canvas, adjusting parameters to achieve the desired effect for your artwork.

Figure 5.14 shows all the available settings in the **Ink** section:

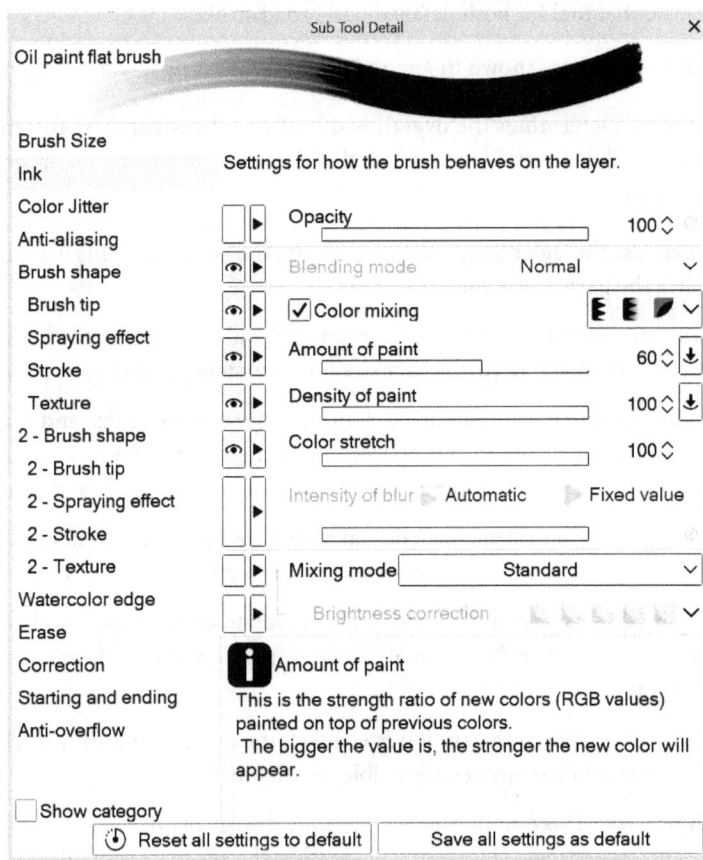

Figure 5.14 – The Ink settings

Let's start by analyzing **Opacity**, which is the first setting you can modify.

Opacity

Opacity determines the transparency level of your brushstrokes. A higher opacity setting produces more solid and opaque lines, while a lower setting produces lighter, more transparent strokes.

You can set brush dynamics that modify opacity by clicking on the icon to the right:

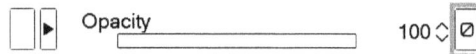

Figure 5.15 – Icon for opacity dynamics

> **Important note**
>
> Using both pen pressure and opacity dynamics simultaneously can make it challenging to achieve consistent results as each stroke's thickness and transparency will vary simultaneously. This can lead to unpredictable outcomes and a lack of precision in your work. Instead, decide which aspect is more critical for your current task.

Blending mode

Blending mode determines how the brushstroke interacts with colors and layers beneath it. It works the same as layer blending modes, but it will affect each brushstroke instead of affecting the whole layer. An in-depth explanation of each blending mode is provided in *Chapter 9, Mastering Layer Blending Modes for Stunning Colors*. Experimenting with these modes can help you create depth and save time in your art process.

Color mixing

The **Color mixing** setting allows you to blend your current brush color with the colors already on the canvas, simulating traditional painting techniques. This is particularly useful for creating realistic shading and blending effects as it mimics how colors interact in real-life media:

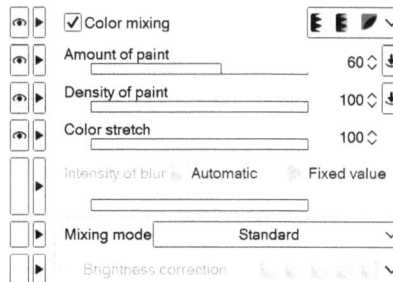

Figure 5.16 – The Color mixing settings

On the right-hand side of **Color mixing**, you can choose from three different ways to mix colors:

- **Blend** (left icon): This option lets you mix the drawing color with all the colors the brush passes through, creating a smooth transition.
- **Running Color** (center icon): This technique mixes only the drawing color with the color the brush passes through, allowing for more controlled blending.
- **Smear** (right icon): Like **Blend**, this method mixes the drawing color with all the colors the brush touches, creating a smudging effect.

Both the **Blend** and **Running Color** methods allow you to paint with transparency. Below those, there are more settings you can use to customize your brush further, as shown in the following figure:

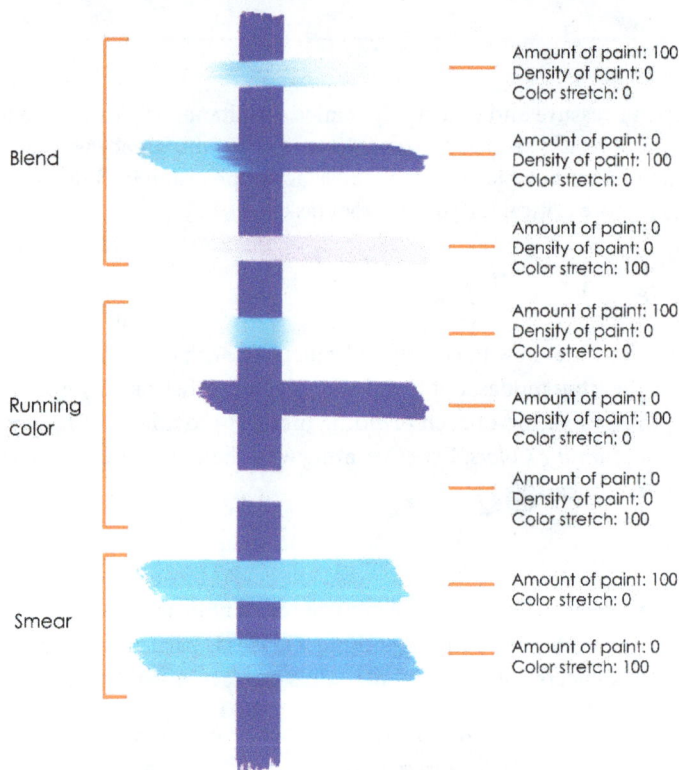

Figure 5.17 – The different Color mixing settings create different effects

Here's a breakdown of the settings and how they influence the brushstroke:

- **Amount of paint**: This setting controls the ratio of the RGB color components that are mixed during blending. A higher value increases the RGB mixing ratio, meaning more of the brush's color will blend with the existing color.

- **Density of paint**: This setting adjusts how much the transparent components of the color will mix with the existing color. A higher value increases the transparency ratio, allowing more of the paint's transparency to blend with the underlying colors. This adjustment is available when **Color mixing** is set to **Blend** or **Running Color**.

- **Color stretch**: This setting determines how long the initial color remains visible before it starts blending with the surrounding colors. A higher value extends the distance over which the color blends, affecting how the brushstroke transitions.

- **Intensity of blur**: This setting controls how much the existing color is blurred outward from the brushstroke. You can choose **Automatic** if you wish the blur effect to follow the brush size or **Fixed Value** to manually set the blur width using a slider or numerical value. This setting can be adjusted when **Running Color** is selected.

- **Mixing mode**: This setting lets you choose between **Standard** and **Perceptual** modes for color mixing, as shown in *Figure 5.18*. **Standard** follows the traditional method from CSP Ver. 1.0, while **Perceptual** provides a more realistic and vivid color blend, something that was introduced in CSP Ver. 2.0, reducing dullness in the mix. This setting also influences two **Color Jitter** settings – **Change brush tip color** and **Randomize per stroke**:

Perceptual: Standard:

Figure 5.18 – Mixing mode options

- **Brightness correction**: This setting is available when **Perceptual** mixing mode is active. It offers five levels of brightness adjustment for fine-tuning how colors blend, helping you achieve your desired visual effect.

Figure 5.17 shows some extreme examples of color mixing so that you can see what each one does. When working with color mixing, you'll usually use less extreme values, such as **50** for **Amount of paint**, **60** for **Density of paint**, and **20** for **Color stretch**. Experiment with each of them to see what best suits your needs in a given process.

Note that you can tap the **Dynamics** icon to enable stylus inputs to influence **Amount of paint** and **Density of paint**.

With the **Ink** settings thoroughly explored, let's move on to **Color Jitter**. This feature will help you add dynamic variation to your strokes, making your artwork more vibrant and engaging.

Color Jitter

Color Jitter lets you add variety to your artwork by randomizing the hue, saturation, and luminosity of your brushstrokes or by having these attributes change based on brush dynamics. The following screenshot shows the **Color Jitter** settings:

Figure 5.19 – The Color Jitter settings

The first setting is **Change brush tip color**. It modifies your stroke's hue, saturation, and luminosity and allows color blending between your main drawing color and the secondary (sub) drawing color. The higher the value in the scale, the greater the change to the brush color. All settings under **Change brush tip color** allow dynamic stylus inputs when you click on the right-most icon near each setting.

When **Blend with sub color** is turned on, you can blend your primary color with the sub-color to create varied effects. The higher the value you set, the more dominant the sub-color becomes in the mix.

Next comes **Randomize per stroke**, which introduces random changes to the hue, saturation, brightness, and color mixing for the sub-drawing color with each new brushstroke. By increasing the values in these settings, you can achieve more dramatic and varied color changes, adding an element of randomness to your strokes for a more exciting appearance. This is an excellent setting to turn on when you're creating organic backgrounds and adding variation to repetitive patterns.

You can turn **Change brush tip color** and **Randomize per stroke** on or off by tapping the checkboxes next to their names.

Lastly, there's the **Change** setting. When using a brush tip that incorporates both the main and sub-drawing colors or if you have **Blend with sub color** turned on, this option allows you to determine where the **Change brush tip color** and **Randomize per stroke** settings will be applied. You can choose to affect **Main color**, **Sub color**, or both colors together. This setting helps you control how the color dynamics influence your artwork.

Having understood how to use **Color Jitter** to bring your strokes to life with dynamic variations, let's explore **Anti-aliasing**. This crucial feature will ensure your lines and borders appear smooth and refined, enhancing the overall quality of your artwork.

Anti-aliasing

Anti-aliasing is a setting that smoothens out jagged edges in your lines and borders, resulting in smoother, more refined outlines. Its settings are shown in the following screenshot:

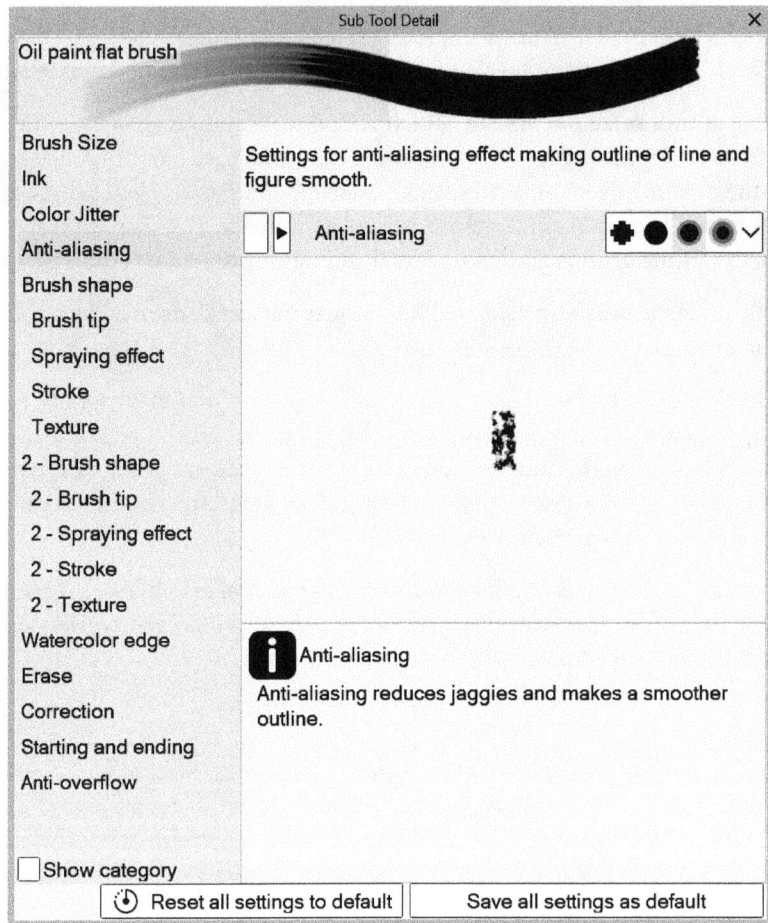

Figure 5.20 – The Anti-aliasing settings

You can adjust the level of anti-aliasing that's applied to your lines by setting it to **None**, **Weak**, **Middle**, or **Strong**. Choose **None** if you want to maintain crisp, unsoftened edges in your artwork. Select a higher level of anti-aliasing for smoother and more refined lines.

With **Anti-aliasing** set to adjust line smoothness, we can turn our attention to **Brush shape**. This will guide you in selecting and customizing the brush shape to better suit your artistic needs and style.

Brush shape

The **Brush shape** settings offer essential tools for defining the form of your brush. This feature allows you to choose from preset shapes or use custom materials to craft unique brush tips that suit your artistic vision. All available **Brush shape** settings are shown in *Figure 5.21*:

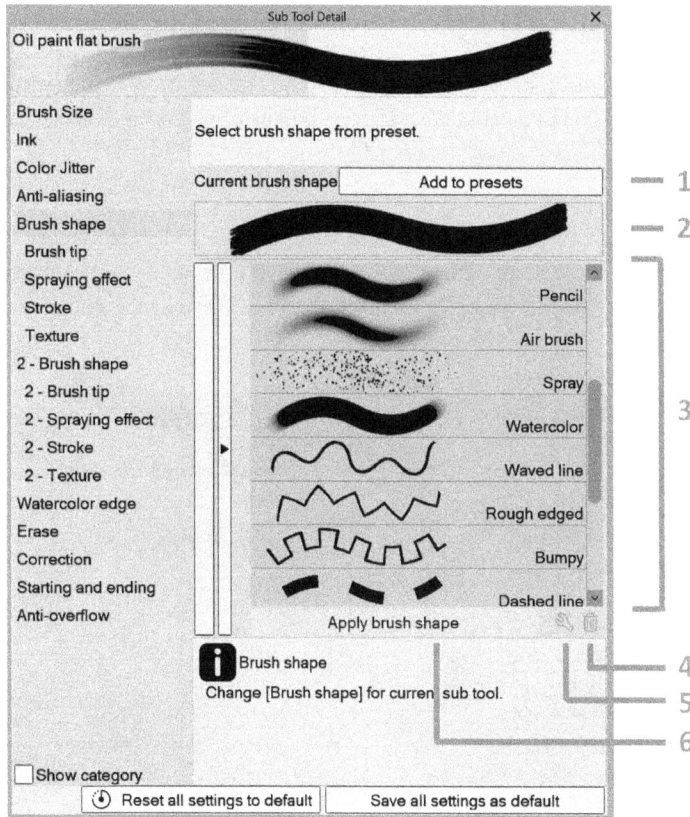

Figure 5.21 – The Brush shape settings

Here's how you can manage the **Brush shape** menu:

1. **Add to presets**: Here, you can save your custom brush tip shapes, spraying effects, strokes, and textures as presets for future use. To add your current settings to the list of brush tip shape presets, simply configure your desired settings and tap the **Add to presets** function.

2. **Brush shape preview**: Displays a preview of the selected brush tip shape, helping you see how your strokes will appear before you apply them.

3. **Brush shape**: Lists all available brush tip shape presets. Tap on any item in the list to select it.

4. **Delete a brush shape**: Tap to remove a brush tip shape preset from the list. Deleting a preset will permanently remove it from your list of available brush shapes.

5. **Change the name of the selected brush shape**: Tap this option to open the **Preset of brush shape settings** dialog, where you can rename the currently selected brush tip shape. This helps you keep your presets organized and easily identifiable.

6. **Apply brush shape**: Tap to apply a selected brush tip shape preset to your current sub-tool. Applying a preset will update your sub-tool's shape settings to match those saved in the selected preset.

Within **Brush shape**, there are four subcategories you can explore by navigating to the left-hand side menu of the **Sub Tool Detail** palette. We'll start with **Brush tip** and the effects it can have on your brush.

Brush tip

Brush tips are essential for defining your brushstroke's texture, style, and impact. Understanding how to select and customize these shapes allows you to tailor your brush so that you can achieve a wide range of effects, from precise lines to complex textures. *Figure 5.22* shows the available settings for **Brush tip**:

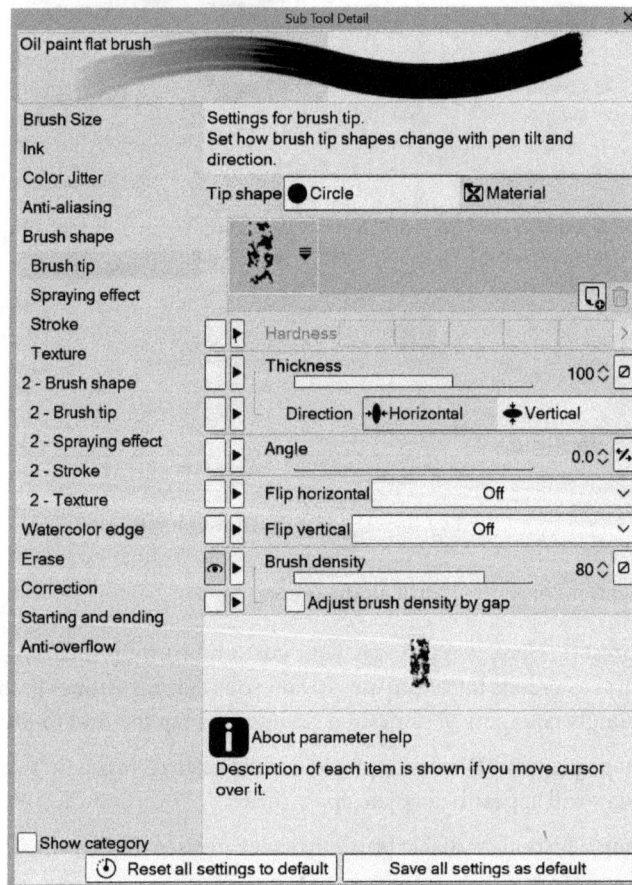

Figure 5.22 – The Brush tip settings

Here's a breakdown of the available features and settings:

- Using the **Tip shape** setting, you can choose between **Circle**, which is a standard round brush tip, or **Material**, which allows you to use an image material as your brush tip shape.

- **Brush tip** icons display the shapes that have currently been set for the selected sub-tool. This is available when **Tip shape** is set to **Material**. Tap the arrow next to the brush shape to choose a brush tip shape. When there are multiple tip shapes, you can rearrange them by dragging and dropping.

- Below the **Brush tip** icons, on the right-hand side, there are two buttons. The first is **Add brush tip shape**, which allows you to use multiple shapes for one brush, making the brush more varied and organic. Tap it to open the **Select Material** dialog, where you can choose and apply a new brush tip shape. The second button is **Delete selected brush tip shape**, which removes a specific brush tip shape from your brush settings.

- Using the **Hardness** setting, you can adjust the hardness of circular brush tips by using the slider or setting a value number when you click on the arrow on the right-hand side. A lower value will create a more blurred and softer brush tip, while a higher value will make it harder. This setting is only available when **Tip shape** is set to **Circle**.

- The **Thickness** setting adjusts the brush tip's size in the direction specified under **Direction**. You can link this setting to pen pressure, tilt, and stroke speed by tapping the **Dynamics** icon.

- The **Direction** setting controls the orientation of the brush tip's thickness and determines whether the **Thickness** setting changes horizontally or vertically.

- The **Angle** setting allows you to adjust the angle of the brush tip's shape from **0** to **360** degrees by using the slider or setting a numbered value. You can link this setting to brush dynamics by clicking the **Dynamics** icon, something we covered in the *Understanding brush dynamics* section.

- The **Flip horizontal** and **Flip vertical** settings let you choose to flip the brush tip shape horizontally or vertically, respectively, and provide options such as **Off**, **Flip**, **Random**, and **Flip on reversed strokes**. The **Flip on reversed strokes** option is available when the **Repeat** method inside **Stroke** is set to **Reverse**.

- The **Brush density** setting controls the opacity of the selected brush tip shape. This setting can be linked to brush dynamics.

- When the **Adjust brush density by gap** setting is enabled, it reduces brush density as the brush tip gap becomes narrower under **Stroke**. This will maintain density so that it's approximately constant:

Figure 5.23 – Adjust brush density by gap

Now that we've explored the versatility of brush tip customization, let's delve into **Spraying effect** so that you can enhance your brush dynamics and artistic possibilities.

Spraying effect

The **Spraying effect** settings enable you to add a textured, stippled look to your brushstrokes, simulating the effect of spraying paint or ink. This feature is handy for creating dynamic textures and realistic effects that can enhance the depth and richness of your artwork. The **Spraying effect** settings are shown in *Figure 5.24*:

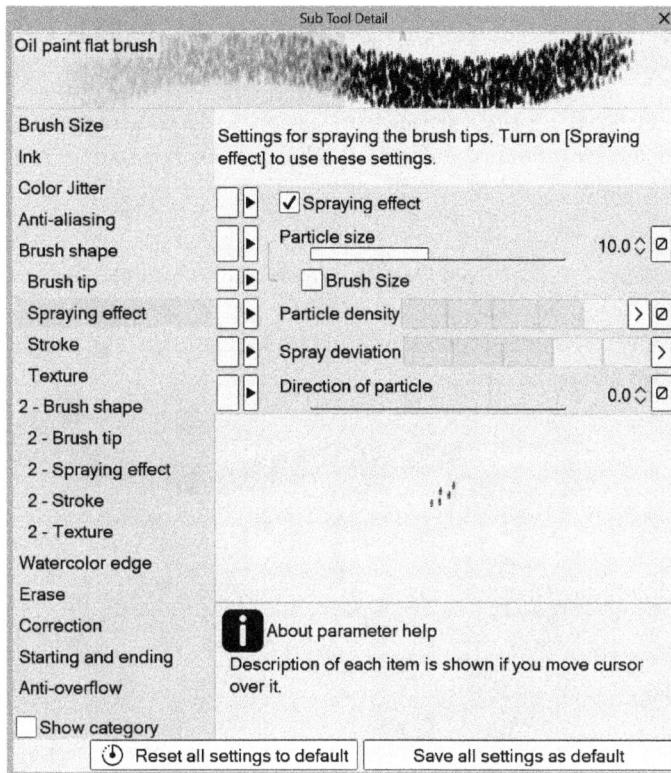

Figure 5.24 – The Spraying effect settings

Let's look at the key components of the **Spraying effect** settings:

- **Spraying effect**: This toggle activates the spraying effect for the selected brush. When turned on, your brushstrokes will appear as a series of dots or particles rather than a continuous line.

- **Particle size**: Adjust this setting to change the size of the individual particles in the spray. Smaller particles create a fine, delicate texture, while larger particles produce a more pronounced and bold texture. This setting can be linked to brush dynamics.

- **Brush size**: When turned on, the size of your particles will increase or decrease proportionately due to changes in brush size.

- **Particle density**: This setting controls how many particles are sprayed with each stroke. A higher density will result in a more solid, continuous spray, while a lower density will create a more scattered, textured effect.

- **Spray deviation**: This setting adjusts how much the sprayed particles will deviate from the stroke you make with your stylus.

- **Direction of particle**: This setting allows you to set an angle for each particle.

I use **Spraying effect** frequently – it's great for adding light particles, ashes, and other graphic elements that make the artwork more dynamic.

By mastering the **Spraying effect** settings, you can achieve a wide range of textures and effects that add depth and interest to your digital artwork. Next, let's explore settings related to **Stroke**.

Stroke

The **Stroke** section in the **Sub Tool Detail** palette in CSP is essential for defining the behavior and appearance of your brushstrokes. This section allows you to customize how your brush applies paint or ink to the canvas, giving you control over the smoothness, spacing, and dynamics of each stroke. *Figure 5.25* shows all **Stroke** settings:

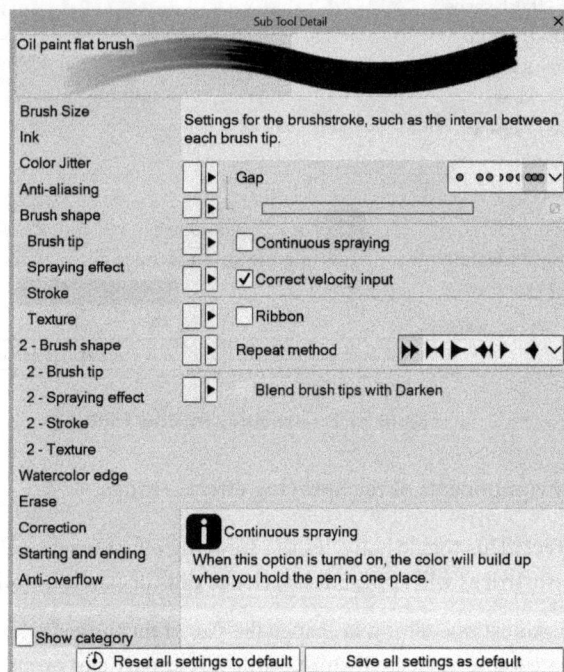

Figure 5.25 – The Stroke settings

Here's a breakdown of the key functions:

- **Gap**: This setting controls the spacing between each brush tip imprint along the stroke path. A smaller gap results in a smoother, more continuous line, while a more significant gap can create a dotted or dashed effect.

- **Continuous spraying**: When this setting is toggled on, the color will build up when you hold the stylus in one place, like real-life ink on paper.

- **Correct velocity input**: This setting changes how the velocity input for tool dynamics is calculated. When toggled on, the change in speed will be consistent across different devices.

- **Ribbon**: When toggled on, the brush tip shape will match the pen stroke, forming a continuous pattern. It's great for decorative brushes.

- **Repeat method**: When the brush tip is set to **Material** and there are multiple materials, you can set the order of the tip shapes.

- **Blend brush tips with Darken**: When turned on, brushstrokes will layer similarly to the **Darken** blending mode – which means only the darkest color will appear. It's frequently used in watercolor brushes to replicate real watercolor.

By fine-tuning the **Stroke** settings, you can achieve a variety of line qualities and effects, from smooth and continuous to dynamic and textured, enhancing the overall look and feel of your artwork. The following section is about texture, which will add a new layer of complexity to your brushes.

Texture

The **Texture** section in the **Sub Tool Detail** palette allows you to add intricate surface details to your brushstrokes, mimicking the appearance of traditional media such as canvas, paper, or rough surfaces. This group of settings provides various options you can use to enhance your digital artwork's tactile quality. You can see all **Texture** settings in *Figure 5.26*:

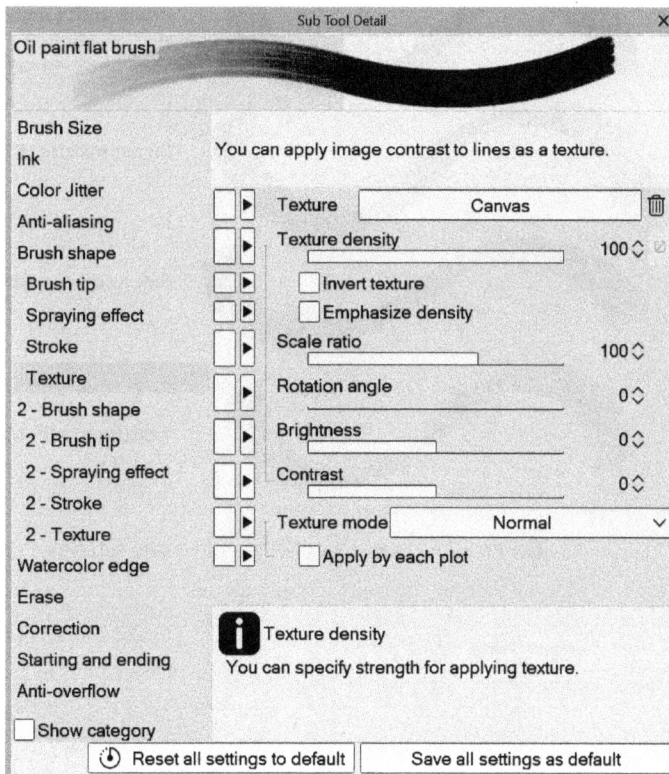

Figure 5.26 – The Texture settings

Here's how you can utilize the **Texture** settings:

- **Texture**: When you click the texture's name (or **None**, if no texture is selected), the **Select paper texture material** dialog will open. From here, you can choose from a range of pre-defined textures or import custom textures you wish to apply to your brush. This texture will be overlaid on your brushstrokes, adding depth and variation.

- To import your custom textures, you must register them as image materials by navigating to **Edit | Register Material | Image…**. The details of this process can be found in *Chapter 3, Setting Up Materials for Consistency and Speed*.

- **Texture density**: This setting adjusts the strength of the texture effect on your brushstrokes. Higher intensity values make the texture more pronounced, while lower values create a subtler effect.

- **Invert texture**: This setting reverses the light and dark areas of the texture, creating a different visual effect.

- **Emphasize density**: This setting emphasizes the contrast of the texture.

   Figure 5.27 shows how different **Texture** functions can affect the stroke:

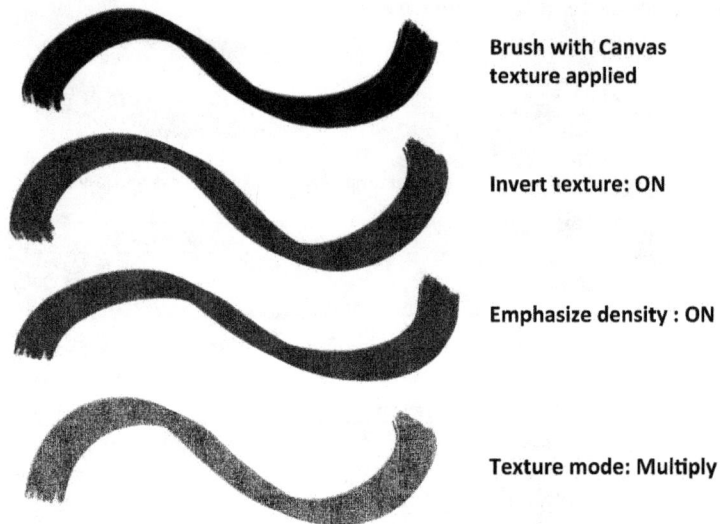

Figure 5.27 – Examples of different Texture settings

- **Scale ratio**: This setting adjusts the size of the texture relative to the brushstroke. Smaller scales make the texture appear more detailed, while larger scales give a coarser effect.

- **Rotation angle**: This setting allows you to change the orientation of the texture, giving you further control over the appearance of your brushstrokes.

- **Brightness** and **Contrast**: Both settings adjust the relationship between the darkest and lightest areas of the texture, making it more or less pronounced.

- **Texture mode**: This setting determines how the texture interacts with the colors of your brushstrokes. Different modes can produce varying effects, such as darkening, lightening, or adding contrast.

- **Apply by each plot**: When toggled on, the texture becomes less visible as the brushstrokes overlap. When toggled off, the texture is applied to each stroke as a whole. You can see how this function modifies the stroke in *Figure 5.28*:

Apply by each plot

OFF: ON:

Figure 5.28 – Apply by each plot

Using the **Texture** settings, you can add a rich, tactile quality to your digital paintings, making them feel more organic and realistic.

Dual brush (2 - Brush shape)

The **Dual brush** feature in CSP lets you combine two different brush shapes and properties to create a unique, complex brush that offers more versatility and creative potential. It allows you to paint two brushes simultaneously, one on top of the other. This feature is particularly useful for artists looking to add more depth and variation to their strokes. *Figure 5.29* shows the **2 - Brush shape** settings:

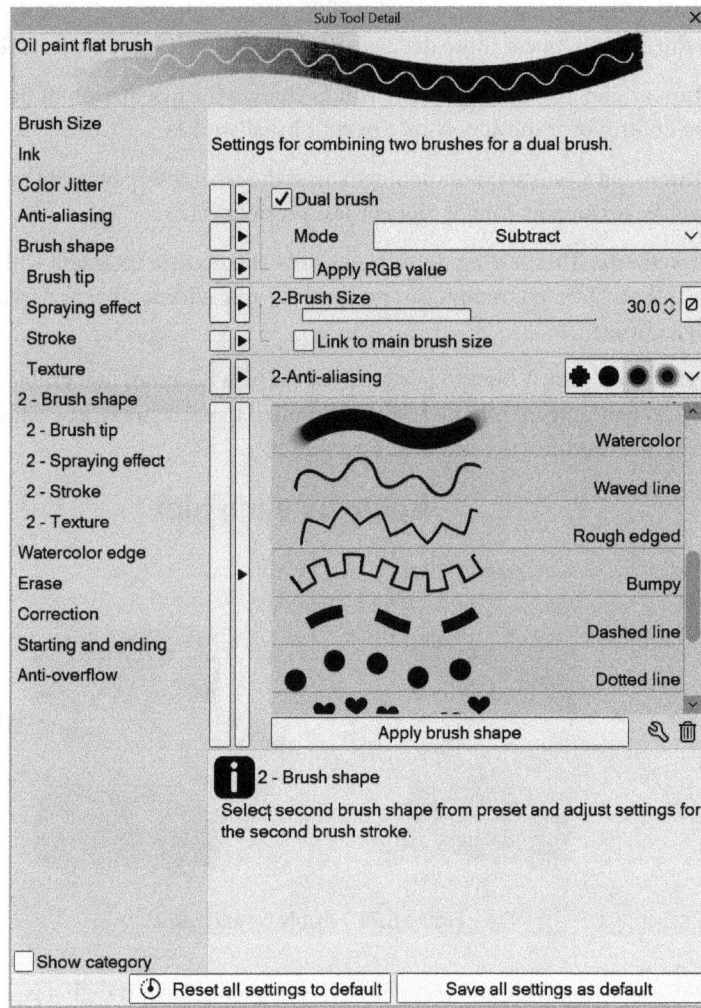

Figure 5.29 – The 2 - Brush shape settings

Here's how to make the most of the **2 - Brush shape** settings:

- **Dual brush**: Turn on this setting to activate the **Dual brush** feature so that you can blend two brush tips into one.

- **Mode**: Determine how the secondary brush blends with the primary brush. Different blend modes will affect how the two brushes interact, such as overlaying, multiplying, or adding to each other. You can see examples of this in *Figure 5.30*:

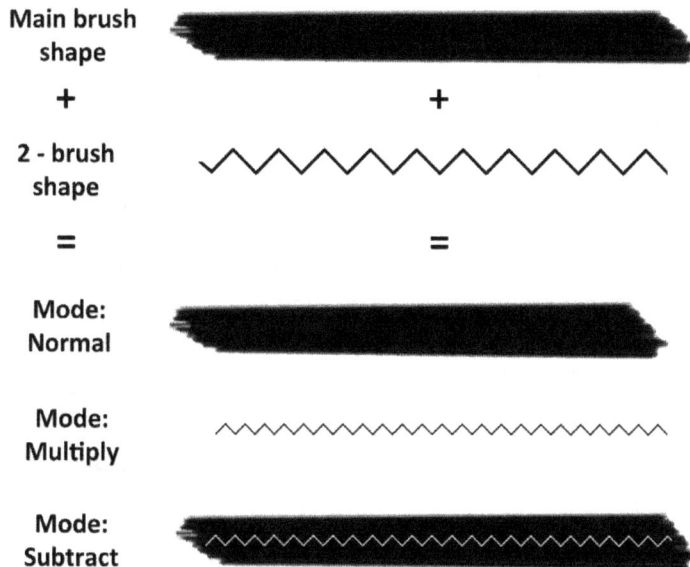

Figure 5.30 – Example combinations of 2-brush shapes and modes

- **Apply RGB value**: When toggled on, the RGB value of the second brush will be applied using the selected blending mode. When it's off, only the opacity of the second brush will be applied.

- **2-Brush Size**: You can set a specific size for the second brush and link it to input dynamics.

- **Link to main brush size**: When toggled on, the second brush size will adjust automatically to changes in the main brush size.

- **2-Anti-aliasing**: Defines the anti-aliasing of the second brush shape.

- List of 2-Brush tip shape: Shows a list of available brush shapes to apply. If your desired brush shape is not available in this list, you must select the desired brush and navigate to **Sub Tool Detail** | **Brush shape** | **Add to presets**. Then, it will be available for **Dual brush** settings in other brushes.

- **Apply brush shape**: Once you've decided on a brush shape, click this button to apply it to the **Dual brush** setting.

Many of the settings available for the main brush are also available for the secondary brush: **Brush tip**, **Spraying effect**, **Stroke**, and **Texture**. Making a change to one of these settings will completely change your dual brush, so experiment with them until you find your desired brush!

> **Important note**
>
> The dual brush will be placed on top of the main brush, so switching which is the main and which is the dual brush can completely change the result.

One valuable and unique way to use the **Dual brush** feature is by making it an optional second part of the brush that you can toggle on and off. To illustrate this, I'll use the **Zipper** decorative brush, which comes with CSP, as an example. The **Zipper** brush has the **Dual brush** feature turned on, creating a closed zipper. However, if you prefer it to be only one side of an open zipper, you can simply toggle the **Dual brush** feature off –the main brush shape will display only the single side!

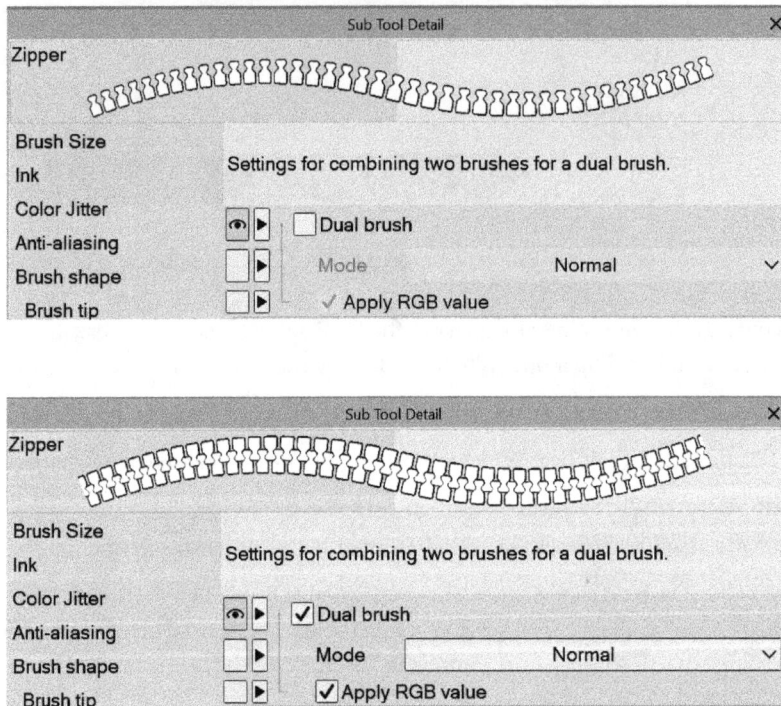

Figure 5.31 – You can use Dual brush to create complementary brushes

By mastering the **Dual brush** settings, you can create highly customized brushes that offer a wide range of artistic possibilities, from intricate textures to complex patterns, enhancing the expressiveness and uniqueness of your art.

Watercolor edge

The **Watercolor edge** feature simulates the natural, irregular edges often seen in traditional watercolor paintings. This setting is crucial for creating realistic watercolor effects in your digital artwork, giving your brushstrokes a more organic and authentic look. *Figure 5.32* shows the **Watercolor edge** functions:

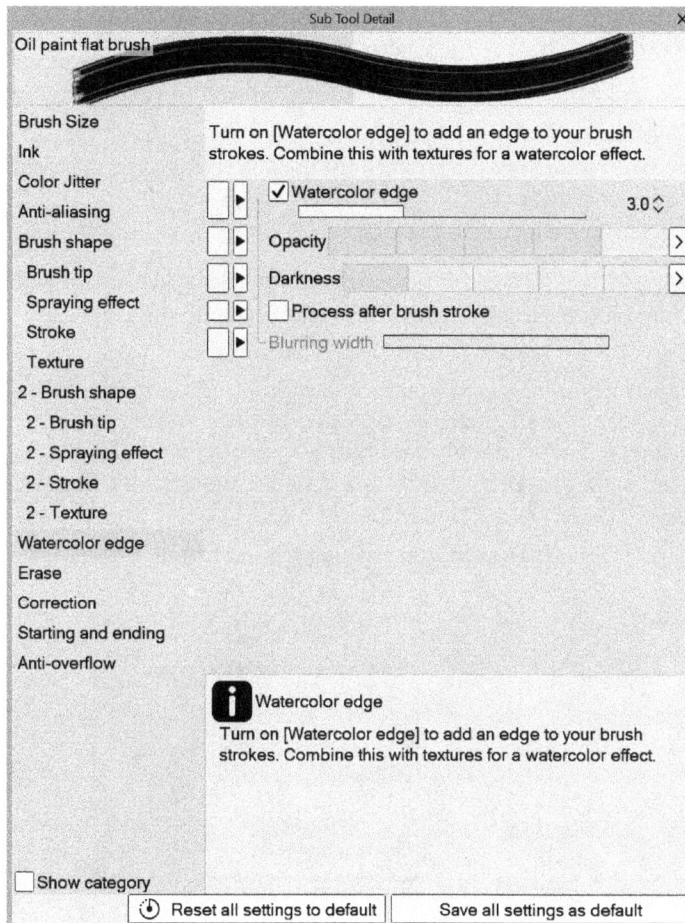

Figure 5.32 – The Watercolor edge settings

Here's how to utilize the **Watercolor edge** settings:

- **Watercolor edge**: Activate this setting to apply a watercolor edge to your brushstrokes. Use the sliders to configure the width of the dark line border on the inside. The larger the value, the wider the dark border will be.

- **Opacity**: Specifies the opacity of the outline. The higher the value, the more opaque the line border becomes.

- **Darkness**: Sets how dark the line border is. The higher the value, the darker the line border becomes.

- **Process after brush stroke**: Applies the watercolor edge after the line is fully drawn, allowing you to process the effect faster.

- **Blurring width**: This setting configures the strength of the blur on the edge. The larger the value, the more blurred the border area will be displayed. This setting is only available when **Process after brush stroke** is toggled on.

> **Important note**
>
> Items in the **Watercolor edge** category can't be used on vector layers or layers with **Monochrome** as their **Expression color**.

By experimenting with the **Watercolor edge** settings, you can add a unique and realistic touch to your digital watercolor paintings, enhancing their overall aesthetic and depth.

Erase

The **Erase** function in CSP allows you to modify your brush tool so that it acts as an eraser, providing you with a seamless way to correct mistakes and refine your artwork. You can see the **Erase** settings in *Figure 5.33*:

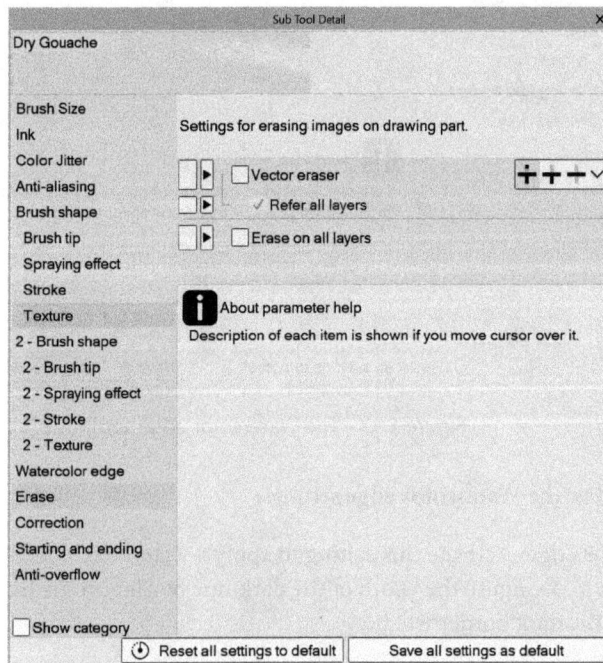

Figure 5.33 – The Erase settings

Here's how to use the **Erase** settings:

1. Inside the **Sub Tool Detail** palette, navigate to **Ink** and set **Blending mode** to **Erase**.

2. Now, you can go to **Erase** and toggle **Erase on all layers** on. This will make your brushstroke erase everything in all visible layers.

3. If you're working on a vector layer, the **Vector eraser** setting can be toggled on and adjusted to suit your needs. We'll see this in detail in *Chapter 6, Enhancing Your Lines with Vector Layers*.

Using the **Erase** settings, you can refine your artwork with precision, ensuring that your corrections blend seamlessly with the rest of your piece.

Correction

The **Correction** setting helps you refine and stabilize your brushstrokes, making it easier to achieve smooth and precise lines. This feature is especially beneficial for inking and line art, where clean and consistent strokes are essential.

This setting is versatile, encompassing various tools such as the **Pen** and **Liquify** tools, as well as shape-drawing tools such as **Figure**, **Balloon**, and **Frame Border**. The available settings vary depending on the tool that's been selected. *Figure 5.34* shows the available **Correction** settings:

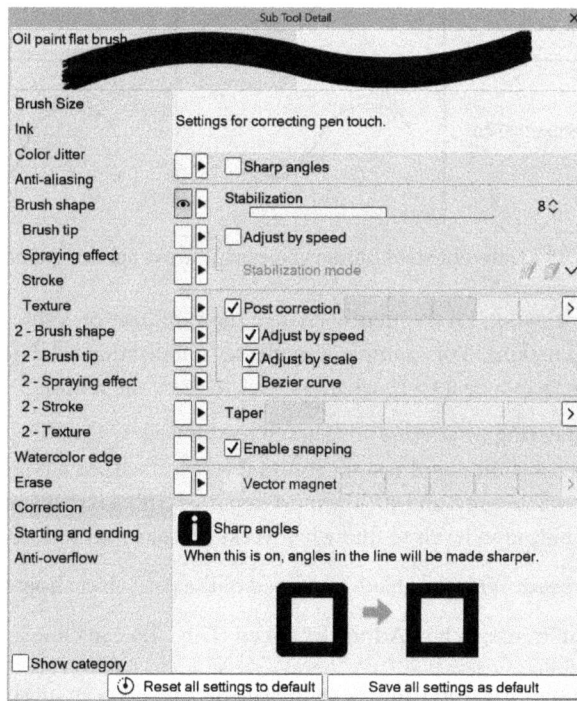

Figure 5.34 – The Correction settings

Here's how to utilize the **Correction** settings:

- **Sharp angles**: When enabled, angles drawn in the line will become pointed.

- **Stabilization**: This setting delays your brushstrokes, allowing you to draw smoother lines. While this might sound like the dream feature, it's essential to learn how to control it properly; otherwise, your lines may look dull and lifeless.

  There's a slider and a number value you can use to change how much your lines will be stabilized. The further you move the slider to the right and the higher the number, the more stabilization will be applied. High stabilization is ideal for creating controlled, flowing lines. It's especially useful for inking, technical illustrations, and smooth curves.

  However, if you try to make quick strokes with high stabilization, you'll be very disappointed and frustrated with the result. Low stabilization is better suited for more natural, freehand strokes. It's beneficial for sketching, expressive lines, hatching, and cross-hatching.

  Figure 5.35 shows how different stabilization values and stroke speeds change the result:

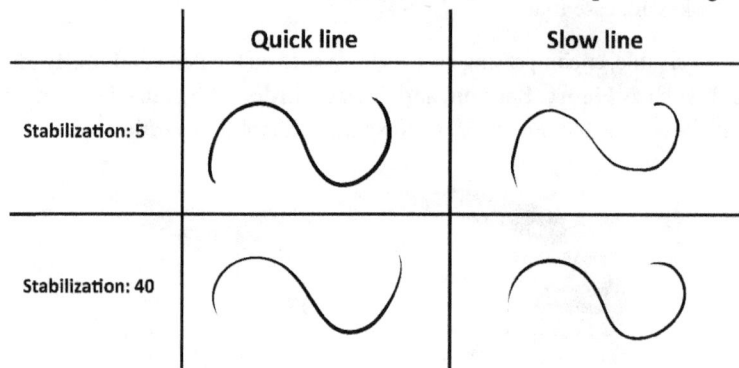

	Quick line	Slow line
Stabilization: 5		
Stabilization: 40		

Figure 5.35 – Different stabilization values and stroke speeds create different results

In a single drawing, I'll frequently change the stabilization value based on what part of the drawing I'm making. For example, I might set stabilization to 40 for outlining the face of the character, then reduce it to 13 when it's time to draw the mouth.

If you're wondering what value you should use for each type of line, I can't give you this answer – it's a personal choice, and you must find it for yourself. As a reference, my line stabilization usually ranges between 8 and 40. The most important thing is that you experiment with it and test different stabilization levels to find what works best for your style and the specific task at hand.

- **Adjust by speed**: When enabled, the speed of the pen affects how stabilization is applied.

- **Stabilization mode**: When **Adjust by speed** is on, you can choose a stabilization mode:

  - **Increase stabilization when drawing slowly**: Stabilizes small shakes when drawing slowly. This setting is disabled if the **Stabilization** value is set to 30 or higher.

- **Reduce stabilization when drawing quickly**: Fixes lagging lines by decreasing stabilization as the pen moves faster.

Which **Stabilization mode** option is best depends on your art process, so you can try both and decide what feels most natural.

- **Post correction**: This setting smooths the line *after* you've completed the stroke. It works independently of the **Stabilization** setting. The strength of this setting can be adjusted using an indicator or a numerical value. On a vector layer, a higher **Post correction** value results in fewer control points, while on a raster layer, curves can become more angular, depending on the setting.

When toggled on, three settings become available:

- **Adjust by speed**: Adjusts the strength of **Post correction** based on the stroke speed. I usually leave it on; when it's off, quick curves will show several angles.

- **Adjust by scale**: Adjusts the strength of **Post correction** according to the display ratio of the canvas.

- **Bezier curve**: Changes how curves are corrected post-stroke. When enabled, lines become quadratic Bezier curves after correction; when disabled, lines become spline curves. This is visible when drawing on a vector layer or using control points with tools such as the **Balloon** tool.

- **Taper**: This setting adjusts the length of the stroke as pen pressure decreases. Higher values extend the line's tapering effect beyond the point the stylus touched the tablet, simulating a brush with a long tip.

- **Enable snapping**: This setting allows you to draw as if you were snapping to a ruler. When disabled, your drawing will not snap to the ruler, even if ruler snapping is enabled. For shape-drawing tools, it snaps to guidelines and perspective rulers but not other rulers.

- **Vector magnet**: This allows you to snap to previously drawn lines on a vector layer. If possible, lines will be merged into one. An indicator can adjust the strength of the snap, with higher values allowing more distant lines to snap together.

By leveraging the **Correction** settings, you can create more polished and professional-looking artwork, with clean and precise lines that enhance the overall quality of your piece.

Starting and ending

The **Starting and ending** settings allow you to customize the appearance of your brushstrokes at the beginning and end, providing greater control over the dynamics of your lines. These settings are shown in *Figure 5.36*:

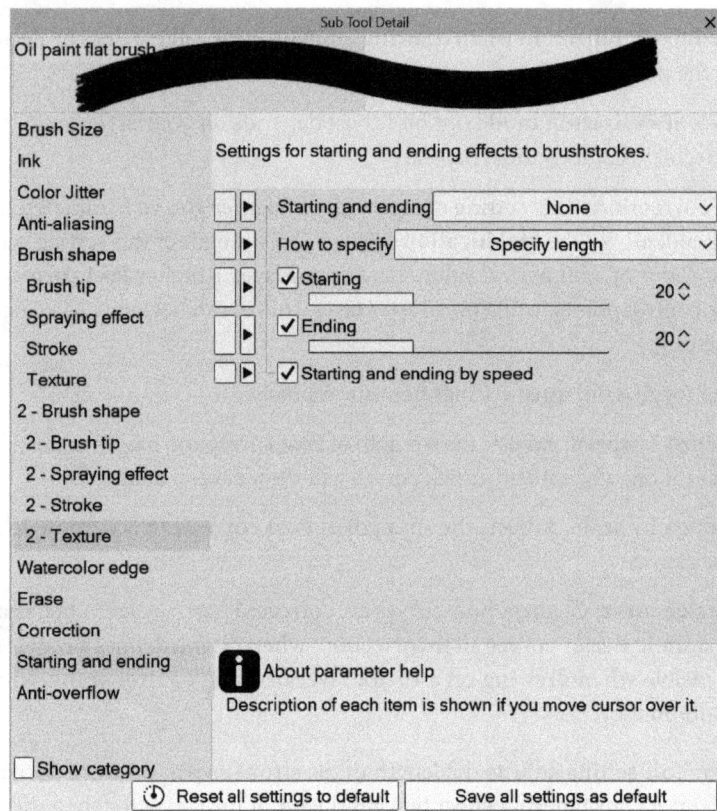

Figure 5.36 – The Starting and ending settings

> **Important note**
>
> The **Starting and ending** settings simulate pen pressure dynamics, so they're helpful if pen pressure is unavailable.

Here's how to use the **Starting and ending** settings:

- **Starting and ending**: This setting displays **Starting and ending effect dynamics**, allowing you to set **Brush Size**, **Brush density**, and more. Check the boxes for settings that you want to apply to the start and end of the stroke. Multiple settings can be selected for the starting and ending effects of brushstrokes.

- **How to specify**: Changes how **Starting and ending** is set. Here are some of the options you can use:

  - **Specify length**: Specifies the brushstroke length numerically. Higher values will apply the effect for a longer distance within the brushstroke.

- **By percentage**: Sets values as percentages of the line to draw.

- **Fade**: Applies only the **Ending** setting to the stroke. It gradually changes settings from the start of the drawing to reach the **Minimum value** option that's been set for **Ending**. Once reached, **Minimum value** remains until the end of the stroke.

- **Starting**: Enables settings for the beginning of a stroke. The stroke starts at **Minimum value** set at **Starting and ending** and gradually increases to the maximum value (**100%**). The **Starting** range can be set with a slider. If **How to specify** is set to **Fade**, **Starting** settings cannot be used.

- **Ending**: Enables settings for the end of a stroke. The stroke starts at **Minimum value** set at **Starting and Ending** and gradually decreases. The **Ending** range can be set with a slider, with values depending on the **How to specify** setting.

- **Starting and ending by speed**: Factors speed into the **Starting and ending** effects. Slower lines will have less dramatic effects.

By fine-tuning the **Starting and ending** settings, you can add a unique and dynamic touch to your brushstrokes, enhancing the expressiveness and fluidity of your lines.

Anti-overflow

The **Anti-overflow** feature is designed to prevent your brushstrokes from spilling over into unwanted areas, ensuring clean and controlled paint application. *Figure 5.36* shows how the brush should be spilling outside of the square border, but the paint is only applied within those borders:

Figure 5.37 – An example application of the Anti-overflow feature

This setting is particularly useful when you're working with complex shapes and layers. The following screenshot shows the available **Anti-overflow** settings:

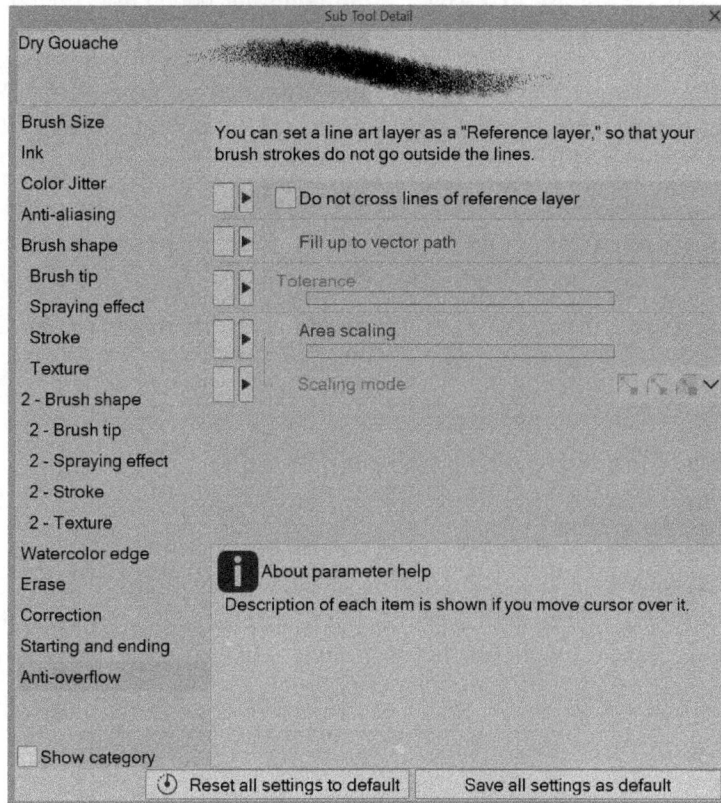

Figure 5.38 – The Anti-overflow settings

Here's how you can utilize these functions:

- **Do not cross lines of reference layer**: Prevents you from drawing over lines on the reference layers. The brush will only paint on the side with the majority of the brush shape.

- **Fill up to vector path**: Refers to the center line of the vector when a vector layer is used as a reference layer.

- **Tolerance**: Adjusts the tolerance for recognizing a color as the same as that of a line drawn on the reference layer. Higher numbers include more areas of different colors in the reference.

- **Area scaling**: Enlarges or shrinks the paint area by the number of pixels specified by the slider.

- **Scaling mode**: When **Area scaling** is on, you can set the corner shape to **Round**, **Rectangle**, or **To Darkest Pixel**.

With a solid understanding of brush properties, you're now equipped to create varied and expressive lines. However, to achieve truly professional results, you must know how to create custom brushes. The next section will delve into the step-by-step process you must follow to craft personalized brushes.

Creating custom brushes

Creating custom brushes is an essential skill for any digital artist looking to tailor their tools to their unique artistic style and workflow. In this section, we'll delve into the practical work you must do to design custom brushes.

To create custom brushes, follow these steps:

1. Select an existing brush that has similar characteristics to what you wish to create.
2. Right-click your chosen brush and select **Duplicate sub tool…**. A new popup will appear:

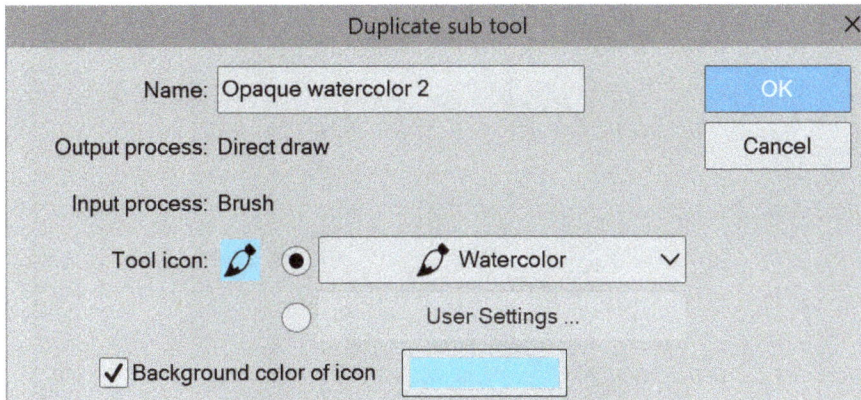

Figure 5.39 – The Duplicate sub tool dialog

3. Customize the new brush's appearance. You must rename it so that you don't mistake it for another. You can also change the icon and attribute a color to it.
4. Once the brush has been duplicated, you can edit it using the **Sub Tool Detail** palette. Using all the settings and tools we've covered in this chapter, you can customize it fully to your liking.

If you want to create a new brush tip shape, register it as an **Image** material by following these steps:

1. Go to **Edit | Register Material(J) | Image…**.
2. The **Material property** dialog will open.
3. Create a name, choose a saving location, and add a tag to this material.
4. Make sure you select **Use for brush tip shape**.
5. Press **OK** to save your brush tip material.

> **Important note**
>
> When you register a new brush tip shape, the original layer's **Expression color** will change how your brush behaves.
>
> If you leave **Expression color** set to **Color**, the brush will be saved with its RGB information – whatever color you used to paint it. Maintaining colors is useful when you're creating decorative brushes, such as bushes and trees, that you wish to save fully colored.
>
> When the layer's **Expression color** is set to **Gray**, you can change the brush's color using any of the color palettes. This setting is most useful for regular brushes, such as pens, pencils, ink, and paintbrushes.

To change **Expression color**, navigate to the **Layer Property** palette and choose **Expression color | Gray**, as shown in *Figure 5.40*:

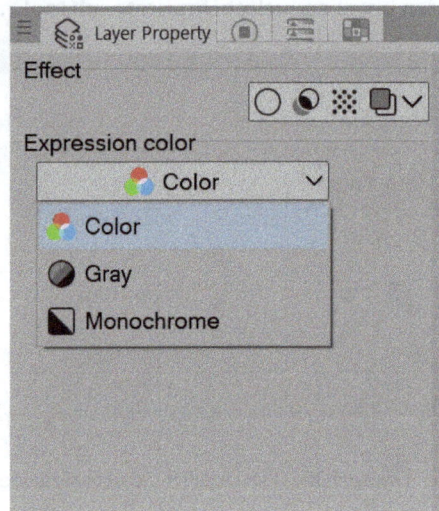

Figure 5.40 – How to change Expression color

Once you have created your desired brush tip shape, go to the **Sub Tool Detail** palette and choose **Brush tip**. Choose **Tip shape: Material** and select your newly-created brush tip shape.

One of the biggest questions artists ask themselves when creating custom brushes is, "How can I create textured brushes that feel natural and real?" A common mistake is to use only the **Texture** setting in the **Sub Tool Detail** palette. With this setting, you get an even texture throughout the brush, but its edges remain the same. For example, if we place a rock texture on a round brush, this is the result:

Figure 5.41 – Using the Texture setting

That is usually not enough to create realistic textured brushes since the edges remain rounded. Dual brushes are the secret technique you need to master to create realistic textured brushes in CSP since they can change the edges of your brush to make it more realistic. We covered dual brushes extensively in the previous section, *Mastering brush properties for complete customization*. Next, I will demonstrate how to create a textured brush using dual brushes so that you can apply this technique to your custom brushes.

We'll start with an uneven rectangular brush. I created this shape by drawing it on a new canvas and registering it as a material, something we covered previously in this section. Here is the base brush tip shape we'll be using:

Figure 5.42 – A custom brush tip shape (left) and a brushstroke created with it (right)

While it is a little uneven, it doesn't even come close to being as textured as I want. Because of that, I will turn on 2-Brush settings and choose an irregular shape, as shown here:

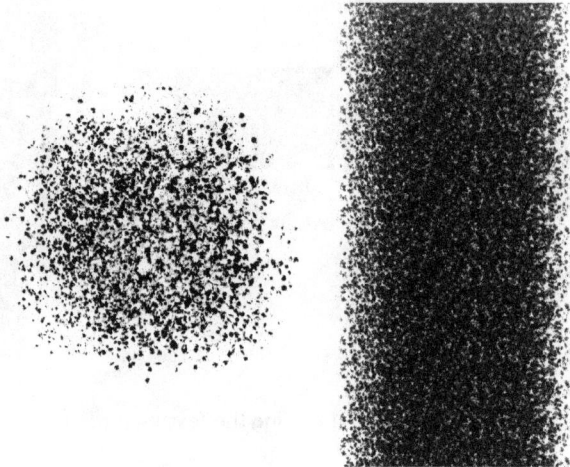

Figure 5.43 – The dual brush tip shape (left) and a brushstroke created with it (right)

Et voilà! We have a fully customized textured brush in CSP. To make sure this dual brush operates how I want, I've set its blending mode to **Multiply** under **Sub Tool Detail | 2 - Brush shape**. The type of texture you'll get largely depends on the combination of the base brush tip shape, the dual brush tip shape, and the dual brush blending mode. Some different alternatives can be seen in the following figure:

Figure 5.44 – Different combinations of base and dual brush tip shapes

I suggest you experiment with the brush tips and other settings when creating your brushes. Don't settle for less: you deserve the perfect brush that complements your painting skills! So, take your time creating and tweaking your brushes until they feel completely natural to you.

Creating custom brushes opens up a world of possibilities for digital artists, allowing greater control, flexibility, and individuality in your work. You can craft tools that perfectly align with your artistic vision and needs by crafting your own brushes. Embrace the process of creating custom brushes as a vital component of your artistic toolkit, empowering you to push the boundaries of your creativity and achieve remarkable results in your digital art endeavors!

Summary

In this chapter, we explored the comprehensive world of brush customization to enhance your digital art. We began by delving into brush dynamics, where you learned how pen pressure, tilt, and other factors can affect your strokes, allowing for more natural and expressive drawing. Next, we covered mastering brush properties for complete customization, guiding you through the **Sub Tool Detail** palette and explaining how to adjust brush size, opacity, texture, and more to suit your specific needs. Finally, we walked through creating custom brushes, giving you the tools to design and fine-tune brushes that align perfectly with your artistic vision and workflow.

With a solid grasp of these brush customization techniques, you're now equipped to create more personalized and efficient tools that will enhance your digital artwork.

As we move forward, in *Chapter 6*, *Enhancing Your Lines with Vector Layers*, we'll explore how you can further strengthen your drawings by leveraging the power of vector layers. This will enable you to achieve even greater precision and flexibility in your line work.

Get This Book's PDF Version and Exclusive Extras

UNLOCK NOW

Scan the QR code (or go to `packtpub.com/unlock`). Search for this book by name, confirm the edition, and then follow the steps on the page.

Note: Keep your invoice handly. Purchase made directly from packt don't require one.

6

Enhancing Your Lines with Vector Layers

Vector layers provide unmatched flexibility and precision inside **Clip Studio Paint** (CSP), making them indispensable for artists who depend heavily on line work, such as comic and manga artists. By mastering vector layers, you will gain the ability to create, edit, and perfect your line art with ease, transforming your digital drawings into polished and professional pieces.

In this chapter, we're going to cover the following main topics:

- Understanding what vector layers are and how to create them
- Editing and transforming vector lines
- Erasing vector lines

By the end of this chapter, you will be proficient in creating and utilizing vector layers to achieve perfect line art, including making vector layers, editing and transforming vector lines through pinching, rotating, scaling, and adjusting control points, changing the brush shape and size of vector lines for different visual effects, and employing various methods to erase vector lines for clean, professional results. These skills will help you enhance your technical capabilities and produce polished, high-quality artwork.

Now, let's dive into the world of vector layers and start improving your lines with these powerful tools!

Understanding what vector layers are and how to create them

Vector layers are a powerful tool for artists, particularly those who rely heavily on line art, such as comic and manga creators. Unlike raster layers, which are composed of individual pixels, vector layers use mathematical equations to create lines and shapes. This allows for infinite scalability without any loss of quality, making vector layers ideal for creating clean, precise lines that can be easily edited and transformed.

Vector lines are composed of **control points**, which can be freely created, erased, and manipulated.

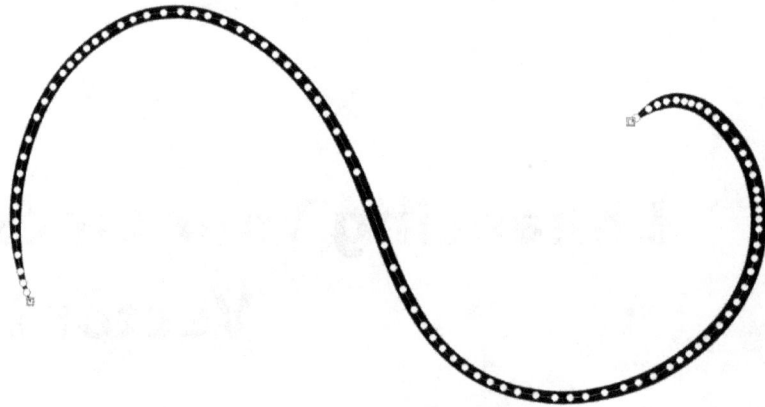

Figure 6.1 – Control points

Not all tools are available for vector layers inside CSP. The tools available are **Pen**, **Pencil**, **Brush**, **Airbrush**, **Decoration**, **Eraser**, and **Figure**. If you wish to use the **Fill** tool, for example, you need to create a raster layer for it. We will cover this process in detail in *Chapter 8*, *Maximizing Efficiency and Organization with Layers*, where we'll cover reference layers, and *Chapter 11*, *Applying Color Quickly with Pro Techniques*, where we'll cover the **Fill** tool extensively.

Now that you know what vector layers are, let's cover how to create vector layers.

Creating vector layers from scratch

Creating vector layers from scratch allows you to take full advantage of the precise and flexible nature of vector art. In this section, you will learn how to set up a new vector layer in your project, giving you the foundation to produce clean and scalable line art.

To create a vector layer, follow these steps:

1. Navigate to the **Layer** menu | **New Layer** | **Vector layer…**.
2. A dialog box will appear, where you can configure **Name**, **Expression color**, and **Blending Mode**, as shown in *Figure 6.2*:

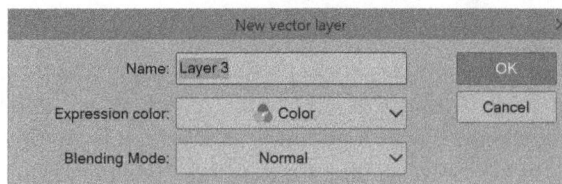

Figure 6.2 – New vector layer

3. Expression colors in vector layers are used to define and manage color properties, allowing dynamic adjustments and precise control over the appearance of vector lines and shapes.

When the **Gray** or **Monochrome** expression colors are selected, you can set the drawing colors – the black and white squares that appear on the right side of the **Expression color** drop-down menu. The effect changes depending on which expression color you selected:

	Gray	Monochrome
Only black	The drawing colors will be grayscale, from black to transparent	The drawing color will be black only
Only white	The drawing colors will be grayscale, from white to transparent	The drawing color will be white only
Both black and white	The drawing colors will be grayscale, from black to white	The drawing color will be black and white only

Table 6.1 – How expression colors affect vector layers

4. Select a **Blending Mode** for the vector layer. We'll cover blending modes extensively in *Chapter 9, Mastering Layer Blending Modes for Stunning Colors.*

5. Hit **OK** and the layer will be created.

Because of the way vector lines are processed, they might have a different appearance compared to their raster versions. This difference is more pronounced when you convert a raster layer to a vector layer.

There are two more ways to create vector layers besides starting from scratch: importing **Scalable Vector Graphics** (**SVG**) file formats from Adobe Illustrator and other softwares into CSP or converting a raster layer into a vector layer. Let's cover how to import SVG files first.

Importing SVG files from other software

Importing SVG files from other software allows you to incorporate external vector graphics into your projects seamlessly. SVG files, known for their ability to maintain quality at any size, are perfect for detailed illustrations, logos, and designs that require scalability.

To import an SVG file into CSP, follow these steps:

1. Open or create the file in which you wish to include the SVG file. You cannot import SVG files without an open project.

2. Once you have an opened file, go to the **File** menu | **Import** | **Vector....**

3. Choose the SVG file from your computer.

    Once imported, the SVG file will appear as a vector layer in your project, retaining all its editable vector properties. This feature is particularly useful for artists who create their initial designs in software such as Adobe Illustrator and want to continue refining their work in CSP. By importing SVG files, you can take advantage of CSP's robust vector editing tools, ensuring an efficient workflow and high-quality results.

4. Notice you can also export your CSP vector layer as SVG. Simply select the layer and navigate to the **Edit** menu | **Copy vectors as SVG**. Then, you can paste this information into your destination software.

After learning a process that ensures your imported vector graphics integrate smoothly with your existing vector layers, let's see how to convert layers next.

Converting raster layers into vector

You might realize in the middle of a process that you need a layer to be vectorized. In these moments, converting raster layers into vector layers provides more flexible and precise editing options.

Here are the steps to convert a raster layer into a vector layer:

1. On the **Layer** palette, select the layer you wish to convert.

2. Right-click the layer to open the **Layer** menu and select **Convert Layer(H)…**.

3. In the popup that appears, set **Type(K)** as **Vector layer**.

4. Once you have selected the vector layer type, the **Vector settings…** option will become available. When you tap it, you can customize your new layer even further:

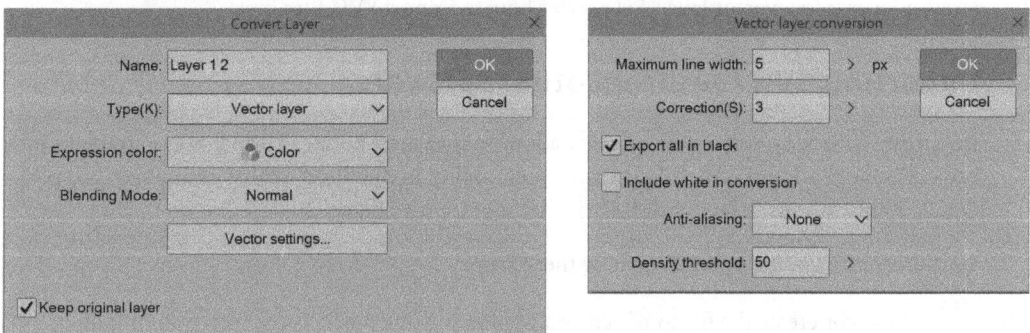

Figure 6.3 – Convert Layer and Vector layer conversion dialogs

These are the possible customizations inside the **Vector layer conversion** dialog:

A. **Maximum line width**: Sets the maximum line width of a vector line. Any raster line that is thicker than this value will be recognized as a fill color.

B. **Correction**: Sets the number of control points. The larger the **Correction** value, the fewer control points will be created—like brush **Stabilization** and **Post correction** settings, which we covered in *Chapter 5, Unlocking the Full Potential of Brush Settings.*

C. **Export all in black**: When this option is checked, it converts all vector lines to black, and one vector line is created per RGB value of the original image.

> **Important note**
>
> When **Export all in black** is turned off and the original image has more than 16 colors, it cannot be converted into a vector layer.

D. **Include white in conversion**: When this setting is checked, white pixels will not be converted into vector lines.

E. **Anti-aliasing**: Like **Anti-aliasing** with a brush, it softens the edge of the line. You can set **Anti-aliasing** to **None**, **Weak**, **Middle**, or **Strong**.

F. **Density threshold**: Sets the opacity threshold for converting pixels into vector lines. Pixels with opacity higher than the specified value will be converted into vector lines.

It's also possible to convert a vector layer into a raster layer by following the same procedures and selecting **Raster layer** for **Type(K)**.

Notice you can also convert a vector layer into a *vector image material layer*. Those are layers that can have both raster and vector images, and the vector images can be scaled up or down without losing quality. However, *vector lines cannot be edited in a vector image material layer*, and if the vector layer includes a layer mask, it will be converted without the layer mask.

By mastering vector layer creation and conversion, you can produce artwork with clean, crisp lines that are perfect for resizing and further editing, making your workflow more efficient and your final pieces more professional.

Now that you understand what vector layers are and how to create them, let's explore the various ways you can edit and transform vector lines to enhance your artwork.

Editing and transforming vector lines

Editing and transforming vector lines is a fundamental skill that allows you to refine your artwork with precision. In this section, you will learn how to manipulate vector lines through pinching, rotating, scaling, and adjusting control points. These techniques will give you the flexibility to make detailed adjustments and achieve the exact look you desire for your line art.

There are two tools you can use to edit vector layers:

- The **Operation** tool (with its **Object** sub tool.)

- The **Correct line** tool.

With both options, you can select multiple vector lines. To do so, create a selection with any **Selection** sub tool (e.g., the **Rectangle** sub tool). Once the selection is created encompassing the area you wish to modify, there are two options:

- Navigate to the **Select** menu and click **Select Overlapping Vectors**, and any vectors that overlap the selection will be included in the selection.

- Navigate to the **Select** menu and click **Select Vectors Within Area**, and only vector lines that are entirely contained within the selection will be selected.

You can see the difference between each option in the following figure:

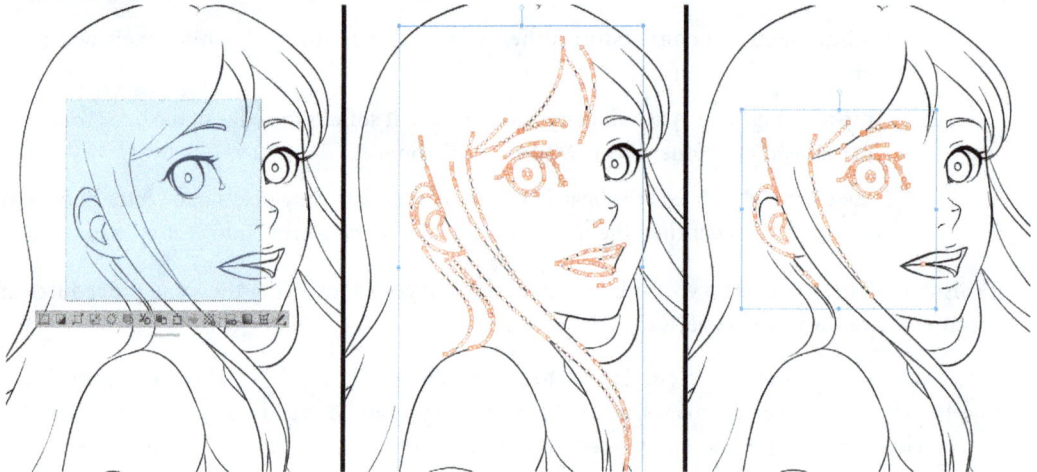

Figure 6.4 – The original selection (highlighted blue on the left) and the resulting vector selections with Select Overlapping Vectors (center) and Select Vectors Within Area (right)

Once you have selected your desired area, a **Transformation** control box will appear. Use it to edit the selection as you would any other object: you can scale it up and down and rotate it with the rotation handle at the top of the box.

Now that you know how to select multiple lines, let's cover how to edit vector lines with the **Object** sub tool.

Transforming vector lines with the Object sub tool

When you have a vector layer and select the Object sub tool, any lines you click on will show their control points, and you'll be able to move each control point freely.

In *Figure 6.5*, you can see the **Tool Property** palette when you select a vector line with the **Object** sub tool.

Figure 6.5 – The Tool Property palette when Object is selected

There are a few different settings you can change:

- **Operation of transparent part**: Determines what happens when you tap an empty area on a layer. You can choose between options such as **Switch to different layer** and **Operate object by dragging**.

- **Selectable object**: Only objects toggled on in this list will be selectable. Make sure **Vector** is toggled on before you proceed.

- **Selection mode**: Allows you to choose how you want to select the vector lines for editing. You can switch between different modes:

  - **New selection**: Each click will delete previous selections and create a new one.

  - **Add to selection**: Each click will add the selected line or control point to the current selection.

  - **Remove from selection**: Each click will remove the selected objects or control points from the current selection.

- **Toggle selection**: Allows you to select or deselect an object or control point with each tap. Tapping an unselected item adds it to the selection, while tapping an already selected item removes it from the selection. This flexibility lets you select and manipulate the parts of your vector line that need adjustment.

- **Main color**: You can change the main color of the selected vector line.

- **Brush Size** and **Brush shape**: Allow you to change the brush size and shape of the selected vector line. Changing the brush shape and size of vector lines can dramatically alter the visual impact of your artwork, enabling you to switch from delicate, grainy pencil lines to bold, thick, oil-paint strokes. This versatility allows you to adapt your line art to different artistic styles and preferences.

- **Adjust line thickness when scaling**: When you transform the selected vector by scaling it up or down, it will make the line thicker or thinner to maintain its proportions.

- **Mode**: Determines what type of transformation you can operate. You can choose between **Move control points & Scale/Rotate**, **Move control points**, **Scale/Rotate**, **Scale**, **Rotate**, **Free Transform**, **Distort**, **Skew**, and **Perspective**. Select whichever best fits the transformation you wish to apply to the selected vector line or control point.

With the **Object** sub tool, you can transform vector lines freely. Tap any single point, drag it, and the line will be moved accordingly:

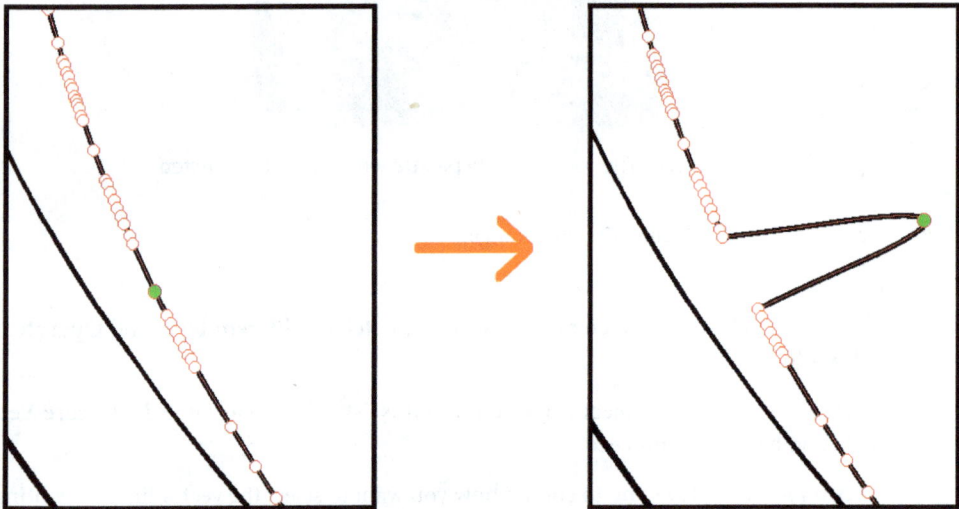

Figure 6.6 – Transforming vector lines with the Object sub tool

What if you want to delete or create control points, though? That's easy! Just head to the **Correct line** tool and modify it however you wish. Let's see more about the **Correct line** tool next.

Editing vector lines with the Correct line tool

Correct line is your tool when you want to have full control over the control points of a line, make the line thicker or thinner in a single point, and more. To use the **Correct line** tool, navigate to **Correct line** and select one of its **Sub Tool** options:

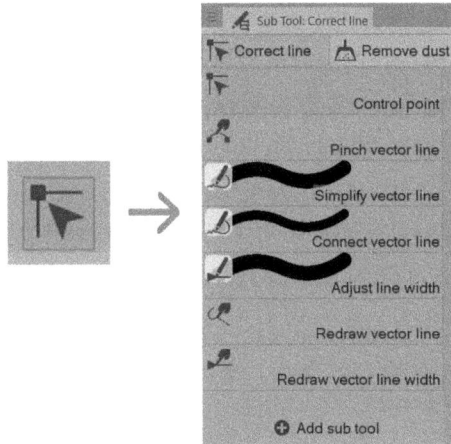

Figure 6.7 – The Correct line tool and its sub tools

Let's see what each of these sub tools can do.

Control point sub tool

The **Control point** sub tool offers complete control over vector points, enabling precise adjustments and modifications. With this tool, you can easily move, add, or delete control points, as well as adjust line width and opacity. Just select your desired action from the **Tool Property** palette, as shown in *Figure 6.8*:

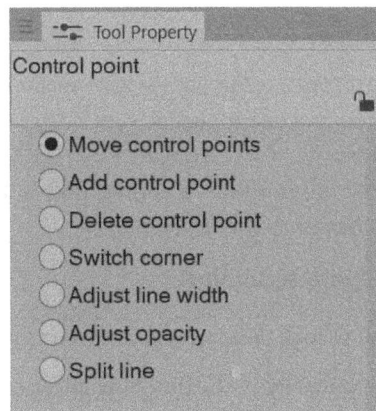

Figure 6.8 – Tool Property for Control point

Let's see in detail each of the options:

- **Move control points**: Drag and release control points to move them.
- **Add control point**: Add a new control point exactly where you click on the vector path. If you select an existing control point, you can drag and move it as well.
- **Delete control point**: Tap a control point and it will be deleted.
- **Switch corner**: Tap a control point in a corner to turn it into a curve, and vice versa.
- **Adjust line width**: Tap and drag a control point. If you drag it to the left, the line around the control point will become thinner, and to the right will make it thicker.
- **Adjust opacity**: Like **Adjust line width**, tap and drag a control point to the left or right side. Left will make it more transparent, and right will make it more opaque.
- **Split line**: Tap a control point and the vector line will be split in two at that point.

The **Control point** sub tool allows you to manipulate your vector lines with unparalleled precision, enhancing the quality of your line art. Next, we will explore the **Pinch vector line** sub tool, which allows for broad line adjustments.

Pinch vector line sub tool

The **Pinch vector line** sub tool drags part of the line and reshapes it completely. In *Figure 6.9*, you can see the difference between **Control point | Move control points (center)** and **Pinch vector line (right)**:

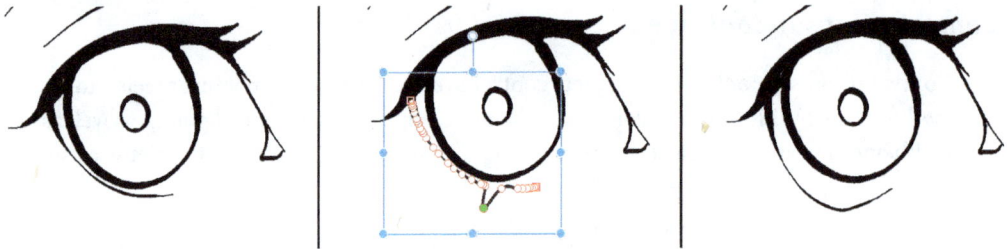

Figure 6.9 – The original vectors (left), transformation with Move control points (center), and transformation with Pinch vector line (right)

While **Move control points** lets you move single control points, **Pinch vector lines** does not show the control points and applies changes to the entire line.

There are seven settings inside **Pinch vector line**:

- **Fix end**: Choose whether to lock the start and end points in place.
- **Pinch level**: Adjusts the intensity of the pinching effect on the line. Higher values increase the effect.

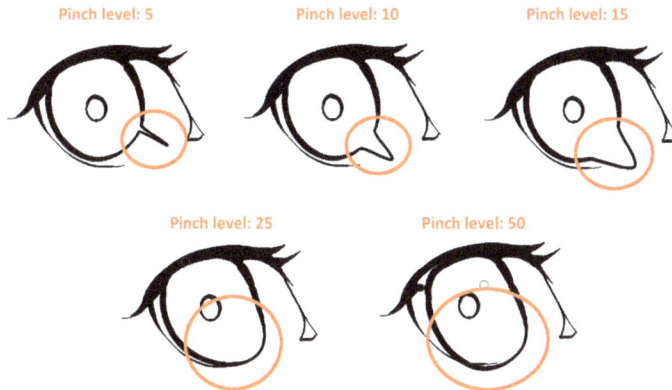

Figure 6.10 – Pinch levels

- **Pen pressure**: When enabled, higher pen pressure increases the pinch level. This is enabled by default.

- **Effect range**: Sets the size of the pinching area around the cursor. A smaller range offers more precision, while a larger range allows adjustments further from the clicked point.

- **Add control point**: When toggled on, this adds control points to the line after editing.

- **Connect lines**: When toggled on, dragging and overlapping the ends of two lines will connect them.

- **Snap to symmetry ruler**: When toggled on, transformations will be reflected if a symmetry ruler is active.

Utilizing the **Pinch vector line** sub tool can help you achieve finer details and more complex shapes in your vector artwork. Moving forward, let's look at the **Simplify vector line** sub tool to streamline your vector lines.

Simplify vector line sub tool

The **Simplify vector line** sub tool reduces the number of control points, making it cleaner. You can see its settings in *Figure 6.11*:

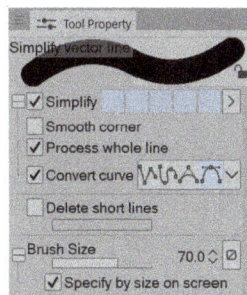

Figure 6.11 – Tool Property for Simplify vector line

The following settings are available:

- **Simplify**: Adjusts the degree of simplification. Higher values remove more control points.

- **Smooth corner**: Enable to smooth out angles. When off, corner shapes remain unchanged.

- **Process whole line**: Simplifies the entire line when clicking anywhere on it.

- **Convert curve**: Changes the curve type during simplification. This is available when **Process whole line** is enabled. Options include **Polyline**, **Spline**, **Quadratic Bezier**, and **Cubic Bezier**. Each will simplify the line differently, and in some cases, the number of control points might increase.

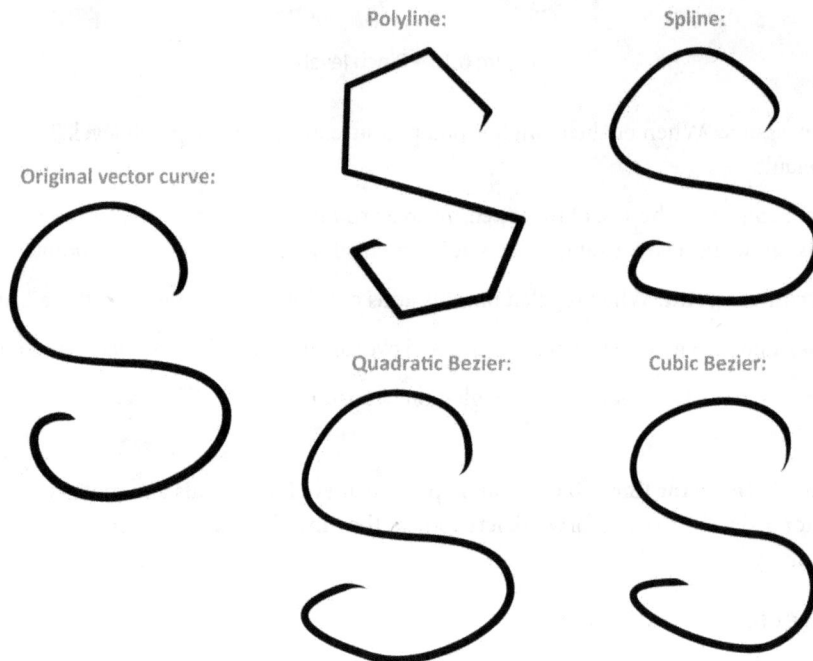

Figure 6.12 – Convert curve options

- **Connect lines**: Connects nearby lines. You can adjust the strength with the slider.

- **Delete short lines**: Removes short lines in the target area. Adjust the strength with the slider.

- **Brush Size**: Adjusts the tool size. You can apply input dynamics to this setting.

With the **Simplify vector line** sub tool, you can clean up your vector lines, making them easier to manage. Next, we will discuss the **Connect vector line** sub tool, which ensures seamless line connections.

Connect vector line sub tool

The **Connect vector line** sub tool allows you to seamlessly join the ends of vector lines that are close to each other, creating continuous paths. *Figure 6.13* shows its settings inside the **Tool Property** palette:

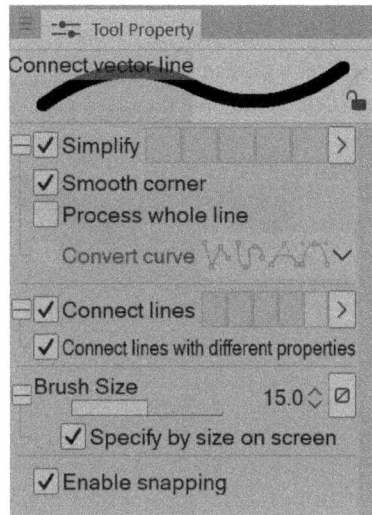

Figure 6.13 – Tool Property for Connect vector line

The following settings can be modified:

- **Simplify**: Adjusts the simplification level. Higher values remove more control points. When **Simplify** is enabled, you can customize it with the following options:

  - **Smooth corner**: When enabled, sharp points will become smooth curves with rounded shapes.

  - **Process whole line**: When enabled, processes will be applied to the entire line, not only the areas to which you applied **Connect vector line**.

  - **Convert curve**: Changes the curve type during simplification. This is available when **Process whole line** is enabled. Options include **Straight line**, **Spline**, **Quadratic Bezier**, and **Cubic Bezier**. They each will simplify the line differently, and in some cases, the number of control points might increase, similar to what we saw in *Figure 6.12*.

- **Connect lines**: Connects nearby lines. You can adjust the strength with the slider.

- **Connect lines with different properties**: Connects lines even if they have different colors or brush tip shapes. When connected, these lines will have one single color.

- **Brush Size**: Adjust the tool size.

- **Enable snapping**: When checked, the **Connect vector line** sub tool will snap to rulers.

Leveraging the **Connect vector line** sub tool ensures your vector artwork has fluid, uninterrupted lines, enhancing its overall cohesion. Now, let's delve into the **Adjust line width** sub tool to modify the thickness of your lines.

Adjust line width sub tool

The **Adjust line width** sub tool scales the line width up or down without reducing line quality. When selected, the following settings determine how the line width will be adjusted:

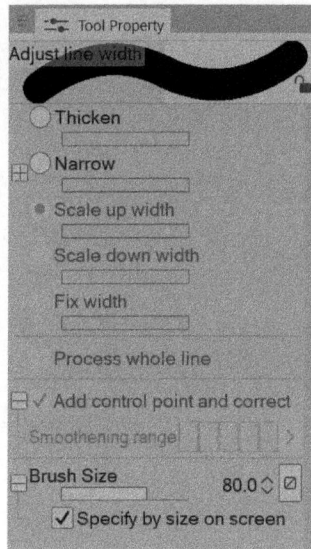

Figure 6.14 – Tool Property for Adjust line width

Here is how each setting affects this sub tool:

- **Thicken**: Increases the line thickness by a specified amount. For example, if you set the value at 5, it will increase the width by 5 pixels. Tapered lines become rounded at the ends.

- **Narrow**: Decreases the line thickness by a specified amount. Tapered lines become rounded at the ends.

  - When you select **Narrow**, you can determine a minimum width of **At least 1 pixel**, which prevents lines from disappearing when narrowed.

- **Scale up width**: Increases the line thickness based on the current width and a specified scale, multiplying it by a ratio. Tapered lines remain pointed.

- **Scale down width**: Decreases the line thickness based on the current width and a specified scale, multiplying it by a ratio. Tapered lines remain pointed.

- **Fix width**: Determines how to change line width and the degree of it.

After you have selected one of these options, you can customize it further with the following settings:

- **Process whole line**: Applies changes to the entire line, not just touched areas.
- **Add control point and correct**: Allows you to add a control point and change the width from the middle of the line. This setting can only be enabled when **Process whole line** is off.
  - When **Add control point and correct** is enabled, you can set a **Smoothening range** value, which specifies the smoothening range for both end points of the line.
- **Brush Size**: Adjusts the tool size.

With the **Adjust line width** sub tool, you can dynamically alter line thickness, adding depth and emphasis to your vector art. Following this, we will cover the **Redraw vector line** sub tool for refining your existing lines.

Redraw vector line sub tool

The **Redraw vector line** sub tool lets you refine and correct existing vector lines by redrawing them as you move your stylus. This tool updates the control points of the line to align with your new stroke, and its settings are shown in *Figure 6.15*:

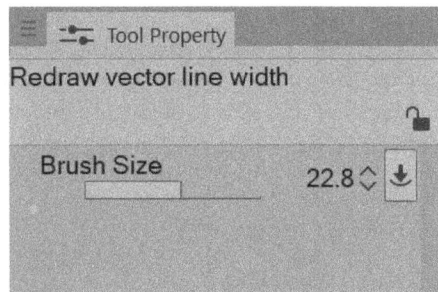

Figure 6.15 – Tool Property for Redraw vector line

Here is how each function works inside the **Tool Property** palette:

- **Fix end**: Choose whether to lock the start and end points in place.
- **Connect lines**: Connect overlapping ends of two lines when dragging.
- **Simplify**: Adjust the simplification level. Higher values remove more control points.
- **Stabilization**: Adjusts the stabilization of the pen.

Using the **Redraw vector line** sub tool provides a straightforward way to perfect your vector lines, ensuring they meet your artistic vision. Finally, we will explore the **Redraw vector line width** tool to customize your linework further.

Redraw vector line width sub tool

The **Redraw vector line width** sub tool allows you to trace a vector line to change its width. You can set up input dynamics for this sub tool:

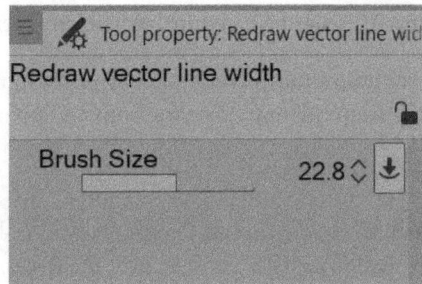

Figure 6.16 – Tool property: Redraw vector line width

To use this sub tool, select a **Brush Size** value and draw over your vector path. The area you have drawn over will match the width you set for **Brush Size**. You can use this sub tool to increase or decrease the vector line width.

The **Redraw vector line width** sub tool empowers you to customize the thickness of your vector lines, giving your artwork a distinctive and polished look. This concludes our exploration of vector line editing tools. By understanding these editing and transformation techniques, you'll be able to create polished, professional-looking lines that elevate the quality of your artwork. Now, let's move on to another powerful feature of vector layers—the erasing process.

Erasing vector lines

Vector erasers are specifically designed to work with vector lines, offering more precise and controlled erasing options. Unlike a regular eraser, which simply removes pixels from a raster layer, the vector eraser allows you to erase vector lines up to specific intersections, remove entire segments, or erase only the portions of lines you touch. This precision makes the vector eraser an indispensable tool for artists working on detailed line art, such as comics and illustrations, where clean, precise lines are crucial.

There are two ways to use vector erasers. The first is in the brush **Sub Tool Detail** palette:

1. Inside the **Sub Tool Detail** palette, navigate to **Ink** and set **Blending mode** to **Erase**.
2. Go to **Erase** and check the **Erase on all layers** option if you wish to affect all visible layers.

3. Turn the **Vector eraser** setting on, as seen in *Figure 6.17*:

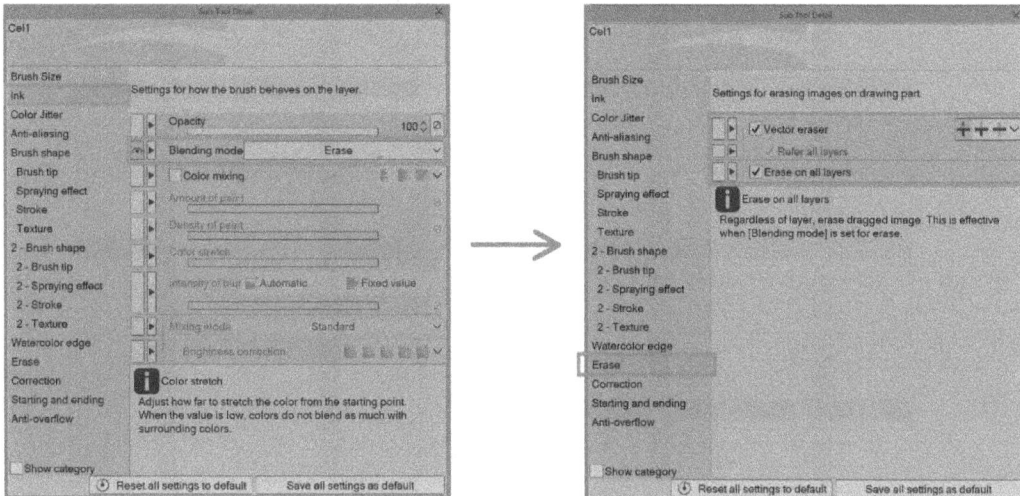

Figure 6.17 – Setting a brush as a vector eraser

The second method is by using the **Eraser** tool:

1. Select the **Eraser** tool.

2. Any of the sub tools inside of **Eraser** can be used for vector layers if you follow the same procedure explained previously: navigate to the **Sub Tool Detail** palette | **Erase** | turn **Vector eraser** on.

3. Once you turn **Vector eraser** on, new options will become available on the right side:

Figure 6.18 – Vector eraser options

These are the options:

I.   **Erase touched areas**: All areas touched by the eraser will disappear.

II. **Erase up to intersection**: Removes the line up to where it intersects with another line.

III. **Whole line**: Deletes entire vector strokes with a single click.

In *Figure 6.19*, you can see how each of these options affects vector lines. The green stroke marks the eraser:

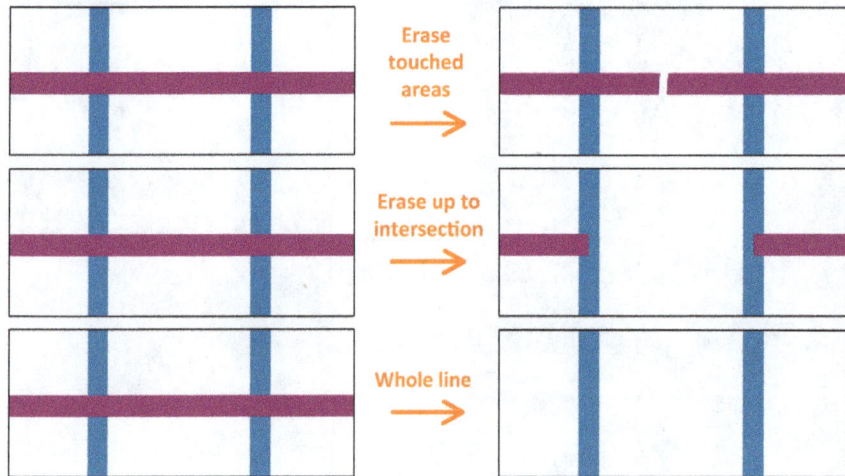

Figure 6.19 – Vector eraser types

Understanding and utilizing the different methods for erasing vector lines will significantly improve the quality and clarity of your line art. With these skills, you can easily correct mistakes and refine your illustrations. Having explored these essential techniques, you are now well-equipped to enhance your lines with vector layers, taking your artworks to the next level.

Summary

In this chapter, you've learned the fundamentals of vector layers and how to create them, enabling you to produce a clean and easily editable line art. You also explored how to edit and transform vector lines, customize their brush shapes and sizes, and efficiently erase them. Mastering these techniques allows for greater flexibility and precision in your artwork, particularly for line-intensive art styles.

In the next chapter, we'll delve into utilizing rulers and guides to achieve even greater precision in your drawings.

7

Utilizing Rulers and Guides for Precision

Rulers and guides are essential tools for creating accurate, symmetrical, and perfectly aligned drawings. In this chapter, we delve into these often-overlooked **Clip Studio Paint** (**CSP**) tools, which are essential for artists striving for precision and consistency in their work. Whether you're creating intricate symmetrical designs, dynamic perspective-based compositions, or simply ensuring that your lines and shapes are perfectly aligned, mastering rulers and guides will elevate the quality and accuracy of your art.

In this chapter, we're going to cover the following main topics:

- Understanding guides in CSP
- Using Linear, Curve, and Figure rulers
- Making the most out of the Ruler pen and the Special ruler
- Applying a Perspective ruler for dynamic images
- Optimizing your use of the Symmetrical ruler

By the end of this chapter, you'll have a solid grasp of how to use rulers and guides to improve the precision and efficiency of your artwork, making your creative process smoother and more professional.

We'll start by thoroughly covering the different types of guides, how to use them, and how they can enhance the precision and accuracy of your work.

Understanding guides in CSP

CSP provides a few different types of guide tools, and you must understand the differences between them before we can dive into complex subjects such as special rulers.

Rulers and guides are on-screen reference lines that help you control and direct your brush strokes with precision. You can snap your brush strokes and other tools to any of the guide lines we cover in this chapter, ensuring that all elements are perfectly aligned. In *Figure 7.1*, you can see the difference between lines that snap (left) and lines that do not snap (right):

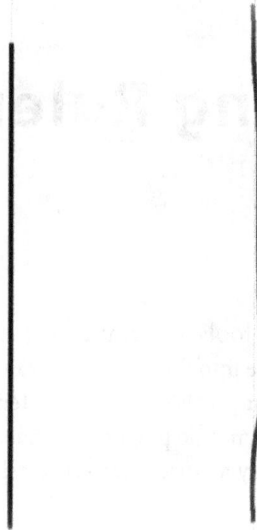

Figure 7.1 – Snapping lines versus non-snapping lines

To enable snapping, follow these steps:

1. Navigate to **View** | **Snap to Ruler**, **Snap to Special Ruler**, or **Snap to Grid**.
2. Make sure the tool you're using also enables snapping. To toggle it on/off, go to **Tool Property** | **Sub Tool Detail** | **Correction** | **Enable snapping**, as we covered in *Chapter 5, Unlocking the Full Potential of Brush Settings*.

Now that you know how to turn snapping on and off, let's fully understand each of the types of guides. We'll start by covering the **Ruler bar**, which appears by default when you first launch CSP.

The Ruler bar

The Ruler bar appears around the canvas, on the left and top sides. It is useful for measuring parts of your artwork in real-life size (millimeters) and dividing the canvas into equal parts. You can see it highlighted in orange in *Figure 7.2*:

Figure 7.2 – The Ruler bar

There are two ways to toggle the Ruler bar on/off:

- Navigate to **View** | **Ruler Bar**.

- Press the shortcut *Ctrl/command + R*.

Its default measurement is set to millimeters, and the start position is at the top left of the canvas. You can change the start position by following these steps:

1. Navigate to **View** | **Grid/Ruler bar Settings**.
2. The **Grid/Ruler bar settings** dialog will open (*Figure 7.3*):

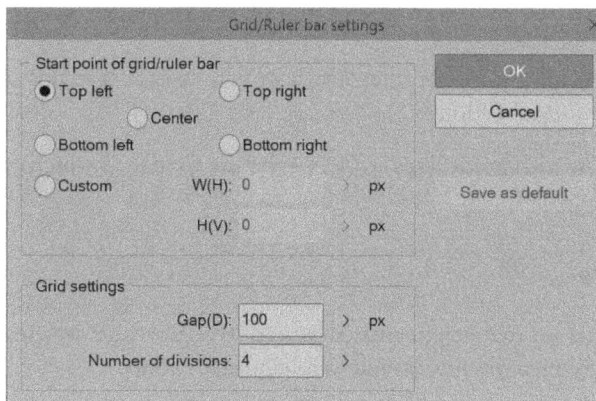

Figure 7.3 – Grid/Ruler bar settings

3. Decide the **Start point of grid/ruler bar**. You can set it to **Top left**, **Top right**, **Center**, **Bottom left**, **Bottom right**, or **Custom**. If you choose **Custom**, you get the following options:

- **W(H)**: Determines the starting point of the width (horizontal) in pixels.

- **H(V)**: Determines the starting point of the height (vertical) in pixels.

4. Press **Save as default** to save those settings for the next time you use the Ruler bar, or just hit **OK** to apply it once.

Now that you understand the Ruler bar, it's time to explore another tool for maintaining precision in your artwork: guide lines.

Guide lines

Guide lines are a type of ruler that create completely vertical or horizontal lines. With these lines, you can align elements of your art perfectly, be it drawings or text. It is very useful for creating precise work.

There are three ways to create guide lines:

- Navigate to the **Ruler** tool and select the **Guide** sub tool.

- Navigate to the **Ruler** tool, select the **Special ruler** sub tool, navigate to **Tool property**, and set **Special ruler** to **Guide**.

- When the Ruler bar is visible, you can drag and drop guide lines on the canvas:

    A. Click on the ruler bar and hold.

    B. Drag until the point where you wish to position the guide line.

    C. Release the click. The guide line will be positioned.

If you wish to remove a guide line, perform the opposite motion: click on the line, drag and drop it back to the Ruler bar.

Guide lines operate like the Linear ruler, which we will cover later in this chapter in the *Using Linear, Curve, and Figure Rulers* section.

Now that you know what guide lines are, let's cover the **Grid** tool, which creates a structured overlay to aid your drawings.

The Grid tool

The **Grid** is a visual aid that helps artists align and structure their drawings with ease and accuracy. It acts as a guide for creating precise and well-aligned artworks.

When enabled, it overlays your canvas with evenly spaced horizontal and vertical lines, forming a grid pattern (*Figure 7.4*). This can be helpful when working on layouts and checking proportions, ensuring elements are aligned correctly.

Figure 7.4 – The Grid tool

The Grid can be toggled on and off easily, allowing you to switch between a guided and freehand approach as needed. To toggle it on/off, navigate to **View | Grid**.

You can customize some elements of the Grid to suit your needs, adjusting the **Gap** and **Number of divisions** to better fit the project you're working on. To customize the Grid, follow these steps:

1. Navigate to **View | Grid/Ruler Bar Settings**.
2. The Grid/Ruler bar settings dialog will open (as shown in *Figure 7.3*.)
3. Decide the **Gap** value (in pixels).
4. Set the **Number of divisions**.
5. If you wish to save those settings for the next time you use the Grid, press **Save as default**.
6. Hit **OK** to apply the Grid.

Having explored the Grid, let's move on to understanding how to use rulers to further enhance your drawing precision.

The Ruler tool

Rulers are powerful tools that allow you to create consistent, accurate lines and shapes, giving you control over your artwork's structure and composition. They allow artists to draw perfectly straight lines, curves, and shapes with precision.

There are several types of rulers available, such as the **Linear ruler** for straight lines and the **Perspective ruler** for detailed perspective grids. You can even create custom rulers by drawing directly on the canvas, which can be used to guide your pen strokes. Once the ruler is set, you can customize it; the extent of customization varies based on the type of ruler selected. We'll cover how to edit each ruler type later in this chapter.

To use the Ruler tool, follow these steps:

1. Select the **Ruler** tool in the **Tool** palette.

2. Choose a sub tool from the list:

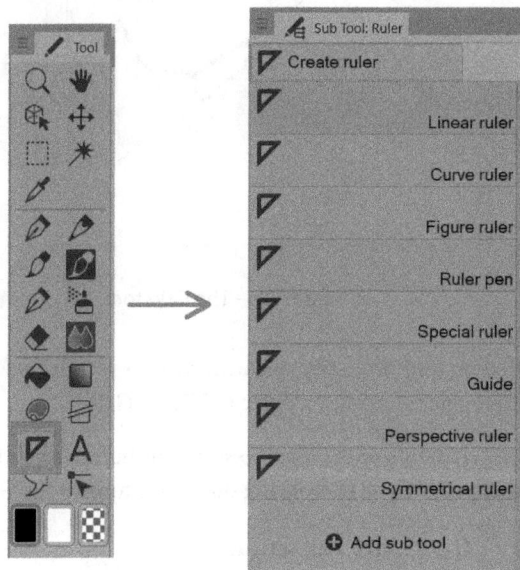

Figure 7.5 – The Ruler tool and its sub tools

3. Apply the ruler by clicking or drawing on the canvas. You can either create the ruler on your current editing layer or on a new, dedicated layer. To change this setting, follow these steps:

    A. Navigate to the **Tool property** palette.

    B. Toggle **Create at editing layer** on/off.

If you want to position the ruler at a specific angle, there are two options:

- Navigate to the **Tool property** palette and toggle on the **Snap angle** feature. You can determine the angle with the value slider or by typing a number (*Figure 7.6*).

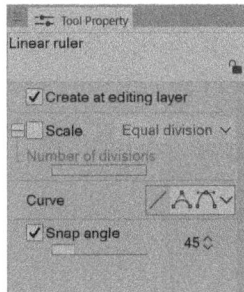

Figure 7.6 – The Snap angle settings inside of Tool Property

- Hold *Shift* while dragging, and the ruler will move in 45-degree increments. When using the Figure ruler, you can choose the angle after determining the figure size and releasing, then pressing *Shift* to move it in 45-degree increments.

  This operation does not work with the Ruler pen, and the Guide sub tool can only be set at 90 or 180 degrees.

To edit a ruler after it is placed on canvas, follow these steps:

1. Select the **Operation** tool | **Object** sub tool.
2. Inside **Tool property**, select a transformation **Mode**, such as **Rotate**, **Scale**, **Distort**, or **Skew**.
3. Click on the existing ruler. A transformation box will appear, as shown in *Figure 7.7*:

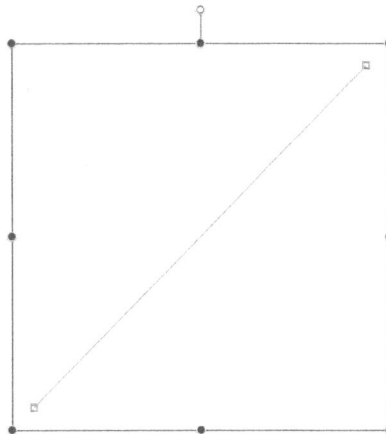

Figure 7.7 – A transformation box (blue) around a Linear ruler (purple)

4.   Use the transformation box to apply changes based on the Mode selected in *step 2* or click on one of the control points to adjust it. If you wish to move the entire ruler without modifying any part of it, press *Shift + click and drag* to your desired position.

A layer with an active ruler will show a ruler icon inside the Layer palette, as shown in *Figure 7.8* (left).

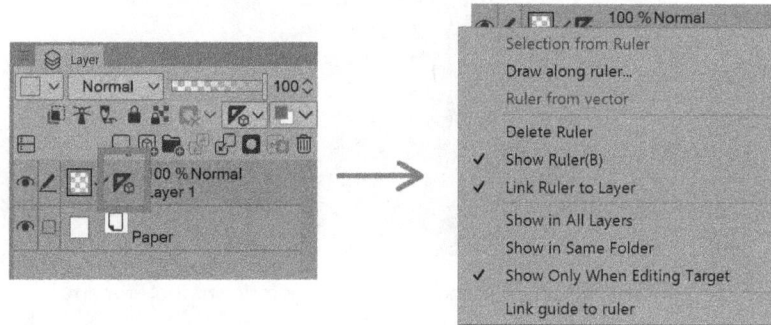

Figure 7.8 – The ruler icon and its operations

You can click this icon and drag it to another layer. Right-clicking the ruler icon will show new operations (*Figure 7.8*, right):

- **Selection from Ruler**: This operation is available for close-shaped rulers. A selection will be created considering the ruler shape. You can also create a selection from a ruler by pressing *Ctrl* and clicking on the ruler icon.

- **Draw along ruler…**: Creates a brush stroke following the ruler. The brush stroke will be hard-edged and continuous, without any width variations. You can determine the brush width for it in the **Draw along ruler** dialog.

- **Ruler from vector**: Select a vector layer with the **Object** sub tool and apply this operation to create a ruler shaped exactly like the vector drawing. If you only have one vector line selected, only this line will be considered for the new ruler.

- **Delete Ruler**: Deletes the selected ruler. If no ruler is selected with the **Object** sub tool, it will delete all rulers on the current layer.

- **Show Ruler**: Toggle it on/off to show or hide the ruler. You can also *Shift + click the ruler icon*, and it will show/hide the ruler.

- **Link Ruler to Layer**: When toggled on, the rulers will move with the layer when the layer is moved with the **Move** layer tool.

- **Show in All Layers**: The ruler will affect all layers. New lines in any Raster, Vector, or Selection layer, as well as lines in Quick mask and the Balloon tool, will snap to it.

- **Show in Same Folder**: The ruler will affect layers within the same folder.

- **Show Only When Editing Target**: The ruler will affect only the current layer.

- **Link guide to ruler**: When toggled on, this setting links the ruler to layers created above it, and rulers and guides are moved together with the **Move** tool.

The main difference between a Ruler and other guiding tools is that the Ruler is an active drawing aid that allows full customization, while the Ruler bar is a passive visual guide, and the Grid does not allow full customization.

Understanding guides in CSP equips you with the tools to maintain consistent alignment, balance, and precision throughout your artwork. By mastering the use of guides, you'll find it easier to create polished, professional-looking pieces with elements that are perfectly aligned. These foundational skills not only improve the visual harmony of your work but also streamline your creative process, allowing you to focus more on the artistic elements and less on technical alignment.

Now that you have a solid understanding of guides, it's time to explore the different types of rulers available. By mastering Linear, Curve, and Figure rulers, you'll be able to add depth, precision, and creativity to your drawings with ease.

Using Linear, Curve, and Figure rulers

The Linear, Curve, and Figure rulers are versatile options for artists looking to create clean, precise lines and shapes. These rulers help you draw with accuracy, whether you're creating straight lines, smooth curves, or perfect geometric shapes. In this section, we'll delve into how to use each type effectively, enhancing your ability to produce refined and structured artwork. Let's start with the **Linear ruler**, which creates straight lines at any angle.

The Linear ruler

The **Linear ruler** allows you to create straight lines by dragging on the canvas. Whether you're drawing architectural elements, horizon lines, or other linear components, this ruler allows you to achieve perfect alignment effortlessly.

To use the Linear ruler, select the **Ruler** tool and the **Linear ruler** sub tool. Then, click and drag on the canvas to place it.

Once the Linear ruler is on the canvas, drawings made near it will snap and follow the line, as shown in the following figure:

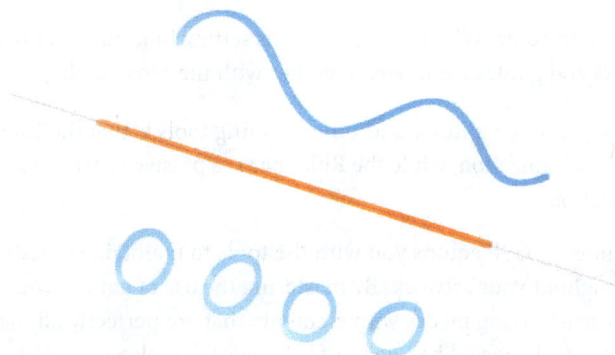

Figure 7.9 – The Linear ruler

In *Figure 7.9*, you can see that a line (orange) drawn close to the ruler (purple) will snap and become completely straight. From a certain distance, you can draw freely (blue). You must experiment to learn what the distance is.

Mastering the Linear ruler gives you the foundation for structured, straight designs. Now, let's explore how to create curves with the **Curve ruler**.

The Curve ruler

The **Curve ruler** is your go-to tool for creating smooth, flowing curves. Ideal for inorganic and organic rounded shapes, this ruler offers various options for drawing curved lines with precision.

You can adjust various methods for drawing curves using the **Tool Property** palette, such as polylines and Bezier curves, as shown in *Figure 7.10*:

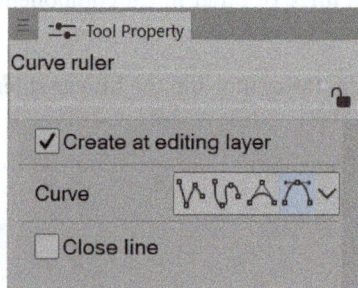

Figure 7.10 – Tool Property for the Curve ruler palette

Here's how each of the Curve modes behaves:

- **Straight line**: Each click on the canvas will create a straight line connected to the previous one, and there are no curves on the line.

- **Spline**: This is the default Curve mode. In this mode, tap to place multiple points along the curve, then double-tap the final point to establish the curve ruler. With each new tap, moving your cursor will change the angle of the previous lines.

- **Quadratic Bezier**: This curve comprises anchor points and direction points that define the line shape. To draw a Quadratic Bezier curve, follow these steps:

    A. Place the line's starting point on the canvas with a click.

    B. Click on the spot where you want to place the direction point to control the curve.

    C. Move the cursor to adjust the specifics of the curve.

    D. Click again to finish the first curve.

    E. Every new click will continue the Curve ruler. After creating as many points as you wish, double-click or press *Enter* to create the ending point of the Curve ruler, as shown in *Figure 7.11*:

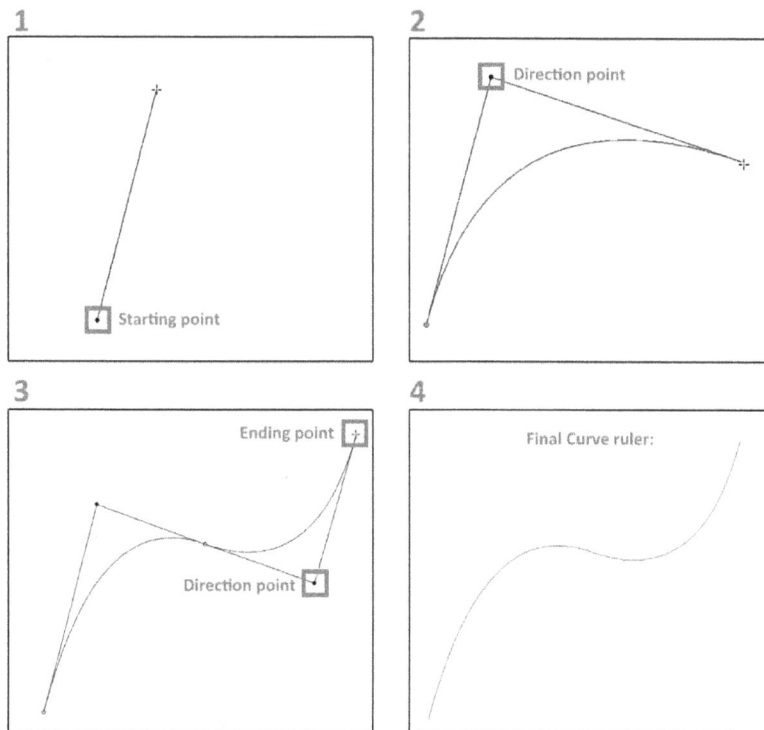

Figure 7.11 – Creating a Curve ruler with Bezier curve

If you want to make the anchor point a corner instead of a curve, hold *Alt* as you click on the canvas.

- **Cubic Bezier**: Like the Quadratic Bezier, the Cubic Bezier also consists of anchor points and direction points. However, when you click on the second point, you must drag the cursor to change the shape of the curve.

By using the Curve ruler, you can effortlessly integrate elegant curves into your designs. Next, let's explore the versatility of the **Figure ruler** for creating geometric shapes.

The Figure ruler

The **Figure ruler** allows you to create rulers following geometric shapes such as rectangles, ellipses, and polygons. This tool is perfect for constructing the foundational elements of your design.

To select the geometrical shape of the Figure ruler, navigate to **Tool Property | Figure** and select one of its options:

- **Rectangle**: Creates a rectangular shape of your desired size and proportion.
- **Ellipse**: Creates an ellipse of your desired size and proportion.
- **Polygon**: Creates a polygon of your desired size and proportion. To select the number of corners, navigate to **Number of corners**, below **Figure**, and choose a value between **3** and **32**.

When Rectangle or Polygon are selected, it's possible to round the corners of the shape, as shown in *Figure 7.12*:

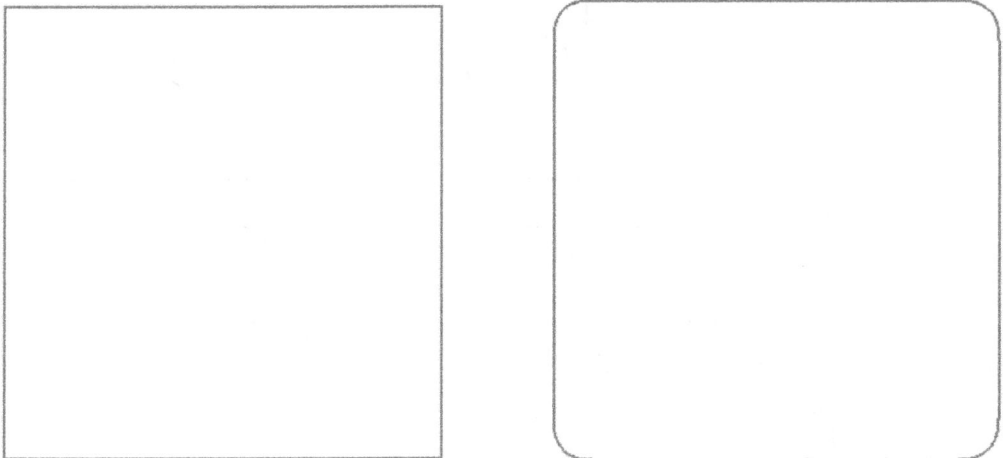

Figure 7.12 – Figures with (right) and without (left) round corners

To round the corners, follow these steps:

1. Toggle on **Roundness of corner** inside the **Tool Property** palette.

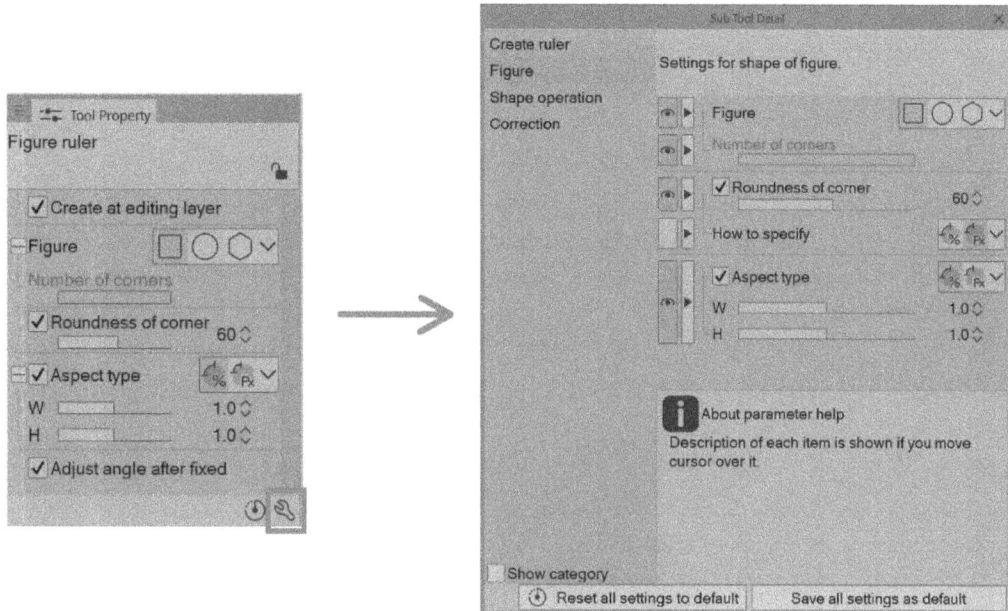

Figure 7.13 – The Tool Property palette for the Figure ruler and Sub Tool Detail | Figure

2. Go to **Sub Tool Detail | Figure.**
3. Set **How to specify**, which controls the way CSP rounds off the corners.

    *   **Specified ratio** rounds the corners proportionally based on a percentage (%) of the figure's sides.
    *   **Specify length** rounds the corners by setting a fixed distance from the corner's center.

You can also determine the **Aspect type** of the shape, changing the relationship between the vertical and horizontal side. This is useful when you have a ruler with specific proportions. Follow these steps:

1. Navigate to **Tool Property**.
2. Toggle on **Aspect type**.
3. On the right side, there will be two options:

    *   **Specified ratio**: Changes ratio based on a percentage (%) of the figure's sides.
    *   **Specify length**: Changes ratio by setting a fixed distance from the center of the figure. It sets a specific size for the shape, which cannot be enlarged or reduced unless you use the **Object** sub tool.

4. Use the sliders **W** and **H** to determine width (horizontal) and height (vertical) proportions.

After determining the shape of your ruler, click and drag on the canvas to determine its size. Once you release, move the cursor to rotate the Figure ruler.

Another useful setting is the **Start from center** option. To find it, navigate to the **Sub Tool Detail** palette and select **Shape operation**. This feature determines how the shape is drawn: when enabled, the point you click becomes the center of the figure. When disabled, the point you click marks the corner of the figure.

With a solid understanding of linear, curve, and figure rulers, you can now expand your toolkit by exploring the **Ruler pen** and the **Special ruler**. These advanced tools offer unique functionalities that can simplify complex drawing tasks, enabling you to create intricate patterns, parallel lines, and more—with minimal effort.

Making the most out of the Ruler pen and the Special ruler

The Ruler pen and the Special ruler provide advanced options for artists looking to push their work to the next level. These tools are designed to handle more complex drawing tasks, such as creating free-handed lines, parallel lines, and radial lines. By learning how to effectively use these rulers, you'll be able to add a new dimension of precision and creativity to your artwork.

We'll start with the **Ruler pen**, which allows you to create custom hand-drawn rulers by sketching directly on the canvas in any shape you want to follow.

The Ruler pen

The **Ruler pen** provides the freedom to create custom, hand-drawn rulers. This tool is perfect for artists who want to maintain control over their lines while still benefiting from the precision of a ruler. It allows you to create custom hand-drawn rulers by sketching directly on the canvas in any shape you want to follow.

To use the Ruler pen sub tool, select it from the **Ruler** tool and draw on the canvas. Your drawing will become a ruler to which lines will snap.

To modify the ruler you've created with the Ruler pen, select and move individual control points using the **Object** sub tool:

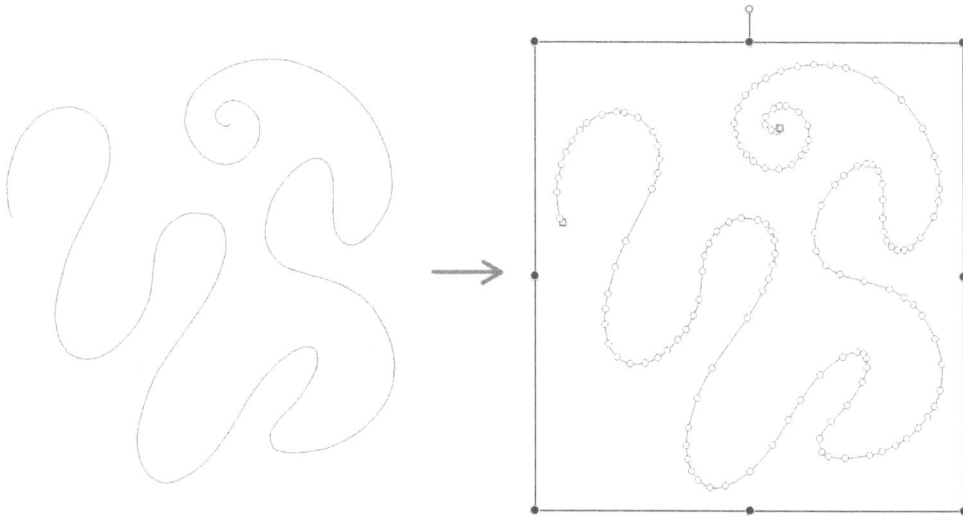

Figure 7.14 – A ruler created with the Ruler pen (left) and its control points (right)

You can apply stabilization and post correction to the Ruler pen as if it were a brush. Navigate to the **Sub Tool Detail** palette | **Correction** and adjust it as you wish. For details on these settings, refer to *Chapter 5, Unlocking the Full Potential of Brush Settings*.

It's important to notice you can also create a ruler from a vector drawing by following the next steps:

1. Right-click the layer you wish to convert into ruler.
2. Select **Ruler/Frame** | **Ruler from vector**.
3. The drawing will be copied into a ruler, which you can drag and drop on any layer.

The Ruler pen combines the best of both worlds—precision and creative freedom. Next, let's look at the **Special ruler**, designed for more complex tasks, such as creating parallel and radial lines.

The Special ruler

The **Special ruler** is an advanced sub tool that allows you to create complex designs, including parallel lines, radial lines, and concentric circles, which are particularly useful for comic work. These rulers are perfect for adding depth and dynamic effects to your artwork. One key aspect to notice when using special rulers is their unique line-guiding function: unlike the Figure ruler and Ruler pen, which snap lines only to their specific designs, special rulers allow you to create multiple lines across different areas—all following the same guiding lines. You can choose the type of Special ruler you need from the **Tool Property** palette, creating many intricate designs:

Figure 7.15 – Types of Special ruler

Based on *Figure 7.15*, let's discuss the types of Special ruler in more detail:

1. **Parallel line**: This ruler allows you to draw parallel lines. Drag from the starting point to the endpoint on the canvas to set the ruler. Each new line on the canvas will be parallel to the ruler.

2. **Parallel curve**: Similar to Parallel line, this type of Special ruler allows you to create a curved guide, ensuring that all lines you draw run parallel to the curve. The default setting is **Spline**, allowing multiple curves by tapping on the canvas. Double-tap or press *Enter* to finalize the ruler.

3. **Multiple curve**: This ruler is for drawing dynamic curves that follow along the path of the ruler.

4. **Radial line**: This ruler creates a central point where lines converge. This is ideal for comic effects.

5. **Radial curve**: This ruler creates curved lines that converge on a center point. Tap to set the center, then add points to define the curve.

6. **Concentric circle**: This allows you to draw concentric circles. Tap to set the center and drag to adjust the size and angle of the ruler.

The curved rulers – Parallel curve, Multiple curve, and Radial curve – all allow you to choose the type of Curve between Straight line, Spline, and Quadratic Bezier, which were explained in the previous section, *The Ruler pen*.

You can easily create intricate designs that add a professional touch to your work using the Special ruler. Having explored the versatility of the Ruler pen and the Special ruler, it's time to dive into one of the most powerful tools in CSP: the **Perspective ruler**. This tool is essential for artists looking to create dynamic, realistic scenes with depth and perspective, adding a professional touch to their compositions.

Applying a Perspective ruler for dynamic images

The **Perspective ruler** is invaluable for artists aiming to create dynamic and realistic scenes. By setting vanishing points and horizon lines, this tool lets you draw with accurate perspective, making your scenes come to life.

These rulers help you draw lines that naturally converge toward vanishing points, ensuring that your artwork accurately reflects the principles of perspective. By mastering Perspective rulers, you'll be able to construct scenes with a sense of depth and space, bringing your compositions to life with professional-grade accuracy.

> **Important note**
>
> The Perspective ruler is ideal for creating perfectly straight lines. The more you use such perfect lines, the more artificial your drawing will look. This can be useful in a sci-fi environment but can hurt your drawings in a natural landscape.
>
> If you're drawing organic scenery or characters, I suggest you use the Perspective ruler only to create a sketch and turn the ruler off when it's time to draw the line art. That will allow you to add small mistakes, bumps, and wiggles, making everything look more natural.

There are multiple ways to create a Perspective ruler:

- Through the **Layer** menu:

    A. Navigate to **Layer | Ruler/Frame | Create Perspective ruler**.

    B. In the **Create Perspective Ruler** dialog, select which type you wish (1-, 2- or 3-point perspective) and hit **OK**.

    C. After it is created, you can edit it with the **Object** sub tool to suit your needs.

- With a 3D model:

    A. Place the 3D material onto the canvas.

    B. Adjust it to the desired camera angle. We'll cover this process in detail in *Chapter 13, Manipulating 3D Objects on the Canvas*.

    C. Tap the ruler icon on the 3D layer to reveal the Perspective ruler.

- With the Ruler tool:

    A. Select the **Perspective ruler** sub tool.

    B. Modify its settings in the **Tool Property** palette. You can see the available settings in *Figure 7.16*:

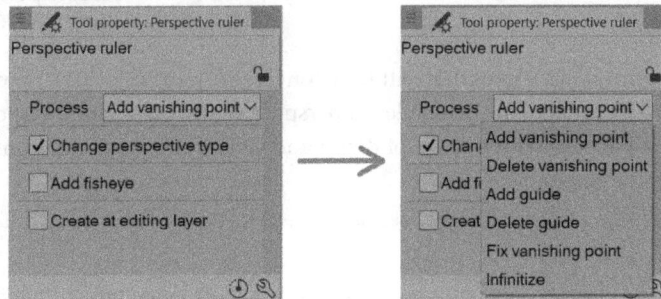

Figure 7.16 – Tool property palette for the Perspective ruler

You can customize the Perspective ruler settings as follows:

- **Process**: You can choose between **Add vanishing point**, **Delete vanishing point**, **Add guide**, **Delete guide**, **Fix vanishing point**, and **Infinitize**:

    - **Add vanishing point**: Creates a new vanishing point. Use this **Process** to start a new Perspective ruler or add more points to an existing one.

    - **Delete vanishing point**: Deletes an existing vanishing point.

    - **Add guide**: Creates a new guide line, which radiates from the vanishing point.

    - **Delete guide**: Deletes a guide line.

    - **Fix vanishing point**: Locks a vanishing point in place, so it cannot be moved or edited.

    - **Infinitize**: Switches a vanishing point to infinity.

- **Change perspective type**: When toggled on, changes the perspective type (1-, 2- or 3-point perspective) automatically when a vanishing point is added to an existing ruler.

- **Add fisheye**: When toggled on, creates a fisheye Perspective ruler.

- **Create at editing layer**: When toggled on, the ruler will be created on the current layer. If toggled off, a new layer will be created with it.

Now that we have covered the **Tool Property** palette for the Perspective ruler, let's dive into the specifics of using the Perspective ruler.

Using the Perspective ruler for 1-, 2-, and 3-point perspectives

Using the Perspective ruler allows you to create precise, dynamic drawings by aligning your lines to vanishing points and perspective grids. In this sub-section, you'll learn how to effectively apply the Perspective ruler to enhance your compositions and streamline the process of creating perspective-based artwork.

When creating a new Perspective ruler with the Ruler tool, you must have in mind what kind of scene you want to create. Is it seen from above, a bird's eye view, or from below, a worm's view? Can we see the vanishing point within the canvas, or is it outside? To solve these questions, I suggest you draw a quick sketch first. That way, you'll know where to place the perspective lines.

To create a Perspective ruler, set the **Process** at **Add vanishing point**. Then, follow these steps:

1. To set up the vanishing point, you'll intersect two lines; the center will be the vanishing point. To do so, first click on the canvas. One line will appear, and you can drag the cursor up and down to change its angle. In *Figure 7.17*, this first line is **Line A**.

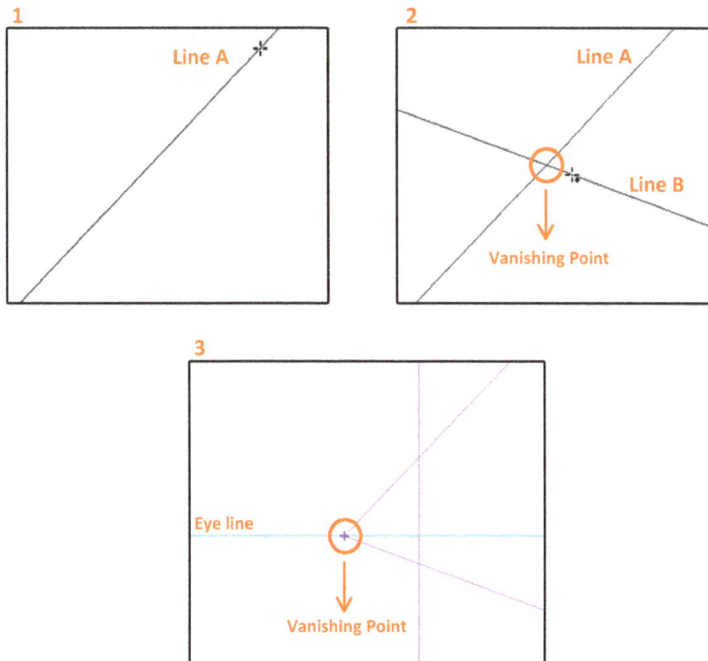

Figure 7.17 – Steps to create a Perspective ruler

If you press *Shift* as you drag up and down, the ruler will move in 45-degree increments. Release the click when you're satisfied with its placement.

2.   Now that you have one line placed, it's time to determine the vanishing point. Click anywhere on the canvas and modify the new line's angle until the two lines intersect at your desired vanishing point position. This second line is **Line B** in *Figure 7.17*. Notice that their intersection is the **Vanishing Point**.

3.   When the two lines intersect, the **Eye line**, or horizon line, will be automatically created.

4.   You now have a 1-point Perspective ruler. Although only one guide line is visible, every brush stroke will now either converge towards that point, move completely vertically, or move completely horizontally.

5.   If you wish to add a second vanishing point, repeat *steps 2 and 3*. If the new vanishing point is located outside of the Eye line, the Eye line will rotate to connect the two vanishing points. To horizontalize the Eye line again, right click on the ruler and select **Horizontalize eye level**.

6.   For more vanishing points, repeat *steps 2 and 3*.

If you decide to modify the Perspective ruler after you have placed it, you might notice several new control points and buttons near it. We'll analyze these thoroughly next.

Understanding the parts of a Perspective ruler

When you select a Perspective ruler with the Object sub tool, several control points appear next to it. Understanding these is essential to manipulate the ruler and suit it to your needs.

Figure 7.18 shows each of the control points:

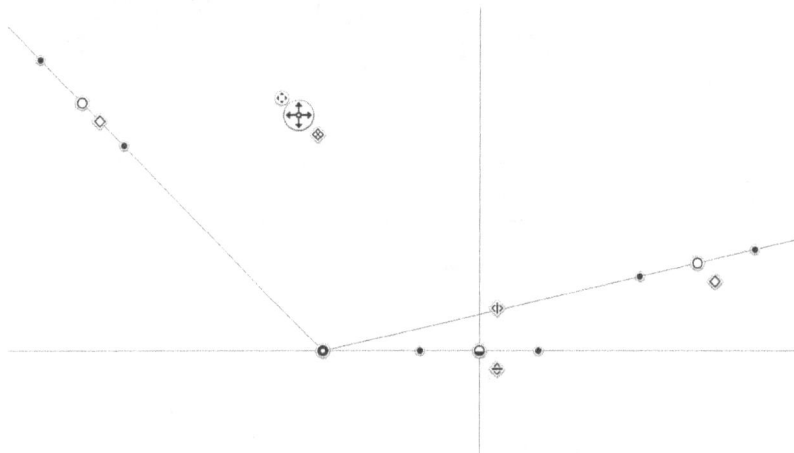

Figure 7.18 – Parts of a Perspective ruler

Let's see each of their functions:

- **Whole perspective ruler handle**: With this handle, you can move the whole Perspective ruler anywhere on the canvas. It has three parts:

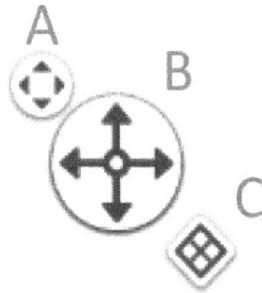

Figure 7.19 – Parts of the Whole perspective ruler Handle

A. **Move**: When you drag this point, it moves the **Whole perspective ruler handle**.

B. **Move perspective ruler**: Dragging it moves the entire Perspective ruler.

C. **Switch snap to perspective ruler**: Use this to toggle the snapping feature on/off. When on, all lines will converge to the ruler; when off, you can draw freely.

- **Line Orthogonal to Eye Level**: An auxiliary line perpendicular to the eye level. It's visible when using 1- and 2-point Perspective rulers:

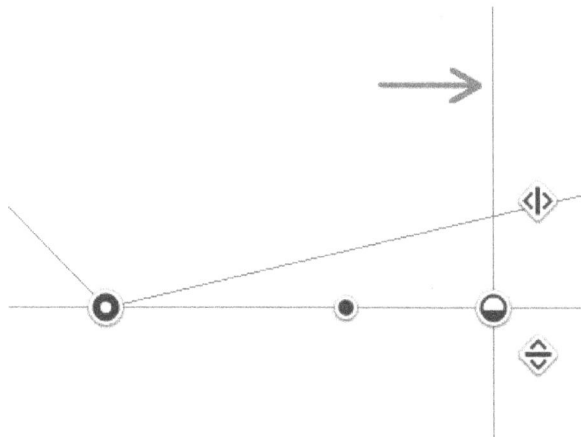

Figure 7.20 – The arrow points to the Line Orthogonal to Eye Level

- **Handle for Line Orthogonal to Eye Level**: When toggled on, this handle allows you to draw lines that are perfectly perpendicular to the eye level:

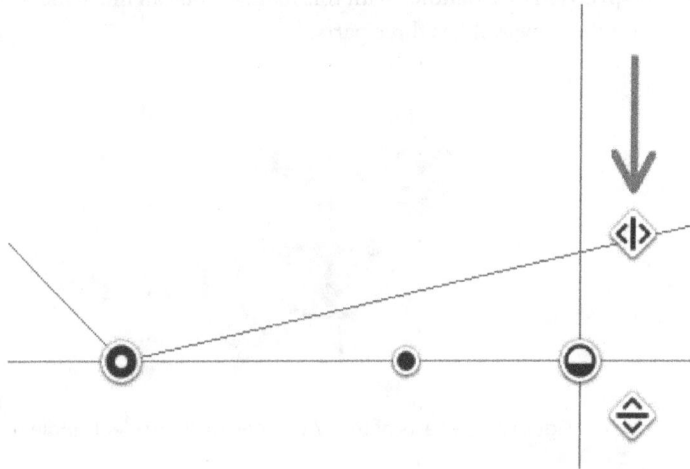

Figure 7.21 – The arrow points to the Handle for Line Orthogonal to Eye Level

- **Eye level handle**: This lets you move and rotate the eye level. You can see this control in detail in *Figure 7.22*:

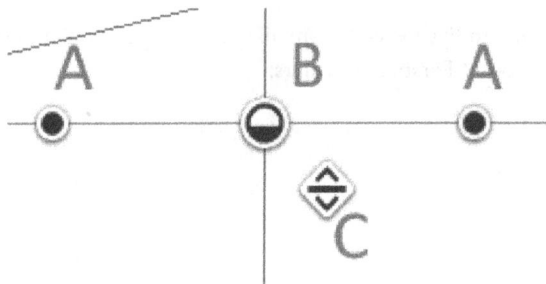

Figure 7.22 – Parts of the Eye level handle

The **Eye level handle** consists of three parts:

A. **Rotate eye level**: Dragging it rotates the eye level around its center point.

B. **Move eye level**: Dragging it moves the eye level both horizontally and vertically. As the eye level shifts, the vanishing points will also move while maintaining their relative distance from the **Eye level handle**. This movement generates new converging guide lines, altering the perspective of your drawing.

C. **Switch snap to eye level** (one-point perspective): This option toggles the snap function to the eye level, enabling you to draw lines that align with the eye level when using a 1-point perspective. It appears only when the 1-point Perspective ruler is selected.

- **Guide line**: Lines that radiate from the vanishing point and can be used as references when drawing with the Perspective ruler:

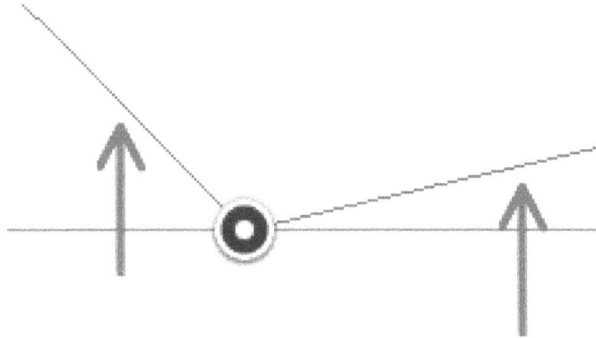

Figure 7.23 – Arrows point to guide lines

- **Guide/Vanishing Point Handle**: This handle allows you to adjust the guides or move the vanishing point. You can see its parts in the following figure:

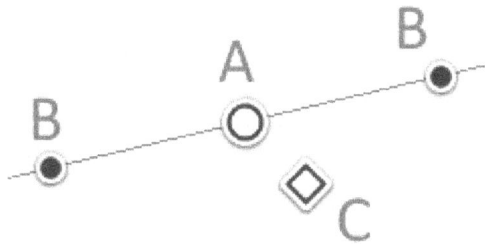

Figure 7.24 – Parts of the Vanishing Point Handle

A. **Move Guide**: Dragging it moves only the guide line, without affecting the vanishing point.

B. **Move Vanishing Point**: Dragging it adjusts the direction of the guide line, moving the vanishing point accordingly.

C. **Switch Snap to Vanishing Point**: This option toggles the snap function to the vanishing point, allowing you to draw lines that snap directly to it when Switch snap to perspective ruler is enabled.

Now that you understand how to modify the Perspective ruler, let's see a practical example of how to use it.

Using the Perspective ruler in practice

Perspective rulers are incredibly useful for showing distance and depth in your drawings. In this section, we'll cover how to use them in practice. When you select the Perspective ruler, you'll create its guide lines by clicking and dragging – when you release, the guide line is created.

Before placing any guide lines, I always start with a simple, free-hand sketch. This way, I have an idea of where the ruler will go. In *Figure 7.25*, you can see an initial sketch (left) and the first guide line of the ruler (right). I've highlighted the Perspective ruler's initial guide line in orange, so you can see it more clearly.

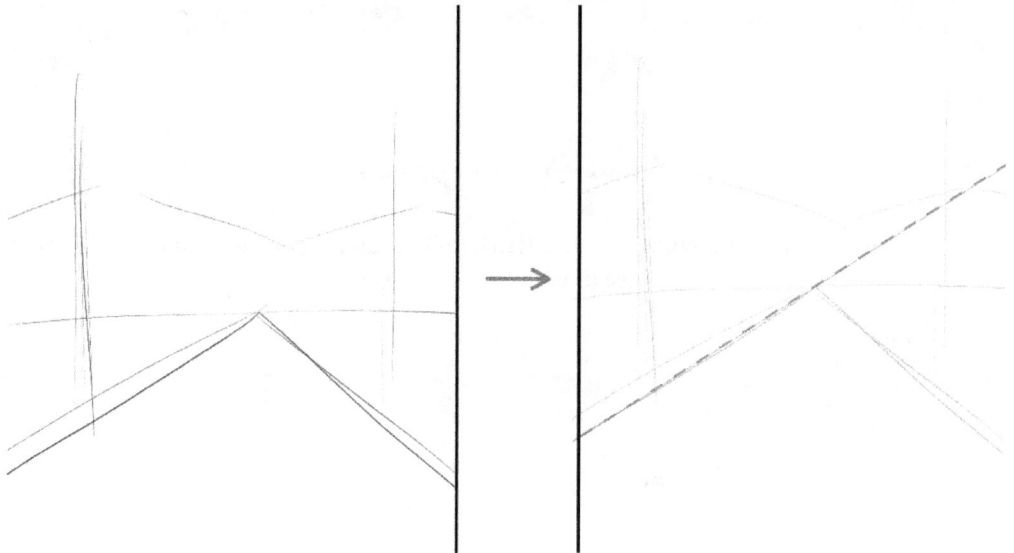

Figure 7.25 – Initial sketch (left) and the first guideline of the Perspective ruler (right)

Once you've placed the first guide line, your next click-and-drag will place the second guideline, as you can see in *Figure 7.26*:

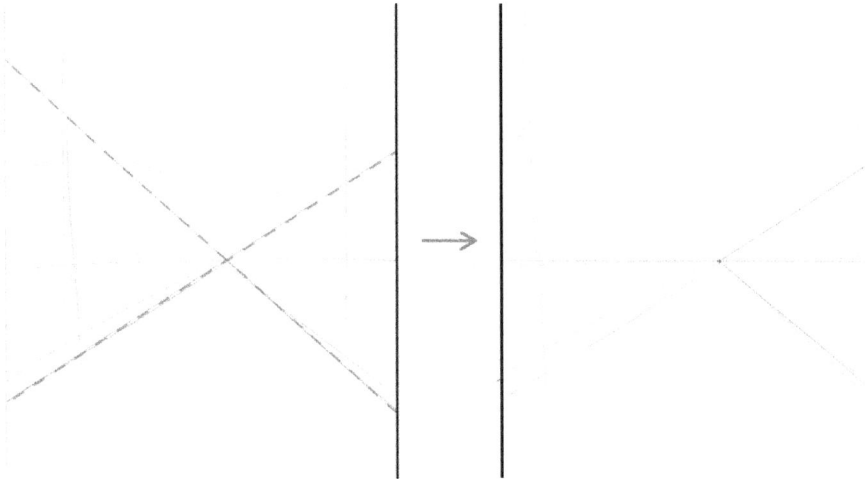

Figure 7.26 – The two guide lines (left) and the resulting Perspective ruler (right)

Once the ruler is correctly positioned, release your click, and the Perspective ruler will be created, as you can see on the right side of *Figure 7.26*. From then on, any lines you create will follow this ruler.

After the ruler is created, I like creating the structure of the drawing with it (*Figure 7.27*, left). However, if I'm drawing natural scenery, I'll use this structure only as a basis, and actually make the final drawing free-hand (*Figure 7.27*, right). That's because lines created with the ruler are too stiff and perfect, which does not suit natural elements.

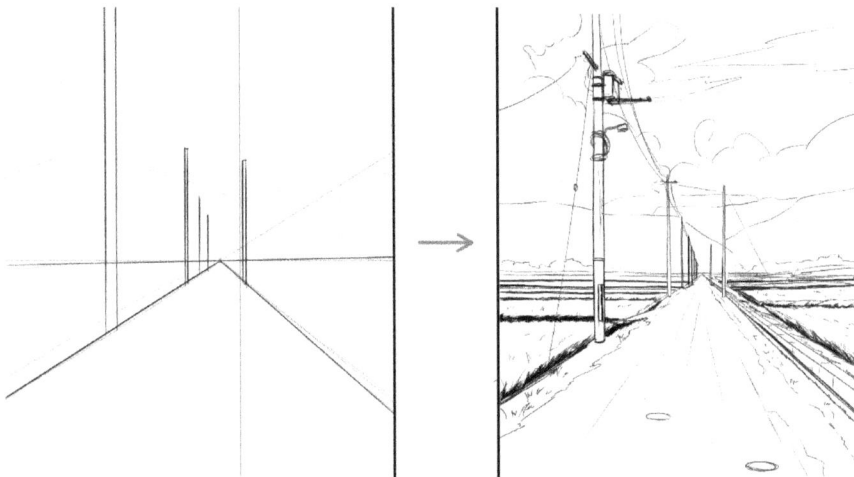

Figure 7.27 - A structure created with the Ruler (left) and the final, free-handed drawing (right)

You can apply this method to any perspective scene you want to create. Just start with a sketch, place the guide lines accordingly, and finalize it.

After mastering Perspective rulers, the next step is to learn about the **Symmetrical ruler**. This tool is perfect for creating balanced and mirrored designs, whether you're working on character designs, intricate patterns, or architectural drawings.

Optimizing your use of the Symmetrical ruler

The **Symmetrical ruler** is a powerful tool in CSP that allows you to easily create perfectly mirrored designs. This feature is particularly useful for artists who want to ensure balance and symmetry in their work, whether for character illustration, decorative patterns, or architectural elements. By mastering the Symmetrical ruler, you can significantly speed up your workflow and achieve consistent, professional results.

Here's how you can use the Symmetrical ruler:

1. Select the **Ruler** tool | **Symmetrical ruler** sub tool.

2. Go to **Tool Property| Number of lines** to determine how many symmetry lines will be generated from the center point. If you need just two identical parts, such as when drawing a face, set the value to 2; if you make a complex design that requires several equal parts, such as a mandala, use a larger number, up to 16:

Figure 7.28 – Symmetric patterns with 2 sides (left) and 10 sides (right)

3. Click on the canvas, and the ruler will be centered where you clicked. When **Number of lines** is set to 2, the ruler will be placed as a perfectly vertical line. When you set **Number of lines** to 3 or more, there will always be one line that is completely vertical. If that is not the angle you want to use, tap and drag outward to position it differently.

Mastering the symmetrical ruler opens up a world of possibilities for creating balanced, intricate designs with minimal effort. Whether you're designing characters, crafting patterns, or working on architectural elements, this tool ensures that your work is consistently precise and aesthetically pleasing. With this knowledge, you can confidently tackle any symmetrical drawing challenge, setting the stage for even more advanced techniques in your artistic journey.

Summary

In this chapter, you've explored the powerful tools of rulers and guides in CSP to enhance the precision of your artwork. Beginning with the basics, you learned how to manipulate the Ruler bar and Grid, setting a solid foundation for utilizing these essential tools.

We delved into the various types of rulers, including the Linear, Curve, and Figure rulers, each offering unique benefits for creating straight lines, complex curves, and geometric shapes. The Ruler pen and Special ruler were introduced to provide even more control and creativity in your line work. We also explored the use of the Perspective ruler to establish accurate depth and vanishing points in your compositions. Lastly, we covered the Symmetrical ruler, a tool that simplifies creating balanced, mirrored designs.

By mastering these rulers and guides, you've equipped yourself with techniques to streamline your drawing process, maintain consistent proportions, and achieve greater accuracy in your digital art.

In the next chapter, we'll shift our focus to maximizing efficiency and organization with layers: you'll discover how to optimize your workflow by effectively managing layers, ensuring your projects are well organized and easy to navigate.

Part 3: Time-Saving Painting Techniques

With your drawings in place, it's time to focus on painting efficiently and effectively. This part of the book is all about accelerating your painting process while maintaining quality. You'll learn how to organize your layers for maximum control, use blending modes to create rich and dynamic color interactions, and perfect your selections to work faster and with more precision. These techniques will help you paint smarter, not harder, and give your illustrations a professional finish in less time.

This part has the following chapters:

- *Chapter 8, Maximizing Efficiency and Organization with Layers*
- *Chapter 9, Mastering Layer Blending Modes for Stunning Colors*
- *Chapter 10, Perfecting Your Selections*
- *Chapter 11, Applying Color Quickly with Pro Techniques*
- *Chapter 12, Enhancing Your Art with Post-Processing Adjustments*

8

Maximizing Efficiency and Organization with Layers

Layers are one of the most powerful digital art tools available in **Clip Studio Paint** (**CSP**). They are the backbone of digital art, allowing you to stack, adjust, and modify your work in ways impossible in most traditional mediums.

Layers are like transparent sheets stacked on top of each other, each holding different elements of your artwork. By working on individual layers, you can isolate parts of your drawing—such as sketches, colors, or shading—without affecting the rest of the image. This non-destructive approach allows for easy adjustments, edits, and refinements, giving you more control and flexibility in your creative process. Layers are fundamental to efficient digital painting, enabling artists to build up their artwork step by step while keeping everything organized and easy to modify.

In this chapter, we're going to cover the following main topics:

- Navigating the Layer palette
- Customizing your layers with the Layer Property palette
- Optimizing your layers with pro techniques

Beyond the basics of adding and removing layers, there are powerful features such as **Reference** layers, **Draft** layers, and specialized properties that allow you to streamline your art creation process. By understanding how to navigate the **Layer** palette, customize layer properties, and optimize your layers with advanced techniques, you will gain greater control over your artwork and work more efficiently.

Throughout this chapter, you'll learn how to efficiently navigate the **Layer** palette and uncover time-saving tips, such as quickly locating specific layers in your project. You'll also discover how to add effects to layers using the **Layer Property** palette, which includes practical techniques such as applying outlines and converting layers to screen tones. Finally, we'll delve into pro techniques that take advantage of features such as transparency lock, layer lock, and clipping masks to refine your layers and create cleaner, more polished results.

By the end of this chapter, you'll know how to organize your layers and unlock the full potential of these tools for faster and more precise art creation. We'll start by covering the **Layer** palette, the central hub for managing and organizing your layers.

Navigating the Layer palette

The **Layer** palette is the control center of your artwork, providing an overview of every layer in your project and the power to manipulate them efficiently. In this section, we'll dive into the essentials of the Layer palette, showing you how to manage layers for a more organized workflow. You'll learn how to adjust layer visibility, lock layers, group them, and use essential features such as **Reference** and **Draft** layers that can significantly speed up your process. Mastering this tool will ensure you never feel overwhelmed by a complex project again, making it easier to keep track of everything on your canvas.

This is the layout of the **Layer** palette:

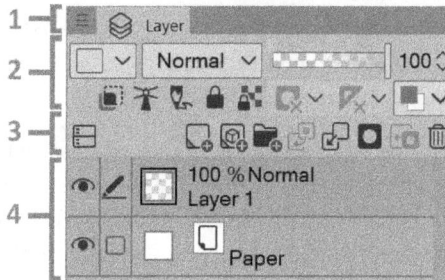

Figure 8.1 – The Layer palette

These are its parts:

1. **Layer** palette's menu
2. Property bar
3. Command bar
4. Layer list

We'll cover each of these in detail, starting with the **Layer palette's** menu.

The Layer palette's menu

The **Layer** palette's menu, represented by three bars in the top-left corner of the **Layer** palette, provides access to the same commands found in the **Layer** menu, such as creating and deleting layers and creating selections from a layer:

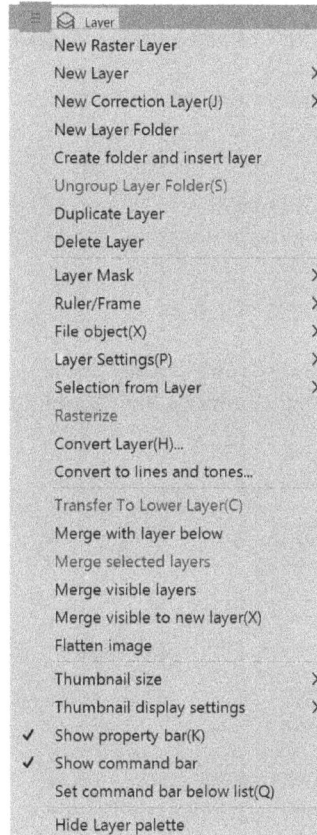

Figure 8.2 – The Layer palette menu

There are, however, some specific settings at the bottom of the Layer palette menu. They work as follows:

- **Thumbnail size**: Allows you to adjust the size of layer thumbnails in the Layer palette.

- **Thumbnail display settings**: This setting lets you customize how layer thumbnails are shown. You can choose to display thumbnails that reflect the layer within the entire canvas, or only the layer area.

- **Show property bar(K)**: Enabling this option will display the property bar at the top of the Layer palette. We'll learn more about this property bar in the next section, *The Layer palette's property bar*.

- **Show command bar**: Controls the visibility of the command bar, located below the property bar.

- **Set command bar below list(Q)**: Moves the command bar directly beneath the list of layers in the Layer palette, instead of having it fixed above the layer list. This positioning might make it more convenient depending on your workflow.

- **Hide Layer palette**: Selecting this option will hide the entire Layer palette from your workspace. This is useful if you want more screen space to focus on your artwork. You can bring back the Layer palette when needed by navigating to the **Window** menu and tapping on **Layer**.

Knowing how to use the Layer palette menu ensures that you can access essential commands swiftly and organize your workspace exactly how you want it. You can create an efficient and comfortable working environment by adjusting thumbnail sizes, displaying toolbars, or even hiding the entire palette. With the Layer palette menu understood, let's now move on to the property bar, which offers essential tools for quickly adjusting the properties of individual layers.

The Layer palette's property bar

The property bar consists of the top two rows of icons that let you easily modify the currently selected layer's properties. *Figure 8.3* shows the property bar's appearance:

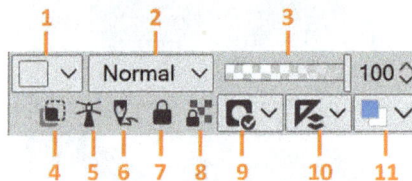

Figure 8.3 – The Layer palette's property bar

It contains the following functions:

1. **Change palette color**: Applies a color mark to the selected layer in the **Layer** palette, making it easy to identify. You can see it in action in *Figure 8.4*:

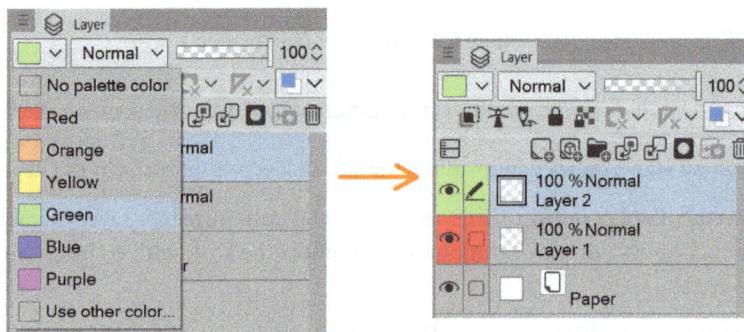

Figure 8.4 – The Change palette color function in action

You can choose from a drop-down list of colors or select **Use other color…** to open the **Color settings** dialog box and make a custom selection.

2. **Blending mode**: This drop-down menu allows you to set the blending mode for the selected layer. For more details, refer to *Chapter 9, Mastering Layer Blending Modes for Stunning Colors*.

3. **Opacity** slider: Adjusts the layer's opacity. Lower values increase transparency, while higher values make the layer more opaque.

4. **Clip to Layer Below**: Allows you to limit the visibility of a layer's content to the non-transparent areas of the layer directly beneath it, as shown in *Figure 8.5*:

Figure 8.5 – An unclipped layer (left) versus a clipped layer (right)

This can be used for adding details, textures, shadows, or color adjustments to specific areas of your artwork without affecting other parts of the image.

5. **Set as Reference Layer**: Marks the selected layer or layer folder as a **Reference** layer, indicated by a lighthouse icon. A **Reference** layer is a special layer used as a point of reference for tools and functions such as **Fill**, **Auto-select**, and even brushes. This function allows you to work on other layers while referencing the Reference layer's content.

6. **Set as Draft Layer**: Designates the selected layer as a **Draft** layer. A **Draft** layer is used to designate a layer as a non-final layer, usually intended for rough sketches, notes, or initial compositions. When a layer is marked as a Draft layer, it won't be considered for certain functions such as printing or exporting. Additionally, certain tools, such as the **Fill** and **Selection** tools, can exclude **Draft** layers. **Draft** layers are marked with a purple vertical line on the left side of the thumbnail and a pencil icon on the far right:

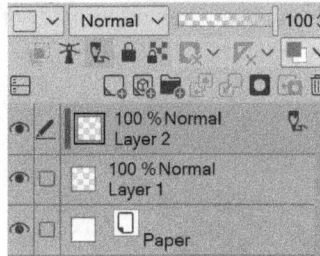

Figure 8.6 – You can recognize a Draft layer by the purple line and the pencil icon

7. **Lock Layer**: Prevents changes to the layer's settings and restricts further drawing. Once a layer is locked, you cannot paint, move, adjust or delete it until it's unlocked. Use this to preserve the integrity of a layer while working on other parts of the artwork.

8. **Lock transparent pixels**: Locks the transparent parts of a raster layer, allowing you to draw only on existing areas without affecting transparent sections. This gives more control when refining existing content on a layer without affecting its transparency.

   Don't confuse it with the **Lock Layer** function: while **Lock Layer** prevents any edits to the entire layer, **Lock transparent pixels** allows you to continue editing non-transparent areas.

9. Mask settings: This drop-down menu has two functions you can use when a **Layer Mask** is active:

   • **Enable Mask**: Controls whether the mask on a layer is active or not. When the mask is enabled, it will affect the layer's visibility, and areas hidden by the mask will not be visible. If you disable the mask, the layer will return to its full visibility, regardless of what parts the mask is hiding. This function is useful when you want to temporarily disregard the mask and view the entire layer without deleting or permanently altering the mask. You can easily toggle the mask on or off to compare different visual outcomes.

   • **Show Mask Area**: Visually indicates which areas of the mask are hidden by displaying them with a purple overlay. This feature is purely for reference and doesn't affect the artwork itself; it simply shows which parts of the layer are being masked. Showing the mask area helps you keep track of hidden and revealed sections, especially in complex masking situations.

10. **Set ruler range**: Determines which layers will display the ruler and snap to it. The same functions are available when you right-click the ruler icon, which we covered in *Chapter 7, Utilizing Rulers and Guides for Precision*, under the *Understanding guides in CSP* section.

11. **Change layer color**: This option toggles the **Layer color** effect, which changes the entire layer to a specified color. By default, the layer is converted to blue, but you can customize this by selecting different colors from the drop-down menu. The **Layer color** option replaces all *black* pixels with your chosen color, while the **Sub color** option replaces all *white* pixels with the selected color. These changes are not permanent: you can toggle them on and off by clicking on the **Change layer color** function.

In *Figure 8.7*, you can see a comparison between an image with its original colors (left) and how it looks when **Change layer color** is toggled on (right):

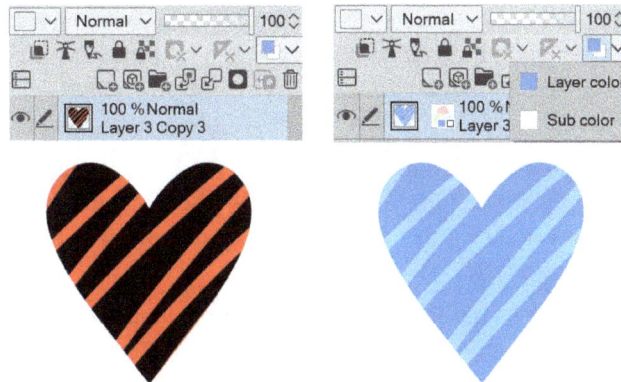

Figure 8.7 – How Change layer color works

Mastering the Layer palette's property bar allows you to efficiently customize your layers with just a few clicks, significantly speeding up your workflow. By understanding how to quickly adjust properties such as opacity, blending modes, or locking transparent pixels, you gain full control over your layers. This knowledge empowers you to make precise changes with ease, saving time and enhancing the quality of your work.

After getting familiar with the property bar, it's time to explore the command bar, where you'll find quick access to fundamental actions such as adding, locking, and masking layers.

The Layer palette's command bar

The **Layer** palette's command bar, the bottom row of icons, provides quick access to essential commands such as adding new layers, clipping layers, and creating layer masks. *Figure 8.8* shows the command bar and its functions:

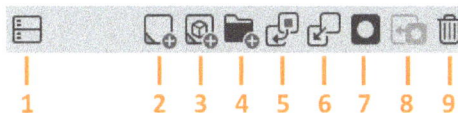

Figure 8.8 – The Layer palette's command bar

Its functions include the following:

1. **Show layer in 2 panes**: This command splits the Layer palette into two sections, allowing you to view different parts of your layer stack at the same time. This is useful when working with multiple layers spread across various folders, providing an easier way to navigate your layers without constant scrolling.

2. **New Raster Layer**: Creates a new raster layer, which is the standard type of layer used for drawing and painting. Raster layers allow you to use brushes and other tools to create pixel-based art.

3. **New vector layer**: Creates a new vector layer. Unlike raster layers, vector layers store your artwork as lines and curves rather than pixels, allowing you to scale and edit line work without losing quality. We thoroughly covered vector layers in *Chapter 6, Enhancing Your Lines with Vector Layers*.

4. **New Layer Folder**: Adds a new layer folder, which you can use to organize layers. This is especially helpful for keeping your project tidy when working with a large number of layers, grouping similar layers together for better management—as we covered in *Chapter 4, Organizing Your Projects Effectively*.

5. **Transfer to Lower Layer**: This command merges the content of the selected layer with the layer directly beneath it without deleting the original layer. It's useful when you want to combine layers but still keep the original layer, which becomes empty.

6. **Merge with layer below**: Combines the selected layer with the layer directly beneath it, permanently fusing them into one. This is useful when you've finished editing separate layers and want to simplify your layer stack by merging them.

> **Important note**
>
> When merging layers with different blending modes, the resulting merged layer will adopt the blending mode of the bottom layer.
>
> If there are no clipped layers involved, the blending effects will only apply within the overlapping area of the two layers. For example, if you merge an **Overlay** layer with a **Normal** layer, the blending mode (**Overlay**) will be applied to the pixels where the two layers overlap. Any pixels from the **Overlay** layer outside the **Normal** layer's pixels will lose the blending effect and revert to a normal appearance.

7. **Create layer mask**: Adds a mask to the selected layer, allowing you to control the visibility of certain areas of that layer without permanently erasing any content. Masks are essential for non-destructive editing.

8. **Apply Mask to Layer**: This command permanently applies changes made using the layer mask to the selected layer. Once applied, the mask is removed, and any hidden areas are permanently erased.

9. **Delete Layer**: Deletes the selected layer from the **Layer** palette. If you accidentally delete a layer, you can undo this action by pressing *Ctrl/command + Z*.

To hide the command bar, follow the next steps:

1. Navigate to the palette menu.
2. Select **Show command bar**.

Additionally, you can reposition the command bar to the bottom of the **Layer** palette:

1. Navigate to the palette menu.
2. Select **Set command bar below list(Q)**.

Understanding the **Layer** palette's command bar is a crucial step in optimizing your digital art process. With quick access to frequently used functions such as creating new layers and adding masks, you can enhance your efficiency and layer organization. Mastering these commands makes it easier to keep your layers structured and apply essential functions without slowing your creative flow.

Having covered the command bar, we now arrive at the core of the Layer palette—the layer list, where all your active layers are organized and managed.

The layer list

The layer list is the heart of your layer management system in CSP. It serves as the visual representation of all layers in your project, allowing you to see and manage each layer's contents, order, and attributes. *Figure 8.9* shows the layer list and its functions:

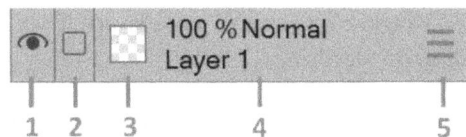

Figure 8.9 – The layer list

These are the functions within the layer list:

1. Visibility: This icon controls whether the layer is visible or hidden. An eye icon indicates a visible layer. Right-clicking the eye icon opens a context menu with options to show or hide multiple layers quickly. The functions are the following:

    - **Show/Hide this layer(C)**: This option toggles the visibility of the selected layer. If the layer is within a hidden folder, it will remain invisible. Use the **Show This Layer And Parent Folders** option to make the layer visible.

- **Show This Layer And Parent Folders**: Ensures that the selected layer is visible along with its parent folders.

- **Show All Other Layers**: Makes all layers visible, including any previously hidden layer.

- **Hide All Other Layers(N)**: Hides every layer except the one currently being edited, which is the one with a pencil icon on its layer status column. Hold *Alt* and tap the **Visibility** icon to toggle **Hide All Other Layers** on/off.

- **Hide All Except Selected Layer**: Hides every layer except the ones you have selected. Unlike **Hide All Other Layers**, you can choose multiple layers to remain visible, while all unselected layers will be hidden.

2. Layer status: Icons in this column display the status of each layer. The active layer shows a pencil icon. Selected layers, other than the active one, will display a checkmark. You can select or deselect multiple layers by holding *Shift* or *Alt* and clicking on the layer status boxes. Alternatively, you can click on the checkmark in a layer's status box and drag it over other checkboxes to select all the layers it passes over. **Reference** layers are marked by a lighthouse icon, and **Light table** layers in the **Animation Cels** palette are indicated by a light table icon.

3. Layer thumbnail: The thumbnail previews the content on each layer. Tap the thumbnail while holding *Ctrl/command* to create a selection from the layer.

4. Layer details: This section shows layer information such as the name, opacity, and blending mode. The currently selected layer is highlighted in light blue. Double tap this field to rename the layer. On *Windows/macOS*, you can reorder layers by dragging them up or down within this area.

5. Grip (tablet): Mobile devices use the grip icon, represented with three lines on the right side, to rearrange layers. Drag the grip icon to move layers. If you have multiple layers selected, all selected layers will move together.

The layer list is the core of your layer management in digital art. Knowing how to navigate and organize this list effectively ensures that you always have quick access to the right layer, which is essential for maintaining clarity and efficiency in your projects. Keeping your layers organized allows you to easily make changes and corrections, making your overall workflow more streamlined and effective.

Now that you've mastered the basics of navigating layers, let's explore how to customize them further using the **Layer Property** palette, where you can enhance the visual properties and functionality of each layer.

Customizing your layers with the Layer Property palette

The **Layer Property** palette lets you fine-tune your layers appearance and behavior. In this section, we'll cover how to add outlines to your layers, convert them to screen tones, and apply effects to enhance your artwork. Learning to customize your layers will open new creative possibilities and give you greater control over the visual impact of your work.

The functions available in the **Layer Property** palette depend on the type of layer selected. *Figure 8.10* shows the **Layer Property** palette for a raster layer with a layer mask:

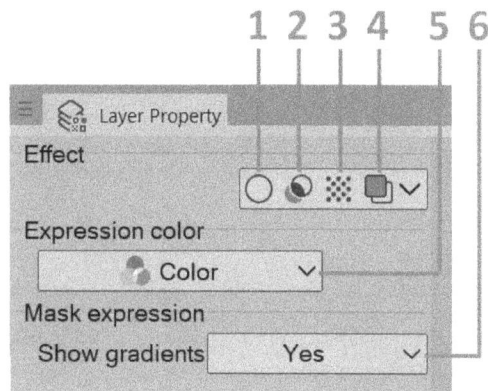

Figure 8.10 – The Layer Property palette of a raster layer with a layer mask

These are the functions available:

1. **Border effect**: Adds a border around the drawn content of a layer.
2. **Extract line** (EX Only): Allows you to isolate lines and black-fill areas from a selected layer. The settings for this are identical to those found in the **Convert to lines and tones** dialog under the **Layer** menu.
3. **Tone**: Displays the layer as screentone dots.
4. **Layer color**: Displays the entire layer in a selected color.
5. **Expression color**: Determines how colors are displayed on a layer. You can choose between **Color**, **Gray**, or **Monochrome**.

6. **Mask expression**: Lets you control whether partial masking is allowed using gradients. This option appears when the layer has a layer mask.

When you select a layer with a 3D material or an image material on it, there are new options, as shown in *Figure 8.11*:

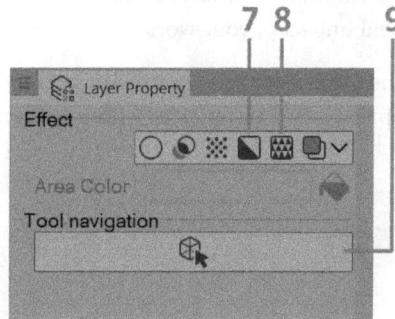

Figure 8.11 – The Layer Property palette of a layer with a 3D material

These are the new options:

7. **Display decrease color**: Allows you to preview an image material or 3D material in limited colors, such as **Gray** or **Monochrome**, without altering the expression color mode.

8. **Overlay texture**: Allows you to apply a texture overlay to the layer. This setting is available for image material layers only.

9. **Tool navigation**: Displays available tools and sub-tools for editing the selected layer.

Lastly, there is a different setting when working on an animation with a **Light table** layer:

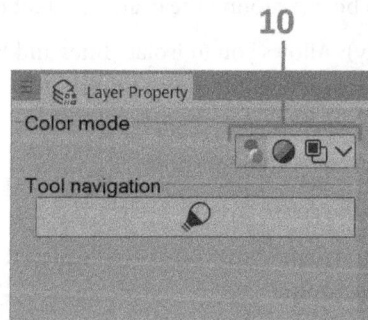

Figure 8.12 – The Layer Property palette of a Light table layer

The setting is the following:

10. **Color mode**: Defines how colors are displayed on the **Light table** layer, with options for **Color**, **Half Color**, and **Monochrome**. This setting applies only to **Light table** layers.

As you can see in the preceding list, not all functions are available for all layer types. The following table shows us the settings available for each layer type:

	Raster	Vector	Gradient	Fill	3D	Tone	Paper	Frame	Image material	Correction	Light table
Border effect	✓	✓	✗	✗	✓	✗	✗	✗	✓	✗	✗
Extract lines	✓	✓	✗	✗	✓	✗	✗	✗	✓	✗	✗
Tone	✓	✓	✓	✓	✓	✓	✗	✗	✓	✗	✗
Layer color	✓	✓	✓	✓	✓	✓	✓	✗	✓	✗	✗
Expression color	✓	✓	✗	✗	✗	✗	✗	✗	✓	✗	✗
Display decrease color	✗	✗	✗	✗	✓	✗	✗	✗	✓	✗	✗
Mask expression	✗	✗	✓	✓	✗	✓	✗	✗	✓	✓	✗
Tool navigation	✗	✓	✓	✓	✓	✓	✗	✓	✓	✗	✗
Overlay texture	✗	✗	✗	✗	✗	✗	✗	✗	✓	✗	✗
Color mode	✗	✗	✗	✗	✗	✗	✗	✗	✗	✗	✓

Table 8.1 – Layer properties available for each layer type

We'll analyze each of these settings in detail, starting with **Border effect**.

Border effect

Adding borders around elements in your artwork can be a simple yet impactful way to enhance visibility and create a distinct style. In the next image, you can see examples of border styles:

Figure 8.13 – An image without any effects (left), with a white edge (middle), and with Watercolor edge (right)

There are two border styles available:

- **Edge**: Creates a solid color outline around the content. When **Border effect** is set to **Edge**, you can adjust the thickness, color, and anti-aliasing of the border.

- **Watercolor edge**: Gives a subtle, soft edge that resembles a watercolor stain. When **Border effect** is set to **Watercolor edge**, you can control the range, opacity, darkness, and blurring width of the effect, as shown in *Figure 8.14*:

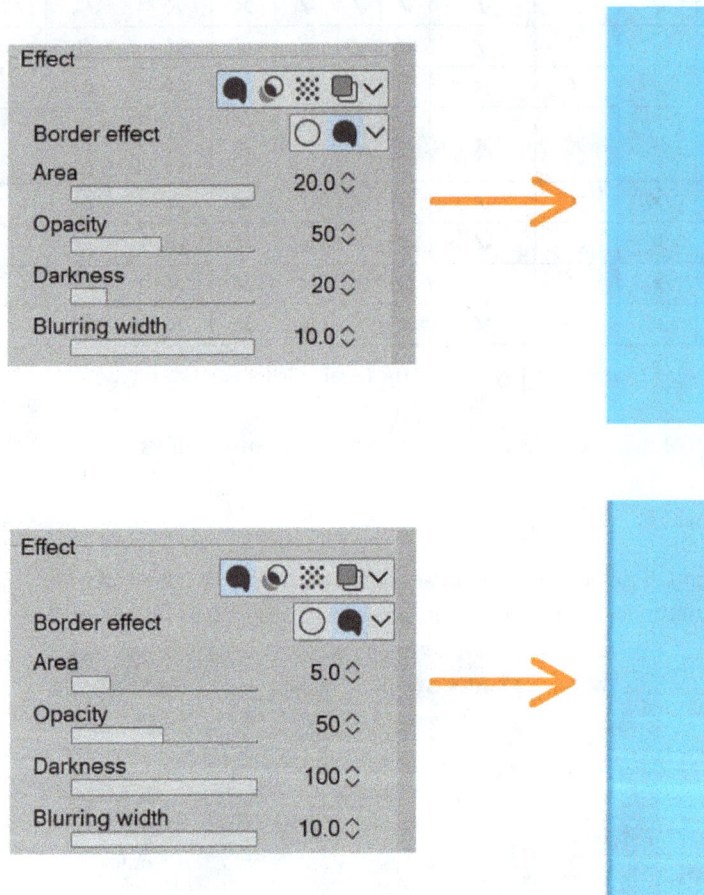

Figure 8.14 – Different Watercolor edge settings create different effects

The color of the **Watercolor edge** effect is based on the original color of the layer.

> **Important note**
> When the layer's opacity is lowered, the border effect will apply not only to its edges but across the entire layer.

Having covered the **Border effect** setting, let's now explore a function that will speed up your process: **Extract lines**.

Extract lines (EX only)

When you want to isolate lines from a layer for further refinement or adjustment, the **Extract lines** feature is invaluable— especially for creating clean, defined line art.

This tool allows you to extract lines and black-filled areas from a selected layer, breaking the content into separate layers. This is extremely useful: you can turn photos and 3D models into lines, expediting your drawing process. You can see an example in *Figure 8.15*:

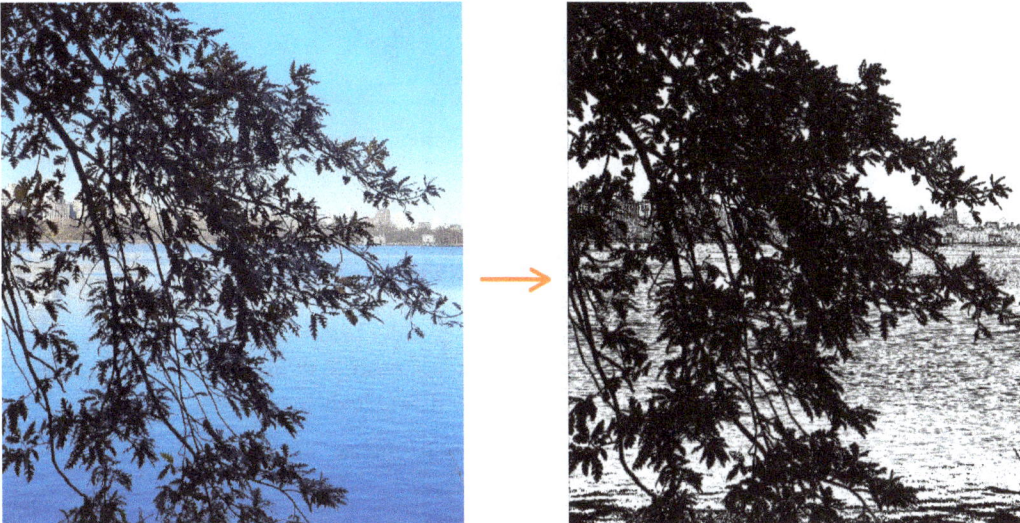

Figure 8.15 – The Extract lines effect

You can extract lines from images and 3D models, each with its own specificities. Let's see next how to extract lines from images.

Extracting lines from images

When an image is selected, you can extract its lines. To do this, follow the next steps:

1. Select the layer on which you wish to apply the effect.

2. Tap the **Extract lines** icon inside of the **Layer Property** palette.

3.   New options will appear inside the **Layer Property** palette:

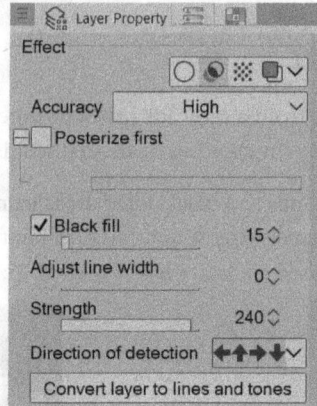

Figure 8.16 – Available settings for Extract lines

They work as follows:

- **Accuracy**: Sets the display accuracy of line detection.

- **Posterize first**: If enabled, the original layer is posterized before extracting the outline. You can adjust the gradient using the levels slider below it—this slider represents different shading levels. You can adjust the nodes horizontally to modify the gradient, add new nodes by clicking on the bar, or remove them by dragging the nodes vertically.

- **Black fill**: Sets the areas to be filled in black. You can modify the threshold using a value number or a slider.

- **Adjust line width**: Determines the width of the extracted lines. Adjust via the value number or slider.

- **Strength**: Sets the number of lines to detect.

- **Direction of detection**: Sets the direction in which edges will be detected.

4.   When you are satisfied with the settings, you have two options:

- Leave it as it is, and the line extraction can be toggled on/off by clicking on the **Extract lines** icon.

- Press **Convert layer to lines and tones** to apply changes permanently. The **Convert to lines and tones** dialog will open—which is the same as navigating to the **Layer** menu and clicking on **Convert to lines and tones…**.

When you use **Convert to lines and tones**, a new layer folder will be created with all the lines, tones, and fill layers inside. Your original layer will be maintained, and its visibility will be automatically turned off.

Now that you can extract lines from images, let's see how to extract lines from 3D models, which can further enhance your workflow.

Extracting lines from 3D models

When a 3D layer is selected, you can follow the same steps as the one used to extract lines from images:

1. Select the layer you wish to convert.

2. Tap the **Extract lines** icon inside of the **Layer Property** palette or navigate to the **Layer** menu | **Convert to lines and tones…**.

3. Adjust the settings within the dialog that opens.

4. Use the **Preview** option to check the result before applying the conversion.

5. Once satisfied, click **OK** to proceed.

The same settings discussed in the previous section, *Extracting lines from images*, will still apply when selecting the process from the **Layer Property** palette. However, when using the **Convert to lines and tones…** process, additional settings become available, as you can see in *Figure 8.17*:

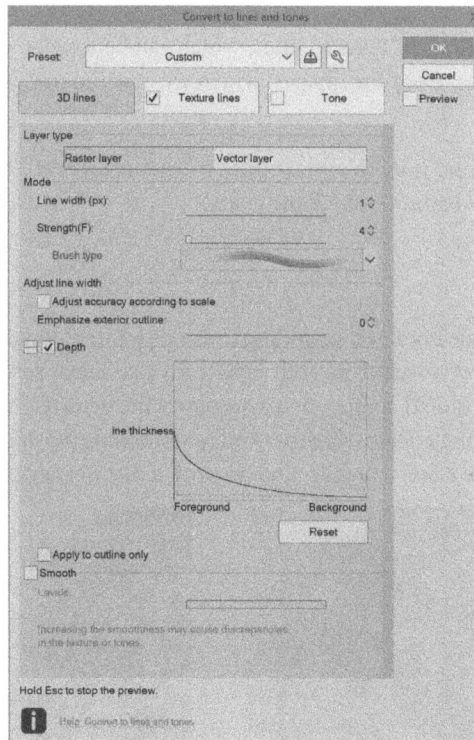

Figure 8.17 – The Convert to lines and tones dialog when a 3D material is selected

There are two categories of settings for converting 3D layers into lines. The first category is **3D lines**, and its functions are as follows:

- **Layer type** [**Raster layer/Vector layer**]: Choose whether to extract lines as a raster layer or vector layer.

- **Adjust line width**: Determines the width of extracted lines. Adjust via the value box or slider.

- **Strength(F)**: Sets the number of lines to detect.

- **Brush type**: Adjusts the appearance of extracted lines. This setting is only available when **Vector layer** is selected under **Layer type**.

- **Adjust line width**: Sets the thickness of extracted lines. You can toggle on **Adjust accuracy according to scale**, which will change line width depending on the model size. When **Adjust accuracy according to scale** is toggled on, you can emphasize the exterior outline with a value number and a slider.

- **Depth**: Adds depth to outlines. Adjust this with the provided graph or limit the effect to outer outlines by enabling **Apply only to outer line**.

- **Smooth**: Enables smoothing for 3D outlines. Larger values result in smoother lines.

The other category of settings is **Texture lines**, which can be toggled on and off. When toggled on, its settings are the same as those for images, which we covered in the previous section, *Extracting lines from images*.

Now that you've understood how to extract lines from images and 3D models, let's move on to an effect that adds depth and texture—the **Tone** effect.

Tone

Creating a traditional comic book feel or adding textural elements to your work is achievable through the **Tone** effect. This effect transforms your layer into a series of screentone dots, mimicking the halftone patterns seen in printed comics. You can control the density, frequency, and shape of the dots to create a variety of shading effects. Whether you're simulating a printed texture or adding depth to your illustration, the **Tone** effect can give your artwork a distinct aesthetic:

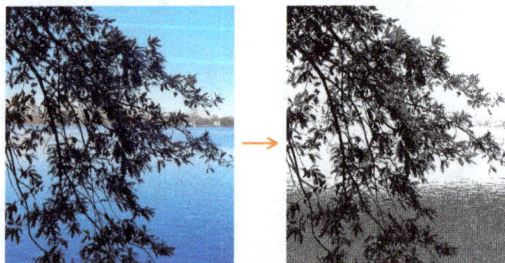

Figure 8.18 – The Tone effect

To use the **Tone** effect, follow the next steps:

1. Select the layer on which you wish to apply the effect.

2. Tap the **Tone** icon inside of the **Layer Property** palette:

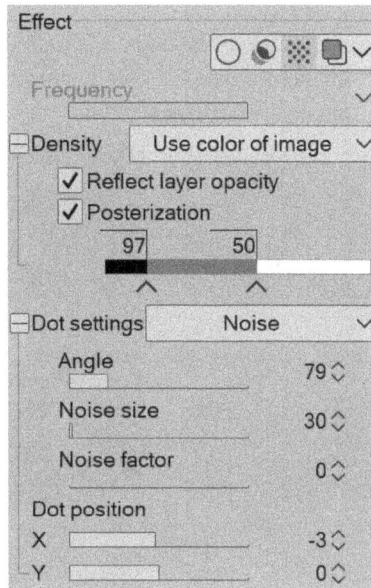

Figure 8.19 – Available settings for the Tone effect

3. New options will appear inside the **Layer Property** palette:

   • **Frequency**: Controls the number of screentone lines per inch. A higher frequency creates smaller dots.

   • **Density**: Specifies the density of tones. You can base the density on the original colors or brightness of the image, with darker areas resulting in denser tones. When you tap the + icon on the left side of **Density**, two more options appear:

     • **Reflect layer opacity**: When toggled on, this option adjusts the size of screentone dots based on the layer's opacity while keeping the dot color unchanged.

     • **Posterization**: When toggled on, it will use different tone densities for a poster-like effect. This setting allows you to modify the tone's density using a slider (this option is not available for **Fill** layers).

- **Dot settings**: Specifies the type of halftone used. You can choose between a variety of shapes, such as **Circle**, **Square**, **Noise**, and even shapes such as **Star** or **Heart**. When you tap the + icon on the left side of **Dot settings**, two more options appear:

  - **Angle**: Defines the angle of the pattern.

  - **Noise size**: Defines the size of the noise without altering its shape. This setting is only visible when **Noise** is selected as the **Dot settings** type. *Figure 8.20* shows examples of how different settings create varying results:

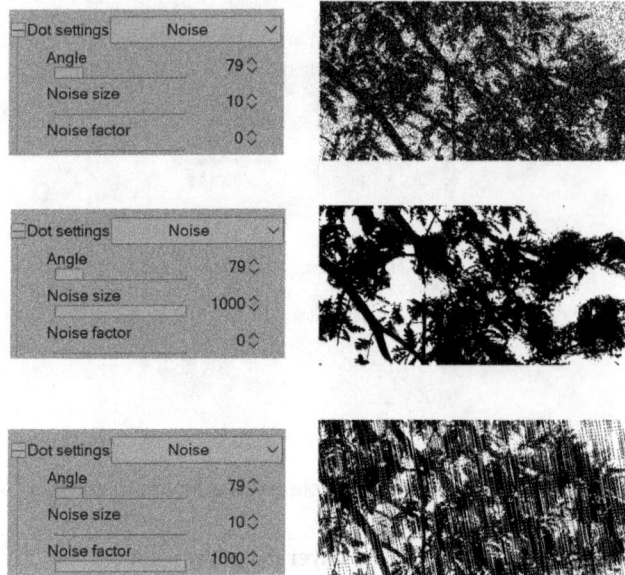

Figure 8.20 – Examples of Noise size and Noise factor in action

- **Noise factor**: Defines the noise factor. The higher the value, the longer each noise particle will become. This setting is only visible when the **Dot settings** type is set to **Noise**.

- **Dot position**: Allows you to shift the position of dots horizontally and vertically.

With **Area color**, you can add a color overlay to tone areas, making them easily distinguishable. To apply this overlay, navigate to **View | Show tone area**, and the *area color* will be applied only to selected layers.

When you are satisfied with the settings, you have two options:

1. Leave it as it is, and **Tone** can be toggled on/off by clicking on its icon.
2. Navigate to **Layer | Convert layer to lines and tones…** to apply changes permanently. A **Convert to lines and tones** dialog will open.

3. Use the **Preview** option to check the result before applying the conversion.

4. Once satisfied, click **OK** to proceed.

> **Important note**
>
> When you use the **Tone** effect under **Layer Property**, you can toggle it on/off by clicking its icon.
>
> When you use **Convert layer to lines and tones**, the **Tone** effect cannot be toggled on/off. A new layer folder will be created with all lines, tones, and fill layers inside. Your original layer will be maintained, and its visibility will be automatically turned off.

Moving from the **Tone** effect, which transforms your layer into screentone dots, we now shift to the **Layer color** option, which allows you to display your entire layer in a selected color for added visual control.

Layer color

Color consistency across your artwork can unify your design or correct specific areas. **Layer color** is a simple yet effective tool for this. By applying a selected color to the entire layer, you can quickly change how the layer appears without affecting its content. This effect is perfect for making quick color adjustments or for focusing on specific areas of your project. *Figure 8.21* shows examples of **Layer color** applications:

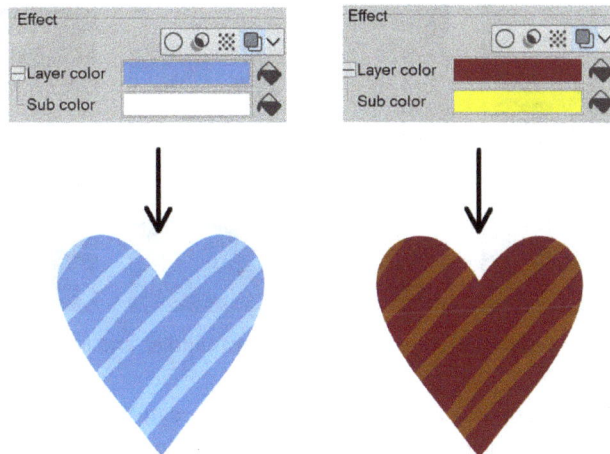

Figure 8.21 – Examples of Layer color settings

Clicking the **Set layer colors** bar opens the **Color settings** dialog, where you can choose a custom color. The selected layer color will replace black pixels. Additionally, you can specify a **Sub color** option to replace white pixels. This function has the same effect as the **Change layer color** function in the **Layer** palette.

Layer color is a setting you can toggle on and off by clicking its icon. To make this change permanent, you must rasterize the layer. There are two ways to rasterize a layer:

- Right-click on the layer name inside the **Layer** palette and select **Rasterize**.
- Navigate to the **Layer** menu and select **Rasterize**.

> **Important note**
>
> Once you rasterize the layer, the **Layer color** effect cannot be undone by simply switching back to the original mode.

From changing the entire layer's color, we now move to fine-tuning how colors are displayed with **Expression color**.

Expression color

Sometimes you need to adjust how color information is processed across a layer, which is where **Expression color** comes into play. With this setting, you can change how colors are interpreted on a selected layer, as shown in *Figure 8.22*:

Figure 8.22 – Expression color: Color (left), Gray (middle), and Monochrome (right)

There are three options: **Color**, **Gray**, or **Monochrome**. These modes allow flexible experimentation with different tonal values and styles, from full-color illustrations to black-and-white compositions. This feature is great for testing different visual styles without permanently committing to a color change. When changing to a lower-information mode such as **Gray** or **Monochrome**, a preview allows you to adjust the settings before confirming.

When converting a layer to **Monochrome**, you can fine-tune how the original colors are translated into black and white by clicking the + icon on the left side of **Monochrome**. You can change these settings:

- **Color threshold**: Determines the line between black and white.

- **Alpha threshold**: Controls the boundary between black, white, and transparency based on opacity.

- **Reflect layer opacity**: This option lets you decide to consider the original layer's opacity. When enabled, the drawing color is separated into black, white, and transparent based on the original colors and layer opacity. When disabled, opacity is applied to the layer after it has been converted to **Monochrome**.

When you are satisfied with the appearance, tap on **Apply expression color of preview** to permanently apply the **Expression color** effect.

Important note

Once confirmed, the **Expression color** effect cannot be undone by simply switching back to the original mode.

You have learned how to permanently change the expression color of your artwork, which is a handy function. Sometimes, you don't want to change the expression color; you only want to preview your work in limited color formats. That's where **Display decrease color** steps in.

Display decrease color

Previewing an image in a simplified color palette without permanently altering its color scheme is crucial when working with varied tones or preparing an image for monochrome output. **Display decrease color** lets you temporarily display an image or 3D material in **Gray** or **Monochrome** without changing its expression color mode.

This setting takes the place of the **Expression color** option, which is unavailable for image material layers. Although **Display decrease color** produces a similar visual effect as **Expression color**, it cannot be applied permanently.

For **Monochrome** layers, you can adjust the **Color threshold** setting to control how colors are divided between black and white. Similarly, the **Alpha threshold** setting determines how transparent areas are treated. You can also choose to reflect the layer's opacity in the conversion. These functions have been explained in detail in the *Expression color* section.

Display decrease color is especially helpful when you want to check how your work will appear when reduced to a simpler value scheme, such as for print or specific stylistic purposes.

Having covered **Display decrease color**, let's understand how **Mask expression** works.

Mask expression

Controlling transparency and masking areas of your layer requires precision, which is exactly what the **Mask expression** feature offers. When working with a layer mask, **Mask expression** gives you the ability to allow or restrict partial masking using gradients. You can see this setting in effect in *Figure 8.23*:

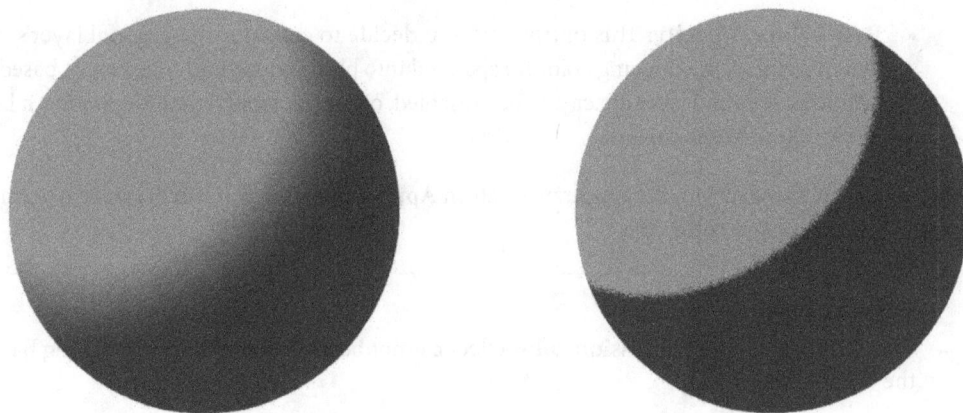

Figure 8.23 – Mask expression | Show gradients: Yes (left), No (right)

With **Show gradients** toggled on, you can create smooth transitions between masked and unmasked areas, making it perfect for applying subtle adjustments and soft blends. When turned off, using any color above a certain opacity will fully mask the area. That way, a flat look will be applied, which is useful depending on your art style. You can adjust the threshold in the **Mask expression** settings.

From masking, we now shift to a more navigational function—**Tool navigation**.

Tool navigation

Efficiency in digital art is often increased through a streamlined workflow, and **Tool navigation** helps achieve this by giving you quick access to the tools and sub tools available for editing the currently selected layer. This setting is available for vector, gradient, fill, 3D, tone, frame, and image material layers.

Tool navigation allows quick switching between options without opening additional menus, keeping you focused on your work. For example: on a vector layer, it offers shortcut icons for the **Object** tool, the **Control point** sub tool, the **Pinch line** sub tool and the **Adjust line width** sub tool. The faster you can access these functions, the more fluid your creative process will be. Which options appear on the Tool navigation will depend on the type of layer that is selected.

Next, let's look at a more specialized effect for adding texture to image material layers with **Overlay texture**.

Overlay texture

When working with texture-heavy designs or adding surface details, **Overlay texture** becomes an essential tool for depth and richness. This setting is specifically available for image material layers, allowing you to apply texture overlays to enhance the surface quality of your artwork. To use this setting effectively, select an image with a texture you want to apply to your artwork and place it on top of all other layers. *Figure 8.24* shows examples of the **Overlay texture** effect:

Figure 8.24 – Examples of different Strength values for the Overlay texture effect

The **Strength** value of the texture effect can be adjusted to create subtle or pronounced texture, adding an extra layer of complexity to your image.

After focusing on texture overlays, let's delve into how colors are displayed on the light table using **Color mode**.

Color mode

For animators working with light tables, the way colors are displayed can greatly affect the clarity of your work. **Color mode** applies exclusively to **Light table** layers, which are cels and layers that are registered in the **Animation cels** palette.

Color mode offers three display options: **Color**, **Half Color**, and **Monochrome**.

These options allow you to adjust how underlying layers are viewed, giving you flexibility when working with complex animations. Depending on your needs, you can maintain full color, reduce the palette, or convert everything to monochrome for easier distinction.

We have now completed our exploration of layer customization using the **Layer Property** palette. With this section, you've gained the knowledge to fully utilize this palette, expanding your range of creative tools. Next, we'll dive into advanced techniques that will take your workflow efficiency even further by utilizing pro layer techniques!

Optimizing your layers with pro techniques

To maximize your efficiency, you need to adopt pro-level techniques for layer management. In this section, we'll cover techniques to optimize your use of tools such as transparency lock, clipping mask, and layer lock. By mastering these techniques, you'll be able to create faster and with greater accuracy, ensuring that your layers work together seamlessly.

The first technique I want to cover is the use of **Reference** layers. When you set a layer as **Reference**, the **Fill** tool and the **Selection** tool can take the Reference layer into account even as you work on another layer. To make these tools consider the **Reference** layer, follow the next steps:

1. Navigate to the **Tool** palette.
2. Select either the **Fill** tool or the **Selection** tool.
3. Go to the **Tool property** palette.
4. Toggle on **Refer multiple**.
5. Select **Reference layer**.

There are two ways in which I frequently use **Reference** layers:

- Set my line art layer as a **Reference** layer. This way, I can use the **Fill** tool on a layer below it, and it will use the lines from the line art layer to determine edges.

- Set my base colors layer as a **Reference** layer. This way, I can use the **Auto select** tool to select specific parts of it, such as hair or skin, and paint only within this area. By using **Reference** layers like this, you can speed up your process considerably.

The second helpful technique you should know is the use of **Draft** layers. As we mentioned inside *The Layer palette's property bar* section, **Draft** layers can be disregarded by the **Fill** tool and the **Selection** tool. This is especially useful in a few settings:

- Set your sketch layer as a **Draft** layer. This way, those tools will ignore the sketch, and you'll be able to paint easily without having to hide it. An additional bonus is that the sketch layer will not be exported in the final image.

- Set your texture layer as a **Draft** layer. Paired with setting the line art layer as **Reference**, you can now paint considering only the line art, which will allow for a much cleaner result.

> **Important note**
>
> After you have finished using the **Fill** tool and the **Selection** tool, don't forget to toggle **Draft layer** off so that the texture will show in the final exported image.

When you apply these **Draft** layer techniques to your artwork, you'll have a much smoother workflow.

The third pro technique uses the **Lock Layer** function to disregard a layer when using the **Eyedropper** tool. This is especially useful when dealing with a **Correction Layer**, such as **Tone Curve** and **Level Correction**. When you create one such layer on top of all others, you might still want to paint the layers below. However, if you color pick, it will modify the resulting color because it will consider the **Correction** layer's colors (*Figure 8.25*):

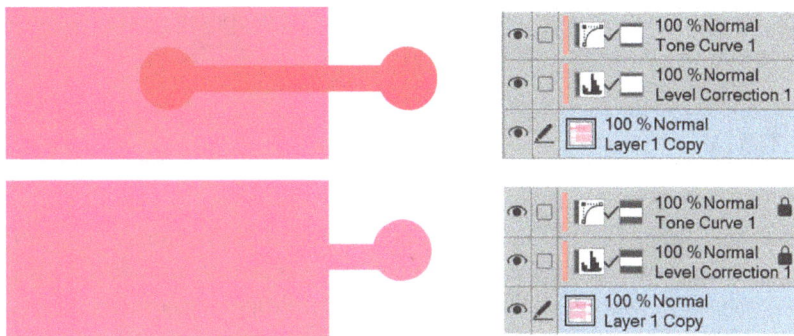

Figure 8.25 – Color-picking with an unlocked Correction Layer (top) and a locked Correction Layer (bottom)

To solve this issue, you can lock your **Correction** layer. Then, follow these steps:

1. Select the **Eyedropper** tool.
2. Select the **Obtain display color** sub tool.
3. Go to the **Tool property** palette.
4. Find **Exclude** | select **Exclude locked layers**.

You might notice this **Locked** layer technique works like the **Draft** layer we mentioned before, which might cause you to think they are the same. However, there's a reason why you should use this one for correction layers: **Correction** layers cannot become **Draft** layers.

Lastly, I want to give you a suggestion when painting an image that requires blending colors. Keeping separate layers will make the blending process very difficult, so you should do the following:

1. Navigate to the **Layer** menu | **Create folder and insert layer**, or press *Ctrl/command + G*. This will group all selected layers.

   - I recommend you group different elements separately, such as one group for the character, one group for the trees, one group for the sky, and so on.

2. Navigate to the **Layer** menu | **Duplicate Layer**, or press *Ctrl/command + J*. This will duplicate the selected group.

3. Turn off visibility for the original group in the **Layer** palette. This invisible group is your backup.

4. Still in the **Layer** palette, select the new folder, right-click its name and opacity details, and click on **Merge selected layers**.

5. Your layers will be merged, and you can paint and blend freely. You also have a backup of your original layers in case you need to go back to your previous step.

With these advanced techniques under your belt, you'll be able to push the boundaries of what you can achieve with layers, reducing unnecessary steps and enhancing your overall workflow. These methods ensure that your layers remain organized and purposeful, allowing you to focus on the creative aspects of your work.

Summary

In this chapter, you gained a solid understanding of essential layer features that can elevate your digital art process. You learned how to efficiently navigate the **Layer** palette using techniques that allow you to locate and manage layers quickly and discovered how to maximize the utility of **Reference** and **Draft** layers. Additionally, you explored the power of the **Layer Property** palette, learning how to manipulate layers by adding outlines, converting to screen tones, and much more. Finally, you enhanced your workflow with advanced techniques using tools such as **Reference** layers, locked layers, and layer groups, ensuring that your projects are both efficient and polished.

Armed with these new skills, your ability to organize and enhance your art has reached a new level of efficiency. Now, it's time to move on to another powerful topic: *mastering layer blending modes for stunning colors*, where you'll learn how to make the most of blending modes to create dynamic and beautiful effects in your artwork.

9

Mastering Layer Blending Modes for Stunning Colors

Layer blending modes are powerful tools inside **Clip Studio Paint** (**CSP**) that can transform your artwork, adding depth, light, and dynamic effects that elevate your creations from good to truly stunning. Understanding how these modes work and mastering their use can make a significant difference in your digital painting process. In this chapter, we'll dive deep into the world of blending modes, focusing on how to use them effectively to enhance your art.

You'll learn practical techniques for applying blending modes in various scenarios, from creating realistic shadows to adding luminous highlights. We'll explore all of the blending modes, dissecting how each one influences color in different ways.

In this chapter, we're going to cover the following topics:

- Understanding blending modes
- Enhancing shadows
- Illuminating your artwork
- Refining contrast, hue, saturation, and color
- Applying blending modes to a real painting

By the end of this chapter, you'll be equipped with the skills to manipulate shadows, light, and color in ways that will make your artwork stand out. You'll understand how blending modes work and be able to apply them with confidence in your own artwork. Whether you're working on character designs, environments, or complex illustrations, the techniques covered here will enable you to create rich, vibrant images that capture attention and convey emotion.

Understanding blending modes

Before diving into specific techniques, it is crucial to develop a solid understanding of blending modes and how they function. Blending modes control how layers interact with one another. They are a powerful way to manipulate color, tone, and contrast, enabling you to create effects ranging from subtle shading to dynamic light and color changes. By adjusting how one layer blends with the layers beneath it, you can quickly and precisely transform the look of your artwork.

The same colors can create very different results depending on the blending mode. *Figure 9.1* shows the difference between the **Normal** mode (left) and the **Overlay** mode (right), which we'll cover in the *Refining contrast, hue, saturation, and color* section.

Figure 9.1 – Same colors with the Normal mode (left) and the Overlay mode (right)

At their core, blending modes use mathematical algorithms to determine how the colors on one layer will blend with those on the layer beneath it. Each blending mode has its specific way of combining the values of the two layers. For example, darkening modes might compare the color values of two layers and retain the darkest values, while lightening modes might do the opposite, retaining the lightest values.

In addition to the visual effects, the order and opacity of your layers play a significant role in determining the result. As you experiment with different blending modes, you'll notice that changing a mode or layer position can dramatically alter the look of your artwork. It's this combination of layer stacking, blending modes, and opacity that allows for a high degree of flexibility in your digital workflow.

Blending modes are particularly powerful when used in combination. For example, you might use **Multiply** for shadows and **Saturation** to enhance the vibrancy of your colors. The ability to blend and stack these effects opens up a multitude of creative possibilities. By experimenting with different modes, you'll discover new ways to enhance your artwork, all while maintaining efficiency and control over the final look.

> **Important note**
>
> It's frequently hard to predict how strong the effect will be. If you're not satisfied with the resulting color, go to **Edit | Tonal correction | Hue/Saturation/Luminosity**, or press *Ctrl/command + U* to adjust it. If the color is good but the effect is too strong, go to the **Layer** palette and reduce the blending layer opacity. With time, you'll instinctively understand how colors and blending modes interact, speeding up your process.

Every new layer is created with the **Normal** blending mode, and colors are placed on top of others without any special effect. This is the default blending mode; if you wish to change it, you can select a layer blending mode by following these steps:

1. Navigate to the **Layer** palette.

2.   Select **Mode**.

The list of blending modes will appear:

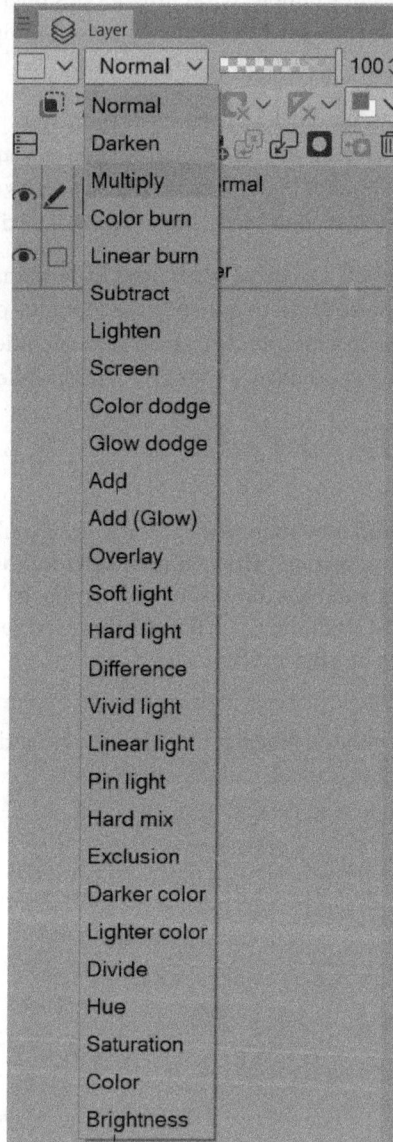

Figure 9.2 – List of blending modes

3. Select the blending mode you wish to apply.

4. The blending mode name will appear in the layer details:

Figure 9.3 – The blending mode is visible in the layer details

There are 28 blending modes, but you don't need to include all of them in your workflow. In fact, after experimenting with them, you'll probably have a handful of favorite modes and rarely use the others. As we cover layer blending modes, remember that all of these modes also apply to specific tools such as brushes and decorative tools. To apply them to specific tools, follow these steps:

1. Select the tool you wish to paint with, such as a brush.

2. Navigate to the **Tool Property** palette.

3. Tap on the wrench icon to open the **Sub Tool Detail** palette.

4. Go to **Ink | Blending mode** and select the desired mode.

Now that you have a solid understanding of blending modes and how to select them, you're ready to start applying these concepts. In the upcoming section, we'll delve into specific techniques for enhancing shadows using blending modes such as **Darken** and **Multiply**, which will help you increase the depth and dimension of your artwork.

Enhancing shadows

Shadows are essential for adding depth and realism to your artwork. In this section, we'll dive into the art of enhancing shadows using specific blending modes. You'll learn how to create rich, dynamic shadows that not only add contrast but also bring a sense of weight and volume to your subjects. We will explore darkening blending modes such as **Darken**, **Multiply**, and **Color burn**, and how to use them effectively to enhance your artwork. By mastering these modes, you can quickly add shadows and fix values to establish a solid foundation.

Each darkening layer mode has its specificities. Let's start with **Darken**, the first darkening blending mode on the list.

Darken

The **Darken** blending mode compares the pixel values of two layers and retains the darkest values:

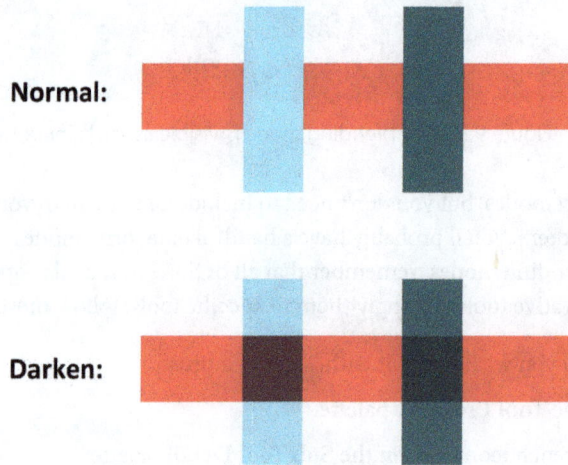

Figure 9.4 – Normal mode (top) and Darken mode (bottom)

Using this blending mode will slightly darken the pixels and combine their colors, as seen in *Figure 9.4*. This mode is useful for reducing brightness and decreasing contrast. The hues are combined, so when they are on opposite sides of the color wheel, the difference is more visible than when they are similar hues:

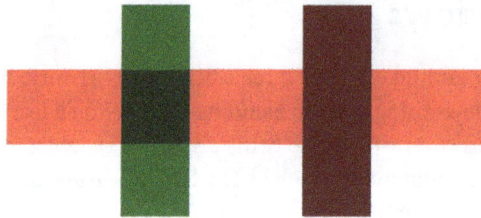

Figure 9.5 – How changing the hue can affect the result with Darken

In the preceding figure, the combination of green and red is much more visible than the combination of maroon and red because of the hue difference.

Having understood **Darken**, we'll now cover **Multiply**, my favorite blending mode for shading.

Multiply

The **Multiply** blending mode is one of the most used darkening techniques. It multiplies the RGB values of the blending layer and the underlying layers, creating rich shadows. It is more intense than **Darken**:

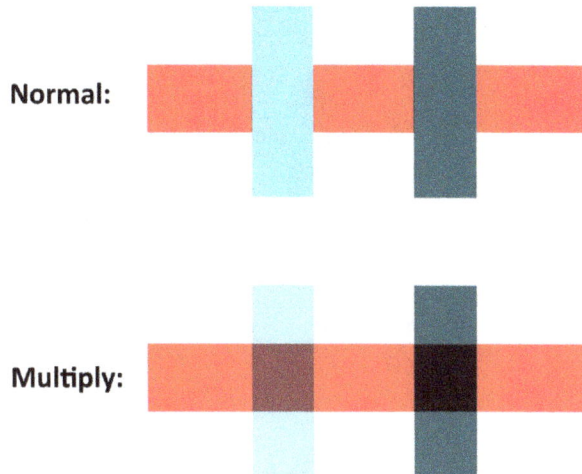

Normal:

Multiply:

Figure 9.6 – Normal mode (top) and Multiply mode (bottom)

Because it multiplies the values, every pixel will become darker and, frequently, more saturated. For this reason, I usually choose desaturated colors for the **Multiply** layer to reduce the intensity of the result. If the layers have different hues, the result will be a combination of both hues:

Figure 9.7 – How changing the hue can affect the result with Multiply

Multiply is great for placing shadows and making small value fixes. Use it to place all sorts of shadows on your image, whether they are cast shadows, form shadows, or occlusion shadows.

Once you've mastered **Multiply**, you might want to enhance shadows with more intensity using **Color burn**, which adds dramatic shading effects.

Color burn

Color burn amplifies the darkness of shadows by increasing contrast between the layer colors, making it perfect for adding bold, intense shadow effects.

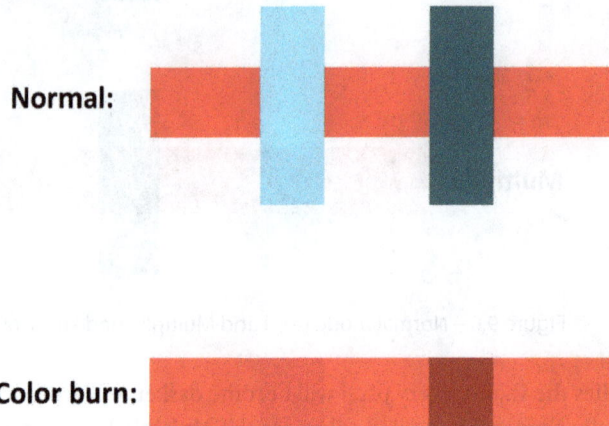

Figure 9.8 – Normal mode (top) and Color burn mode (bottom)

If the blending mode's value is brighter than the underlying layer's colors, the effect is very discrete. Not only that but depending on the blending layer's color, the hue might not change compared to the underlying layer, as shown in *Figure 9.8*. **Color burn** will frequently increase saturation dramatically, but it doesn't darken the values as much.

Another great blending mode for shadows is **Linear burn**, which provides a more abrupt transition in darker areas, allowing for stronger shading.

Linear burn

Linear burn offers a darker alternative to **Color burn**. It darkens the colors of the underlying layers to blend the colors of the blending layer.

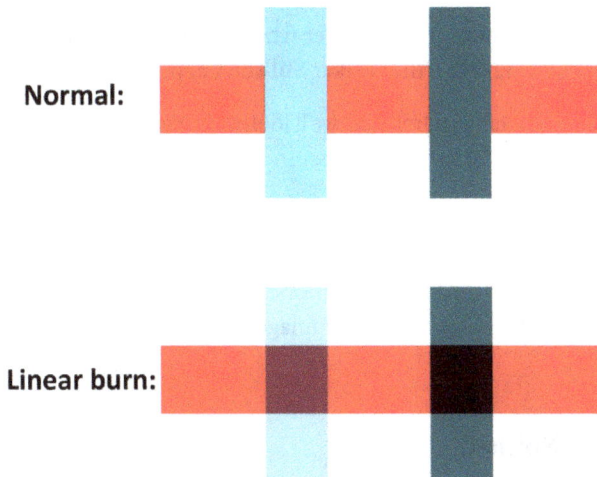

Figure 9.9 – Normal mode (top) and Linear burn mode (bottom)

This blending mode can look similar to **Multiply** or **Color burn**, but it creates a darker look. It frequently results in less saturated colors than **Color burn**.

After exploring **Linear burn**, we'll introduce **Subtract**, a blending mode that subtracts color to create unique effects.

Subtract

Subtract is a more intense blending mode that removes color from the layer, resulting in a darker image with completely different hues that can give your image a distinctive, dramatic look.

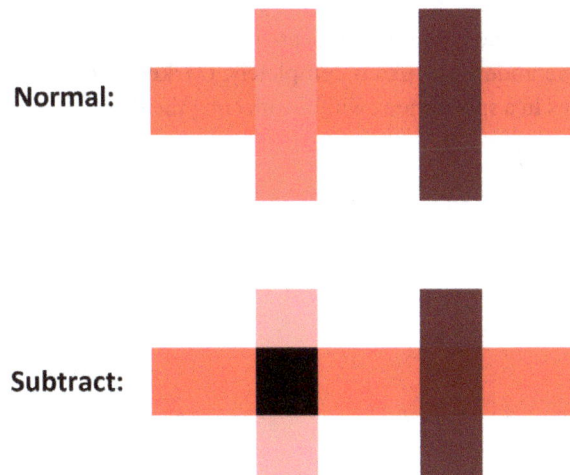

Figure 9.10 – Normal mode (top) and Subtract mode (bottom)

Because **Subtract** removes colors, it is stronger when the blending color is lighter and has a similar hue. The darker the blending color, the weaker **Subtract** appears.

Next, to round out our darkening techniques, we'll look at **Darker color**, which provides a non-contrast-based approach to retaining the darkest pixels.

Darker color

Darker color is a straightforward blending mode that keeps the darkest colors without blending, offering a simple and subtle way to darken an image without altering the darkest pixels.

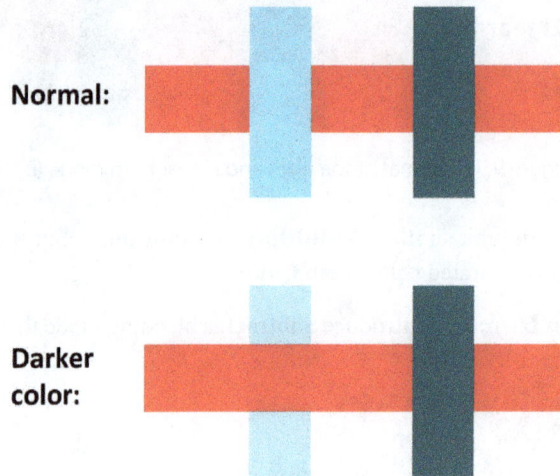

Figure 9.11 – Normal mode (top) and Darker color mode (bottom)

It is a yes-or-no mode. If the blending pixels are lighter, they disappear. If the blending pixels are darker, they cover the underlying pixels completely. **Darker color** is the best blending mode for toning down the lights in a specific area without affecting the shadows. I frequently use this mode to reduce contrast subtly.

We've now covered all the darkening blending modes. In the following figure, you can see a comparison between each of them:

Figure 9.12 – A comparison between each darkening blending mode

With your newfound skills, you can confidently build depth and change contrast through skillful shadow work using blending modes. In the next section, we'll shift our focus from shadows to light and discover how to illuminate your artwork using blending modes that brighten and enhance highlights.

Illuminating your artwork

While shadows create depth, light is what brings your artwork to life. In this section, we'll explore how to use blending modes to illuminate your work, adding highlights and enhancing the sense of light in your scenes. You'll learn about blending modes such as **Screen**, **Lighten**, and **Add**, which are excellent for enhancing light sources, highlights, and other illuminated areas.

We'll start with **Lighten**, the first brightening blending mode on the list.

Lighten

The **Lighten** blending mode compares pixel values and retains the lightest ones, allowing you to subtly brighten your artwork without overexposing the darker areas:

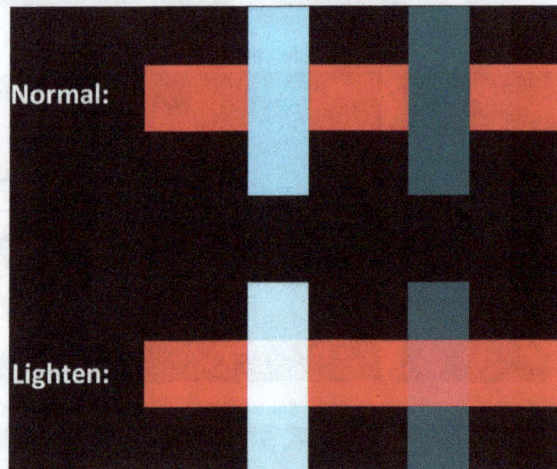

Figure 9.13 – Normal mode (top) and Lighten mode (bottom)

Using this blending mode will slightly lighten the pixels and combine their colors. Lighten is useful for increasing brightness and decreasing contrast – it is the exact opposite of the **Darken** blending mode we covered in the previous section, *Enhancing shadows with blending modes*.

After learning how to softly brighten your image with **Lighten**, we'll dive into **Screen**, a more powerful mode for creating lighter effects and enhancing highlights.

Screen

The **Screen** blending mode is a go-to method for creating brighter areas. It inverts the base colors and multiplies them with the colors of the blending layer, which is the opposite effect of the **Multiply** mode:

Figure 9.14 – Normal mode (top) and Screen mode (bottom)

I choose **Screen** when I want a soft, bright effect. The result typically appears less saturated than the color on the blending layer.

With **Screen** under your belt, let's move on to **Color dodge**, a dynamic blending mode for adding intense, glowing highlights that make your artwork pop.

Color dodge

Color dodge dramatically brightens areas by boosting the intensity of highlights, making it perfect for adding radiant light effects and vibrant color transitions:

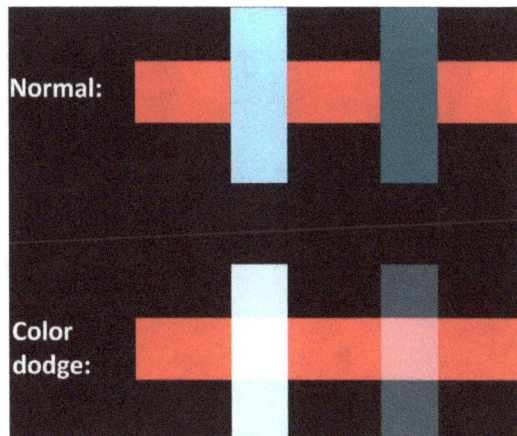

Figure 9.15 – Normal mode (top) and Color dodge mode (bottom)

This blending mode lightens the colors of the underlying layer and reduces contrast, creating saturated mid-tones and bright highlights.

Next, we'll take that glow a step further with **Glow dodge**, which enhances brightness with even more vibrancy for eye-catching luminosity.

Glow dodge

Glow dodge amplifies light even more than **Color dodge**, infusing your artwork with intense, glowing highlights that create a powerful sense of light:

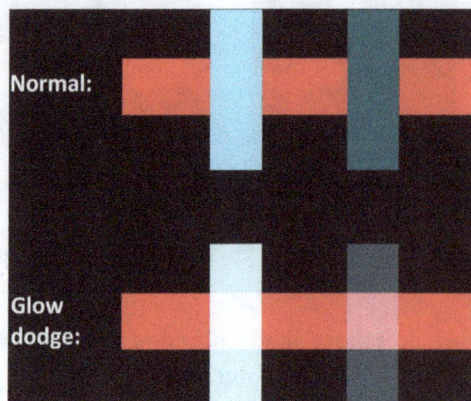

Figure 9.16 – Normal mode (top) and Glow dodge mode (bottom)

I frequently use **Glow dodge** for special effects, such as sparkles and robust, direct light. It often creates a saturated edge, which is excellent when painting bright sunlight on the skin, as shown in the next example:

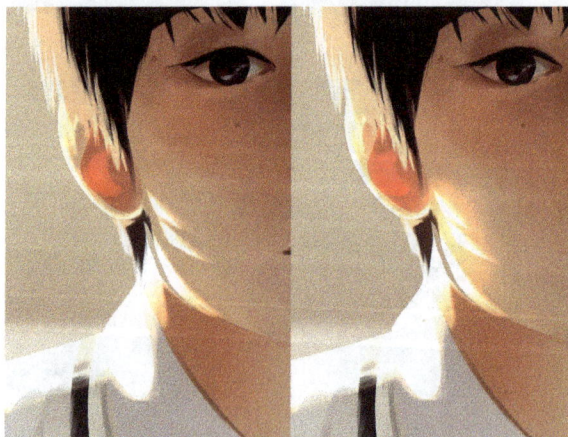

Figure 9.17 – Sunlight on skin without Glow dodge (left) and with Glow dodge (right)

Once you've tried **Glow dodge**, you'll want to experiment with **Add**, which offers a stronger way to combine layers for brighter results.

Add

The **Add** blending mode increases the brightness of overlapping areas by combining the pixel values:

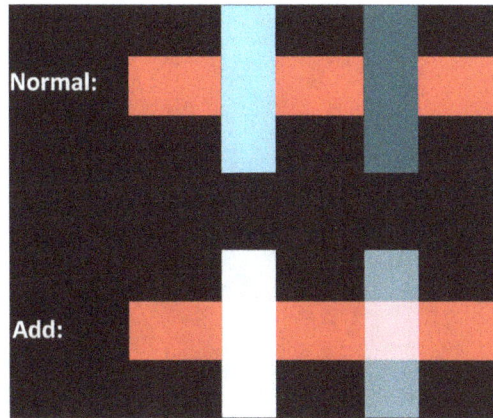

Figure 9.18 – Normal mode (top) and Add mode (bottom)

Add results in even brighter and less saturated results than other blending modes, such as **Screen**.

Now, let's intensify these effects further with **Add (Glow)**, a blending mode that takes the glow effect to the next level by adding intensity while maintaining smooth transitions.

Add (Glow)

Add (Glow) creates a stronger effect than **Add**. It enhances your image by adding a soft, luminous glow to the brightest areas, providing a beautiful finishing touch to your highlights. Below you see examples of **Add (Glow)** in action:

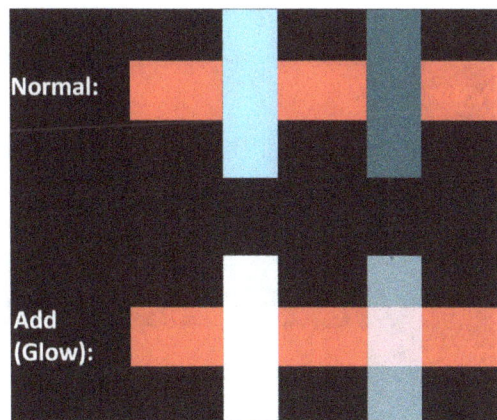

Figure 9.19 – Normal mode (top) and Add (Glow) mode (bottom)

Like **Glow dodge**, it often creates an edge of saturation around the colored area, which can result in beautiful effects. Comparing these blending modes, **Add (Glow)** creates a brighter result with less contrast, while **Glow dodge** increases contrast and saturation:

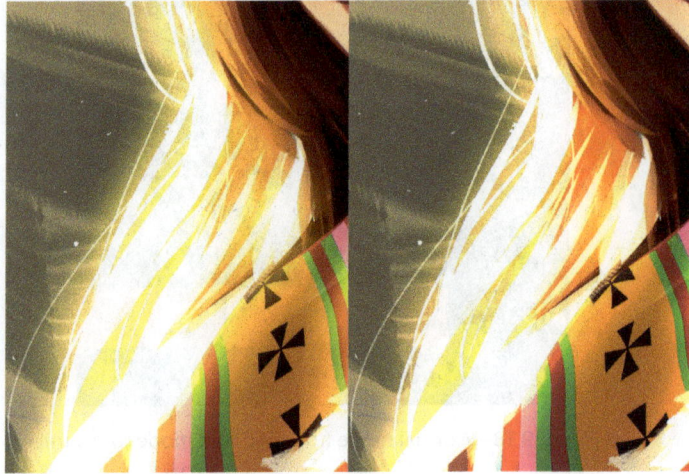

Figure 9.20 – A comparison between Add (Glow) (left) and Glow dodge (right)

With a solid understanding of **Add (Glow)**, we are now ready to dive into the **Divide** blending mode, which enhances bright areas by dividing color values.

Divide

With the **Divide** blending mode, the RGB values of the underlying layer are multiplied by 255 and then divided by the RGB values of the blending layer. This changes the hue and might lighten the image:

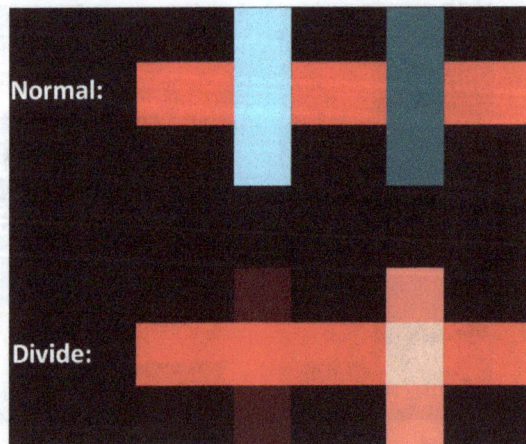

Figure 9.21 – Normal mode (top) and Divide mode (bottom)

This mode can be used to remove dark areas or create a glowing, washed-out look. In *Figure 9.22*, you can see an example of **Divide** in action:

Figure 9.22 – The cyan light in Normal mode (left) and Divide mode (right)

Divide can be particularly useful for achieving a bright and ethereal look with unusual hue combinations. Next, let's discuss **Lighter color**, which is great for subtle value fixing.

Lighter color

Lighter color compares the brightness of the blending layer and the underlying layer and shows the color with the higher value. It is the exact opposite of the **Darker color** blending mode we covered in the *Enhancing shadows* section. You can see **Lighter color** in action in the following figure:

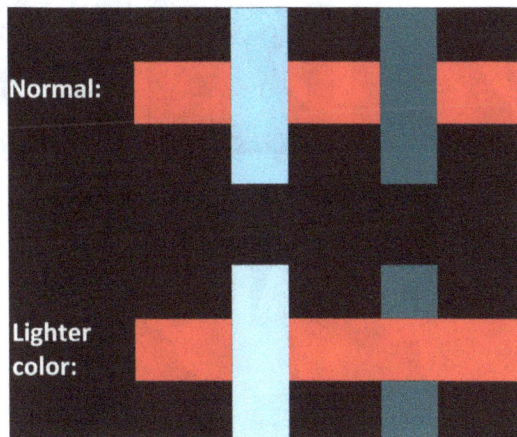

Figure 9.23 – Normal mode (top) and Lighter color mode (bottom)

Like **Darker color**, this is a yes-or-no mode. If the blending pixels are darker, they disappear. If the blending pixels are lighter, they cover the underlying pixels completely. **Lighter color** is the best blending mode for increasing the lights in a specific area without affecting the shadows. I frequently use this mode to increase brightness while reducing contrast subtly.

We've now covered all the brightening blending modes. In the following figure, you can see a comparison between each of them:

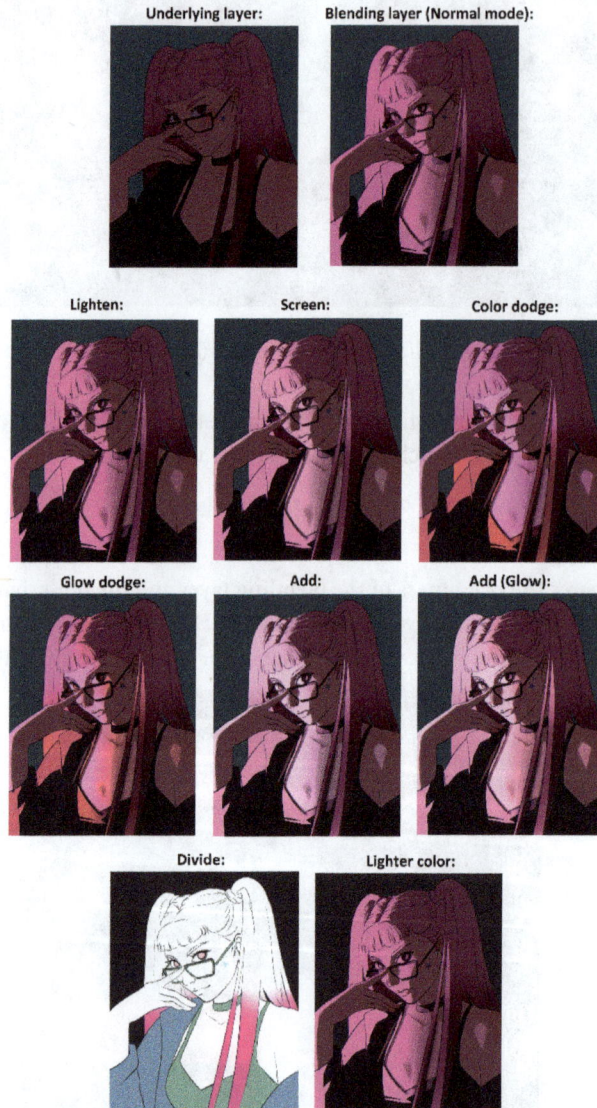

Figure 9.24 – A comparison between each lightening blending mode

Now that you've mastered the techniques for adding light and highlights, you're ready to explore the next step in enhancing your artwork. In the following section, we'll delve into the subtler yet equally impactful task of adjusting tone and saturation and how blending modes can improve these aspects.

Refining contrast, hue, saturation, and color

To bring your artwork to its full potential, it's important to fine-tune every detail, from contrast to hue and saturation. This section will explore advanced blending modes such as **Difference**, **Vivid light**, **Linear light**, and **Hue**, which give you precise control over these aspects. You'll learn how to use these modes to achieve precise color and contrast adjustments, allowing you to perfect your image's overall appearance. By mastering these blending modes, you'll be able to manipulate the final look of your artwork with expert precision. We'll start with **Overlay**, a blending mode that changes hue and contrast.

Overlay

The **Overlay** blending mode is one of the most versatile and commonly used blending modes. It behaves like the **Screen** mode in bright areas and the **Multiply** mode in dark areas, enhancing contrast:

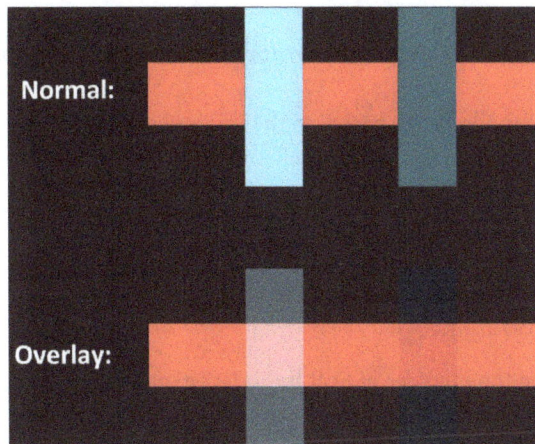

Figure 9.25 – Normal mode (top) and Overlay color mode (bottom)

Overlay is a powerful tool for artists looking to intensify highlights and shadows, resulting in a more dramatic and polished finish. By applying this mode strategically, you can achieve a vibrant and dynamic look in your art. This blending mode is especially useful for adding textures, increasing the richness of colors, or refining lighting in your artwork without losing essential details. I typically use **Overlay** when I want to add a hint of color on top of the image and for some special effects, such as subsurface scattering.

Now that we've explored **Overlay** and its ability to enhance contrast, let's delve into the next blending mode, **Soft light**, which can brighten and darken your image.

Soft light

Soft light is a versatile blending mode that gently alters the appearance of the layer beneath it, either darkening or lightening based on the tones of the blending layer. Despite its name, it does not only brighten colors. This effect adds a subtle yet dynamic shift to your image, creating smoother transitions between light and shadow. You can see **Soft light** in action here:

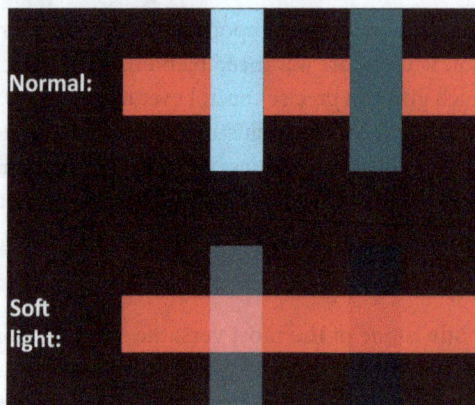

Figure 9.26 – Normal mode (top) and Soft light mode (bottom)

The effect of **Soft light** mode varies based on the brightness of the color applied. Lighter colors on the blending layer will brighten the image, similar to *dodge* modes, while darker colors will darken it, like *burn* modes. When applied to white areas, any color will appear white. This mode creates a more gradual and natural effect compared to other blending modes such as **Overlay** or **Hard light**. It is often used to enhance lighting and contrast in a less harsh, more delicate manner, making it a great option for adjusting overall mood or adding depth to an image without overexposing highlights or deepening shadows excessively.

Now that we've covered the nuances of **Soft light**, let's explore the bolder impact of the **Hard light** blending mode and how it interacts with light and dark areas in your artwork.

Hard light

Hard light is a powerful and more intense blending mode that emphasizes contrast by amplifying the light and dark areas of your image. Despite its name, it does not only brighten colors. It's particularly effective when you want to create a stronger, more defined effect:

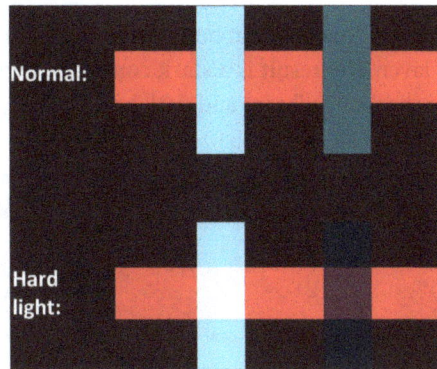

Figure 9.27 – Normal mode (top) and Hard light mode (bottom)

The effect of **Hard light** is influenced by the brightness of the blending color. Brighter colors on the blending layer produce a lightening effect similar to the **Screen** mode, while darker colors create a darkening effect like the **Multiply** mode. **Hard light** delivers a bold, dramatic look, making it useful for sharp highlights, strong shadows, or when you want to emphasize key features in your artwork. However, it requires careful control, as it can easily result in an image that appears too harsh or overly contrasted.

Hard light is your go-to mode for dramatic lighting effects and strong contrast. I frequently use it when I have a strong, colored light source, such as a green or bright blue spotlight. Now that we've explored **Hard light**, let's delve into the next blending mode, **Difference**, which creates a strikingly different effect by inverting colors based on the applied layer.

Difference

The **Difference** blending mode creates striking contrasts by comparing the difference between the underlying layer and the blending layer:

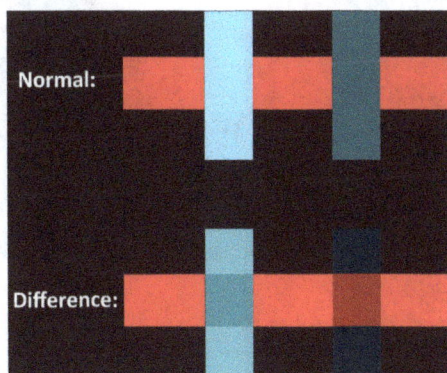

Figure 9.28 – Normal mode (top) and Difference mode (bottom)

This mode compares the values of the pixels in both layers and subtracts the colors of the blending layer from the underlying layer. The result is a stark contrast where similar colors produce light tones, and contrasting colors generate vibrant and dark results. Here, you can see an example of the **Difference** mode in action:

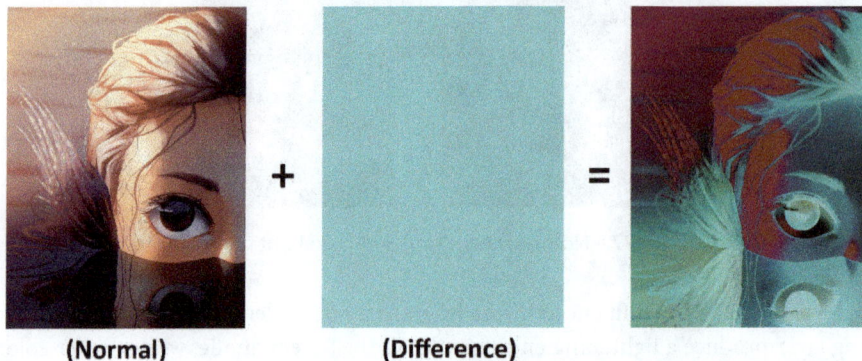

(Normal)   (Difference)

Figure 9.29 – An example of the Difference blending mode

The **Difference** mode can add dynamic contrast and unique color shifts to your artwork, making it perfect for experimenting with color variation. Next, let's explore **Vivid light**, a blending mode that combines brightness and contrast adjustments.

Vivid light

Vivid light offers an intense combination of **Color dodge** and **Color burn**, adding high contrast to your images:

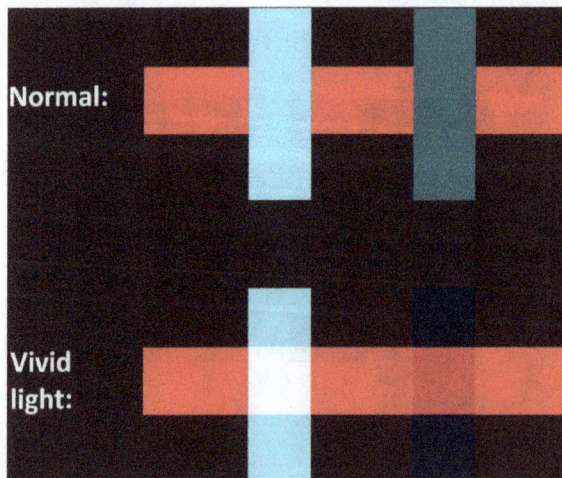

Figure 9.30 – Normal mode (top) and Vivid light mode (bottom)

This blending mode increases or decreases the contrast of the underlying layer based on the brightness of the blending layer. Whether the blended colors will be lighter or darker than the underlying colors depends on the combination of hues and values.

Vivid light is an excellent tool for creating dramatic lighting effects with vibrant colors and strong highlights. It achieves sharp contrast and rich color enhancement, ideal for creating intense lighting effects. Next, let's explore this further with **Linear light**, a similar mode that increases contrast and saturation.

Linear light

Linear light is a powerful blending mode that adjusts brightness and contrast by combining **Multiply** and **Linear burn**:

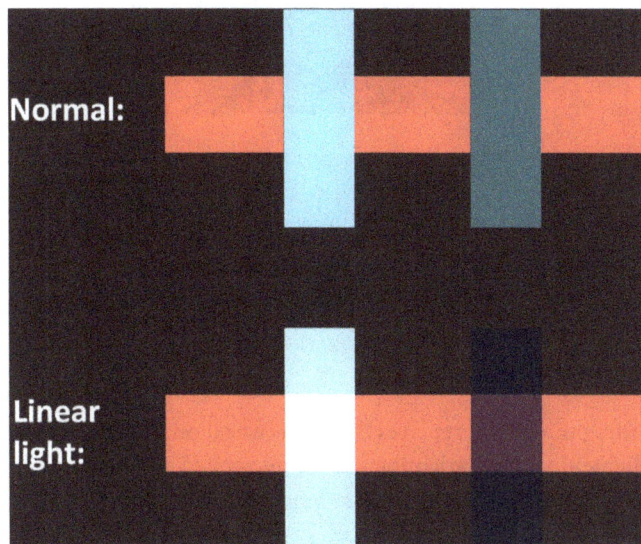

Figure 9.31 – Normal mode (top) and Linear light mode (bottom)

When using **Linear light**, whether the blended colors will be lighter or darker than the underlying colors depends on the combination of hues and values. It is similar to **Vivid light**, but the results are slightly different:

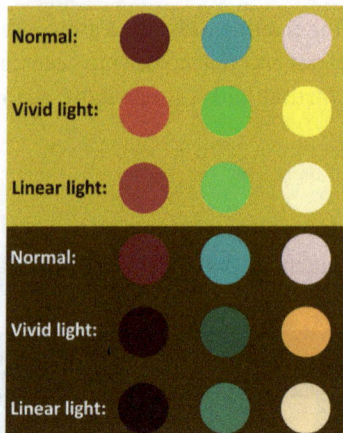

Figure 9.32 – Comparison between Normal, Vivid light, and Linear light

Linear light is perfect for intensifying highlights and shadows in your artwork, providing an intense approach to contrast manipulation. Next, we'll delve into **Pin light**, a blending mode that selectively replaces pixels to change their brightness values.

Pin light

Pin light is a blending mode that replaces the pixels based on the brightness of the blending layer. With this mode, lightening and darkening effects are applied simultaneously. Darker pixels on the underlying layer are blended with the **Lighten** mode, while brighter pixels on the underlying layer are blended with the **Darken** mode:

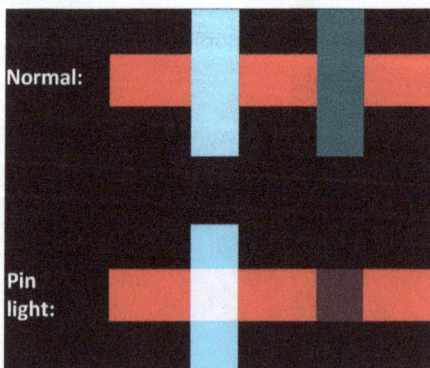

Figure 9.33 – Normal mode (top) and Pin light mode (bottom)

Pin light produces a distinctive effect, which makes it great for artistic experiments. Moving forward, we'll explore **Hard mix**, a blending mode that results in striking, nearly binary color shifts.

Hard mix

Hard mix creates bold, high-contrast effects by adding the RGB values of the blending layer on the underlying layer. If the combined RGB value exceeds 255, it is capped at **255**. If the combined RGB value falls below 255, it is set to **0**:

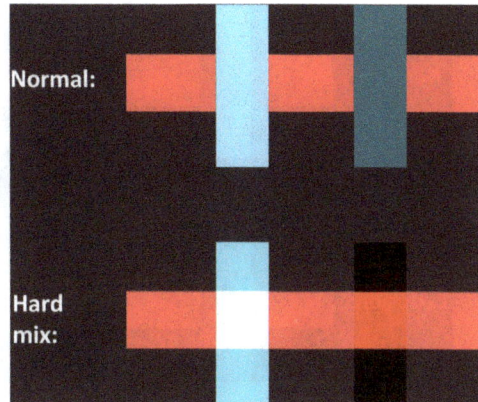

Figure 9.34 – Normal mode (top) and Hard mix mode (bottom)

This results in high contrast and a color palette limited to primary colors in additive and subtractive color models (red, green, blue, cyan, magenta, yellow, black, and white). It's excellent for creating a graphic look with strong, impactful colors:

Figure 9.35 – Normal mode (left) and Hard mix mode (right)

Hard mix delivers a visually intense and limited palette, perfect for bold design statements. Let's transition into **Exclusion**, a blending mode with a more subtle, subtractive effect.

Exclusion

Exclusion is a blending mode that produces an effect similar to **Difference** but with softer and less contrasting results. **Exclusion** compares the colors of the base and blend layers, and it tends to generate more muted and smoother transitions between the colors:

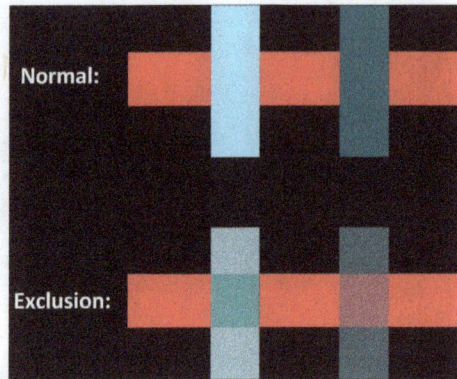

Figure 9.36 – Normal mode (top) and Exclusion mode (bottom)

When the blending layer is white, it inverts the colors of the underlying layer. If the blending layer is black, the underlying colors remain unchanged. This blending mode is ideal for creating soft, dreamy effects with less contrast:

Figure 9.37 – Normal mode (left) and Exclusion mode (right)

Exclusion softens the contrast while still providing unique color interactions, making it a gentler version of the **Difference** mode. Next, let's move on to **Hue**, a blending mode that focuses on adjusting hue without affecting brightness or saturation.

Hue

The **Hue** blending mode changes the hue of the underlying layer while preserving its brightness and saturation:

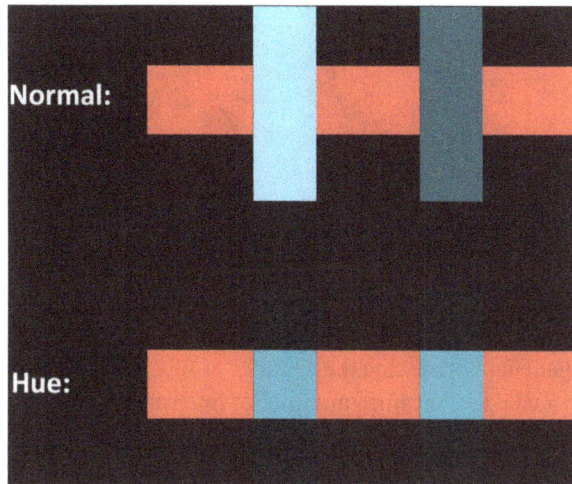

Figure 9.38 – Normal mode (top) and Hue mode (bottom)

Hue is ideal for recoloring areas of your image while maintaining their original tonal qualities, making it perfect for color grading and adjustments.

The **Hue** blending mode is a powerful tool for recoloring and adjusting tones without affecting the values and saturation of the image. Next, let's explore **Saturation**, which controls the intensity of color in your artwork.

Saturation

When using the **Saturation** mode, the colors in the underlying layer are adjusted to match the saturation levels of the blend layer:

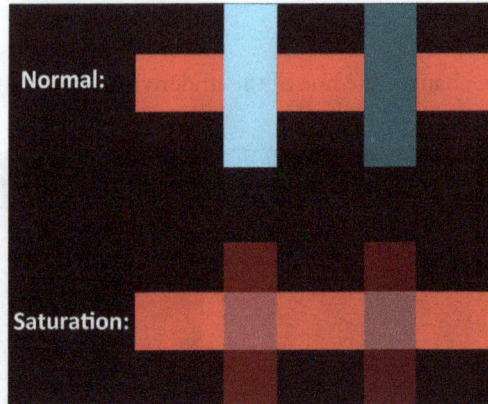

Figure 9.39 – Normal mode (top) and Saturation mode (bottom)

This is perfect for enhancing or reducing the vibrancy of specific areas without affecting their hue or brightness, making it a vital tool for fine-tuning color intensity.

I frequently use a layer in **Saturation** mode to check the values of my image. To check your values with a **Saturation**-type layer, follow these steps:

1. Create a new layer on top of all layers in your image.

2. Go to the **Layer** palette | **Mode** | **Saturation**.

3. Paint the entire layer with gray – any value works well, as long as the color's saturation is zero.

4. Now, your image is completely grayscale while maintaining the original values. You can check whether the values work well or whether anything needs to be fixed.

5. Toggle the visibility for the **Saturation** layer on and off during your painting process to ensure the values continue working well together.

6. You can make this same process with the **Hue** and the **Color** layer modes.

Saturation is helpful for precisely controlling the vividness of your colors, giving you great flexibility over the intensity of the image. Next, let's move on to **Color**, a blending mode that alters both the hue and saturation of your artwork.

Color

The **Color** blending mode changes the underlying layer's colors to match the blending layer's hue and saturation while preserving the underlying layer's original brightness:

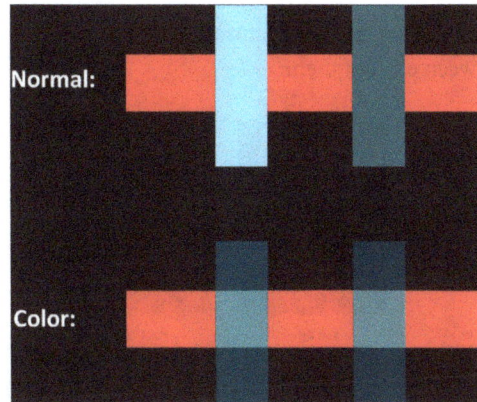

Figure 9.40 – Normal mode (top) and Color mode (bottom)

It's an effective way to recolor an entire image or specific areas without changing the tonal structure, making it invaluable for color corrections and adjustments.

The **Color** mode gives you complete control over recoloring your image without affecting its brightness, allowing for quick color corrections. Finally, let's examine **Brightness**, a mode focused on adjusting the luminosity of your image.

Brightness

When using the **Brightness** mode, the blending layer changes the luminance of the underlying layer while leaving the hue and saturation intact:

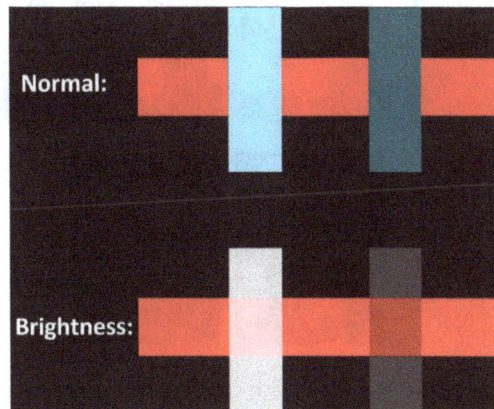

Figure 9.41 – Normal mode (top) and Brightness mode (bottom)

This is a powerful technique for adjusting shadows and highlights in your artwork without distorting the underlying colors.

We've now covered all the contrast, hue, and saturation blending modes. In the following figure, you can see a comparison between each of them:

Figure 9.42 – A comparison between each contrast, hue, and saturation blending mode

Having gained a deeper understanding of how to manipulate contrast, hue, and color, you are now ready to apply everything you've learned in a real-world scenario. In the next section, we'll use these layer modes in an actual painting, where you'll see how these techniques come together to enhance the final result.

Applying blending modes to a real painting

In this final section, it's time to put all your knowledge into practice. We'll walk through a real painting process, where you can see how to apply layer blending modes at various stages. From blocking in shadows to adding highlights, enhancing colors, and refining tones, you'll witness how these techniques can transform an artwork.

The following figure will be our base image:

Figure 9.43 – The base image and its layers

As you can see on the right side of *Figure 9.43*, the layers are divided as such:

- **lines** (**Normal**), the sketch that will guide our painting.

- **blush** (**Normal**), clipped to the layer below.

- **flats** (**Normal**), with all base colors on it. This layer is set to **Reference** so we can select its colors while working on other layers, as we covered in *Chapter 8, Maximizing Efficiency and Organization with Layers*.

- **bg** (**Normal**), the dark green background.

As we covered in *Chapter 4, Organizing Your Projects Effectively*, all layers are named for easy navigation.

With the base layers set, we can set up the light and shadow. We'll start with a **base shading** layer set to **Multiply**:

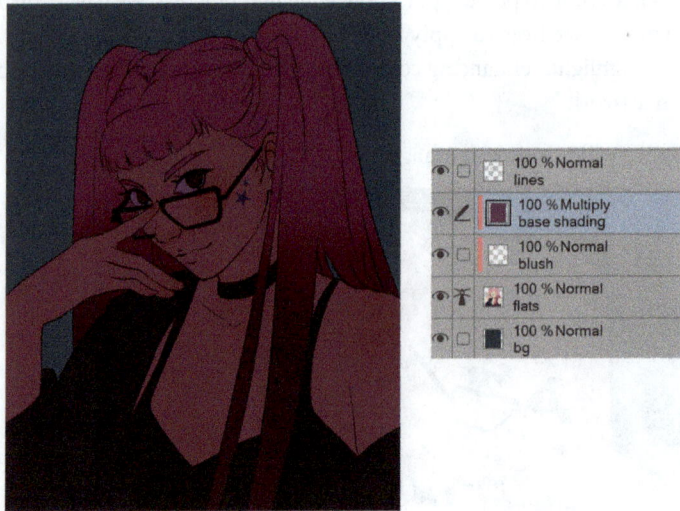

Figure 9.44 – We add a Multiply layer for shading

This base shading starts setting the mood. Next, we can place the lights. We'll have two light sources in this scene: pink and cyan. Let's start with the pink one. We place the colors and set the layer to **Overlay**. With a layer mask, we carve out the shapes:

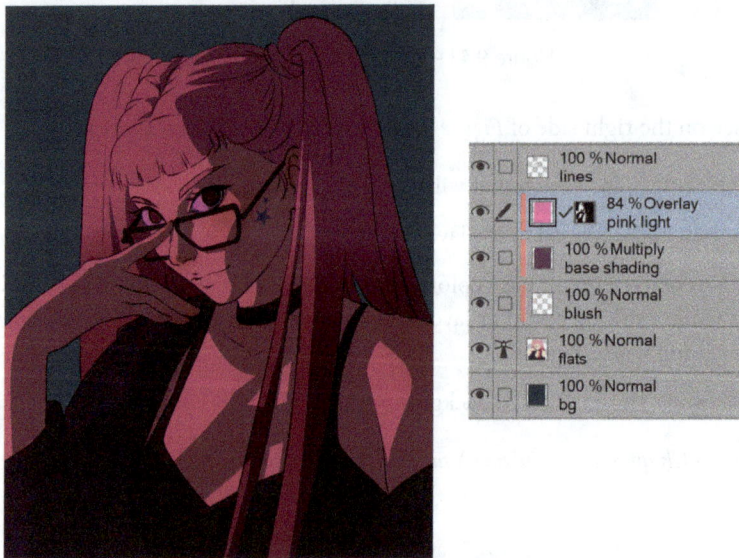

Figure 9.45 – We add an Overlay layer with low opacity for the first light

> **Important note**
>
> Notice the **Overlay** layer's reduced opacity in *Figure 9.45*. Blending modes often create intense results, so tweaking the opacity can help you achieve the desired result.

The image is still dark overall, but let's not worry about it now—we'll increase its brightness later. It's good to start in a controlled environment with a limited value range. Next, let's place the cyan lights. For those, we'll use a **Hard light** layer:

Figure 9.46 – We add a Hard light layer with low opacity for the second light

You might wonder why we're using **Hard light** for the cyan instead of using **Overlay**, as we did for the pink light. There's no particular reason; I tried a few different blending modes and liked **Hard light** the most in this case. You'll frequently experiment with blending modes to find the one you need in each case. In the following figure, you can see how those layers look in full opacity and the **Normal** mode (left), and compare it to the blending mode effects (right):

Figure 9.47 – A comparison between the colors in Normal mode (left) and other blending modes (right)

Next, using the layer mask in the light layers (**pink light** and **cyan light**), we start blending and softening the edges. After that, we can add another **Multiply** layer for darker shadows on a layer named **second shading**:

Figure 9.48 – We add another Multiply layer with low opacity for darker shadows

This secondary shadow layer is essential to add depth to your image. There are multiple types of shadows, and it's useful to create one layer for each of them. For your shadows and highlight layers, remember to change the hue as well – do not just pick the object's color and place it on a **Multiply** layer. Changing the hue is crucial to add depth and life to your painting.

The painting is coming along now, so we can start adding details. After duplicating and merging the current layers to make the rendering process easier, we can create new layers for fine-tuning the light and shadow system. In the following figure, you can see four new layers:

Figure 9.49 – We add more layers with different blending modes to fine-tune the lights and shadows

These are the new layers, in order from top to bottom:

- **glow** (**Glow dodge**): A soft glow around her, using pink for the pink light, and cyan for the cyan light.

- **highlight** (**Screen**): Small areas of strong light, such as the thin, bright streaks of hair.

- **shadows** (**Multiply**): Creating even deeper darks, you can now see more occlusion shadows.

- **sub-surface scattering** (**Overlay**): A soft layer to represent the sub-surface scattering phenomenon that appears when skin is lit.

- **merged** (**Normal**): All the previous layers were duplicated and merged into this one to make it easier. The fewer layers we have, the easier it is to work.

The reason why the **glow** layer is not clipped to the **merged** layer is that we want some of this glow to spill outside of the character's edges. In the following figure, you can see how the image looked without these four new layers (left) and how it looks with them (right):

Figure 9.50 – A comparison between before the new layers (left) and after them (right)

To wrap this up, we'll once again duplicate and merge those layers, then continue rendering. We create a few more layers for light effects:

Figure 9.51 – We add more layers to wrap up the image

These are the new layers, in order from top to bottom:

- **particles (Add (Glow))**: Some flowing particles make the image more dynamic, and when we set it to **Add (Glow)**, it also becomes more magical.

- **Tone Curve (Normal)**: A Correction Layer to fix brightness and contrast. We'll cover Correction Layers in *Chapter 12, Enhancing Your Art with Post-Processing Adjustments*.

- **light (Normal)**: A soft glow from the sides, outside the character, to indicate the light sources. We can leave it at **Normal** because it already looks good – you don't need to change the blending mode if it works the way it is.

- **eyebrow (Multiply)**: Her eyebrow was too light before, so this layer makes it darker. As you can see, the **Multiply** layer can also be used for small adjustments.

- **blue glow (Color dodge)**: The blue light was too weak before. With the new **Color dodge** layer, it becomes brighter.

- **merged (Normal)**: All the previous layers were duplicated and merged into this one to make it easier. The fewer layers we have, the easier it is to work.

- **bg shading (Multiply)**: A soft shading for the background, near the wooden frame.

- **background (Normal)**: The background is below all other layers.

With this real painting demonstration, you now have a clear idea of how to incorporate blending modes into your workflow effectively. These tools will not only help you speed up your process but also bring your art to new heights.

Summary

In this chapter, we've explored the incredible potential of layer blending modes, focusing on how to use them to enhance your digital paintings. Starting with an overview, you understood the principles of each type of blending mode and the transformative effects that can be achieved by layering colors and tones.

You then learned specific techniques for enhancing shadows with blending modes that darken values, such as **Multiply**, **Darken**, and **Color burn**. These modes help create realistic shadows, add depth, and adjust values precisely. Moving into lighter values, you discovered how to use modes such as **Screen**, **Add**, and **Glow dodge**, which effectively add illumination and soft light effects.

Then, you learned about blending modes that modify contrast, hue, saturation, and color, including modes such as **Overlay**, **Soft light**, and **Hue**. This section provided essential tools for adjusting and refining color dynamics, contrast, and overall vibrancy in your artwork. Finally, practical applications were discussed in a real painting context, with tips on choosing modes, setting opacity, and blending for a polished final piece. By experimenting with these modes, you now have the tools to create more dynamic and visually engaging artwork.

The practical applications you've gained will allow you to make more informed choices about which blending modes to use and when to use them. Whether subtly refining an image or making bold, dramatic changes, the skills you've developed in this chapter will be a valuable asset in your artistic toolkit.

In the next chapter, we'll move on to perfecting your selections, where you'll learn how to make precise selections to further refine and control your artwork.

Get This Book's PDF Version and Exclusive Extras

UNLOCK NOW

Scan the QR code (or go to packtpub.com/unlock). Search for this book by name, confirm the edition, and then follow the steps on the page.

Note: Keep your invoice handly. Purchase made directly from packt don't require one.

10

Perfecting Your Selections

Selections are one of the most versatile and powerful tools in **Clip Studio Paint** (**CSP**). When used effectively, they can drastically improve your workflow, allowing you to work with greater precision and speed. Throughout this chapter, you'll learn the practical skills needed to create selections like a pro. You'll discover how to create, modify, and refine selections using various methods, from the standard **Selection area** tool to advanced techniques such as Quick Masks and Selection Layers.

In this chapter, we're going to cover the following topics:

- Using the Selection area tool like a pro
- Mastering the Auto select tool
- Using Quick Masks and Selection Layers
- Optimizing your use of the selection tools

By mastering these skills, you'll be able to work more efficiently, adjusting specific areas, painting within defined boundaries, and manipulating parts of an image. These techniques will give you the confidence to make quick adjustments and improve your overall productivity. With selections becoming second nature, your creative possibilities will expand significantly.

Using the Selection area tool like a pro

The **Selection area** tool allows you to create selections in predefined shapes or paint selection areas as you would with a brush. In this section, we'll dive into its different sub tools, such as **Rectangle**, **Ellipse**, **Lasso**, and **Polyline**, and show you how to use them to make your selection process faster and more intuitive. By the end of the following subsections, you'll be able to easily create and manipulate selections, enabling you to save time and paint more precisely.

To use the **Selection area** tool, navigate to the **Tool** palette and click on the **Selection area** icon. A list of sub tools will become available in the **Sub Tool** palette:

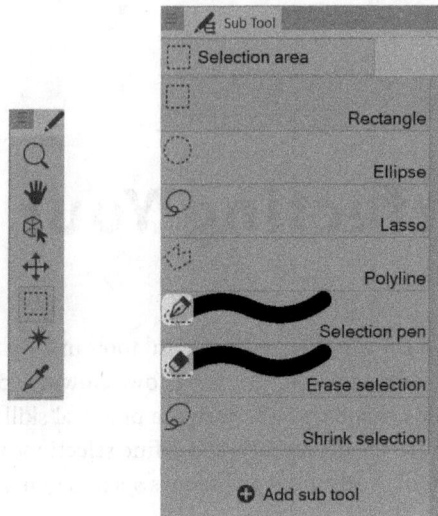

Figure 10.1 – The Selection area tool icon (left) and its sub tools (right)

We'll start by covering the **Rectangle** and the **Ellipse** sub tools, which let you create selections with predefined shapes.

The Rectangle and Ellipse sub tools

The **Rectangle** sub tool lets you create rectangular selections by dragging diagonally across the canvas, while the **Ellipse** sub tool enables you to create elliptical selections in the same way.

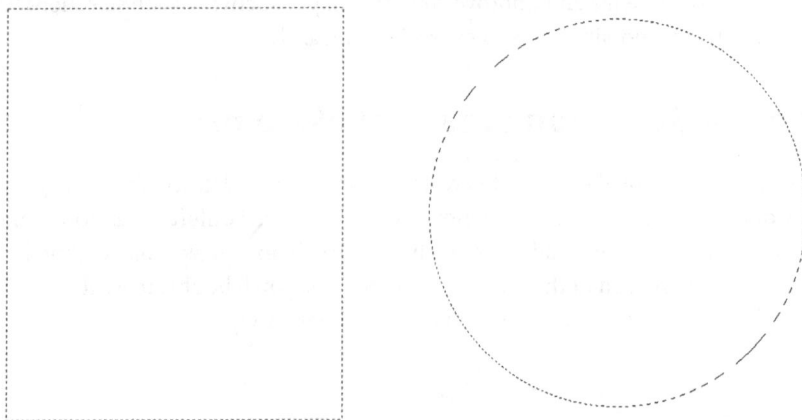

Figure 10.2 – Example of Rectangle selection (left) and Ellipse selection (right)

The **Tool Property** palette shows the following settings for the **Rectangle** and **Ellipse** sub tools:

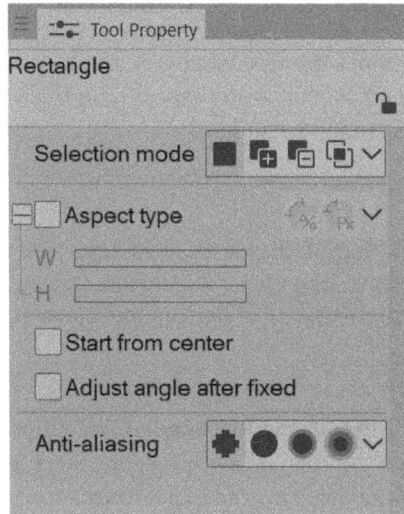

Figure 10.3 – The Tool Property palette for the Rectangle sub tool

These are the settings you can adjust in the **Tool Property** palette:

- **Selection mode**: Determines how new selections interact with existing ones. There are four options:

  - **New selection**: Allows you to create a new selection on your canvas. When this mode is active, your new selection will override the existing one. This setting is typically used when you want to start a new selection from scratch without any interference from previous selections.

  - **Add to selection**: Allows you to extend your current selection by adding new areas. Instead of replacing your previous selection, this setting lets you create additional selections that merge with the current one, expanding the selected area.

    - A modifier key activates this mode; holding the *Shift* key while using your selection tool will enable it temporarily.

  - **Remove from selection**: Enables you to subtract from an existing selection. This is useful when you want to refine your current selection by excluding specific areas, effectively removing parts of the selection that you no longer need.

    - A modifier key activates this mode; holding the *Alt/Option* key while using your selection tool will activate this mode temporarily.

  - **Select from selection**: Helps you refine your selection by choosing only the overlapping area between an existing selection and a new one. This option is ideal when you need to narrow down your selection to specific, intersecting regions.

- A modifier key activates this mode; holding the *Shift + Alt/Option* keys while using your selection tool will activate this mode temporarily.

- **Aspect type**: Determines the aspect between the shape's horizontal and vertical sides. You can leave it toggled off to choose the aspect ratio freely and toggle it on when you have a predetermined aspect ratio to maintain.

> **Important note**
>
> Even when **Aspect type** is toggled off, you can hold down *Shift* while dragging to create perfectly square or circular selections. If you press *Shift* before starting the selection, it will toggle **Add to selection** on. If you press *Shift* after starting the selection, it will turn the selection into a perfect square/circle.

- **Start from center**: By default, the **Rectangular** and **Ellipse** selections start from a corner, not the shape's center. You can change this by toggling **Start from center** on. Then, your pen click will set the center of the shape instead of its corner.

- **Adjust angle after fixed**: Lets you rotate the figure once its size is fixed.

- **Anti-aliasing**: Smoothens out jagged edges in your lines and borders, resulting in smoother, more refined outlines.

Additional settings, such as **Number of corners** and **Roundness of corner** of the selection, can be accessed through the **Sub Tool Detail** palette. These settings are the same as the ones on the **Figure ruler** tool, explained in *Chapter 7, Utilizing Rulers and Guides for Precision*. You can also apply correction to the **Rectangle** and **Ellipse** selections. Go to **Sub Tool Detail | Correction**, and two options appear:

- **Enable snapping**: When toggled on, the selection will snap to rulers. However, even if it's on, the **Rectangle** and **Ellipse** selections only snap to **Guides**, **Symmetrical rulers**, and **Perspective rulers**.

- **Snap to inner border**: When toggled on, the selection will snap to the inner border specified in the comic settings.

Having understood the **Rectangle** and **Ellipse** sub tools, we can now proceed to the **Lasso** sub tool, which lets you make freehanded selections.

The Lasso sub tool

The **Lasso** sub tool is one of the most versatile and frequently used selection tools in digital art. It allows you to create freeform selections by drawing directly on the canvas, giving you complete control over the shape and size of the selection. Its flexibility makes it ideal for selecting irregular or non-geometric areas of your artwork. Understanding how it works, the settings you can adjust, and practical use cases can significantly enhance your workflow.

To create a selection with the **Lasso** sub tool, click and drag to outline the area you want to select. Once you release your stylus, the tool automatically closes the selection, connecting the start and end points. Because you're drawing the selection manually, you can create any shape you need—perfect for organic forms such as characters, intricate details, or areas that don't conform to standard shapes:

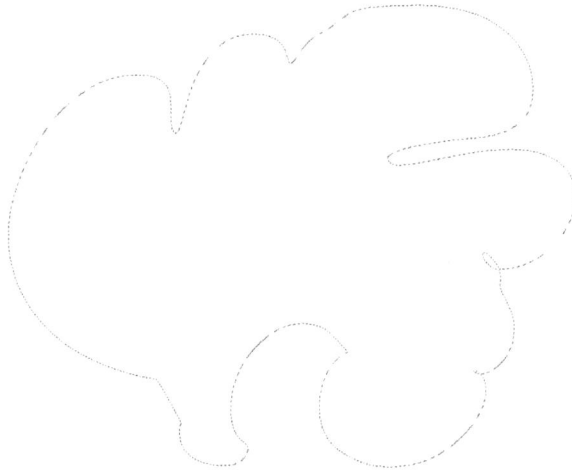

Figure 10.4 – Example of a selection with the Lasso sub tool

You can combine freehand and polyline selections using the same tool. To do this, follow the next steps:

1. Open the **Sub Tool Detail** palette.

2. Go to **Lasso | Lasso selection mode**.

    I.   The default mode is **Single stroke**, which is when you must drag your stylus to create a selection and it's all freehanded.

3. Select **Multiple input**. With this setting enabled, clicking will create straight lines (polyline), while dragging will let you draw freehand. This is especially useful when you need to create a shape that mixes precise, straight edges with more natural, flowing lines.

The various settings available in the **Tool Property** and **Sub Tool Detail** palettes amplify the **Lasso** sub tool's power. These settings allow you to fine-tune how this sub tool behaves. Most of its settings are the same as those of the **Rectangle** sub tool, which we covered in the previous section, *The Rectangle and Ellipse sub tools*. However, one often-overlooked setting in the **Sub Tool Detail** palette can significantly improve your workflow: the **Stabilization** feature.

You can apply **Stabilization** to the **Lasso** sub tool like you would to a brush. This way, your selection can become smoother, helping you create the precise selection you envision. I set my **Stabilization** value at 6, but you can choose any number from 0 to 100. For details on **Stabilization**, refer to *Chapter 5, Unlocking the Full Potential of Brush Settings*.

The **Lasso** sub tool offers a fast and intuitive way to make custom selections, giving you full control over the shapes and areas you want to isolate. However, when you want a little extra help from the software, the **Magnetic lasso** sub tool can be a better option. Let's take a look at how it works and when to use it.

The Magnetic lasso sub tool

A new sub tool was introduced in version 4.0: the **Magnetic lasso** sub tool. It is a handy function that will significantly speed up your selection process. The **Magnetic lasso** sub tool works by snapping the selection to similar pixels on the same layer or on a reference layer. That way, even if your selection is imprecise, the software will snap it to neighboring edges and correct it for you. You can see it in action next.

Figure 10.5 – Example of the Magnetic lasso sub tool in action

In *Figure 10.5*, the green overlay (right) represents the selection created with the **Magnetic lasso** sub tool, while the orange line (left) represents where my stylus actually touched. This tool can speed up your process considerably, as you won't need to worry about being too precise with your selections.

You can determine settings such as **Strength** for the **Magnetic lasso** sub tool as you would do with an automatic selection: the higher the **Strength** value, the more distance the **Magnetic lasso** sub tool will *jump* to touch painted areas.

> **Important note**
> The **Magnetic lasso** sub tool detects the edges of colored pixels against transparent areas. It currently does not distinguish between different colors—it only recognizes the boundary between opaque and transparent regions.

You can turn the **Magnetic lasso** sub tool on and off by going to **Sub Tool Detail** | **Lasso** | **Magnetic lasso** or choose it as a separate sub tool in the **Sub Tool** palette.

Now that you know how to use the **Magnetic lasso** sub tool, let's proceed to the **Polyline** sub tool, which creates straight-edged selections.

The Polyline sub tool

The **Polyline** sub tool creates precise, straight-edged selections by connecting multiple line segments. This tool is particularly useful for selecting areas with angular shapes or where straight lines are needed. Instead of drawing freehand, like with the **Lasso** tool, you click to place points on the canvas, and the tool automatically draws straight lines between these points:

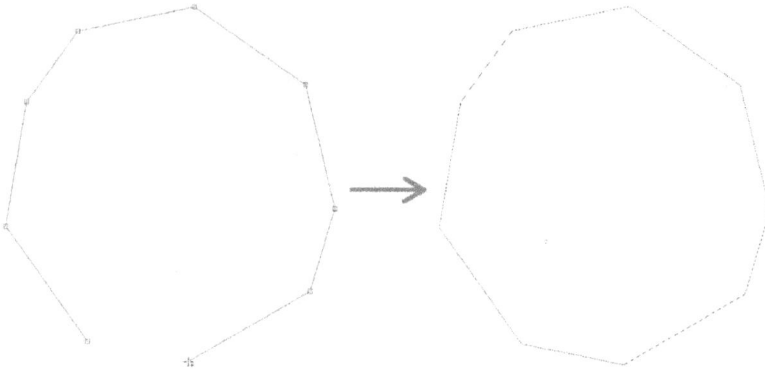

Figure 10.6 – Creating a polyline selection

To use the **Polyline** sub tool, click on the canvas to create the first point, then continue clicking to add additional points. Each click forms a corner, and the tool will draw straight lines between these corners. Pressing *Delete* removes the last corner point while pressing *Esc* cancels the entire selection. Once you're satisfied with the shape, double-tap, click on the first point, or press *Enter* to close the selection.

Additional settings for the **Polyline** sub tool can be adjusted in the **Sub Tool Detail** palette. Most of the settings have already been covered earlier in this chapter, in the *The Rectangle and Ellipse sub tools* section. There are, however, a few settings specific to the **Polyline** sub tool. To find them, go to **Sub Tool Detail | Continuous curve**. The following options will appear:

- **Curve**: This setting controls the behavior of the line segments between points in the polyline selection. With this option, you can choose whether the lines connecting each point should be straight or curved. The default setting is **Straight line**. These **Curve** options work like the ones we covered in *Chapter 7, Utilizing Rulers and Guides for Precision*, in *The Curve ruler* section.

- **How to specify**: Available when the **Curve** method is set to **Cubic Bezier**. This setting determines how to specify control points - **By drag** or **By click**.

- **Show line preview**: Toggling this on shows a preview of the line path as you add each control point. This setting is available when **How to specify** is set to **By drag**.

- **Snap angle**: Snaps the angle of the line segments to specified increments, such as 45° or 90°, when placing control points. You can set any angle value between 1° and 180°.

- **Add/delete control points while drawing**: Allows you to add or remove control points as you create the polyline selection. You can add new points by clicking and remove the last point placed by pressing the *Delete* key. This setting is toggled on by default.

With the **Polyline** sub tool under your belt, let's learn about the **Selection pen** and the **Erase selection** sub tools.

The Selection pen and the Erase selection sub tools

The **Selection pen** and **Erase selection** sub tools are essential for making precise and flexible selections in your artwork. These tools allow you to add or remove parts of a selection by painting directly on the canvas, like using a brush. Their greatest advantage lies in their ability to give artists freehand control over the selection area. They are ideal for detailed and complex selections that would be difficult to achieve with geometric shapes or point-based tools.

The **Selection pen** sub tool works much like a regular brush, but instead of painting color, it paints a selection. When you draw on the canvas with the **Selection pen** sub tool, the areas you cover become part of the active selection. This freehand approach gives you total control over which parts of the canvas you want to include in your selection.

The **Erase selection** sub tool works in the opposite way of the **Selection pen** sub tool. Instead of adding to a selection, this tool erases parts of an active selection, giving you the flexibility to refine the selection. It's like using an eraser to delete unwanted parts of a drawing:

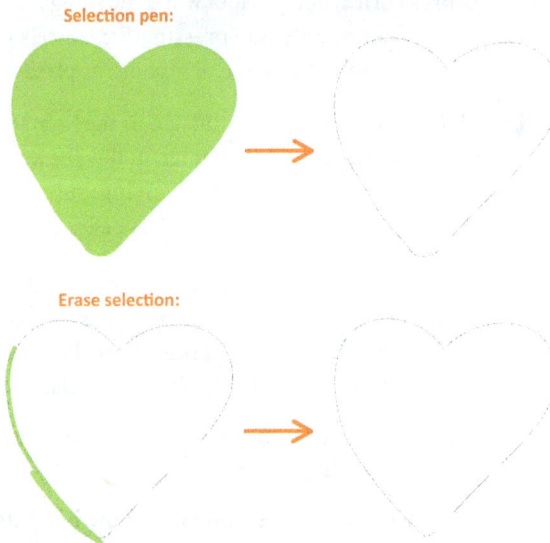

Figure 10.7 – The Selection pen and Erase selection sub tools in practice

Several settings can be adjusted for both sub tools in the **Tool Property** and **Sub Tool Detail** palettes, giving you control over how the sub tools behave. These settings include **Brush Size**, **Brush shape**, **Spraying effect**, and even dual brush. All of these settings are also available for regular brushes. For details, refer to *Chapter 5, Unlocking the Full Potential of Brush Settings*.

One practical way to use these sub tools is by selecting a character's hair. Using the **Selection pen** sub tool, you can trace around the complex, flowing shapes of the hair strands. If you over-select certain areas, you can switch to the **Erase selection** tool to remove the excess, refining the selection without starting over. Adjusting the brush shape, hardness, and opacity of both tools lets you create crisp edges or soft transitions, depending on the effect you want to achieve.

Having covered the **Selection pen** and **Erase selection** sub tools, we'll now focus on the last sub tool inside the **Selection area** tool: **Shrink selection**.

The Shrink selection sub tool

The **Shrink selection** sub tool works by targeting the empty space around a closed shape and creating a selection based on that negative space. Once a selection is created, it shrinks inward toward the edges of the closed area, effectively selecting the entire closed shape in one swift action:

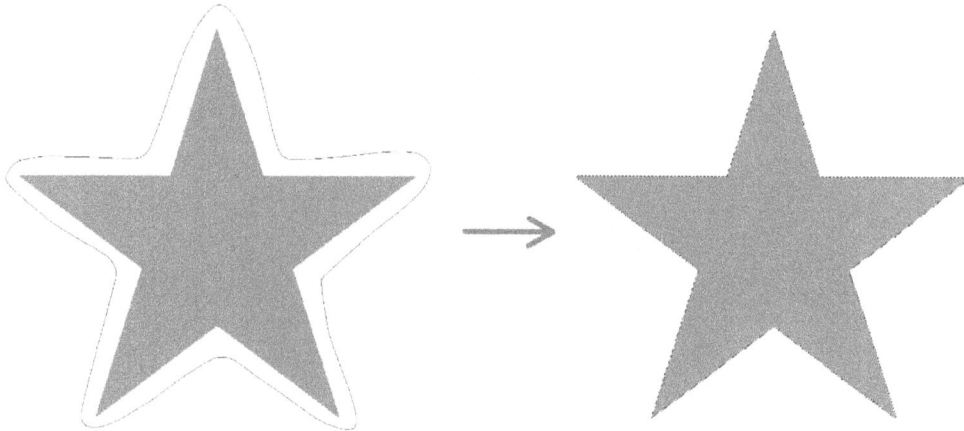

Figure 10.8 – How Shrink selection works

This sub tool is great for quickly selecting complex shapes. It works best when there are transparent, white, or black pixels surrounding the shape you want to select; it does not work in an image where all layers are merged.

Using the **Selection area** tool is the first step in building a strong foundation for your selection skills, and with this, we've covered all of its sub tools. By practicing with it, you'll find that selecting areas on your canvas becomes second nature, making your workflow more fluid and efficient.

Now that you're comfortable with creating precise selections, let's move on to the next essential tool: the **Auto select** tool, which will help you make even more efficient selections.

Mastering the Auto select tool

The **Auto select** tool, often called the magic wand, is an essential tool in CSP that allows you to select areas of your canvas based on color or tone similarity. It's an indispensable tool for tasks such as selecting flat colors, cleaning up line work, or adjusting specific parts of an image. This section will explore how to customize its settings and maximize its potential to make your creative process faster and more accurate.

By clicking on a section of your artwork, the tool selects all neighboring pixels that share similar colors, as you can see in *Figure 10.9*. This makes it especially useful for quickly and efficiently isolating large areas or specific color blocks.

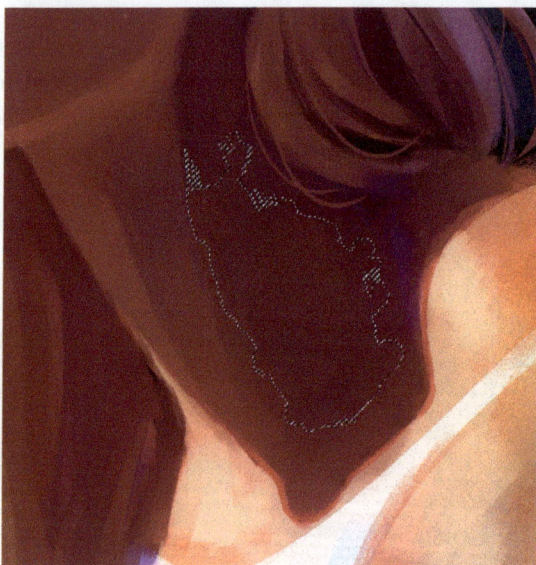

Figure 10.9 – Auto select in action

In the **Tool Property** palette, you'll find a few settings to customize the **Auto select** tool:

- **Apply to connected pixels only**: When this option is enabled, the tool will only select neighboring pixels. When it is disabled, the tool will select all matching pixels across the entire canvas, even if they are not touching.

Figure 10.10 – Apply to connected pixels only on (left) and off (right)

This mode is useful when you want to select only one specific area of a particular color without affecting other parts of your image. On the other hand, disabling it allows you to select all instances of the color, regardless of their position on the canvas, which is great when you wish to quickly modify a color throughout the canvas.

- **Close gap**: Helps prevent the tool from selecting through small gaps in your artwork, allowing the selection to stop at line work or barriers that might not be perfectly closed. This setting is especially useful when working with hand-drawn art where gaps may exist in your line work. You can adjust the gap closure threshold to select within shapes with incomplete boundaries without the selection leaking through the gaps.

- **Tolerance**: Determines how closely the colors need to match for them to be selected. A low tolerance value restricts the selection to only very similar colors, while a high value broadens the selection to include a wider range of shades.

Figure 10.11 – Auto select with Tolerance set to 4 (left) and 16 (right)

This is particularly useful when dealing with gradients or images with slight color variations. For instance, if you're selecting flat colors for shading, a lower tolerance ensures precision, while a higher tolerance can be used to select larger areas of similar colors for adjustments.

- **Area scaling**: Adds a margin around your selection. This can be useful when you need to extend the selection slightly beyond the color boundaries. Adding a margin ensures there are no unselected gaps or visible lines between your selection and adjacent colors, which can happen when pixel boundaries aren't perfectly aligned. You can see an example of **Area scaling** in *Figure 10.12*.

Figure 10.12 – Area scaling set to 1 (left) and 15 (right)

When **Area** scaling is toggled on, you can set a **Scaling** mode. These are the **Scaling** mode options:

- **Rectangle**: Enlarges or reduces the selection area by placing a rectangular boundary around each pixel along the edge of the selection. This often results in a rectangular outline when the area is adjusted.

- **Round**: Enlarges or reduces the selection by placing a circular boundary around each pixel along the edge, creating a rounded outline as the corners of the area are smoothed.

- **To Darkest Pixel**: Expands the selection by identifying the darkest color (or the area with the highest opacity) and extending the selection boundary to reach that point.

- **Refer multiple**: Allows the **Auto select** tool to reference colors from various layers, not just the current one. It can be set to refer to **All layers**, **Reference layer**, **Selected layer**, or **Layer in folder**. This is useful in multilayered compositions. For example, when you're selecting areas of color on a flat color layer but want to ensure the selection respects the lines on a line art layer above, you can enable this option to make the selection tool refer to both layers.

- **Fill up to vector path**: When using a vector layer for your line art and setting it as a reference layer, the **Auto select** tool disregards the pixels of the line art and instead fills up to the vector path, ensuring more precise fills along the actual vector outline:

Figure 10.13 – Fill up to vector path off (left) and on (right)

- **Anti-aliasing**: Smooths the edges of the selection, preventing pixelation or jagged edges.

With a deep understanding of the **Auto select** tool, you can make faster and more precise selections, saving valuable time during your painting sessions. Now, it's time to dive deeper into Quick Masks and Selection Layers, which offer even more control and flexibility in refining your selections.

Using Quick Masks and Selection Layers

Quick Masks and Selection Layers are powerful tools that allow you to refine your selections in ways that aren't possible with standard selection tools. Quick Masks let you paint selections with incredible accuracy, while Selection Layers provide a non-destructive way to save and modify selections at any point in your project. In this section, we'll explore how to use these tools to create highly detailed selections that can be easily adjusted whenever you need them.

These tools share many similarities but have one crucial difference: Quick Masks are designed to be temporary, while Selection Layers are permanent. With that in mind, let's cover how to use these tools, starting with the **Quick Mask** feature.

Quick Mask

Quick Mask is a feature that allows you to create and edit selections with a mask layer. When activated, it overlays a mask on your canvas, showing the selected area as a semi-transparent red, and the unselected area remains untouched. A red overlay appears on top of all other layers, regardless of its position in the **Layer** palette. You can paint on this mask to modify the selection directly. *Figure 10.14* shows an example of a **Quick Mask** overlay and its corresponding selection.

Figure 10.14 – A Quick Mask and its resulting selection

To create a Quick Mask, follow these steps:

1. Navigate to the **Select** menu and click on **Quick Mask**.

2. A **Quick Mask** layer will appear on the **Layer** palette:

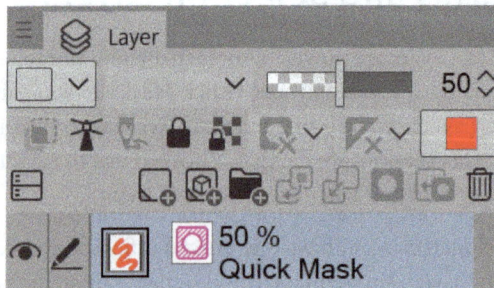

Figure 10.15 – A Quick Mask on the Layer palette

You can choose the color of the mask overlay by clicking the **Change layer color** icon on the **Layer** palette.

3. Draw on the canvas with a drawing tool such as the **Brush** tool. Your brush strokes will be registered on the overlay layer. You can use whichever drawing sub tool you want, making it even more customizable.

4. When you're satisfied with the result, navigate to the **Select** menu and click on **Quick Mask** again. This will create a selection area based on what you drew in the Quick Mask, and the **Quick Mask** layer will disappear.

5. If you do not wish to remove the Quick Mask but still want to create a selection of it, click on the square icon next to the **Layer** thumbnail, and a selection will be created without deleting the **Quick Mask** layer. You can turn the Quick Mask visibility off by clicking the eye icon in the **Layer** palette. You can still create a selection from it, even while it is invisible.

> **Important note**
>
> You can only have one Quick Mask at a time. For multiple Selection Layers, refer to the next section, *Selection Layer*.

Quick Masks are ideal for detailed adjustments of complex selections where traditional selection tools might fall short. Use the **Quick Mask** feature to create irregular or intricate selections that require a more nuanced approach.

Now that we've covered Quick Masks, let's go over Selection Layers, which are designed to be permanent.

Selection Layer

A **Selection Layer** is dedicated to storing and managing selections. This layer retains the shape and position of the selection, allowing easy modifications and applications. When you create a selection, you can save it as a Selection Layer by following these steps:

1. Create your selection with the **Selection area** tool, the **Auto select** tool, or a **Quick Mask**.

2. Go to **Select | Convert to Selection Layer**.

3. Your selection will be converted into a Selection Layer with a green overlay visible above all other layers:

Figure 10.16 – A selection (top) converted to a Selection Layer (bottom)

4. To change the overlay color, click the **Change layer color** icon on the right side of the **Layer** palette:

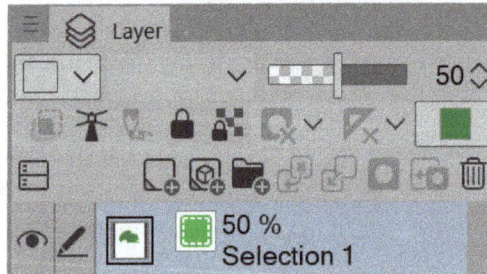

Figure 10.17 – A Selection Layer on the Layer palette

5. If you click on the green icon next to the **Layer** thumbnail, a selection will be created from the Selection Layer.

6. You can modify the layer freely, as with a Quick Mask. Choose a drawing tool and draw and erase as you wish.

7. You can turn the Selection Layer's visibility off by clicking on the eye icon in the **Layer** palette. You can still create a selection from it, even while it is invisible.

> **Important note**
>
> Use Selection Layers to save and switch between multiple selections within a single project. They can help you manage complex selections that must be revisited or adjusted numerous times. I use Selection Layers frequently in my workflow: I create selections for the character's hair, outfit, skin, and so on so that I can always refer to them to make precise adjustments.

Here is an example use of a Selection Layer. The original image is on the left side. I created a Selection Layer for the character's face (middle), and with it, the character's face can be selected anytime (right):

Figure 10.18 – Example use of a Selection Layer

Quick Masks and Selection Layers provide methods to create, modify, and manage selections. Both allow adjustments to selection boundaries and enable more refined control over specific areas of an image. However, there are some differences. A Quick Mask is more dynamic and less formal in terms of storage and later retrieval, and you cannot create multiple Quick Masks simultaneously. A Selection Layer stores selections in a more structured format and is useful for managing multiple selections and maintaining their integrity across various editing sessions.

By mastering Quick Masks and Selection Layers, you'll gain incredible control over your selections, allowing you to make complex adjustments easily. This precision will take your artwork to the next level, especially when editing specific areas of your canvas. Now that you've expanded your selection toolkit, let's focus on optimizing your use of the selection tools to further streamline your workflow and get the most out of your selection techniques.

Optimizing your use of the selection tools

Selections are one of the most versatile and powerful tools in digital art, offering endless possibilities for refining and adjusting your work with accuracy. Beyond their basic function of isolating and moving elements, selections allow you to work efficiently by controlling specific areas of your artwork. In this section, we'll explore a variety of practical and creative ways to optimize your use of selection tools, from repositioning details to fine-tuning colors and controlling edges with ease.

The first tool we'll dive into will be the **Selection Launcher**. It is a powerful feature that appears as a toolbar at the bottom of the screen once you've created a selection using any selection tool, such as the **Lasso**, **Rectangle**, or **Auto select** tool:

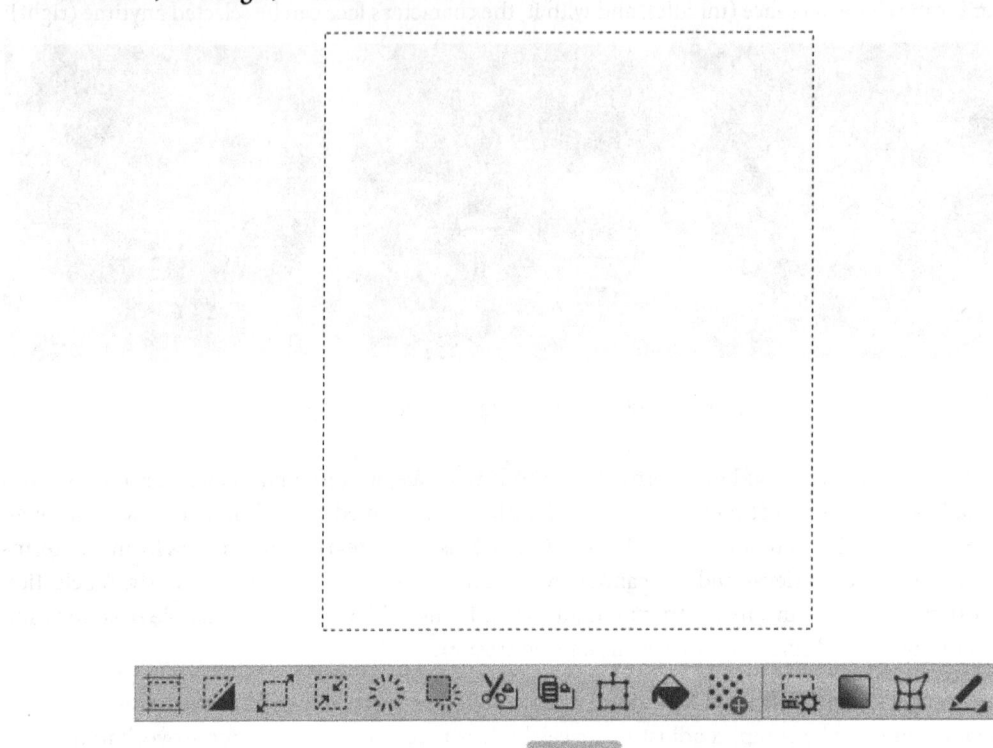

Figure 10.19 – A selection and its Selection Launcher

The **Selection Launcher** contains a range of quick-access buttons that allow you to perform immediate actions on your selection, such as expanding, contracting, or inverting the selection area. You can customize the **Selection Launcher** to show only the tools and actions you use most frequently. This is particularly helpful if you prefer a streamlined interface or want to reduce visual clutter.

To customize the **Selection Launcher**, follow these steps:

1. Go to the **View** menu and open **Selection Launcher Settings...**. A dialog box will open:

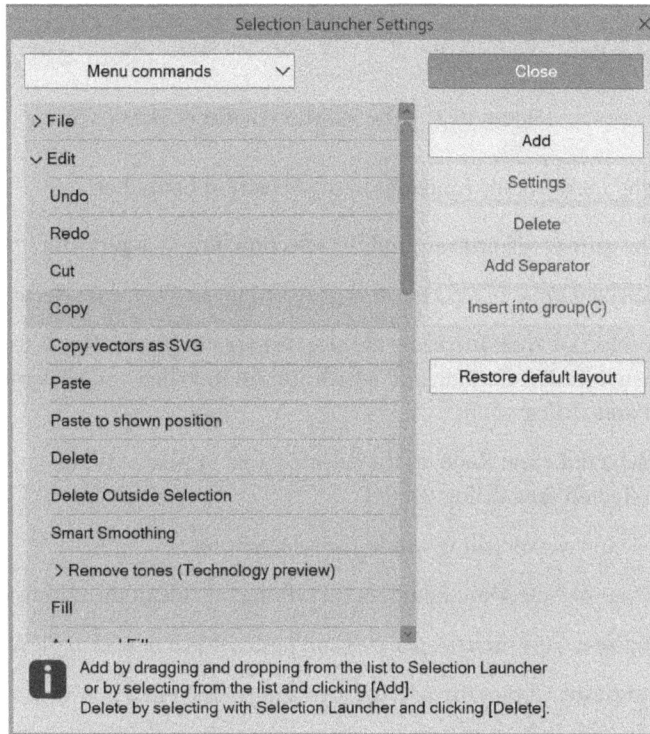

Figure 10.20 – The Selection Launcher Settings dialog

2. On the top left, choose a category. The options are **Menu commands**, **Pop-up palettes**, **Options**, **Tools**, **Auto actions**, and **Drawing color**.

    A list of functions will appear below the category you choose.

3. Click on your desired function and use the buttons on the right to add it to the **Selection Launcher**, delete it, or insert it into a group. You can also add a separator between functions.

4. You can change the settings depending on the function selected:

    *   Selecting **Menu commands**, **Pop-up palette**, **Options**, or **Auto Actions** opens the **Icon Settings** dialog.

    *   Selecting **Tools** opens the **Sub-Tool Settings** dialog.

    *   Selecting **Drawing Color** opens the **Name Settings** dialog.

5. Right-clicking the icon on the **Selection Launcher** will also let you change its settings, delete it, or add a separator.

This customization ensures that your most commonly used commands are at your fingertips when making selections, creating a more intuitive and personal workflow. I've customized my **Selection Launcher** to look as follows:

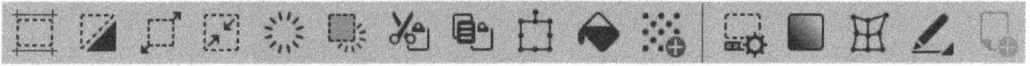

Figure 10.21 – The Selection Launcher Settings dialog

From left to right, these are the functions in my **Selection Launcher**:

- **Crop**: The canvas will crop around the selection, fitting it perfectly.

- **Invert selected area**: Inverts the area of selection, so what was selected is now deselected.

- **Expand selected area**: Increases the selected area in pixels. This is useful for avoiding white spaces between the selection and what's around it. When you click on this icon, the **Expand selected area** dialog opens.

- **Shrink selected area**: Reduces the selected area in pixels. When you click on this icon, the **Shrink selected area** dialog opens.

- **Delete**: Removes everything within the selected area.

- **Delete Outside Selection**: Removes everything outside of the selected area.

- **Cut and paste**: Cuts the selected area and pastes it in a new raster layer.

- **Copy and paste**: Copies the selected area and pastes it in a new raster layer.

- **Scale/Rotate**: Creates a transformation box around the selection, and you can scale and rotate it. When you're satisfied with the result, press **OK** or hit *Enter* on your keyboard to apply changes.

- **Fill**: Fills the selected area with your current color.

- **New Tone**: Fills the area with a tone. When you click on this icon, the **Simple tone settings** dialog opens.

- **Selection Launcher Settings**: Opens the **Selection Launcher Settings** dialog, where you can modify the functions within the **Selection Launcher**.

- **Foreground to transparent**: Selects the **Gradient** tool with the **Foreground to Transparent** sub tool.

- **Mesh Transformation**: Creates a transformation box with a grid, allowing more customization than a regular transformation box.

- **Register Image Material**: Instead of following the **Edit | Register Material(J) | Image...** steps, I can click on this icon and the **Material property** dialog opens, letting me register the image material.

- **Create New from Clipboard**: Creates a new file from the copied image. I typically make a selection, copy it by pressing *Ctrl + C*, then click on the **Create New from Clipboard** icon.

Having covered the **Selection Launcher**, we can now dive into different usages of selections that will enhance your workflow.

Practical uses of selections

There are many ways you can use selections to enhance your process. Here are some ways you can use them:

- **Moving parts of your image**: For example, if you realize that your character's eyes are misaligned, you can select one of the eyes with the **Lasso** tool and reposition it.

- **Selecting specific colors**: I organize my layers so that there's one single layer with all flat colors; then, I can select each area by color on this layer, and on another layer I shade it, paint it, and change it however I want.

- **Edge control**: When using a soft tool such as the **Airbrush** tool, it's usually hard to control edges, and leaving edges completely soft is usually not a good idea. That's why this method is excellent: you make a selection and use the Airbrush tool within it, making one side hard-edged and one side soft-edged:

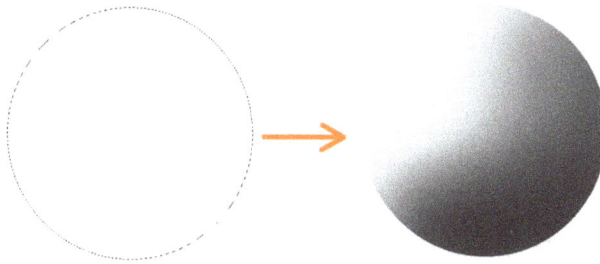

Figure 10.22 – Using a selection to control the Airbrush tool

Here is an example of this technique. On the left, there's the original image. I created a selection with the **Lasso** sub tool around her jaw (middle), airbrushed it with a lighter color, and the result is on the right:

Figure 10.23 – Example use of a selection to control the Airbrush tool

- You can also apply this method when using other types of brush, such as textured brushes. The **Lasso** sub tool will give you the necessary control for scattered and hard-to-control brushes.

- **Correcting tones**: Select specific areas with the **Lasso** sub tool or the **Auto select** tool to apply tonal correction. This way, you can correct your art precisely, ensuring it looks the way you want.

- **Outlining a layer**: When you wish to make a selection with the outlines of an entire layer, press *Ctrl/command* and click on the layer's thumbnail inside the **Layer** palette.

Mastering the various selection tools helps with basic adjustments and opens up more advanced techniques for managing color, controlling edges, and applying precise corrections. By incorporating these methods into your workflow, you'll enhance your ability to fine-tune your artwork efficiently.

Summary

In this chapter, you were given a comprehensive understanding of how to use selection tools to enhance your workflow. You learned to master the **Selection area** tool, optimize the **Auto select** tool, and work with advanced methods such as Quick Masks and Selection Layers. The techniques covered in this chapter will serve you well in many areas of your digital art practice. Incorporating these skills will allow you to work with greater precision and speed, enabling you to make accurate adjustments, save valuable time, and create more polished artworks.

Next, we'll dive into applying color quickly with pro techniques, and you'll learn how to streamline the coloring process and add depth and vibrancy to your artwork quickly and effectively.

11

Applying Color Quickly with Pro Techniques

In this chapter, we'll explore methods that allow you to add color to your artwork quickly and efficiently in **Clip Studio Paint** (**CSP**) without compromising quality. The techniques you'll learn here are invaluable for saving time and creating polished results. We'll focus on tools and processes designed to help you establish base colors quickly and experiment with color choices and shading systems, all while maintaining control over the outcome.

In this chapter, we're going to cover the following topics:

- Using the Lasso fill sub tool for quick color blocks
- Mastering the Fill tool for fast painting
- Applying Color Match and Gradient Maps for quick experimentation
- Saving color sets for quick access to frequently used colors

By the end of this chapter, you'll be equipped to confidently use tools such as the Lasso fill and Fill tools to create efficient, clean color blocks. We'll explore adjusting settings and using reference layers for maximum control with the Fill tool. You'll learn how to incorporate Color Match and Gradient Maps for rapid experimentation, opening up creative opportunities without needing to redo complex color schemes. We'll also explore how to save and use color sets for fast access to the palettes you use the most, which is especially helpful for repetitive tasks such as comic book art or animation. By mastering these time-saving techniques, you can tackle the coloring stage with confidence, efficiency, and professional-level speed.

Using the Lasso fill sub tool for quick color blocks

The **Lasso fill** sub tool is an incredibly efficient function for digital artists looking to block in large areas of color quickly. It combines the free-handed drawing flexibility of the Lasso tool with the instant color application of the Fill tool, allowing you to define and fill shapes with a single action: you create a selection, and when you close it, it fills the selection with color. You can see an example use of the Lasso Fill in the following screenshot:

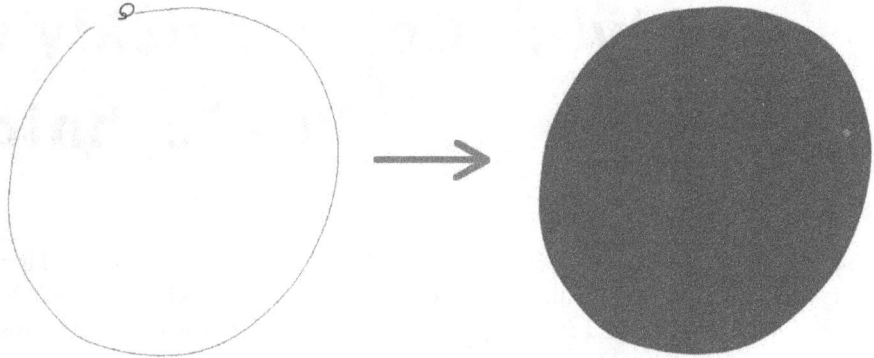

Figure 11.1 – The Lasso fill sub tool in action

This makes it particularly useful for artists who want to work quickly, either in the early stages of their artwork or when needing to fill large or irregularly shaped areas.

To use the Lasso Fill tool, select the **Figure** tool on the **Tool** palette and choose the **Lasso fill** sub tool, as shown in *Figure 11.2*:

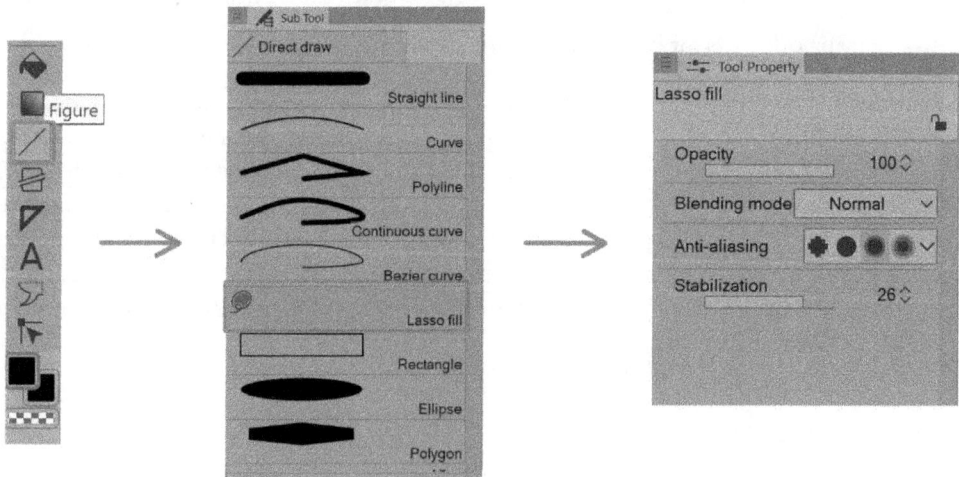

Figure 11.2 – Selecting and modifying the Lasso fill sub tool

You can change its settings in the **Tool Property** palette:

- **Opacity**: Lets you choose how opaque the final color will be. You can choose a range of values between **0** (full transparency) and **100** (full opacity).

- **Blending mode**: Allows you to change the blending mode that will be applied to the color fill. You can choose from a list of blending modes, such as the ones we covered in *Chapter 9*, *Mastering Layer Blending Modes for Stunning Colors*.

- **Anti-aliasing**: Controls how smooth the edges of your filled shape will be.

- **Stabilization**: Controls how much the lines you draw are smoothed as you create your selection. A higher stabilization value means the lines will be more stabilized, reducing hand jitter. We covered stabilization thoroughly in *Chapter 5*, *Unlocking the Full Potential of Brush Settings*.

There are several ways you can use the Lasso Fill tool. Here are some suggestions:

- *Blocking in large areas of color*: The most common use of the Lasso fill sub tool is to block color quickly during the initial stages of your work. I usually choose this sub tool to place the base colors, as well as hard-edged shadows.

- *Quick concept sketching*: When sketching concepts or rough drafts, you can use the Lasso Fill tool to add color quickly without focusing too much on precision. It allows you to focus on the overall composition and color balance of your artwork. In *Figure 11.3*, you can see two examples of concept sketches created mostly with the Lasso Fill tool:

Figure 11.3 – Examples of concept sketches with the Lasso Fill tool

- *Working with irregular shapes*: Unlike the standard Fill tool, which works well with simple shapes or enclosed areas, the Lasso Fill tool is ideal for irregular shapes, allowing you to customize the fill area manually. This is useful when coloring organic objects, abstract designs, or any subject that doesn't fit neatly into geometric shapes. For instance, in the following figure, I used Lasso fill to craft the basic fire shape (top) and then added effects on top with other tools, such as the **Airbrush**, to create the fire (bottom):

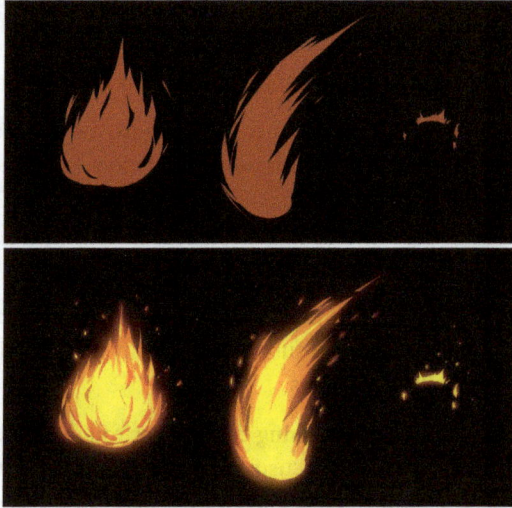

Figure 11.4 – Using the Lasso Fill tool for irregular shapes

- *Creating graphic elements*: For artists working on design elements, the Lasso fill sub tool can help you create bold, graphic shapes quickly.

- *Edge control and masking*: Lasso fill is useful for defining sharp edges when working on detailed areas. For instance, if you need to color within a sharply defined shape or object, this tool helps keep the edges clean without manually painting with a brush.

The Lasso fill sub tool is essential for any digital artist looking to speed up their workflow. Its combination of freehand selection and immediate fill makes it highly efficient for blocking in large areas of color, sketching concepts, and working with irregular shapes. As you progress in your art, experimenting with this sub tool will show you just how versatile it can be.

Next, we'll explore the **Fill** tool. You'll discover how to achieve even greater efficiency using various techniques for different artistic scenarios.

Mastering the Fill tool for fast painting

The **Fill** tool is one of the most powerful tools in CSP for quickly applying flat colors, blocking in large areas, and achieving clean, consistent fills. Mastering this tool can significantly speed up your workflow, especially when working on complex illustrations or when you need to manage multiple layers efficiently.

At its core, the Fill tool detects enclosed areas or boundaries and fills them with a chosen color. Once you select the **Fill** tool in the **Tool** palette, you can click on any enclosed area of your artwork, and the tool will fill that area with the chosen color. Click and drag to fill multiple areas:

Figure 11.5 – Click and drag with the Fill tool for multiple areas

The Fill tool has several sub tools designed for different use cases. Each one has unique functionality for specific needs, whether you're working on the current layer or referencing other layers for more complex coloring tasks. After selecting the Fill tool, go to the **Sub Tool** palette to find its sub tools:

- **Refer only to editing layer**: This is the most basic sub tool on this list. It fills areas only on the active layer you're working on, and it won't consider any information from other layers, which makes it ideal for filling regions enclosed on a single layer. When the line art is on one layer and you are coloring on a separate layer, the color will disregard the line art layer. Instead, it will only consider the colors already present on the coloring layer, as shown in the following figure:

Figure 11.6 – Refer only to editing layer disregards other layers

- **Refer other layers**: This sub tool allows the Fill tool to reference other layers when deciding where to apply the fill. For example, if your line art is on a separate layer from your colors, you can use this sub tool to fill within the boundaries of the line art, even though it's on a different layer. This is perfect for artists who work with line art and color on different layers, allowing you to quickly fill areas under the line art while keeping the layers separate. When the line art is in one layer and you are coloring on a separate layer, the Fill tool will also consider the line art layer, as shown in the next figure:

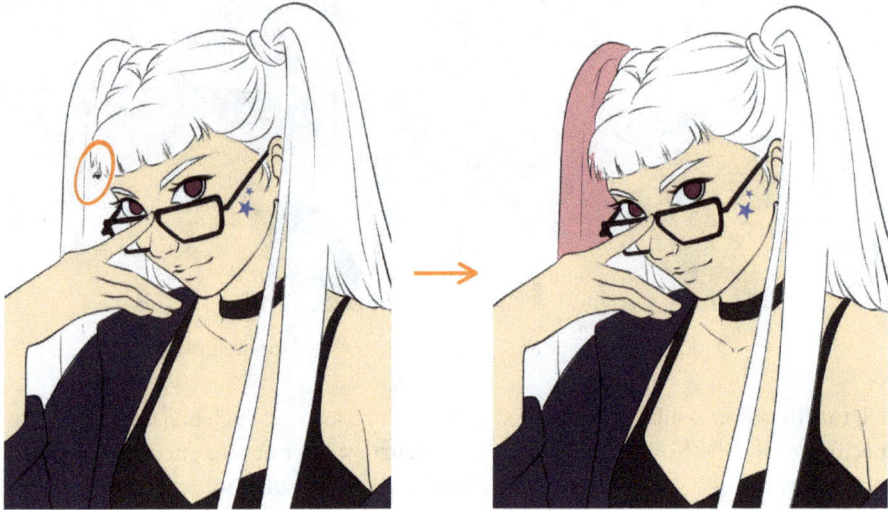

Figure 11.7 – Refer other layers considers information in other layers

- **Enclose and fill**: This sub tool allows you to draw a freeform boundary around an area, and everything inside that boundary will be filled with the chosen color, as shown in *Figure 11.8*:

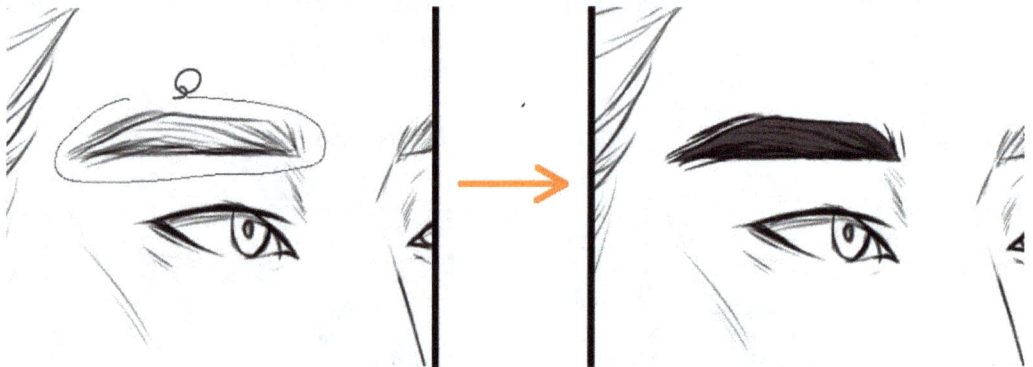

Figure 11.8 – Enclose and fill in action

This is useful when you want to block in color quickly without worrying about precision.

- **Paint unfilled area**: As the name suggests, this sub tool is used to fill any areas that haven't already been filled. It helps to cover gaps or overlooked spots where color didn't reach in earlier filling steps. When in use, it shows a green overlay over areas that will be filled. In *Figure 11.9*, you can see an ear with gaps (left), the green overlay of **Paint unfilled area** (middle), and the fixed image (right).

Figure 11.9 – Paint unfilled area in action

This sub tool is useful for cleaning up places that you might have missed in the initial coloring process, ensuring all areas are filled consistently.

The Fill tool offers a variety of settings in the **Tool Property** palette that allow you to customize its behavior. Adjusting these settings helps you tailor the tool to your specific workflow needs, whether you're filling areas within the current layer or referencing other layers. Below are its settings:

- **Apply to connected pixels only**: When enabled, this option ensures that the Fill tool will only color connected areas, meaning it won't *jump* across disconnected lines or gaps. This is perfect for coloring enclosed areas – for example, within a character's outline or without accidentally filling areas separated by line breaks. When this setting is disabled, the Fill tool will color all areas with the same color, as shown in *Figure 11.10*:

Figure 11.10 – Apply to connected pixels only toggled on (left) and off (right)

- **Close gap**: Allows you to fill areas with small gaps in their boundaries. The tool will attempt to close these gaps when applying the fill. *Figure 11.11* shows this setting toggled on (left) and off (right):

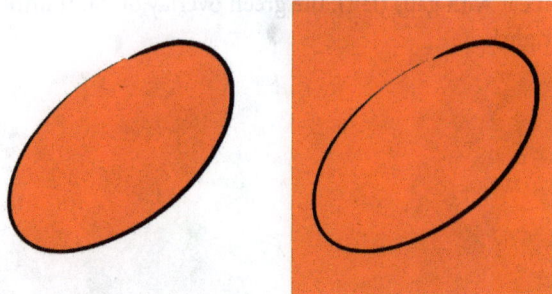

Figure 11.11 – Close gap toggled on (left) and off (right)

This setting is ideal for line art with minor breaks or unconnected lines. The higher the **Close gap** value, the larger the gap it will close.

- **Tolerance**: Controls how much variation in color the Fill tool will tolerate when deciding what to fill. A lower tolerance will only fill areas with very similar colors, while a higher tolerance will fill areas with a broader range of color values. It is useful when you want to fill areas with gradients or slightly varying colors.

- **Area scaling**: Controls how much the filled color will expand beyond the selected area's boundary. You can expand or contract the fill relative to the boundary – values above zero will expand it, and values below zero will contract it. Use this setting to extend the fill slightly beyond the lines of your artwork to prevent uncolored gaps or white fringes around the fill. Contracting the fill can help when you need to keep some edges unfilled. *Figure 11.12* shows how different **Area scaling** settings affect the Fill tool. On the left, **Area scaling** is set to **0**, while on the right, it's set to **15**:

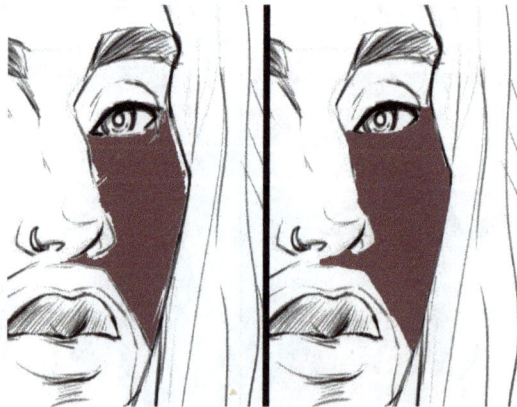

Figure 11.12 – Fill tool with Area scaling set to zero (left) and 15 (right)

- **Refer multiple**: This setting allows you to choose multiple layers the Fill tool can reference when filling. You can refer to reference layers, all layers, or specific groups of layers. It is particularly useful for complex compositions where your line art might be on one layer and your colors on another, as it ensures that the Fill tool works cohesively with all relevant layers.

> **Important note**
>
> For efficiency, I don't switch between the **Refer only to editing layer** and **Refer other layers** sub tools. Instead, I use the shortcut *G* to quickly activate **Refer only to editing layer**, and when I need to reference other layers, I toggle the **Refer multiple** option on.

- **Opacity**: This option controls the opacity of the fill. A lower opacity will make the fill more transparent, while 100% opacity makes the fill fully opaque. It is useful when you want to create semi-transparent fills, such as for shading or subtle effects.
- **Anti-aliasing**: Anti-aliasing smooths the edges of the filled area, preventing jagged or pixelated edges, especially in areas where curves or diagonals are filled.

There are several ways you can use the Fill tool. Here are some suggestions:

- *Flat coloring under line art*: When you have your line art on a separate layer, you can use the **Refer other layers** sub tool to quickly and efficiently fill areas under the line art. This speeds up the base coloring process, allowing you to apply flat colors cleanly.
- *Blocking in backgrounds*: For large, simple shapes such as backgrounds or skies, use the Fill tool to quickly block in these areas without having to rely on perfect outlines. You can easily fill it in with a single click.
- *Fixing small color gaps*: With the **Paint unfilled area** sub tool, fix small color gaps in your art to ensure a professional finish.

Mastering the Fill tool and its sub tools allows you to dramatically speed up your coloring process while maintaining precision and control. Whether you're filling large areas under line art, making color adjustments, or adding tones, the Fill tool provides flexible settings that can adapt to any stage of the painting process. Experimenting with these settings and sub tools will help you find the most efficient workflow for your artistic style.

Next, we'll delve into **Color Match** and **Gradient Maps**, powerful tools that provide even more control over your colors. These techniques will help you take your painting process to the next level, ensuring cleaner, more refined results in your artwork.

Applying Color Match and Gradient Maps for quick experimentation

Color Match (introduced in version 3.0) and **Gradient Maps** are powerful tools for quickly experimenting with color schemes and tones in digital artwork. These tools allow you to explore a wide range of color options without needing to manually repaint sections, making them incredibly useful for fine-tuning color palettes, adjusting moods, or achieving specific artistic effects. This section will show you how these tools work, what settings can be adjusted, and practical ways to use them effectively.

Let's start with Color Match, which is great for taking inspiration from other images and applying it to your own.

Color Match

The **Color Match** function analyzes colors from a reference image and applies a similar palette to your artwork. This is particularly useful for quickly harmonizing colors in a scene or matching your artwork to a particular color aesthetic or reference. You can use this tool to make subtle tweaks or completely overhaul the color palette of your artwork, giving you flexibility in color experimentation. *Figure 11.13* shows a few examples of one image (bottom) with different color schemes (top) applied to it:

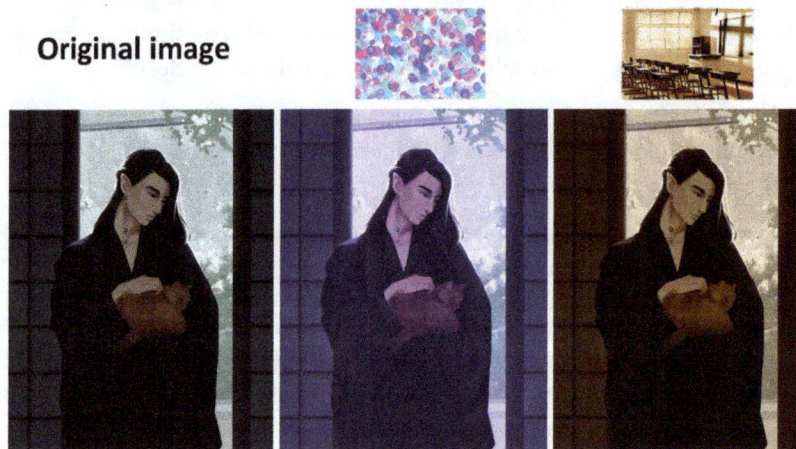

Figure 11.13 – Color Match examples

Follow these steps to apply Color Match to your artwork:

1. Navigate to the **Edit** menu.
2. Select **Tonal Correction(D) | Color Match…**.
3. The **Color Match** dialog will open, and you can specify how the effect will modify your image.

Color Match works on a single raster layer where the expression color is set to **Color**. Currently, you cannot create a Correction Layer with it. If the elements you want to correct with Color Match are spread across multiple layers, you must first merge them into a single layer. To do this, follow these steps:

1. Select the target layers you want to merge.

2. Right-click those layers and select **Duplicate Layer**. This way, you won't lose your original layers.

3. Right-click the selected layers and click on **Merge selected layers**.

4. Alternatively, go to **Layer | Merge selected layers**, or press *Shift + Alt + E*.

5. To include all visible layers, use the **Merge visible to new layer** option.

The settings available in the **Color Match** dialog change depending on whether you're referencing an image or a gradient. *Figure 11.14* shows the settings available when the source is an image:

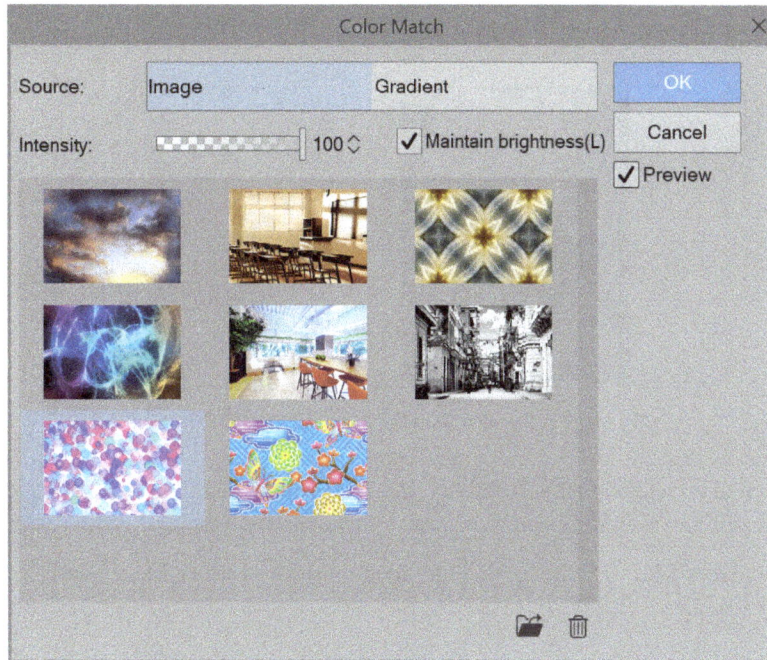

Figure 11.14 – Color Match dialog for an image source

These are the settings for an image source:

*   **Source**: You can set the color source to either **Image** or **Gradient**. **Image** matches the color scheme of the reference image to your current artwork, as shown in *Figure 11.13*. **Gradient** applies a gradient to your image, like the Gradient Map function, which we'll cover in the next sub-section, *Gradient Map*.

- **Intensity**: This slider adjusts how strongly the reference colors are applied. The default is **100**, and lowering the value decreases the reference's influence on your artwork.

- **Maintain brightness(L)**: Toggles the brightness levels of your original image on and off. When it's off, Color Match will adjust the brightness to match the reference more closely:

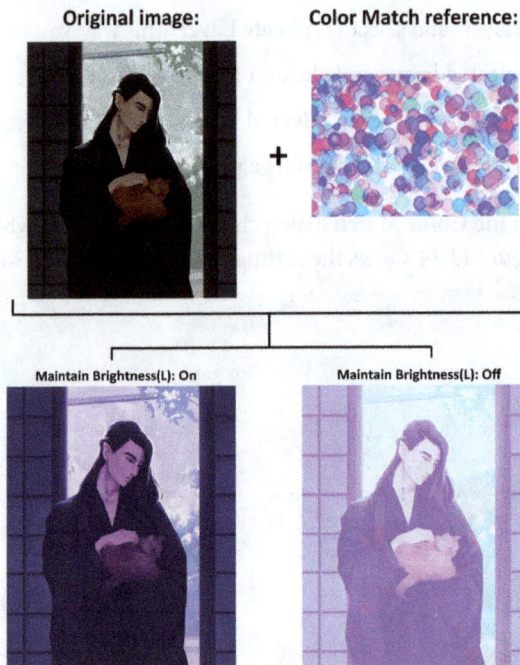

Figure 11.15 – Maintain brightness(L) toggled on and off

- **Image list**: Located below **Intensity**, it displays a thumbnail list of images you can use as a reference. Select a thumbnail to preview its color scheme on your canvas instantly.

- **Select from files**: Use the open folder icon on the bottom right to import an image file as a color reference:

  - **Import from photo library** (tablet): On tablets, you can import images directly from your device's photo gallery to use as a color reference.

  - **Import from camera** (tablet): Allows you to use your device's camera to take a photo and apply its color scheme.

- **Delete**: Use the trash can icon to the right of **Select from files** to remove any unwanted images from the thumbnail list.

- **Preview**: Enables you to see a live preview of the changes made to the layer.

When **Source** is set to **Gradient**, a new set of functions becomes available. *Figure 11.16* shows the settings available when the source is set to **Gradient**:

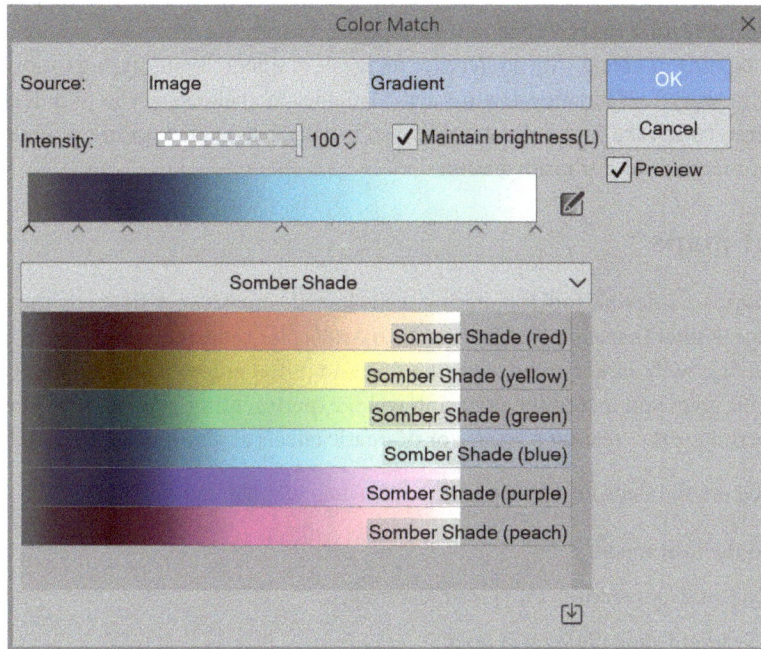

Figure 11.16 – Color Match dialog for a Gradient source

It includes **Source**, **Intensity**, **Maintain brightness(L)**, and **Preview**, like with an **Image** source. These are the exclusive settings available for **Gradient** sources:

- **Color bar**: Shows a preview of the selected gradient below **Intensity**. Tapping the color bar opens the **Gradient** dialog, where you can edit the gradient in detail.

- **Nodes**: Nodes represent each color and its transition within the gradient. They are the upward-pointing arrows at the bottom of the color bar. You can adjust the gradient by dragging nodes horizontally to change the blend, or vertically to delete them. Tap below the color bar to add new nodes.

- **Edit gradient**: The pencil icon on the right side of the color bar opens the **Edit gradient** dialog for further editing of the gradient.

- **Gradient set list**: Displays a drop-down menu of available gradient sets below the color bar. Selecting a set updates the available gradients in the list.

- **Gradient list**: This list shows all gradients within the current set under the Gradient set list. Tap once to select a gradient and apply it to the color bar.

- **Add gradient set from materials**: The icon with a down-pointing arrow at the bottom of the Color Match dialog lets you browse and add new gradient sets from your CSP materials.

The Color Match feature is a powerful tool for rapidly transforming the mood and atmosphere of your artwork by aligning its colors with a reference image or gradient. By mastering Color Match, you can speed up your workflow and elevate your art's visual impact, allowing you to quickly test different styles and moods. To take your color control even further, let's explore **gradient maps**, which offer a different approach to color transformations.

Gradient maps

Gradient maps are a flexible tool for altering the colors of your artwork based on the grayscale values in your image. Rather than simply adjusting the overall color tone, they allow you to apply a gradient over your image, with darker areas receiving one end of the gradient and lighter regions receiving the other. This gives you incredible precision when experimenting with color schemes, making it a must-use technique for creating cohesive or dramatic effects across your work.

The following are the steps for applying a gradient map to a flat image:

1. Go to the **Edit** menu.
2. Select **Tonal Correction(D) | Gradient map…**.
3. The **Gradient map** dialog will open:

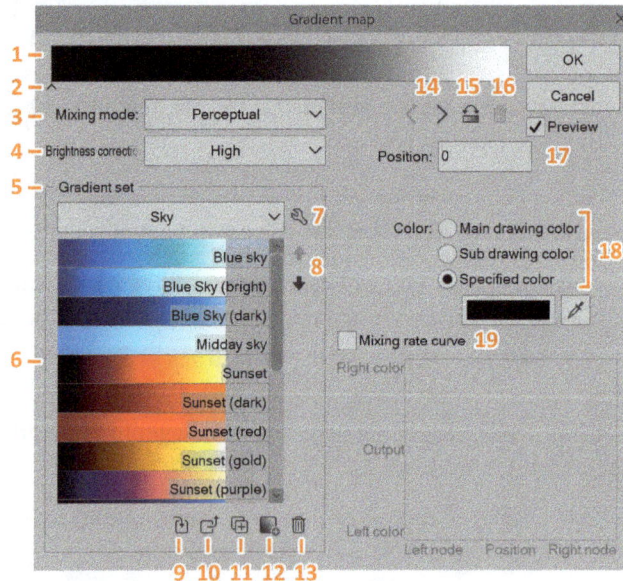

Figure 11.17 – The Gradient map dialog

Here are the settings numbered in the screenshot:

1. **Gradient bar**: A visual preview of the gradient applied to the selected layer.

2. **Node**: These upward-pointing arrows define the colors of the gradient. You can add more nodes by clicking on an empty area of the bar. To adjust, drag the nodes horizontally to change the gradient's transition. Selected nodes are highlighted in white. To delete a node, drag it vertically away from the bar.

3. **Mixing mode**: In version 2.3 or later, the **Edit Gradient** dialog provides four different mixing modes to choose from. These modes allow you to create more vivid and realistic gradients by adjusting how colors blend together.

4. **Brightness correction**: When **Perceptual** is selected as the **Mixing mode**, you can also apply **Brightness correction**, which offers five levels of brightness adjustment for the gradient color mixture, enhancing the overall look of your gradients.

5. **Gradient set**: Displays the available gradient sets for selection.

6. **Gradient list**: Displays the gradients in the current set. Tap a gradient to select it. Double click it to apply it to the color bar.

7. **Show menu**: The wrench icon on the right side opens additional gradient set options, including **Create new set**, **Delete set**, **Duplicate set**, **Change set name**, **Register set as material**, and **Import material set**.

8. **Up/Down**: The arrows on the right side of the gradient list move the selected gradient up or down in the list.

9. **Replace saved gradient**: Replaces the selected gradient with the one currently displayed on the gradient bar.

10. **Load to gradient bar**: Applies the selected gradient on the gradient bar.

11. **Duplicate selected gradient**: Creates a copy of the selected gradient.

12. **Create new gradient**: Adds the currently displayed gradient to the list.

13. **Delete selected gradient from list**: Removes the selected gradient from the list.

14. **Select left node/Select right node**: These arrow icons let you switch to the node on the left or the right of the currently selected one.

15. **Reverse Gradient**: Reverses the direction of the gradient's colors.

16. **Delete node**: The trash can icon deletes the currently selected node.

17. **Position**: Shows the position of the selected node along the gradient bar.

18. **Color**: Indicates the current color of the selected node. You can choose **Main drawing color**, **Sub drawing color**, **Specified color**, or **Pick screen color**. With **Specified color**, you can set a custom color for the node by selecting the color indicator, which opens the **Color settings** dialog. **Pick screen color** uses the eyedropper tool to pick a color directly from the screen (available only on Windows/macOS.)

19. **Mixing rate curve**: Adjust the transition between colors by modifying the curve between nodes. Its horizontal axis represents the node positions, white its vertical axis represents the color mixing ratio between the nodes. A higher value results in a color closer to the right node, while a lower value produces a color closer to the selected node. You can add up to 16 control points by clicking on the curve and dragging them to refine the transition. To delete a control point, drag it outside the graph.

Gradient Maps can only be applied to one raster layer at a time. To apply a gradient map to multiple layers, you must use a Correction Layer. Follow these steps:

1. Go to the **Layer** menu.

2. Select **New Correction Layer(J) | Gradient map…**.

3. The **Gradient map** dialog will open, and you can modify it like you did with the previous option.

There are many ways in which you can use Color Match and Gradient Maps:

- Coloring black and white paintings: If you have a grayscale painting, you can use these tools to color it. Paired with the selection tools we covered in *Chapter 10, Perfecting Your Selections*, these tools give you control over the colors of light and dark areas. In the next figure, you can see examples of coloring a black and white painting with gradient maps:

Figure 11.18 – Examples of gradient maps

- Mood shifts: If you want to change the overall mood of your artwork (e.g., from warm and sunny to cool and mysterious), you can quickly apply colors from a scene with the desired atmosphere.

- Color experimentation: If you're unsure about your piece's color scheme, you can rapidly test different palettes by applying colors from various reference images. This saves time compared to manually adjusting each section of your artwork.

- Consistent series: If you're working on multiple pieces and want to maintain a consistent color tone across all of them, you can apply these tools to ensure harmony across the series.

The Color Match and Gradient Map tools are essential for anyone looking to speed up their color workflow, whether experimenting with different tones or harmonizing the palette of a series. Now that you're familiar with these powerful color adjustment functions, let's move on to **color sets**, which allow you to efficiently organize and access frequently used colors for smoother workflows.

Saving color sets for quick access to frequently used colors

Color sets are an essential feature in CSP that allows artists to quickly access frequently used colors. Whether you're working on a large-scale project or need consistent color usage across multiple illustrations, saving color sets can significantly reduce the time spent searching for specific hues, ensuring a smooth creative process.

To save a color set, you'll need to use the **Color Set** palette, which functions like a customizable swatches palette. If you cannot find the **Color Set** palette, navigate to **Window | Color Set** and it will pop up. In *Figure 11.19*, you can see what it looks like:

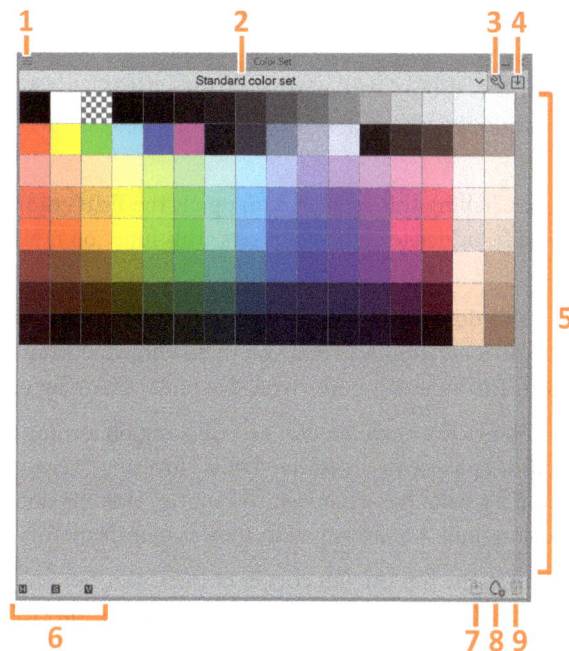

Figure 11.19 – The Color Set palette

These are the functions inside the Color Set palette:

1. **Color Set palette menu**: The three lines in the top-left corner provides options to customize your color sets. It has some unique functions:

   - **Import/Export color set…**: Lets you import color sets from your computer files, or export to your computer.

   - **Register color set as material…**: Allows you to save your color set in the Material palette for sharing or reusing later.

   - **Change color name…**: Lets you rename a color. This setting is also available when you right-click a color in the color set list.

   - **Auto-register color in eyedropper**: Automatically adds colors you pick with the eyedropper tool to your set.

   - **View(S)**: Lets you customize the size and display method of your color tiles, such as small/large sizes or list views.

   - **Show color set bar**: Toggles on and off the color set bar, which is the upper part of the **Color Set** palette and includes the **Show color set**, **Edit color sets**, and **Add color set** functions.

   - **Show command bar**: Toggles on and off the bottom row of icons in the **Color Set** palette, which includes the **RGB/HSV** values, **Replace color**, **Add color**, and **Delete color** icons.

   - **Change order**: Lets you choose to reorganize color tiles by dragging or *Ctrl/command + dragging*.

2. **Show color set**: This drop-down menu displays a list of available color sets with which you can choose to work. It is also available on the Color Set palette menu under the name **Switch color set**.

3. **Edit color sets**: Clicking this wrench icon opens the **Edit color sets** dialog, where you can add, select, modify, or delete entire color sets. This function is also available on the Color Set palette menu.

4. **Add color set** This download icon, on the right of **Edit color sets**, opens the **Add color set** dialog, letting you load color sets that you've downloaded from **CLIP STUDIO ASSETS** or created yourself. This function is also available in the Color Set palette menu.

5. **Color set list**: Shows the current color set. Clicking on a color in the list changes the color in the **Color Slider** palette to the selected one. Hovering over a color lets you see its **RGB** or **HSV** values, and if a color has a name, it will appear. Holding down *Ctrl/command* allows you to rearrange colors, and *Alt* allows you to copy a color to another tile.

6. **RGB/HSV values**: The bottom left corner of the **Color Set** palette shows the RGB or HSV values of the current color. You can switch between RGB and HSV by clicking the numbers.

7. **Replace color**: This downward-pointing arrow in the bottom right corner replaces the selected color tile with the currently active color. This function is also available in the Color Set palette menu and when you right-click a color in the Color Set list.

8. **Add color**: This waterdrop icon adds the currently selected drawing color to the color set. This function is also available in the Color Set palette menu and when you right-click a color in the Color Set list.

9. **Delete color**: The trash can icon deletes the selected color tile from the set. This function is also available in the Color Set palette menu and when you right-click a color in the Color Set list.

There are multiple settings you can adjust within the **Color Set** palette to suit your preferences. For instance, by navigating to the Color Set palette menu and clicking on **View(S)**, you can change the layout of the swatches by adjusting the number of rows and columns, ensuring the palette looks organized and is easily navigable. Another useful feature is the ability to rename individual colors within the set. This is particularly helpful for distinguishing between similar shades, making it easier to identify the exact one you need.

The colors you add to this palette are easily accessible, even across different projects. You can create a new color set by following these steps:

1. Click the **Edit color sets** wrench icon.

2. Select **Create new set**.

3. Name it accordingly. This way, you can organize colors based on themes or artworks. For example, if you're working on a series of portraits, you might create a color set dedicated to skin tones, hair colors, and eye shades.

4. Once the color set has been created, you can begin adding colors to it. Select the color you want to save using the **Color Wheel** palette or any other color palettes, and then click the **Add color** icon on the **Color Set** palette. This stores the selected color, allowing you to quickly access it without needing to pick or replicate it each time.

Practical applications of saving color sets extend beyond convenience. If you need to maintain color consistency for branding, comic series, or a series of illustrations, saving these palettes ensures that you always have the same tones in hand, preventing unwanted variations.

The **Color Set** palette also enables the import and export of color sets, making it ideal for collaborative work. If you're working with a team or switching between devices, you can save a color set as a material and share it with others or use it on a different device. This consistency ensures that everyone working on a project is using the same color palette, maintaining uniformity across all designs and illustrations.

Overall, saving color sets is an invaluable tool for CSP artists, providing quick access to colors and improving workflow and consistency across projects. By organizing and customizing your palettes, you gain better control over color consistency in your artwork and can effortlessly switch between projects without wasting time hunting for the right hues. Whether you're managing a series of illustrations, creating comics, or exploring new color palettes, this feature helps streamline the coloring process while ensuring you can quickly and easily reuse your favorite tones.

Summary

In this chapter, you've learned about a set of powerful tools and methods to help you speed up the coloring process in your digital artwork without sacrificing quality. Starting with the Lasso fill sub tool, you now understand how to create quick and precise color blocks that are ideal for laying down base colors efficiently. Next, you mastered the Fill tool, allowing you to rapidly paint large areas of your canvas with ease, using both reference layers and selections to ensure clean results.

You also learned how to apply Color Match and Gradient Maps for quick experimentation with color schemes. These tools offer a fast and effective way to explore different color harmonies and moods without having to manually repaint your work. Finally, by using color sets, you learned how to access your frequently used colors in a structured and efficient way, making it easier to maintain color consistency across projects and streamline your workflow.

These techniques combine to give you a faster, more professional approach to applying color, ensuring you can focus more on your creations. In the next chapter, *Enhancing Your Art with Post-Processing Adjustments*, we'll dive into the finishing touches that can make your artwork truly stand out.

Get This Book's PDF Version and Exclusive Extras

UNLOCK NOW

Scan the QR code (or go to `packtpub.com/unlock`). Search for this book by name, confirm the edition, and then follow the steps on the page.

Note: Keep your invoice handly. Purchase made directly from packt don't require one.

12

Enhancing Your Art with Post-Processing Adjustments

In this chapter, we'll delve into powerful techniques that can help you enhance and fine-tune your artwork in **Clip Studio Paint** (**CSP**). The techniques covered here are the same time-saving tricks used by professional artists to refine their work quickly and effectively. Whether you need to adjust colors, fix proportions, or alter the mood of your artwork, these methods will streamline your workflow and save you hours of extra work.

In this chapter, we're going to cover the following topics:

- Utilizing correction layers for final touches
- Exploring filters for creative enhancements
- Maximizing the **Liquify** and **Puppet warp** tools for quick structural changes

By the end of this chapter, you'll have learned how to use correction layers such as tone curves, levels, and color balance to add final touches to your work. You'll explore how gradient maps can transform or enhance your color palette, allowing you to tweak color harmony or completely shift the mood of your artwork with a single layer. Finally, you'll discover how to use the **Liquify** tool for quick adjustments to proportions.

These tools not only help you fix mistakes but also provide creative options to improve your final piece. They can be game-changers in your workflow, making sure your art reaches its highest potential with minimal effort. So, let's dive into post-processing magic and take your artwork to the next level with these essential tools!

Utilizing correction layers for final touches

Correction layers are an essential tool in any digital artist's workflow, providing a powerful way to fine-tune the brightness, contrast, and color balance after the initial painting stage. Whether you need to adjust the lighting to match the mood or correct subtle color imbalances, these layers give you complete control over the final look of your art. In this section, you'll explore different types of tonal correction layers, such as levels and curves, to bring out the best in your artwork. By mastering these adjustments, you can ensure that your colors are vibrant, your highlights pop, and your shadows add the right amount of depth.

Correction layers apply changes in tone, color, and values to all layers positioned below them on the layer list. They are a great way to modify multiple layers in one single step, and their non-destructive nature allows you to tweak and experiment with your adjustments freely until you achieve the perfect result. Because they affect all layers below them, if you want one or more layers to be unaffected by the tonal correction, you must change its position on the **Layer** palette. To apply tonal correction only to selected layers, do the following:

1. Go to the **Layer** palette and select the correction layer.
2. Clip the tonal correction layer to the layer or layer folder you want to affect. For details on clipping layers, refer to *Chapter 8, Maximizing Efficiency and Organization with Layers*.

Alternatively, create a folder with the layers you want to affect and place the tonal correction layer inside of it. This way, the tonal correction will only affect layers inside of the folder. After you have created a tonal correction layer, you can modify its setting by double-tapping the layer thumbnail in the **Layer** palette.

> **Important note**
> When setting up any correction layer, be sure to toggle on the **Preview** checkbox to view the effects in real time before applying them.

There are two ways in which you can determine the area where the correction layer will be applied:

- Create a selection, then create a new correction layer. The correction will only be applied within the selection.

- Another option is to erase or add areas in the correction layer's mask as you would to a regular layer mask. The layer mask is visible on the **Layer** palette, near the correction layer's thumbnail. For more details on how to operate layer masks, refer to *Chapter 8, Maximizing Efficiency and Organization with Layers*.

To see the list of correction layers available, go to the **Layer** menu | **New Correction Layer....** We will cover each of them, starting with **Brightness/Contrast**.

Brightness/Contrast

The **Brightness/Contrast** correction layer is a straightforward and effective tool for adjusting the overall lightness and contrast of an image. It allows you to modify how bright or dark the entire image appears while also controlling the contrast, which affects the difference between the dark and light areas. This adjustment layer is particularly useful when your painting looks too flat or washed out, too bright or too dark, and you want to enhance its visual depth without repainting.

When you select **Brightness/Contrast**, the following dialog appears:

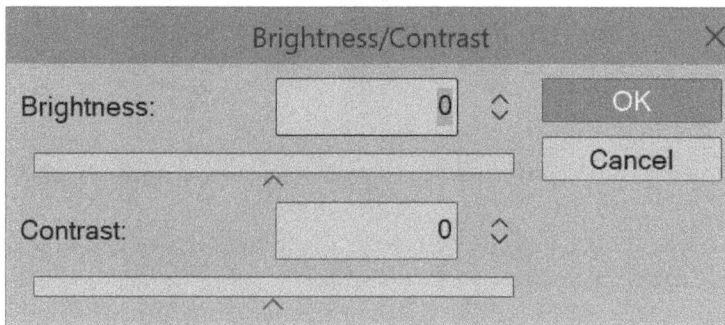

Figure 12.1 – The Brightness/Contrast dialog

While operating the **Brightness/Contrast** dialog, you have two main sliders:

- **Brightness**: This slider controls the overall lightness of your image. Moving it to the right increases the brightness, while moving it to the left darkens the image.

- **Contrast**: This slider adjusts the difference between light and dark areas of your artwork. Increasing contrast makes lights lighter and darks darker, adding depth and dimension to your painting. Lowering the contrast reduces this difference, resulting in a softer, more muted look.

Both sliders can go from **–100** to **100**, with **0** being the original tone. By balancing these two settings, you can ensure that your painting maintains the right level of clarity and impact. Be careful with the adjustments: moving the sliders too much to one side might create a blasted look you're not expecting. Be moderate with this correction for better results. You can see examples of this correction layer in *Figure 12.2*.

Figure 12.2 – Original image (top left) and examples of Brightness/Contrast settings

A practical use for the **Brightness/Contrast** correction layer is when fine-tuning the overall mood of a scene. For example, if you've painted a dramatic sunset but the shadows don't feel strong enough, you can increase the contrast to make them more pronounced. Alternatively, if your image feels too harsh or high in contrast, lowering it can create a softer, more atmospheric feel.

Now that you've understood how to use **Brightness/Contrast**, let's cover **Hue/Saturation/Luminosity**, one of the best color correction layers.

Hue/Saturation/Luminosity

The **Hue/Saturation/Luminosity** correction layer is a versatile tool that allows fine-tuning colors in your artwork by adjusting the three fundamental aspects of color: hue, saturation, and luminosity. This layer lets you modify the color settings with high accuracy, making sure your desired color will be applied. Here is a view of the **Hue/Saturation/Luminosity** dialog:

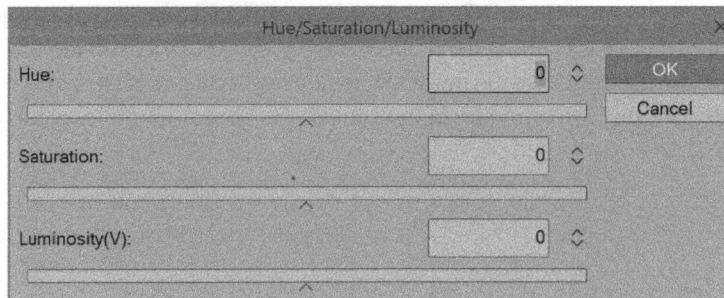

Figure 12.3 – The Hue/Saturation/Luminosity dialog

Let's understand how it works:

- **Hue**: Shifts the colors within your image along the color spectrum. For example, reds can be turned into blues, greens into yellows, and so on. This setting is useful when you want to experiment with color schemes or fix unwanted hues.

- **Saturation**: Controls the intensity of colors. Increasing the saturation will make colors appear more vibrant and bold, while decreasing it will result in more muted or grayscale tones. This is especially useful when you want to create a mood by enhancing or reducing color vibrancy.

- **Luminosity**: Adjusts the brightness of your colors, making your image darker or brighter while maintaining the same hue and saturation. This helps balance light and dark areas in your composition without affecting contrast, similar to the **Brightness** slider in **Brightness/Contrast**.

Notice in *Figure 12.3* that the three color properties can be changed with the slider or with a number value, increasing accuracy even further. By creating a selection and pinpointing the areas you wish to affect, the precision is even higher. Remember, you can also use a layer mask to add or remove parts of the tonal correction as you need. In *Figure 12.4*, you can see an example of a **Hue/Saturation/Luminosity** layer on the character's hair, changing it from dark magenta to teal.

Figure 12.4 – Original image (left) and example of Hue/Saturation/Luminosity correction (right)

If your artwork feels too dull, you can boost saturation and luminosity to make it pop. Conversely, if a section of your piece feels too overpowering, you can subtly reduce the saturation to bring it in line with the rest of the composition. Additionally, it can be a great tool for working with color palettes by testing out different hues in one part of your image while seeing how they interact with other parts.

The **Hue/Saturation/Luminosity** layer provides you with a robust toolkit for color manipulation. As we move forward, there's another fascinating correction layer that offers a more abstract and stylistic approach: **Posterization**.

Posterization

Posterization is a powerful correction tool in CSP that simplifies the color gradient of your artwork by reducing the number of tonal ranges and flattening the image into distinct color areas. Posterization creates bold, graphic-like divisions between tones, giving your artwork a stylized look, as shown in *Figure 12.5*.

Figure 12.5 – Original image (left) and example of posterization (right)

When applying posterization, you control how many tone levels are displayed using the **Levels(N)** slider. For example, if you set the level to two, your image will be reduced to just two distinct color values—one for light areas and one for dark. As you increase the levels, more shades are introduced. This allows for a highly customizable look, depending on the level of abstraction you want. With lower levels, you get more simplified forms, ideal for a graphic, high-contrast style, while higher levels preserve more detail while maintaining that bold separation between shades.

Figure 12.6 – Posterization with two levels (left) and six levels (right)

One practical use of posterization is to create a more graphic look in comic art or illustrations. For example, when designing poster art or promotional materials, a flat and limited color palette can give your work a striking, eye-catching quality. It's also a useful effect when you want to create retro-inspired artwork or emulate certain printing styles, such as screen printing, where fewer colors and sharp tonal boundaries are key.

Posterization is a creative tool that opens new avenues for artistic expression by breaking down color complexity into simpler tonal divisions. As we continue, we'll explore yet another useful tool—**Reverse Gradient**.

Reverse Gradient

Reverse Gradient is a simple but powerful tool in CSP that allows you to instantly invert the colors and values of your image. While this might sound extreme, you can use this effect in selected areas to change the mood and focus of your artwork, making it a great tool for experimentation and fine-tuning color composition.

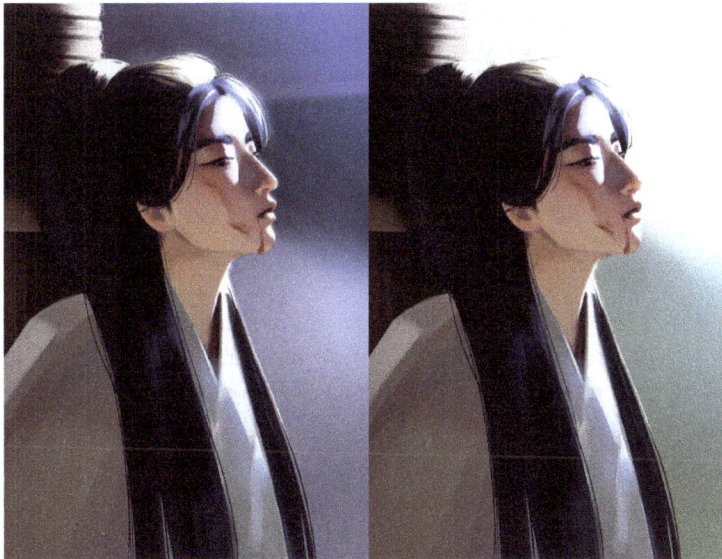

Figure 12.7 – Original image (left) and example of Reverse Gradient on the background (right)

When you create a **Reverse Gradient** layer, it has a layer mask attached to it. Use this mask to select which areas you wish to apply the effect on.

Reverse Gradient is a versatile tool that encourages creative exploration by quickly inverting your colors. As we move forward, we'll delve into **Level Correction**, a more advanced tonal adjustment tool that gives you precise control over the brightness and contrast levels in your image, allowing finer manipulation of light and shadow.

Level Correction

Level Correction is a powerful tonal adjustment tool that lets you fine-tune the brightness, contrast, and tonal range of your artwork. This feature is ideal for balancing the overall lightness and darkness of an image, especially in areas where tonal shifts are necessary to improve clarity or emphasize parts of the composition. By adjusting the levels, you can control how light or dark specific portions of your artwork appear, giving you greater control over how the viewer perceives depth and focus.

Here, you can see the **Level Correction** dialog:

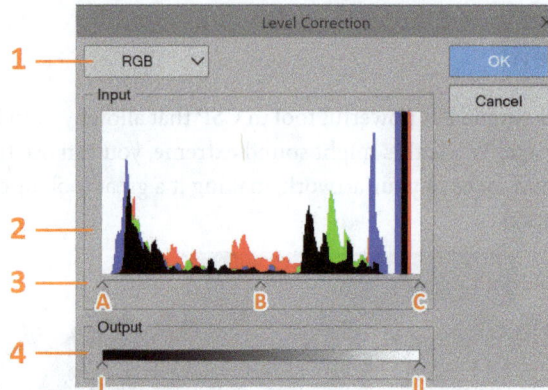

Figure 12.8 – The Level Correction dialog

Let's cover what each of its functions do:

1. **Channel**: This lets you select a color channel to adjust the levels. You can use **RGB**, **Red**, **Green**, or **Blue**. **RGB** applies to all colors on the image, while if you select **Red**, for example, you'll only make changes to tones of red on the image. *Figure 12.9* shows an image before and after changing the **Red** levels.

Figure 12.9 – Original image (left) and modifications on the Red channel (right)

2. **Histogram**: This map shows the amount of shadows (left side) and lights (right side) as mountain peaks. The higher the peak, the more of one tone is present in the image. This is useful for balancing out the contrast, as an image with very low center values is likely to have too much contrast, for example.

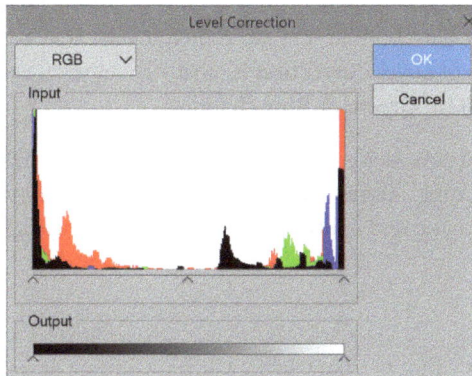

Figure 12.10 – A histogram with low center levels (left) means an image with too much contrast (right)

3. **Input slider**: This lets you control the amount of brightness and darkness of your image with three nodes:

   A. *Shadows*: This arrow on the left side of the slider controls the shadows. When you slide it to the right, the image becomes darker.

   B. *Midtones*: This arrow in the middle of the slider controls the area of midtones on your image. When you drag this arrow to the left, the midtones become brighter, while dragging it to the right makes the midtones darker. When you move the *Shadows* or *Highlight* arrows, *Midtones* will move along.

   C. *Highlights*: The right-sided arrow controls the brightest areas of your image. Drag it to the left to reduce highlights, and to the right to increase them.

   • You can adjust these levels to either compress or expand the tonal range, making dark areas darker, light areas lighter, or adjusting midtones for a more balanced look.

4. **Output**: This controls the maximum tonal value of your image with two nodes:

   I. *Shadows output*: Controls the darkest parts of your image. Drag it to the right to make your image brighter, and to the left to allow the full range of darkness.

   II. *Highlights output*: Controls the brightest parts of your image. Drag it to the left to make your image darker, and to the right to allow the full range of brightness.

Level Correction is particularly useful when working with images that appear flat or lack contrast. For example, if you've scanned a sketch or created an image with subdued lighting, using **Level Correction** can enhance the tonal separation between the darkest and lightest parts of the image, adding depth and richness. I use **Level Correction** frequently to fix the contrast, brightness, and darkness of my paintings. As with other correction layers, I usually prefer small adjustments instead of large ones. My favorite way to use it is to increase the contrast slightly: inside **Input**, I drag the **Shadows** slider to the right, then the **Highlights** slider to the left - both in very small increments. That way, I increase the contrast just a little bit. Although my use of **Level Correction** is mostly about tonal value, you can use this tool for color balance by using the **Red**, **Green**, or **Blue** channels.

Level Correction is an essential tool for artists seeking precise control over the tonal balance of their work. As we move forward to the next topic, **Tone Curve**, we'll explore an even more advanced method for adjusting tonal values with precision and control, allowing you to manipulate the curve of light and shadow across your artwork.

Tone Curve

Tone Curve is a sophisticated tonal adjustment tool that offers precise control over the brightness and contrast of specific tonal ranges in your artwork. Unlike **Level Correction**, which adjusts shadows, midtones, and highlights more globally, **Tone Curve** allows you to manipulate the tonal range more selectively. You can see the **Tone Curve** dialog in *Figure 12.11*.

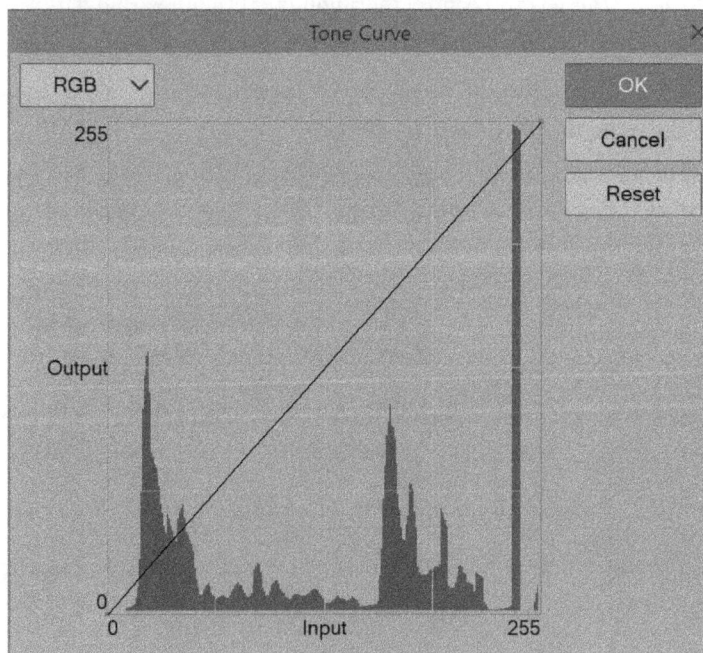

Figure 12.11 – The Tone Curve dialog

As with **Level Correction**, there's a **Channel** drop-down menu in which you can choose between **RGB** (all colors), **Red**, **Green**, or **Blue**. There's also a visual map of the lights and darks of your image - the gray peaks and valleys behind the straight diagonal line. This map can aid in seeing where the darks and lights of your image are.

The tone curve - the straight diagonal line - represents the brightness levels in your image, from shadows on the left to highlights on the right. The **Tone Curve** tool works by letting you create points along the diagonal line that represents the current tonal range of your image. To create a new point, click on the curve. To remove a point, drag it outside of the graph. Dragging a point upward brightens that part of the tonal range while dragging it downward darkens it. This allows you to either boost or reduce the brightness of specific tonal ranges without affecting others. For example, you can darken midtones while keeping both shadows and highlights intact (*Figure 12.12*, top) or lighten shadows to bring out details in dark areas without overexposing the highlights (*Figure 12.12*, bottom).

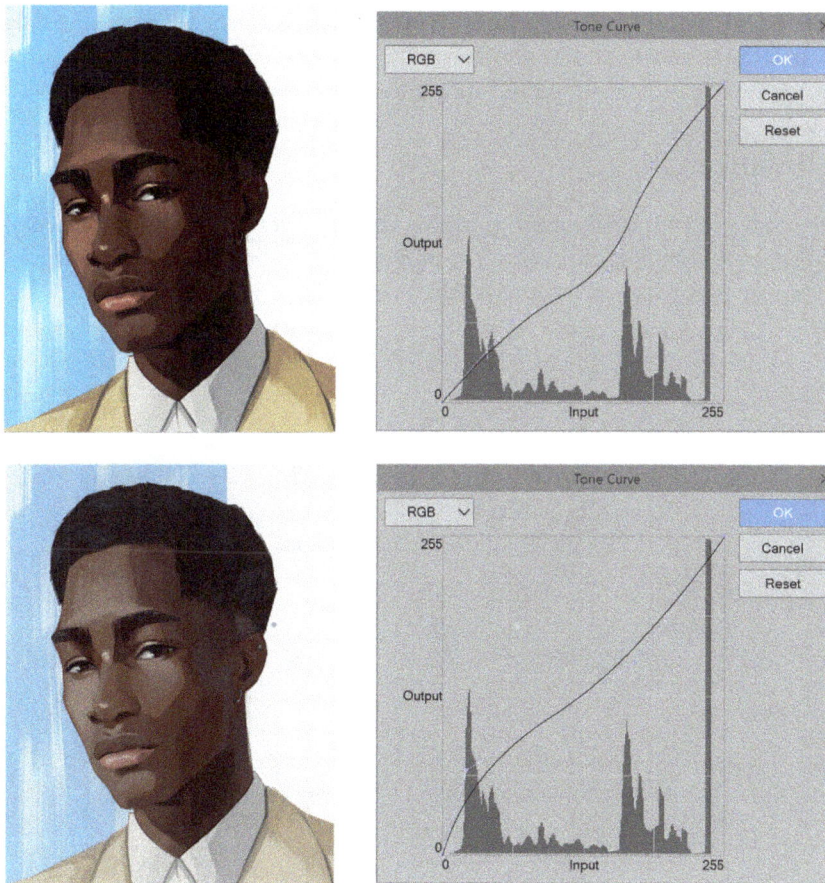

Figure 12.12 – Examples of a tone curve

In practice, the **Tone Curve** tool can be employed to introduce soft tonal transitions or to create dramatic contrast shifts. For example, if you're working on a character illustration, you could deepen the shadows to add mystery or drama or lift the highlights to give the character a more glowing, illuminated look. You could increase the minimum value range to make it brighter or decrease the maximum value range to make it darker.

I use the **Tone Curve** tool frequently to fix the contrast, brightness, and darkness of my paintings. It's similar to how I use **Level Correction**: to increase contrast. I create a point near the bottom left and drag it slightly down, then create a point near the upper right and drag it slightly up. That way, I increase the contrast just a little bit. Just like **Level Correction**, although my use of **Tone Curve** is mostly about tonal value, you can use this tool for color balance as well by using the **Red**, **Green**, or **Blue** channels.

Tone Curve is an indispensable tool for artists looking to refine their control over tonal balance and contrast, offering a higher level of precision than other tonal correction methods. In the next section, we'll dive into **Color balance**, where you'll learn how to adjust color tones across shadows, midtones, and highlights to enhance the mood and atmosphere of your artwork.

Color balance

Color balance is a versatile tonal correction layer in CSP that gives you control over the color distribution within different tonal ranges, allowing you to shift your entire image or specific tones toward warmer or cooler hues as needed. Here, you can see the **Color balance** dialog:

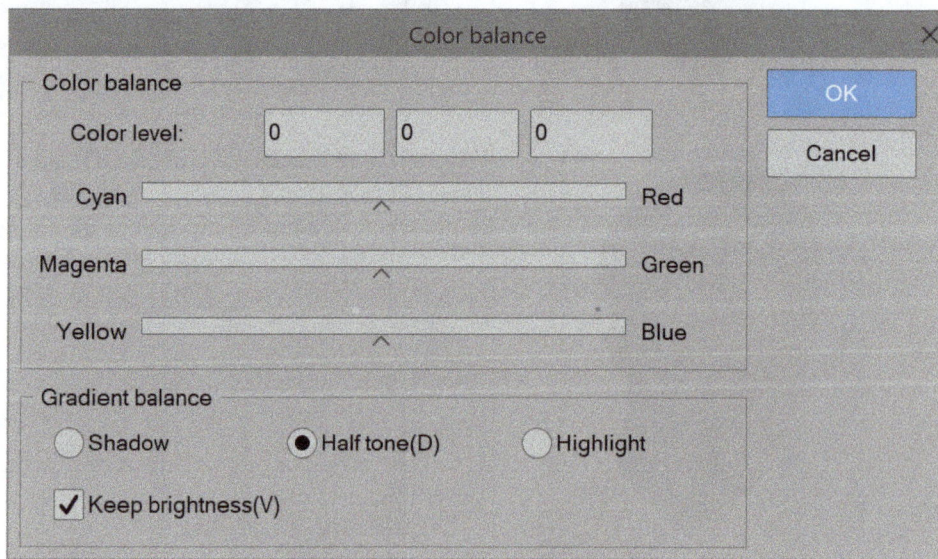

Figure 12.13 – The Color balance dialog

The **Color balance** dialog has two parts. The first is the **Color balance** group of settings, which consists of sliders for the colors **Cyan/Red**, **Magenta/Green**, and **Yellow/Blue**. The value number of each slider appears on the **Color level** setting, and you can manually input value numbers in these fields. By moving the slider toward one end or the other, you can increase the amount of that hue in your image. For example, if you want your image to have more pink, you can drag the **Cyan/Red** slider toward the right (**Red**), and the **Magenta/Green** slider toward the left (**Magenta**). You can see an example of this change in the following figure:

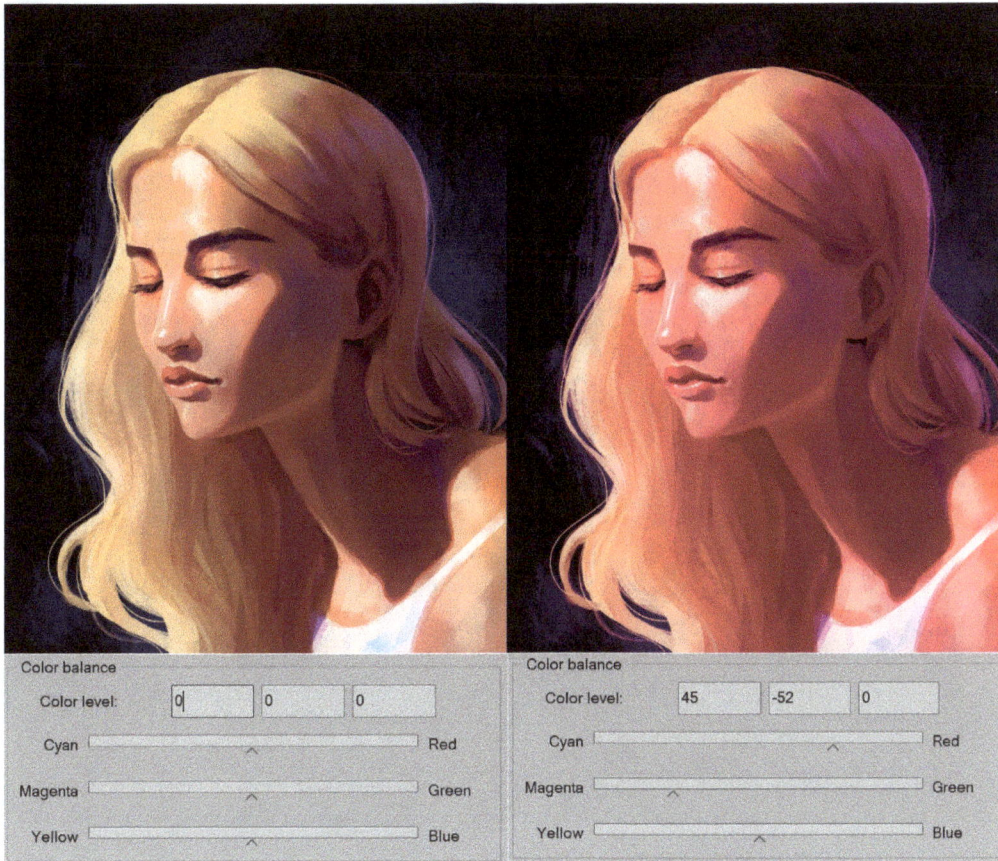

Figure 12.14 – Original image (left) and increased reds and pinks (right)

Below **Color balance**, you'll find **Gradient balance**, which determines which tonal values you'll be affecting. There are three options: **Shadow**, **Half tone(D)**, and **Highlight**. If you select **Shadow**, you'll be changing the hue balance of the darkest parts of your image, while **Half tone(D)** modifies the midtones and **Highlight** modifies the brightest areas. This way, you can adjust each range of tonal value of your image, making it completely customizable.

There's also a **Keep brightness(V)** checkbox below the three options where you can choose to keep the brightness or not. When toggled on, color changes will affect hue and brightness. When toggled off, they will only affect hue, not brightness. You can see the difference in *Figure 12.15*:

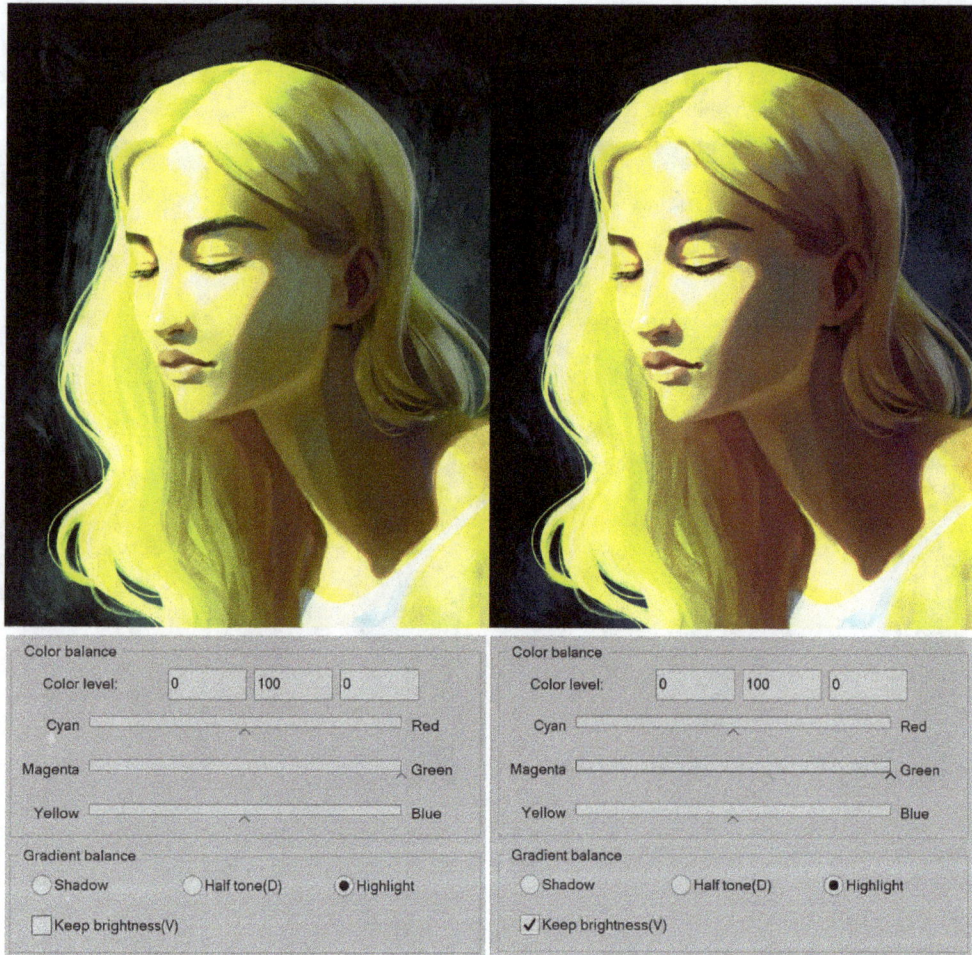

Figure 12.15 – Keep brightness(V) off (left) and on (right)

In practical terms, **Color balance** is ideal for adjusting atmospheric effects and stylizing your artwork. For instance, in a nighttime scene, you might add cyan to the highlights and midtones, creating a cool, mysterious ambiance. On the other hand, a sunset scene could benefit from more red and yellow in the highlights, bringing warmth and vibrance to bright areas.

Overall, **Color balance** provides nuanced control over color distribution in your artwork, enhancing storytelling and emotional appeal. Next, we'll explore **Binarization**, a tonal correction that dramatically simplifies your artwork into high-contrast black-and-white images, creating graphic, impactful artwork.

Binarization

Binarization is a unique and impactful correction layer in CSP that converts an image into a stark, high-contrast black-and-white format by removing all gray tones and reducing each pixel to either black or white. This tool is useful when you want to convert scanned drawings into digital lines or if you want to quickly assess the values in an artwork. By analyzing the tonal range, **Binarization** allows a deeper focus on composition, silhouette, and contrast, highlighting the underlying structure of an image without the distraction of midtones.

The **Binarization** settings are simple but effective, featuring an adjustable **Threshold** slider that determines which pixels become black or white based on their brightness. Any colors brighter than the threshold become white, and colors darker than the threshold become black. Moving the slider left lowers the threshold, increasing the white areas, while moving it right raises the threshold, adding more black areas.

The optimal threshold setting depends on the look you aim to achieve—higher thresholds create shadow-filled compositions, while lower thresholds produce lighter results. This control makes **Binarization** versatile enough to suit diverse needs, from illustration and design to generating high-contrast visual references. In *Figure 12.16*, you can see examples of **Binarization** in practice - one with a value of 50 (left) and the other with 150 (right).

Figure 12.16 – Examples of Binarization with different thresholds

In practice, **Binarization** is useful for testing readability in compositions, especially in small-scale designs such as icons or thumbnails, where simplicity and contrast are crucial. With its ability to sharpen values and emphasize silhouettes, **Binarization** is a straightforward yet powerful tool for artistic refinement. Following this, the **Gradient map** adjustment takes the tonal structure and allows changes in its colors and values with a predetermined set of colors.

Gradient map

The **Gradient map** correction layer is a powerful way to apply custom color schemes based on the underlying grayscale values of an image, offering depth and unique mood customization. We covered practical uses of gradient maps thoroughly in *Chapter 11, Applying Color Quickly with Pro Techniques*, under the *Applying Color Match and Gradient Maps for quick experimentation* section.

Tonal correction layers offer digital artists a non-destructive way to adjust their artwork, providing flexibility and creative control. Whether you're using levels for fine-tuning or color balance for dynamic color changes, these adjustments are key to achieving a polished and cohesive final piece. With just a few thoughtful corrections, your piece can go from good to extraordinary.

By mastering these tools, you can manipulate light and color to amplify the impact of your art. Next, it's time to explore another tool for creative experimentation: filter effects.

Exploring filters for creative enhancements

Filters are powerful tools in CSP that can add unique effects to a piece, from subtle refinements to dramatic alterations. Unlike correction layers, filters directly affect the selected layer's pixels, making them useful for final adjustments or enhancements to specific areas. This section covers CSP's filters, each offering a wide array of effects that can make your work stand out.

> **Important note**
> When setting up any filter, be sure to toggle on the **Preview** checkbox to view the effects in real time before applying them.

To select a filter, go to the **Filter** menu, choose a category, then select the filter of your choosing. We'll dive into these categories and explore how you can use them to take your artwork to the next level, starting with **Blur** filters.

Blur filters

Blur filters are functions that soften, blend, or create motion effects, creating a variety of effects that can add realism, focus, or drama to an artwork. **Blur** filters work by averaging or displacing pixel colors, resulting in softened edges, gentle gradients, or dynamic effects that imply movement. Let's look at the different types of **Blur** filters available and explore the creative potential of each one:

- **Blur**: This provides a light softening that's useful for minor adjustments, such as gently blending colors or reducing the harshness of lines.

- **Blur (strong)(F)**: This is a more intense version of the previous function, **Blur**. **Blur (strong) (F)** is useful for heavier blending where the goal is to obscure details or create a hazy look.

- **Gaussian blur...**: This is one of the most popular blur types due to its smooth and even effect, resulting in a uniform softness. It is highly adjustable, letting you control the blur strength to get the precise amount of softness needed. This blur is frequently used to create **depth-of-field** (**DoF**) effects, where background elements are softened to highlight the subject. In the following figure, I used **Gaussian blur...** to soften the background and emphasize the character:

Figure 12.17 – Example use of Gaussian blur on the background

- **Lens Blur...**: This allows you to create realistic DoF effects, simulating how a camera lens blurs areas that are out of focus. While a Gaussian blur is smoother, a lens blur is more defined and can create sharper light effects. To apply a lens blur effect, go to **Filter** | **Blur** | **Lens Blur**..., which will open the **Lens Blur** dialog. The following are the settings you can adjust:

  - **Strength**: This controls the intensity of the blur. A lower value creates a subtle blur, while a higher value results in a more pronounced, out-of-focus effect.

- **Highlight shape**: Modifies the shape in which light blurs in the scene. Different shapes, such as **Hexagon** or **Triangle**, can create distinct blur characteristics, as you can see in the next figure:

Figure 12.18 – Example of Hexagon (left) and Triangle (right) highlight shapes

- **Highlight intensity**: Controls how bright areas of the image respond to the blur effect. Increasing this value enhances bokeh, the soft glowing effect that appears around blurred highlights, mimicking the look of real camera lenses.

- **Highlight roundness**: When you increase the value of **Highlight roundness**, the highlight shape becomes more circular, softening the edges.

- **Highlight angle**: When using an angular shape such as a triangle or pentagon, you can change its angle with this slider.

- **Motion blur...**: This mimics the effect of objects in motion by stretching the pixels in a specified direction. You can simulate various speeds and movement paths with its adjustable angle and distance settings. This filter is ideal for illustrations where you want to depict motion, such as a character dashing across the screen.

- **Radial blur...**: This applies a circular blur, radiating out from a focal point or in, toward it. This effect is excellent for creating eye-catching visuals, as it draws the viewer's eye to a central point. It gives the appearance of an object jumping out of the screen or jumping in toward its center, which is great for dynamic scenes.

- **Smoothing**: This subtly softens edges, reducing noise and rough textures without significant blurring of details by applying an anti-aliasing effect. This is particularly useful for smoothing out scanned or pixelated lines.

- **Spin blur...**: This adds rotational motion to an image. Unlike **Radial blur…**, which represents objects going in or out of the picture, **Spin blur…** adds a spinning effect that is perfect for adding movement to round objects, such as wheels, or any element that needs to appear as if it's rotating in place. You can set its strength, direction, shape, and tilt.

Figure 12.19 shows examples of **Smoothing** (top left), **Motion blur…** (top right), **Radial blur…** (bottom left), and **Spin blur…** (bottom right).

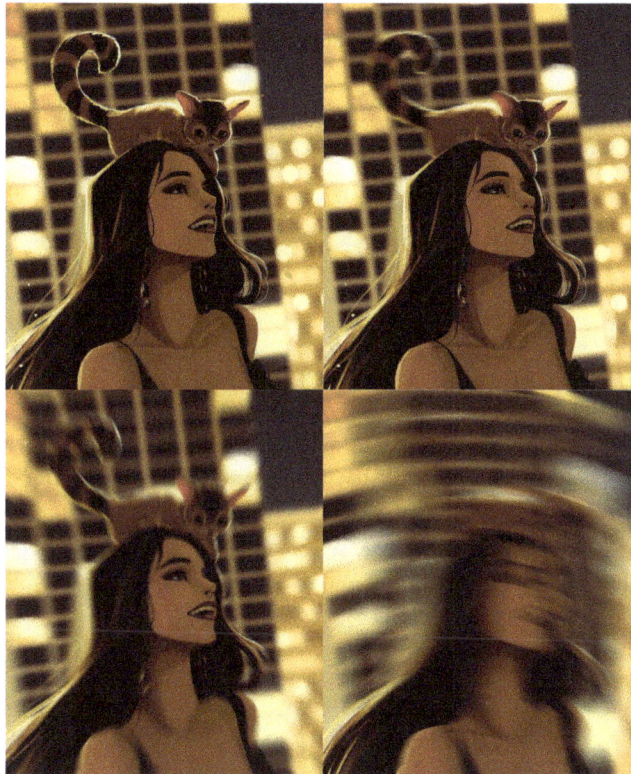

Figure 12.19 – Examples of Smoothing (top left), Motion blur… (top right),
Radial blur… (bottom left), and Spin blur… (bottom right)

Notice how with **Smoothing** we can hardly see any changes; **Motion blur…** on the creature's tail looks like it's in movement; **Radial blur…** on the same image makes it look like something is quickly approaching the character's face, as if to hit her; and **Spin blur…** looks like everything is spinning.

Blur filters soften areas of an image, which can reduce harsh details or create the illusion of depth. Next, we'll see **Correction** filters, which help improve your drawing quality.

Correction filters

Correction filters offer versatile adjustments that help refine an image's appearance. There are two types of **Correction** filters:

- **Adjust line width...**: Changes the width of lines on raster layers. You can make them thicker or thinner, depending on your desired look. By selecting specific areas, you can change the width of only certain parts of your drawing, increasing the sense of depth. Here is an example of this filter in action:

Figure 12.20 – Original sketch (left) and Adjust line width | Thicken (right)

- **Remove dust...**: Detects dust on the selected layer automatically, then erases it up to a specified size and fills the gaps with your main color. This is especially good for scanned drawings. Here is an example of it in action:

Figure 12.21 – Original sketch (left) and Remove dust... (right)

- When you select **Remove dust…**, there are two settings you can change:

  - **Dust size**: Determines the maximum size that will be considered dust.

  - **Mode**: You can choose from four modes:

    - **Remove dust from transparency**: Deletes spots within a layer that are surrounded by transparent areas.

    - **Remove dust from white background**: Deletes non-white spots in areas filled with white.

    - **Fill transparent gaps with surrounding color**: Detects small transparent spots as dust and fills them with the surrounding areas.

    - **Fill transparent gaps with foreground color**: Detects small transparent spots as dust and fills them with your foreground color.

Correction filters are powerful tools for refining details and removing unwanted imperfections from your artwork. Having understood how **Correction** filters work, let's turn our attention to **Distort** filters, which transform shapes, perspectives, and compositions with dynamic and unexpected results.

Distort filters

Distort filters add a variety of transformation effects that allow you to reshape and creatively modify images with specific distortions. Here's an overview of each filter:

- **Convert to Panorama…**: Turns an image into a panorama. We'll cover more about panoramas in *Chapter 16*, *Creating 3D Backgrounds*.

- **Curved surface…**: Applies a reflective distortion that mimics the effect of an image projected onto a cylindrical or spherical surface.

- **Fish-Eye Lens…(D)**: Mimics the distortion from a fish-eye lens, expanding the central portion of the image and leaving outer areas transparent.

- **Geometric distortion…**: Bends the image, creating an effect that makes it appear to curve inward or outward. When you select this filter, the **Geometric distortion** dialog appears, along with a red *X* on the canvas indicating the effect's center. You can drag this mark to reposition the center as needed.

- **Pinch…**: Pulls pixels toward the center point of the effect, creating a pinched distortion.

- **Polar Coordinates…**: Converts an image's coordinates to either polar (circular) or rectangular (grid) format, reshaping the overall structure based on radii and angles.

- **Ripple(Z)…**: Produces a ripple effect that emanates outward from the center, resembling water waves.

- **Twirl(S)…**: Adds a spiral twist to the image around a central point, creating a swirling effect.

- **Wave(F)...:** Transforms the image into a wave shape, applying an undulating effect that alters horizontal and vertical lines.

- **ZigZag(W)...:** Creates a zigzag pattern across the image, distorting its natural lines into a jagged effect.

You can see examples of each of these filters in *Figure 12.22*.

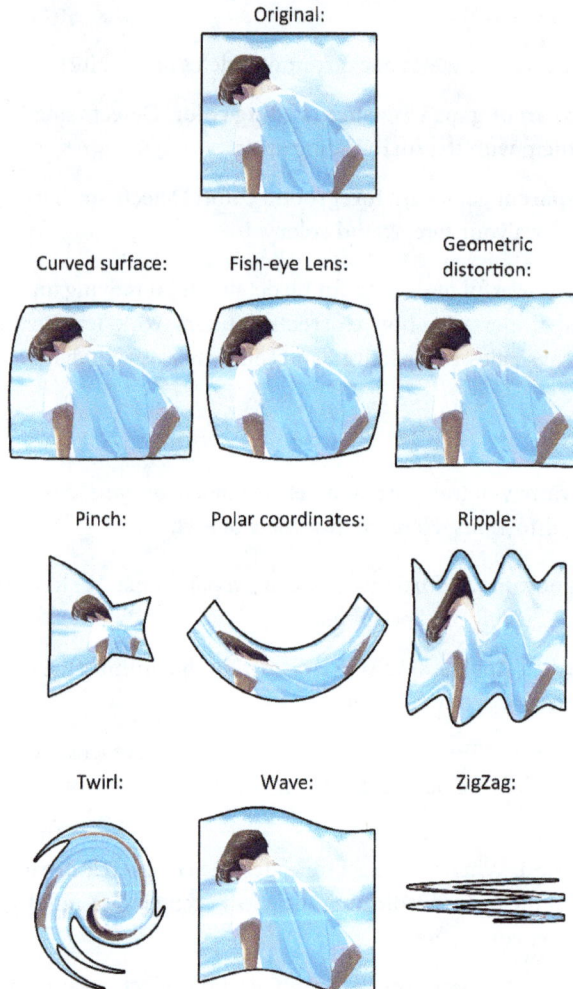

Original:

Curved surface: Fish-eye Lens: Geometric distortion:

Pinch: Polar coordinates: Ripple:

Twirl: Wave: ZigZag:

Figure 12.22 – Examples of Distort filters

Distort filters offer a powerful way to reshape and manipulate images, adding depth, movement, and dynamic focal points to your artwork. Now that we've covered **Distort** filters, let's explore **Effect** filters, which add creative overlays and textures to your work, enhancing its atmosphere and mood.

Effect filters

Effect filters add specialized visual styles to a piece. Here are the **Effect** filters:

- **Artistic...**: Adds an artistic touch to your image, giving it a painterly look. You can choose if there will be lines and colors, lines only, or colors only, as well as determine the appearance of lines and colors in the **Artistic** dialog.

- **Chromatic aberration...**: Applies a chromatic aberration effect, which shows RGB layers slightly separated. When you select this filter, you can adjust its intensity and angle in the **Chromatic aberration** dialog.

- **Crystallize(V)...**: Transforms an image into a pattern resembling stained glass. In this effect, each section of color is called a **cell**. The **Crystallize** dialog allows you to adjust key settings such as **Cell size**, **Randomness**, and **Tiling** to achieve different results.

  - **Cell size**: Controls the size of each individual cell. A lower value creates smaller cells, resulting in a more detailed and intricate pattern. A higher value produces larger cells, reducing the number of color variations in the image.

Figure 12.23 – Crystallize | Cell size at 20 (left) and 100 (right)

  - **Randomness**: Changes the shape of each individual cell. When set to **0**, all cells are uniform squares, producing an effect similar to the **Mosaic** filter. Increasing the randomness value makes the cells more irregular, with each shape differing from the others.

  - **Tiling**: Modifies the **Crystallize** effect to create a seamless, repeating pattern. This is useful for creating textures that loop smoothly without visible seams. After you apply **Crystallize** with the **Tiling** setting on, follow the next steps to create a seamless pattern:

    i.   Right-click the crystallized layer.

    ii. Select **Convert Layer(H)...**.

    iii. In **Type (K)**, select **Image material layer**.

iv.   Use the **Object** sub tool (Operation tool) to select the layer.

v.   Open **Sub Tool Detail | Tiling** and toggle it on.

vi.   Now, when you resize the layer using the transformation box, the image tiles seamlessly. In the following figure, you can see how the image tiles when **Tiling** was toggled off in the **Crystallize** dialog (left) and when it was toggled on (right). Pay close attention to the edges between each tile (bottom):

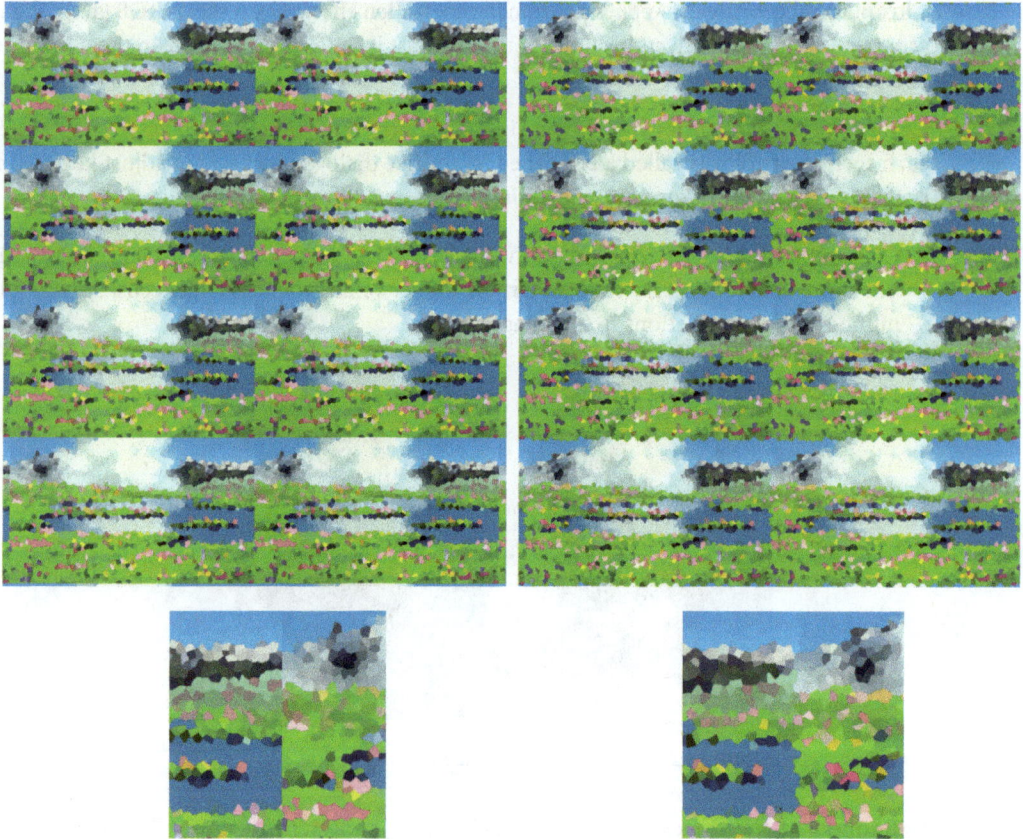

Figure 12.24 – When Tiling is toggled off (left) and on (right) in the Crystallize dialog

- **Mosaic...**: Pixelates your image. When you select this filter, you can determine the size of the tiles in the **Mosaic** dialog.

- **Noise(A)...**: Applies a noise overlay on your image. When you select this filter, you can determine the strength of noise with a slider in the **Noise** dialog.

- **Normal map...**: Converts the image to a normal map for 3D textures in dedicated 3D software.

- **Pencil drawing...**: Transforms your image into a pencil-like artwork with lines and hatching.

- **Remove jpeg noise**: Removes noise generated in images saved in JPEG format, leaving a smooth appearance.

- **Retro film...**: Applies chromatic aberration, noise, and light effects on your image to replicate old photos and films.

You can see examples of each of these filters in *Figure 12.25*.

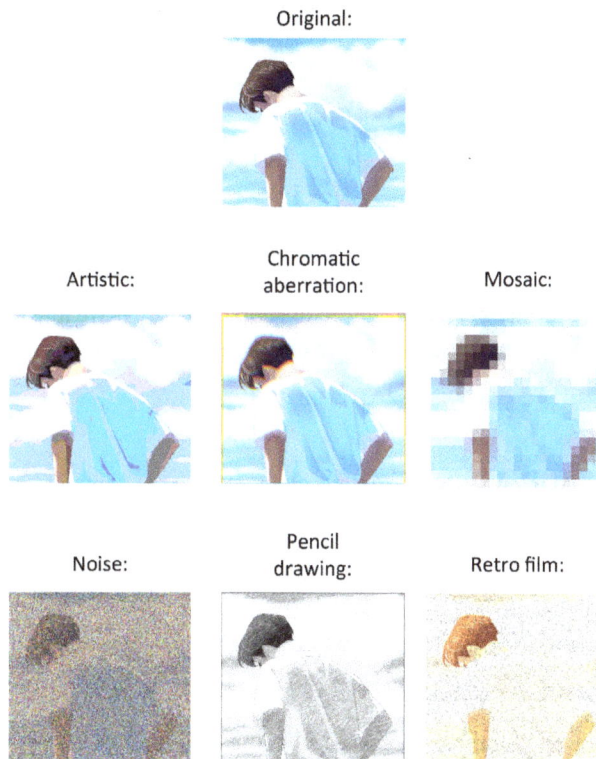

Figure 12.25 – Examples of effect filters

Effect filters allow you to introduce engaging textures and visual effects that can bring a new dimension to your images. Moving forward, we'll examine the **Render** filter, which allows you to add Perlin noise to your image.

The Render filter

There's only one **Render** filter in CSP: **Perlin noise**. It converts the selected layer into an opaque cloud-like pattern. For this reason, this filter should only be used on blank layers - using it on a layer with an image will replace the image. Once a **Perlin noise** layer is created, you can change its opacity, blending mode, and more - like a regular raster layer. Here is an example of the **Perlin noise** filter, set to **Overlay** to show the image below it:

Figure 12.26 – Example of Perlin noise set to Overlay

The **Render** filter can add an interesting texture to your art. As we delve into **Sharpen** filters next, we'll see how sharpening your artwork can enhance detail and bring clarity to your images.

Sharpen filters

Sharpen filters are used to enhance fine details by increasing the contrast between pixels, making an image appear crisper. Careful application of **Sharpen** filters can help define details in specific areas, such as character faces or intricate objects, making them stand out more prominently. There are three filters under **Sharpen**:

- **Sharpen**: Enhances the contrast between separate parts.
- **Sharpen more**: This is a stronger version of the **Sharpen** effect.
- **Unsharp mask…**: Enhances contrast at the image borders. When you choose this filter, you can determine the strength and threshold of the effect.

Sharpen filters are essential tools to refine and clarify details in your work. By enhancing edges and bringing definition to softer elements, these filters ensure that focal points stand out, giving your images a polished finish.

With all these filters covered, you're now equipped to creatively adjust and enhance your work, bringing out the best in every layer and detail. As we continue, we'll explore **Liquify** and **Puppet warp**, two powerful tools that offer even more flexibility in reshaping and refining details to perfect your artwork.

Maximizing the Liquify and the Puppet warp tools for quick structural changes

Making structural adjustments during or after the painting process is a natural part of refining your work. Whether you need to shift proportions, adjust a pose, or subtly enhance facial expressions, having flexible tools at your disposal can save you hours of redrawing. In CSP 4.0, the **Liquify** tool and the new **Puppet warp** transformation offer powerful, intuitive ways to reshape your artwork without compromising quality. In this section, you'll learn how to use both tools to make quick yet precise structural changes that elevate your illustrations and streamline your workflow. We'll start with the **Liquify** tool.

Liquify

The **Liquify** tool is one of the most versatile post-processing tools in digital art, allowing you to reshape, refine, and adjust proportions without having to repaint entire areas. This tool is perfect for making quick fixes to anatomy, adjusting facial expressions, and correcting minor distortions that may have occurred during the painting process. It works like digital clay and lets you push, pull, and warp your artwork until it's just right. By learning how to use **Liquify** effectively, you can easily enhance your composition or correct any structural issues, all while maintaining the integrity of your original work. Here, you can see an example of the **Liquify** tool in action: it is used to push the character's chin, mouth, and nose up.

Figure 12.27 – Example of Liquify in action: the arrows show its direction

To use **Liquify**, go to the **Tool** palette and select **Liquify**. If you installed CSP before version 1.12.0, it will be located as a sub tool under the **Color Mixing** tool. You can see the settings available for **Liquify** on the **Tool Property** palette in *Figure 12.28*:

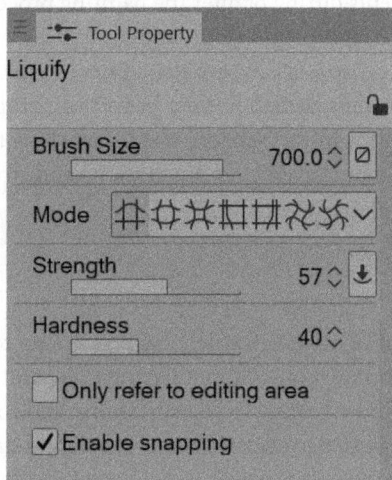

Figure 12.28 – Tool Property palette for the Liquify tool

Let's cover what each of these settings can do:

- **Brush Size**: You can change the size of the **Liquify** tool as if it were a regular brush, modifying the area that will be affected.

- **Mode**: There are multiple modes you can choose, which can dramatically change the effect of the **Liquify** tool.

  - **Push**: As the name suggests, **Push** pushes pixels in the direction of the stroke. If you make a stroke to the left, your pixels will be pushed to the left. This is the most commonly used mode as it is the most versatile.

  - **Expand**: The area you select will be enlarged, as if under a magnifying glass. If you don't drag your brush, only press and hold a position, it will apply the effect more and more to the same area until you release.

  - **Pinch**: Opposite to **Expand**, this mode will contract pixels and reduce the size of the area, as if pinching the painting.

- **Push Left** and **Push Right**: These options determine how pixels are shifted when using **Liquify**. Don't be mistaken by their names: **Push Left** doesn't move pixels toward the left edge; instead, it pulls pixels from the left side of the stroke toward the center. **Push Right** works similarly, pulling pixels from the right side of the stroke toward the center.

- **Twirl Clockwise** and **Twirl Anti-Clockwise**: Rotate pixels around the cursor location.

Here, you can see examples of these modes in action:

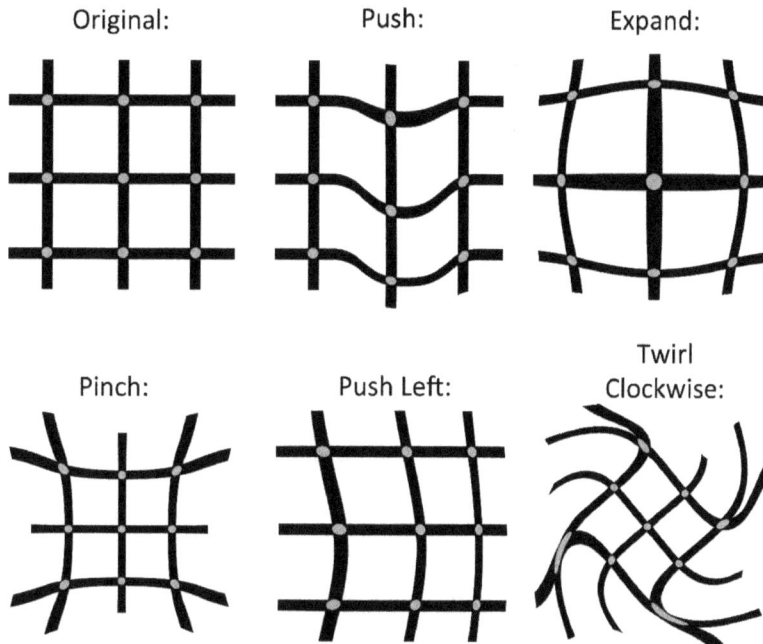

Figure 12.29 – Examples of Liquify modes

- **Strength**: Adjusts the intensity of the **Liquify** effect. You can control this by either using the slider or entering a specific value. I typically set it around 50-60, which offers a balance: it keeps the tool controlled but still allows for noticeable adjustments. Feel free to experiment to find a setting that feels right for you, and keep in mind that a strength of 100 may feel too powerful and challenging to manage.

- **Hardness**: Controls the edge of the **Liquify** effect. You can change this by either using the slider or entering a specific value. When the value is low, the effect will be focused on the center part, and when the value is high, it will affect surrounding areas. I keep it at around 40, but again, you should experiment to find the right amount for your process.

- **Only refer to editing area**: When toggled on, only the image of the edited area is referenced, but the process becomes slower. When toggled off, it will include the image outside the edited area in its calculation. I usually keep it toggled off, as it doesn't change much in the **Push** mode, which I use the most. *Figure 12.30* shows how **Liquify** operates when this setting is toggled on and off:

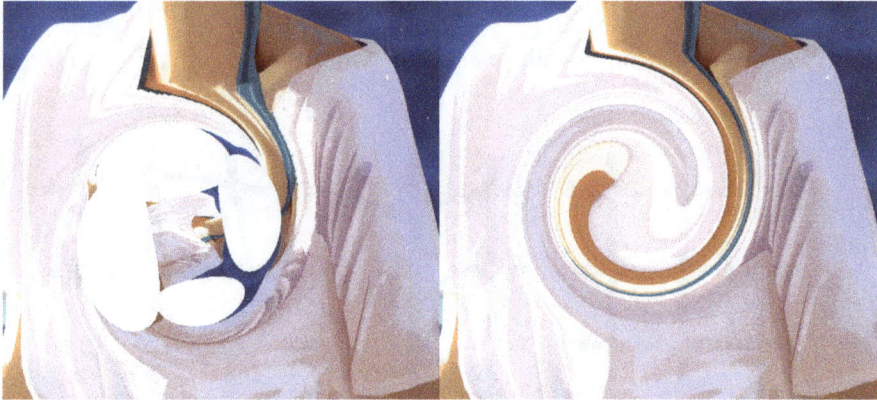

Figure 12.30 – Only refer to editing area on (left) and off (right)

- **Enable snapping**: When toggled on, the **Liquify** tool will snap to rulers, as we covered in *Chapter 7, Utilizing Rulers and Guides for Precision.*

With these settings, you can customize **Liquify** to suit your process and easily fix and enhance your artwork.

There is some important information you should know about **Liquify**:

- Since version 2.0, you can apply **Liquify** to multiple layers by selecting the layers you wish to modify in the **Layer** palette. You can also apply **Liquify** to all of the contents in a layer folder by selecting the folder in the **Layer** palette.
- If you create a selection and then apply **Liquify**, it will only be applied within that selection.
- The more you use **Liquify** in one area, the more its pixels will become blurred. Be careful not to over-use it.

The **Liquify** tool is a powerful asset for artists looking to refine their artwork after the painting phase. Its ability to adjust shapes and proportions quickly and easily makes it a go-to for fixing minor issues and enhancing the overall composition. When used thoughtfully and sparingly, **Liquify** can help elevate your work without compromising the original vision, and by combining this tool with other post-processing techniques, you can fine-tune every aspect of your painting, ensuring that it truly stands out.

While the **Liquify** tool is perfect for organic, fluid adjustments, sometimes you need more control over specific points of transformation—especially when repositioning limbs or adjusting complex shapes. That's where **Puppet warp** comes in. Let's explore how this new feature gives you the ability to bend and reshape your artwork with precision.

Puppet warp transformation

The **Puppet warp** transformation, introduced in version 4.0, is a powerful tool that allows you to manipulate and distort parts of an image with precision. By placing control points on a layer, you can bend, stretch, and reposition different areas without affecting the rest of the image. This is particularly useful for adjusting character poses, fabric flow, or even reshaping organic and mechanical elements with ease.

Here's how to use the **Puppet warp** transformation:

1. Select the layer you want to transform.
2. Go to **Edit | Transform** and select **Puppet warp...**.
3. Once **Puppet warp** is activated, a mesh appears on top of the figure.
4. Click on the mesh to add control points. Each point acts as a pivot for manipulating the structure.
5. Drag the points to reposition, stretch, or bend the image naturally. Next is a list of how to operate the transformation mesh:

    *   **Moving points**: Drag individual points to shift specific parts of the image.
    *   **Rotating points**: Click on the circle around the control point and rotate it to adjust the angle of movement.
    *   **Locking areas**: Place extra points in areas you want to remain fixed while manipulating other sections.
    *   **Grouping points**: Press *Shift* when adding new points to group them together.
    *   **Deleting points**: Press *Alt* and select a point to remove it.
    *   Press *Enter* to confirm the transformation once satisfied.

In the next figure, you can see the original drawing (left), the **Puppet warp** mesh (center), and the final result after pushing the hip and the shoulder points closer:

Figure 12.31 – Example use of the Puppet warp transformation

You can even make one body part overlap another with the **Puppet warp** tool. For that, make sure the body part you want to be in the front will be the last pin you create. You can also separate elements into different layers or make selections and apply **Puppet warp** only to some of them.

The **Puppet warp** tool is a game-changer for artists looking to refine their artwork with flexibility and ease. Whether you're making subtle pose adjustments or dramatic shape changes, this transformation method gives you complete control while maintaining the integrity of your original design.

Summary

In this chapter, you discovered essential post-processing adjustments to add a final layer of polish and professionalism to your artwork. You explored correction layers such as **Brightness/Contrast** and **Hue/Saturation/Luminosity**, which allow you to refine colors, enhance depth, and balance lighting with precise control—all without altering your base layers. These adjustments give your artwork depth and harmony, allowing you to fine-tune elements for maximum visual impact. With filters, you learned how to add unique effects that transform your pieces—whether by softening backgrounds with blur for greater depth, creating dynamic shapes through distortions, or enhancing focal points with specialized effects. Each filter enables you to enhance textures and experiment with visual moods.

Finally, you understood how to use the **Liquify** and the **Puppet warp** tools, which are powerful ways to make quick changes to proportions and balance without redrawing. They allow subtle tweaks or bold shifts, helping refine compositions with flexibility and precision. Together, these post-processing tools bring a polished finish and depth to your work, adding new layers of expressiveness.

With these techniques, your digital artwork can now reach new levels of polish and depth. In the next chapter, we'll explore manipulating 3D objects on the canvas, adding even more dimension and versatility to your compositions.

Get This Book's PDF Version and Exclusive Extras

UNLOCK NOW

Scan the QR code (or go to packtpub.com/unlock). Search for this book by name, confirm the edition, and then follow the steps on the page.

Note: Keep your invoice handly. Purchase made directly from packt don't require one.

Part 4: Leveraging 3D Models and Materials

This part dives into one of Clip Studio Paint's most powerful and often underused features: 3D tools. Whether you're aiming to improve accuracy, speed up complex scenes, or explore new creative possibilities, 3D assets can be game-changers. You'll learn how to manipulate and pose 3D objects and figures to create complex scenes, apply realistic lighting with 3D models, and build immersive environments using 3D backgrounds and panoramas. By the end of this section, you'll be equipped to use 3D elements as flexible tools that enhance your composition, storytelling, and overall workflow.

This part has the following chapters:

- *Chapter 13, Manipulating 3D Objects on the Canvas*
- *Chapter 14, Altering and Posing 3D Figures*
- *Chapter 15, Illuminating Your Artwork with 3D Lighting and Shading Assist*
- *Chapter 16, Creating 3D Backgrounds*

13

Manipulating 3D Objects on the Canvas

In this chapter, we'll delve into the exciting world of 3D objects within CSP and learn how to use and manipulate them to create a dynamic and flexible artistic experience. With 3D functions, you can speed up your process by positioning and customizing digital models, adding depth, perspective, and realism.

In this chapter, we're going to cover the following topics:

- Introducing 3D materials onto your canvas

- Mastering 3D manipulators for precise adjustments

- Modifying the camera angle of a 3D scene

- Maximizing the 3D material hierarchy for easier manipulation

By the end of this chapter, you'll be equipped with the skills to bring 3D elements to life on your canvas, allowing you to create more expressive and realistic compositions.

Introducing 3D materials onto your canvas

Adding 3D materials to your CSP workspace adds a new dimension to your artwork, allowing you to incorporate dynamic models and scenes that can serve as the foundation for realistic poses, accurate proportions, and complex compositions. CSP offers a range of 3D assets, from human figures and props to backgrounds, that can be placed directly onto your canvas. Let's explore how to access, import, and position these 3D materials.

To place a 3D material onto your canvas, follow these steps:

1. Navigate to the **Window** menu and select **Material**.

2. In the **Material** palette, select the **3D materials** folder. Once opened, you'll see categories that organize your resources, such as **Pose**, **Background**, and **Small objects**. Here, you'll find CSP's default assets, as well as any you've downloaded from *CLIP STUDIO ASSETS* and placed into these folders.

3. Click and drag the 3D model or object from the **Material** palette and drop it onto your canvas. You can also select the object and tap on the **Paste Material** icon, something we covered in *Chapter 3, Setting Up Materials for Consistency and Speed*.

4. Once placed, you'll see several controllers around the 3D object, allowing you to manipulate it. You'll discover exactly how to change a 3D object's size and position later in this chapter, in the *Mastering 3D manipulators for precise adjustments* section.

You can also import 3D objects from external sources, so long as they are in a compatible format (CSP supports `.cs3c`, `.cs3o`, `.cs3s`, `.fbx`, `.6kt`, `.6kh`, `.lwo`, `.lws`, `.obj`, `.glb`, `.gITF`, and `.vrm` files). To import 3D materials, follow these steps:

1. Go to the **File** menu.

2. Select **Import**.

3. Choose **3D Data**. A file browser will open where you can locate and select your 3D file.

4. Select the desired file and click **Open**. The 3D file will be placed on your canvas, and control options similar to the ones for CSP's built-in materials will become available.

5. Alternatively, on Windows or macOS, you can drag and drop the 3D file from the *Windows Explorer* or *Finder* area onto the canvas.

> **Important note**
> If your imported 3D file has a texture that's incompatible with CSP, the 3D model will be displayed without texture.

There are different types of 3D materials inside CSP:

*   **3D Body type**: These are human figures with different body shapes.

*   **3D Pose**: These are human figures with different body poses. You can combine 3D body types and 3D poses into one figure, as shown in the following figure. Throughout this book, we'll refer to the combination of 3D body types and 3D poses as *3D figures*:

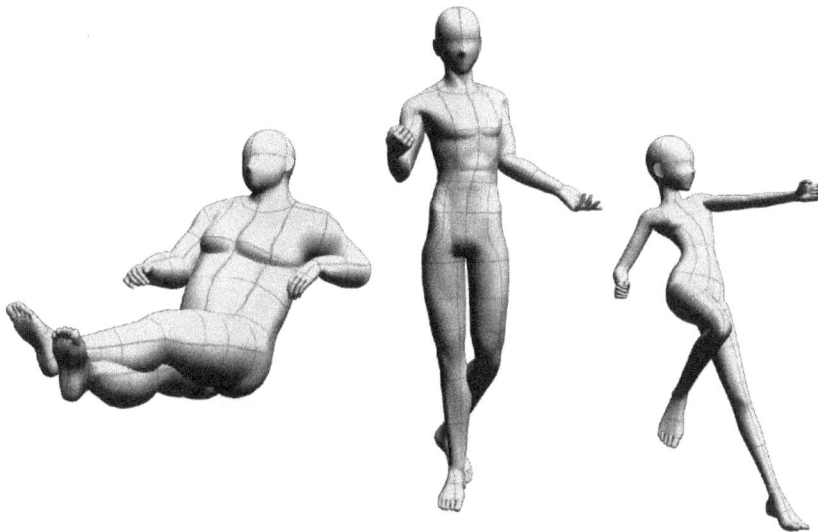

Figure 13.1 – 3D drawing figures

- **3D Head**: These can be customized and saved for each of your characters, ensuring they have the same proportions at any angle:

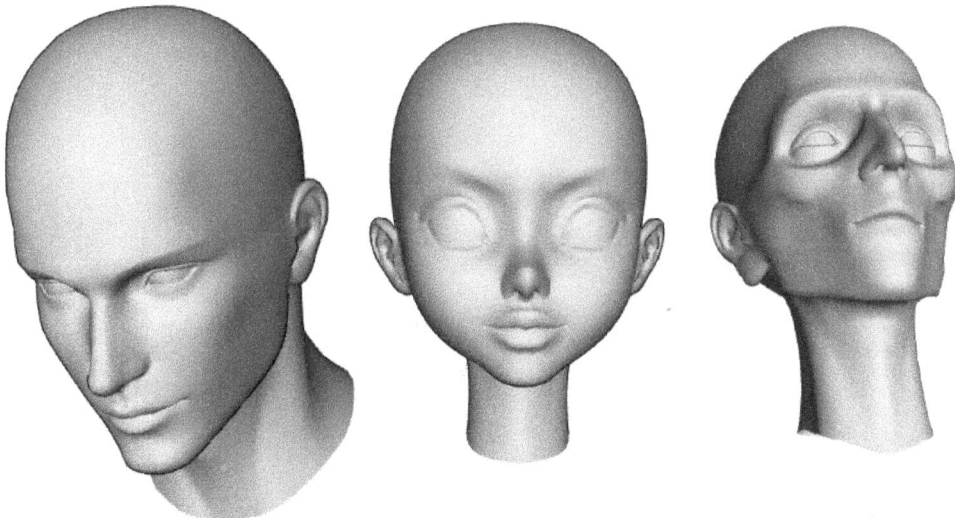

Figure 13.2 – 3D heads

We'll cover how to customize 3D heads and figures in *Chapter 14, Altering and Posing 3D Figures*.

- **3D Character:** These are fully colored and clothed characters whose pose and facial expression can be changed:

Figure 13.3 – 3D characters

You must use the software *Clip Studio Modeler* to set up 3D characters, though you can also download them from *CLIP STUDIO ASSETS*.

- **3D Object**: Materials whose angles, textures, and colors can be changed. In the **Material** palette, **3D Object** materials are located under the **Small object** and **Background** folders. Some object materials contain multiple parts, and you can adjust the size and position of each part. Here are some examples of **3D Object** materials:

Figure 13.4 – 3D Object materials

- **3D Background**: Like **3D Object** materials, the angles, textures, and colors of **3D Background** materials can be modified. However, they don't have individual parts that can be adjusted in terms of size and position - only predetermined parts can be moved. To tell a **3D Object** material apart from a **3D Background** material, select the material on the **Material** palette and check its **Type** value under **Material Details**:

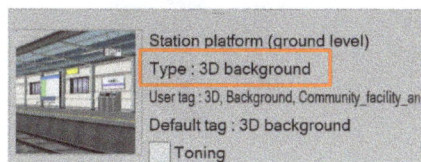

Figure 13.5 – A 3D background (top) and its type in the Material palette (bottom)

- **Panorama**: These are 360-degree background images that are great for 3D works, comics, or illustrations. You can adjust any angle, thus creating a quick and easy background solution. *Figure 13.6* shows an example of **Panorama**. The grayed-out area is outside of the canvas, while the brightly-colored area is within the canvas:

Figure 13.6 – Panorama

- **Primitive**: These are basic shapes such as cubes, spheres, and pyramids:

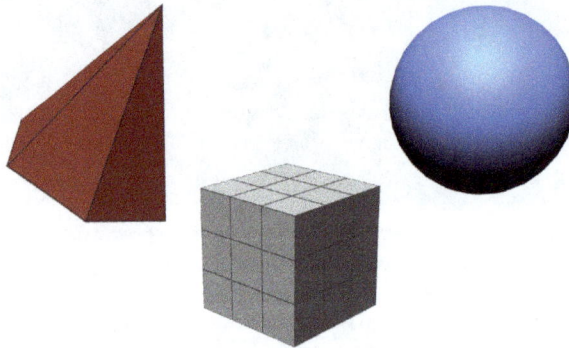

Figure 13.7 – Primitives

You can modify the number of corners, length, width, and depth of a **Primitive** material, as well as colors and textures to add further detail. To make these changes, go to the **Sub Tool Detail** palette and select **Primitive**. In this category, you'll find options to set several divisions, change color, and add texture.

You can draw on 3D drawing figures and primitives as you would on a regular layer. Follow these steps to do so:

1. Place a 3D figure or primitive on the canvas.

> **Important note**
>
> As of CSP Ver. 4.0, you can only draw on top of 3D figures and 3D primitives.

2.   Select a drawing tool, such as **Brush**, **Decorative**, or **Airbrush**.

3.   Select a color from one of the color palettes, such as **Color Wheel**.

4.   Paint on top of the 3D model.

Painting on a 3D model is especially great for drawing in perspective items such as tattoos, scars, swimsuits, and any other type of line you would be able to see on your character. Some example uses of this function can be seen here:

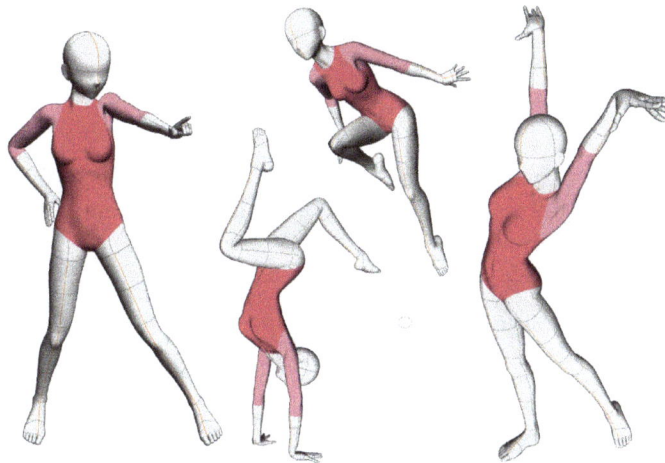

Figure 13.8 – Drawings on top of a 3D figure

If you're working on a series of drawings that contain the same characters, remember to save this 3D model with the drawing on top by following these steps:

1.   Click on the 3D model with the **Object** sub tool (**Operation** tool).

2.   Go to the **Sub Tool Detail** palette and select **3D drawing figure**.

3.   Under **Change body shape**, click the **Register body shape** button.

By registering a body shape with drawings on top, you can easily recover and draw your characters from different angles, including their scars, birthmarks, outfits, and accessories.

When any 3D object is placed on the canvas, a three-point **perspective ruler** is created automatically. This ruler is also hidden automatically, so if you wish to use it to aid your drawings, you must toggle it on by clicking on the ruler icon in the **Layer** palette. When you modify this ruler, the perspective of your 3D object will also change, and if you import a 3D material into a layer that already has a three-point perspective ruler, the material will be positioned to match the ruler.

When you have a 3D layer selected, any new 3D materials that are placed on the canvas will be included in this same 3D layer. This rule does not apply to panoramas, which cannot co-exist: if you place one panorama on top of another, it will replace the existing one. If you wish to have one layer for each 3D object, you have two alternatives:

- Select a non-3D layer before placing the new 3D object on the canvas

- Create a new 3D layer by going to the **Layer** menu and choosing **New Layer** | **3D Layer**

To select a 3D material for your canvas, follow these steps:

1. Navigate to the **Operation** tool.
2. Select the **Object** sub tool.
3. Click on the 3D material and it will be selected.

> **Important note**
>
> When you select a 3D material with multiple parts, such as a 3D figure, you may only select that specific part of the object. When that happens, click on the same part again; the whole 3D material will be selected.

When you place a 3D material on the canvas, the *Movement Manipulator*, *Object Launcher*, and *Root Manipulator* will appear around it, letting you fully customize your 3D material:

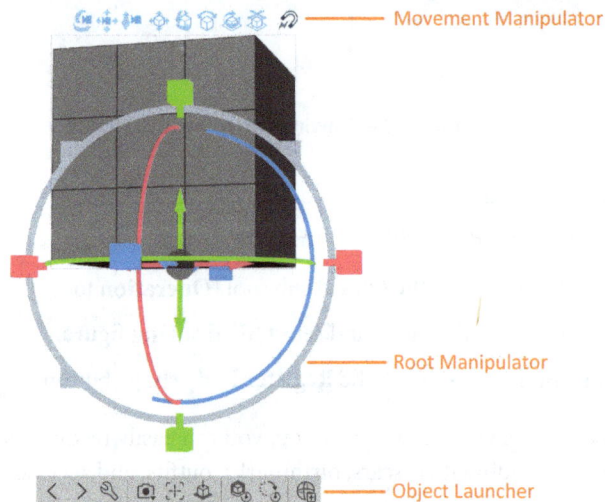

Figure 13.9 – The 3D manipulators

Each of these manipulators includes several functions and tools, and we'll cover them thoroughly throughout the next few sections to ensure you can optimize your 3D operations. Let's start by covering the functions that let you move objects in 3D space.

Mastering 3D manipulators for precise adjustments

Achieving the ideal composition in a 3D scene requires precise control over each element's position, orientation, and perspective. The manipulators available in CSP, including the Movement Manipulator, Object Launcher, and Root Manipulator, are essential tools for making these adjustments with accuracy and ease. These controllers allow you to adjust object placement, scale, and rotation seamlessly, helping you bring your vision to life by fine-tuning each detail. In this section, we'll explore how each manipulator functions and how to use them effectively to shape your 3D scenes exactly as you envision. First, we'll cover the Movement Manipulator, which is great for rotating, translating, and moving 3D materials.

Movement Manipulator

The **Movement Manipulator** is the list of icons that appears on top of the 3D object:

Figure 13.10 – The Movement Manipulator

Here are its functions:

1. **Rotate camera**: Rotates the camera vertically and horizontally. It's as if the camera is being rotated around the scene:

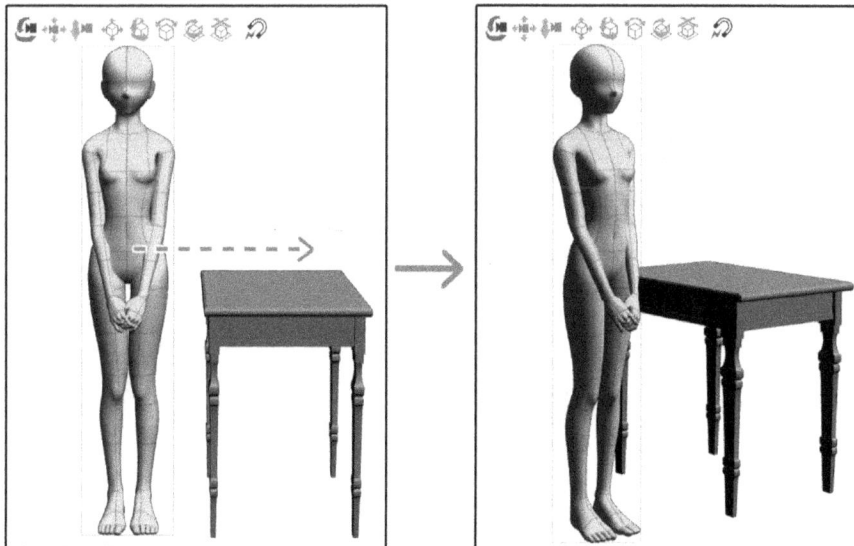

Figure 13.11 – Rotate camera

2. **Translate camera**: Translates the camera up and down, left and right. It's different from the *Rotate camera* function because now it's as if the camera has been moved on a plane:

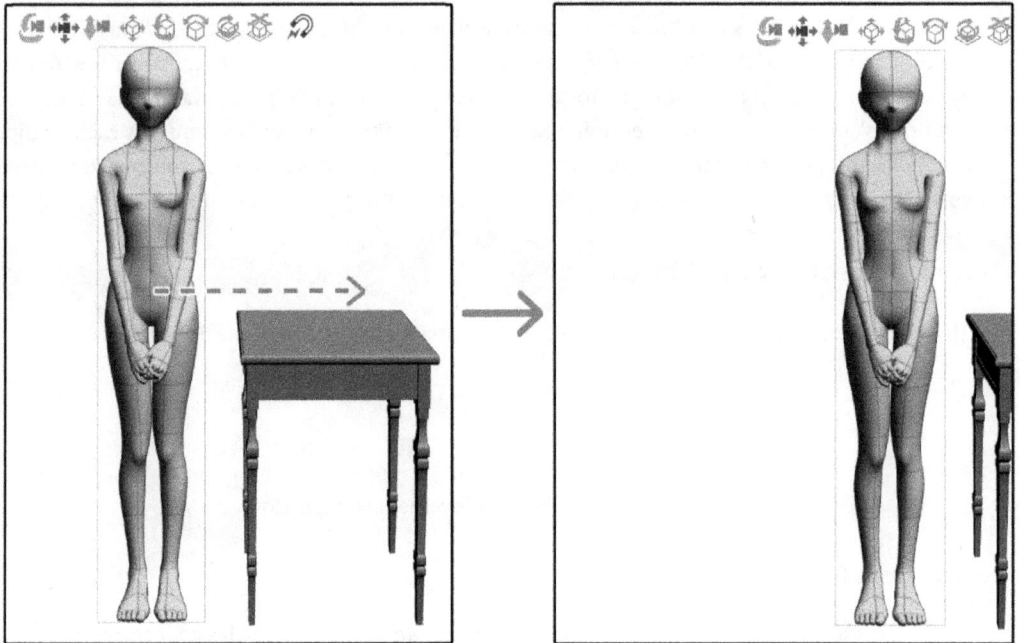

Figure 13.12 – Translate camera

3. **Move camera back and forth**: Moves the camera back and forth, bringing the object closer or taking it farther away:

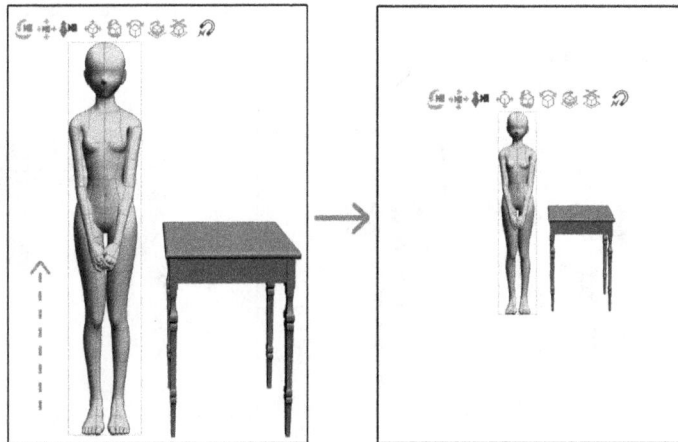

Figure 13.13 – Move camera back and forth

4. **Move on plane**: Moves selected objects or parts on a plane facing the camera:

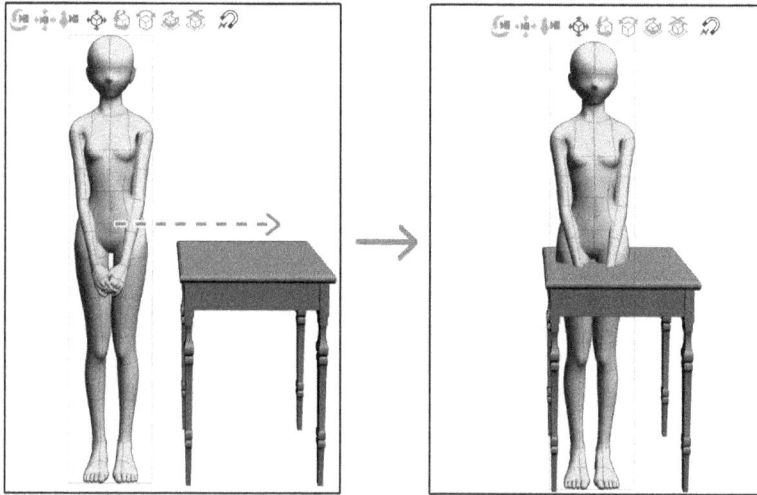

Figure 13.14 – Move on plane

The direction of the dragging motion will change the plane in which the object moves - dragging vertically will move it on the Y axis while dragging horizontally will move it on the X axis.

5. **Rotate relative to camera view**: Rotates selected materials in relation to the camera:

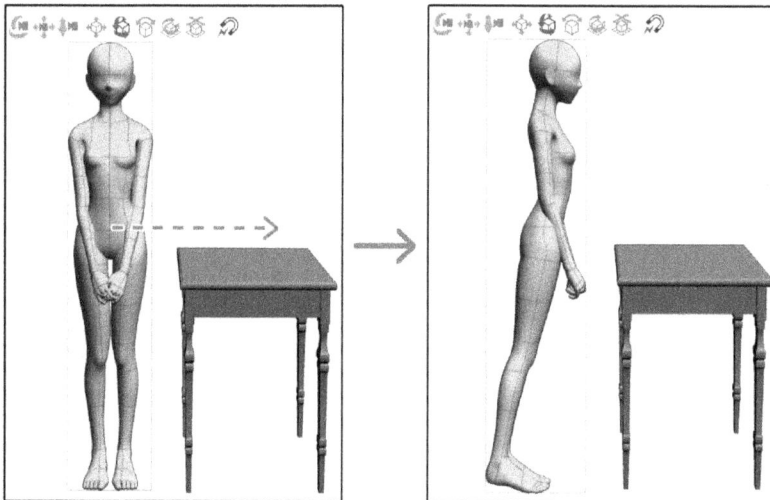

Figure 13.15 – Rotating relative to camera view

6. **Rotate on a plane**: Rotates the selected object around a flat surface, similar to the hands of a clock. For example, if you rotate a character on a plane, its head could tilt sideways until it faces the ground:

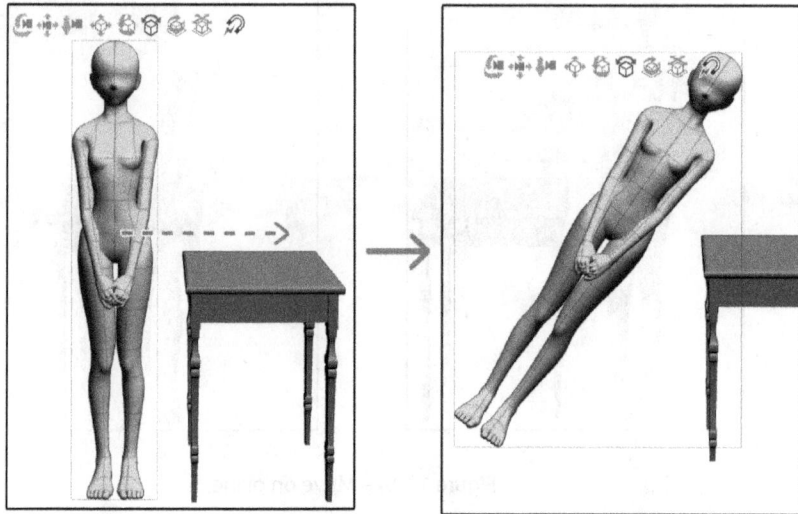

Figure 13.16 – Rotating on a plane

7. **Rotate in 3D space**: Rotates selected materials around their own axes, much like food spinning on a kebab skewer. The object maintains its position while turning in place:

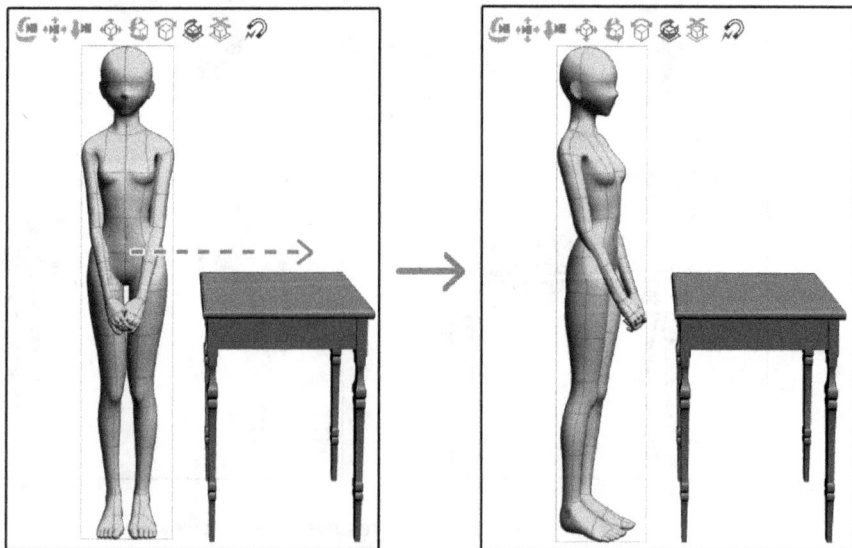

Figure 13.17 – Rotate in 3D space

8. **Snap and move**: Moves selected 3D materials and parts while snapping them to the floor and aligning them with nearby 3D materials:

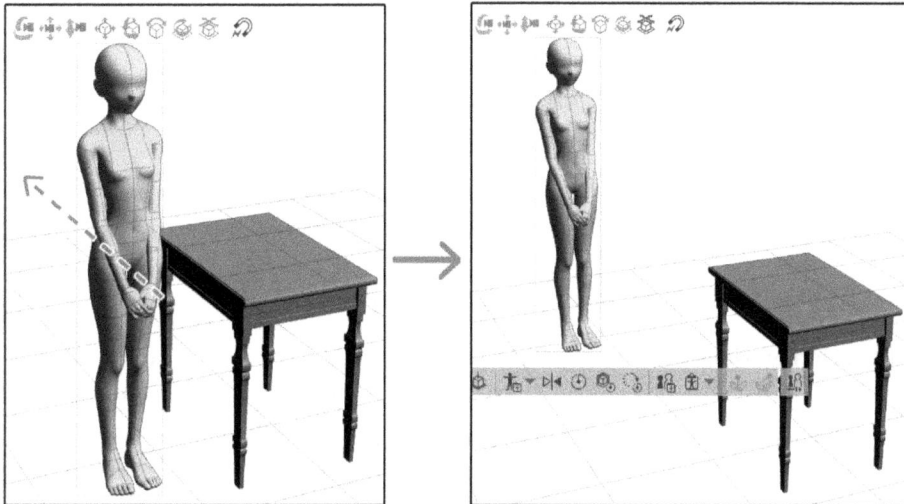

Figure 13.18 – Snap and move

9. **Snap to 3D model**: When toggled on, a bounding box will appear around 3D materials and they will snap to other 3D materials. This is great for aligning 3D objects correctly:

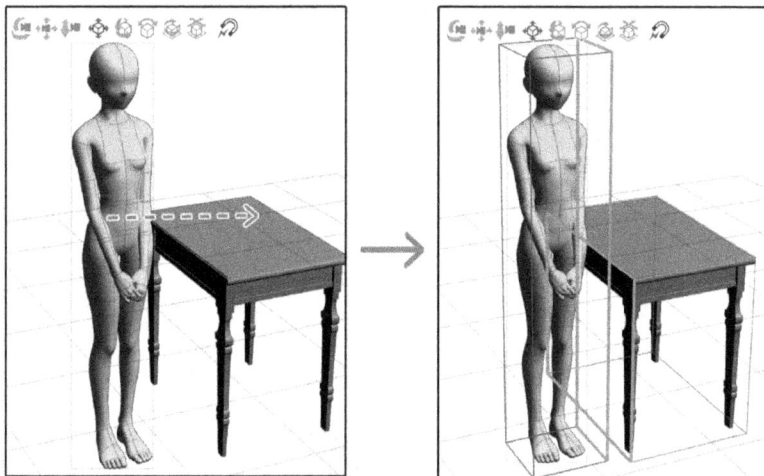

Figure 13.19 – Snap to 3D model

With the Movement Manipulator, you can freely rotate, translate, and move your 3D objects and scenes. Now, let's learn about the Object Launcher, which will allow you to further customize your 3D scene.

Object Launcher

The **Object Launcher** is the list of icons that appear below the 3D material. Its buttons will vary depending on the type of 3D material selected. Here, you can see the functions that are available for all 3D materials:

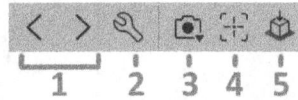

Figure 13.20 – Object Launcher functions common to all 3D materials

These are its functions, numbered according to their positions in *Figure 13.20*:

1. **Select previous/next 3D object**: When working with multiple 3D materials on a single 3D layer, you can toggle between them to select the previous or the next object in the **Object list** area.

2. **Display object list**: This opens the **Sub Tool Detail** palette and displays all 3D materials on the layer. You can select and modify settings for each 3D object from here. The following figure shows an example of the **Object list** area:

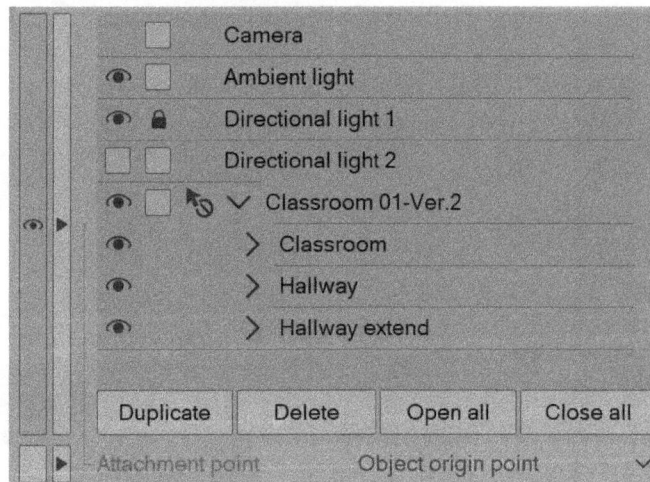

Figure 13.21 – The Object list area

The **Object list** area displays all 3D objects on the same layer. You can use this list to toggle visibility on and off, set material hierarchy, and more. These are its settings:

I. **Material name**: This displays the name of the 3D material. Double-click it to rename the material.

II. **Show/hide**: Click on the eye icon to toggle visibility on and off for a material. When the icon shows an eye, the material is visible on the canvas. When the icon is an empty box, the material is hidden.

III. **Lock**: A locked material cannot be edited. Tapping on the lock icon toggles this function on and off.

IV. **Toggle selection**: This toggles selection on a 3D material on and off. When enabled, you can select the components of a 3D material with multiple parts individually.

V. **Open/close parts**: This arrow on the left side of the material name controls the visibility of part names within the **Object list** area when working with 3D object materials that include pose parts or 3D materials in .lws format. To expand or collapse all hierarchies in the **Object list** area, right-click on the list and choose **Show all** or **Close all** from the menu that appears.

3. **Specify camera angle from preset**: Choose from various default camera angles to adjust your view of the 3D space. This option is unavailable for **Panorama** materials.

4. **Center**: This option adjusts the camera so that it centers on the selected editing target. It's not available for **Panorama** or **3D Background** materials.

5. **Place model on ground level**: This aligns the selected 3D material with the floor of the 3D space. When a specific part of the 3D object is selected, only that part will snap to the base. This option is not available for **Panorama** or **3D Background** materials.

The preceding settings are common to all 3D materials, and there are specific functions for each 3D material type. Let's see the options for 3D figures:

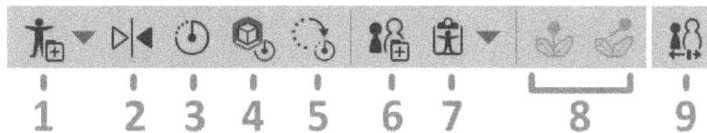

Figure 13.22 – Object Launcher functions exclusive to 3D body types and 3D poses

These are the functions exclusive for 3D figures:

1. **Register full body pose as material**: when you tap this icon, the pose will be saved as a material. If you click the downward-facing arrow on its right-hand side, you can register a hand pose as a material.

2. **Flip model pose horizontally**: reverses the 3D drawing's figure pose horizontally.

3. **Revert model to default pose**: resets the figure to its initial pose.

4. **Reset model scale**: resets the 3D drawing figure to its initial body shape and dimensions.

5. **Reset model rotation**: resets the rotation of the 3D drawing figure to its initial state.

6. **Save body shape as material**: registers the body shape on the **Material** palette.

7. **Use 3D pose material**: with this option, you can apply a pose to the 3D drawing figure. When you click the downward-facing arrow, you can select the following options:

    -   **3D pose (Posemaniacs)**: opens the *POSEMANIACS* website (www.posemaniacs.com), where you can choose a pose from its library and load it onto your 3D model.

    -   **Pose Scanner (image) (Technology preview)**: lets you load an image to be scanned by CSP. The pose inside the image will be applied to the 3D model.

    -   **Hand Scanner (camera)**: opens your device's camera, allowing you to scan your hand and use it for the 3D character.

8. **Lock/release selected joints**: locks or releases the movement of specific joints within a 3D model.

9. **Release all locked joints**: clicking this function will unlock all previously locked joints, allowing you to move and adjust them again.

You'll learn about character posing in more detail in *Chapter 14, Altering and Posing 3D Figures*.

With that, we've covered the functions that are available for 3D figure materials. When you select a **3D Character** material, new functions will appear in the Object Launcher:

Figure 13.23 – Object Launcher functions exclusive to 3D Character materials

The following settings are exclusive to **3D Character** materials:

1. **Switch between enable and disable physical calculation**: enables or disables physical calculations for 3D characters that have physics settings imported from *Clip Studio Modeler*. When enabled, elements such as skirts and hair will move in response to the character's movements.

2. **Select face of character**: loads a list of faces you can choose and place on your character.

3. **Select facial expression of character**: loads a list of expressions you can choose and place on your character.

4. **Select hair style of character**: loads a list of hairstyles you can choose and place on your character.

5. **Select body of character**: loads a list of bodies you can choose and place on your character.

6. **Set display status of accessories of character**: loads a list of accessories you can add to your character.

With this, you can fully customize your 3D character. Now, let's turn our attention to the Object Launcher's functions for 3D Object materials:

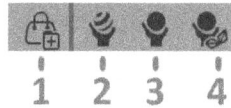

Figure 13.24 – Object Launcher functions for 3D Object materials

Here are the exclusive functions for **3D Object** materials:

1. **Save 3D object to Material palette**: allows you to save the 3D object as a material for easy reuse.
2. **Select material preset**: loads a list of materials you can select to change the tone and texture of the selected 3D object.
3. **Select layout preset**: loads a list of layout options you can select to adjust how the 3D object is positioned and arranged within the scene.
4. **Select movable parts preset**: loads a list of movable parts within the 3D object. Use the slider to adjust the position of these movable parts. This way, you can modify only specific parts of an object.

These same settings are also available for all **3D Background** materials except **Select movable parts preset**. Other 3D materials, such as 3D heads and 3D primitives, have a combination of the functions covered in this section.

The Object Launcher provides a quick and efficient way to access and place 3D objects onto your scene, helping streamline the process of building and customizing your artwork. This tool significantly speeds up the workflow, ensuring you can focus on your creative vision.

Next, we will explore the *Root Manipulator*, which offers precise control over the entire structure of your 3D objects, enabling you to easily adjust and manipulate the base position and scale of elements within the scene.

Root Manipulator

The **Root Manipulator** is a powerful tool in CSP that's designed to give you complete control over the foundation of your 3D objects. By using this tool, you can easily adjust the position, rotation, and scale of your entire 3D object from a single point, making it essential for organizing and positioning complex scenes. The following figure shows it in detail:

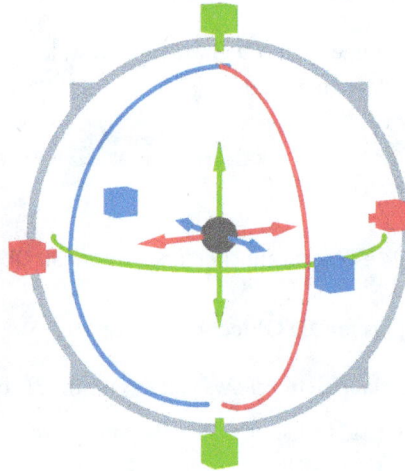

Figure 13.25 – The Root Manipulator

To open the Root Manipulator, tap on a 3D material with the **Object** sub tool. At first glance, it might seem like a complicated function, but it's rather simple. Let's break it down into parts, starting with the gray ones:

- First, the gray ring with arrows determines the size of the object. Drag it outward to increase its size, and inward to decrease it:

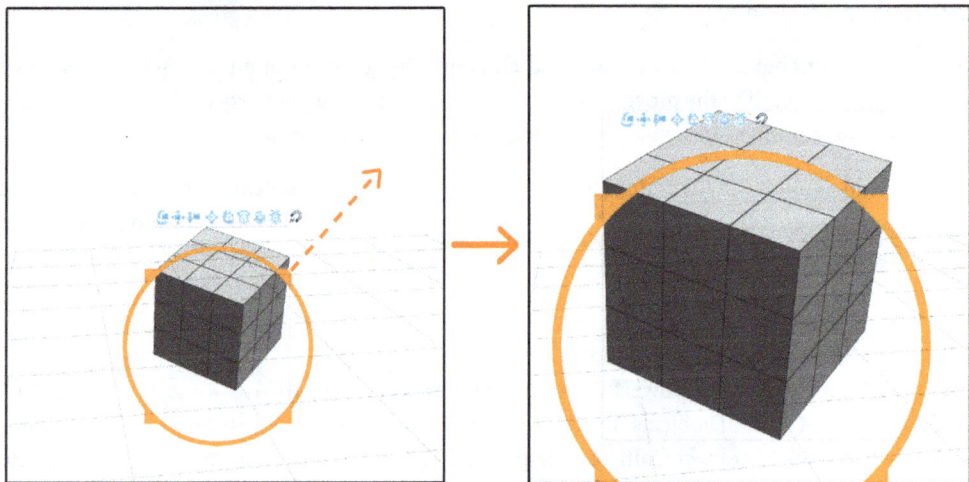

Figure 13.26 – Resizing with the Root Manipulator

- The gray sphere in the center is the *controller*, and you can translate the 3D material in the direction you drag it:

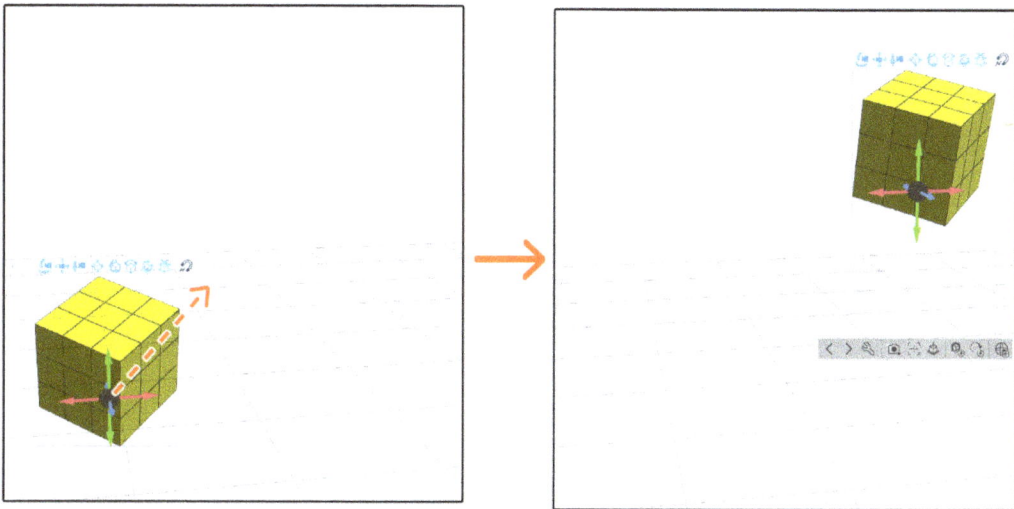

Figure 13.27 – Translating with the Root Manipulator

The other parts are all colored in one of three colors: pink, blue, and pink. These colors indicate the axis in which an operation is performed:

- Pink-colored functions will work horizontally, moving the object from left to right along the X-axis

- Green-colored functions will work vertically, moving the object up and down along the Y-axis

- Blue-colored functions will work along the Z-axis, controlling the depth of the object by moving it forward or backward in 3D space

Each colored part of the manipulator can be used to move and rotate 3D materials:

- **Positioning**: You can drag the arrows to reposition a 3D material on the canvas in the direction the arrow is pointing. In *Figure 13.28*, the cube was dragged toward the camera using the blue arrows:

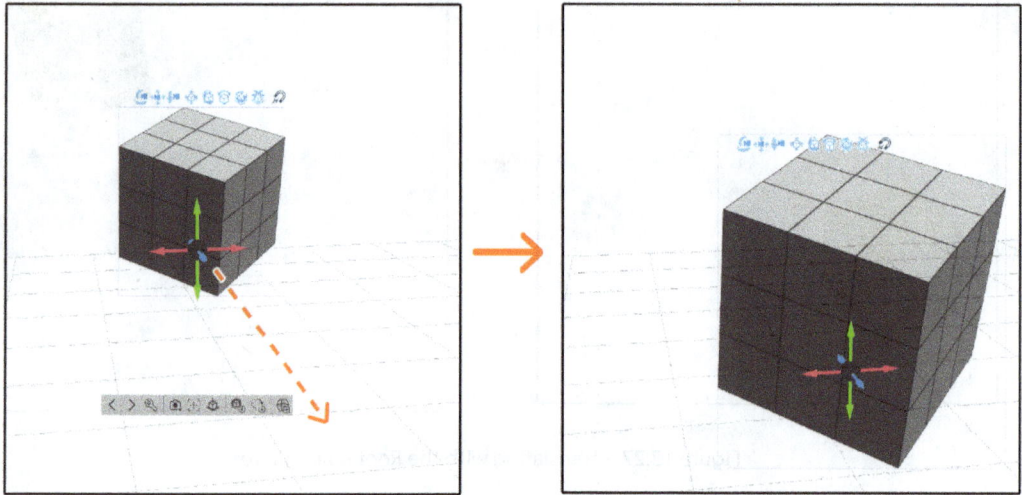

Figure 13.28 – Positioning with the Root Manipulator's arrows

- **Resizing**: Move the squared boxes to resize the 3D material in that axis. In *Figure 13.29*, the cube was resized toward the right-hand side using the pink boxes:

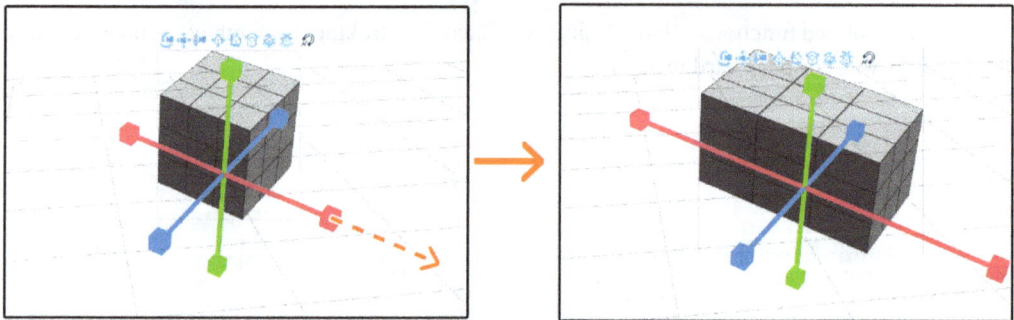

Figure 13.29 – Resizing with the Root Manipulator's boxes

Notice that with this part of the Root Manipulator, you can change the proportions of a 3D material, something you cannot do with the gray outside ring.

- **Rotating**: Click and drag the colored rings to rotate the 3D material. In *Figure 13.30*, the cube was rotated using the blue ring:

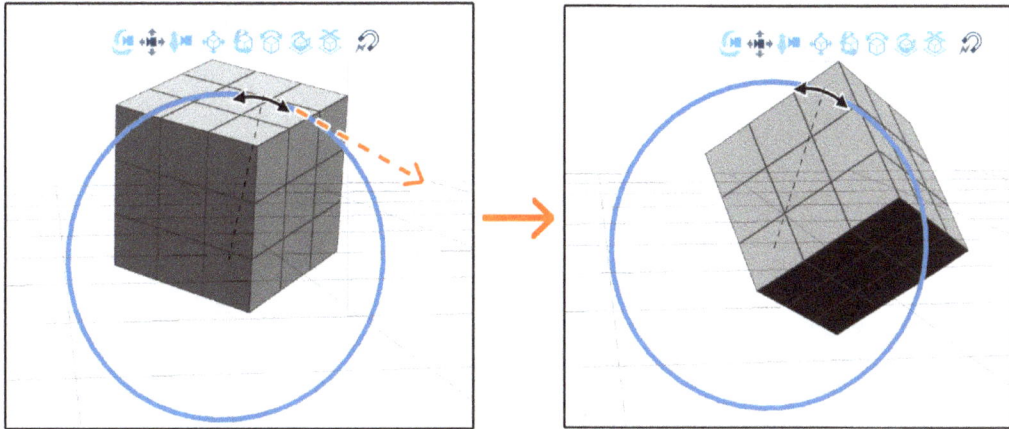

Figure 13.30 – Rotating with the Root Manipulator's colored rings

You can also change the rotation and movement axes. To change these axes, follow these steps:

1. Select the 3D material with the **Object** sub tool (**Operation** tool).

2. Navigate to the **Sub Tool Detail** palette and choose the **Operation** category.

3. Go to the **Movement axis** or **Rotation axis** settings, depending on which axis you want to modify.

4. You can set the axes as follows:

    - **Ground axis**: The Root and Part Manipulator rings align vertically and horizontally with the base (floor) of the 3D space

    - **Object axis**: The Root and Part Manipulator rings align with the angle of the 3D material, matching its current orientation

You can also use the **Sub Tool Detail** palette to transform your 3D material with precision. Go to **Sub Tool Detail | Transform** to find the option to change the object's scale and position and rotate the 3D material on the X, Y, and Z axes.

You can choose which handles are shown by selecting the 3D material, going to the **Tool Property** palette, and adjusting the **On-screen manipulator** setting. Tap the different icons to toggle the visibility of the handles on the manipulator. In the following figure, from left to right, the icons represent **Move**, **Rotate**, and **Scale**:

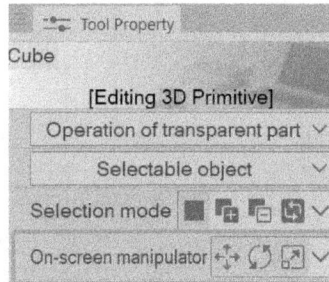

Figure 13.31 – Tool Property | On-screen manipulator

To summarize what we've covered so far, these are the possible methods you can use to manipulate 3D materials on the canvas:

- **Positioning**: Use the Movement Manipulator (**Move on plane** and **Snap and move**), the Root Manipulator (colored arrows or the *controller*), or the **Sub Tool Detail** palette (**Transform | Position**)

- **Rotating**: Use the Movement Manipulator (**Rotate relative to the camera view**, **Rotate on a plane**, and **Rotate in 3D space**), the colored rings on the Root Manipulator, or the **Sub Tool Detail** palette (**Transform | Rotate**)

- **Resizing**: Use the Root Manipulator (gray outside ring) or the **Sub Tool Detail** palette (**Transform | Object scale**)

Once you've arranged the 3D objects to create your scene, it's time to position the camera so that it captures your scene from an ideal perspective and enhances your storytelling. Let's explore more ways to rotate, translate, and move the camera so that you can establish the perfect perspective that complements your scene.

Modifying the camera angle of a 3D scene

In any scene, camera angles play a crucial role in setting the mood, highlighting focal points, and guiding the viewer's perspective. By adjusting the camera, you can completely transform the look and feel of a scene - making it more dramatic, intimate, or balanced according to your artistic vision. Learning to manipulate the camera angle adds depth to your composition and enhances the storytelling power of your art by drawing attention to specific details or interactions within the scene.

As we covered earlier in the *Movement Manipulator* and *Object Launcher* subsections, manipulators let you rotate, translate, and move the camera angle. On top of these manipulators, there are more ways you can move the camera.

The first is the one I use the most: with the 3D layer selected, click outside of the 3D material and drag. This will rotate the camera around the 3D model. To ensure this will work, all icons inside the Movement Manipulator must be deselected.

Another way to set the perspective is with the **Sub Tool Detail** palette. To open this palette and change the camera angle, follow these steps:

1. Select the 3D material with the **Object** sub tool (**Operation** tool).

2. Navigate to the **Tool Property** palette.

3. Tap on the bottom-right wrench icon. The **Sub Tool Detail** palette will open. Alternatively, go to **Window | Sub Tool Detail**.

4. In the **Sub Tool Detail** palette, navigate to the **Camera** category. The following options will appear:

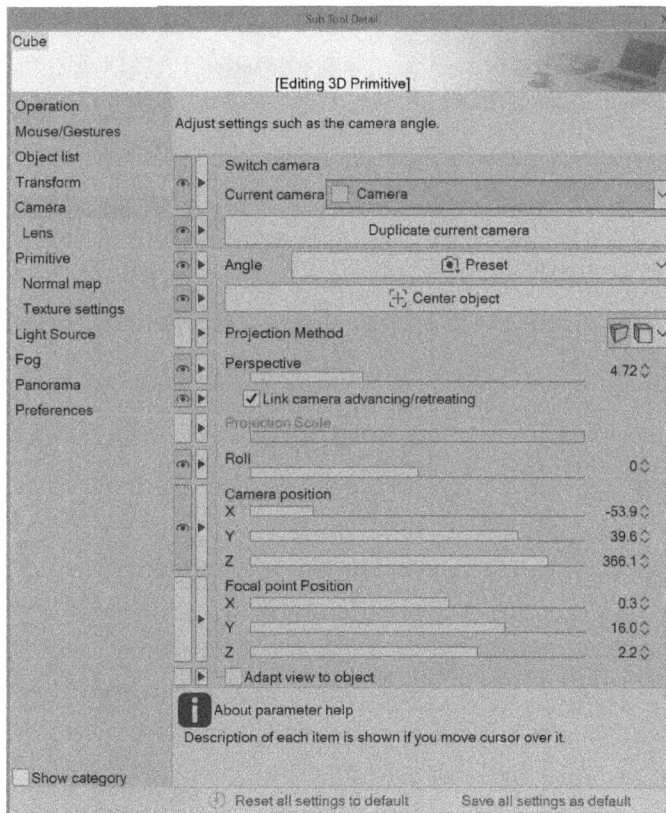

Figure 13.32 – The Sub Tool Detail palette | Camera

They work as follows:

- **Switch camera**: lets you switch between your saved camera angles. We'll cover this topic later in this section. You can also choose **Duplicate current camera**.

- **Angle**: tap the drop-down menu next to **Angle** to show the possible camera angle presets.

- **Projection Method**: choose whether there will be perspective (**Perspective Projection**) or whether lines will be parallel (**Parallel Projection**).

- **Perspective**: use this slider or set a numerical value to determine how much perspective distortion occurs. This setting is visible when you set the **Projection Method** to **Perspective Projection**.

- **Link camera advancing/retreating**: when toggled on, changes in perspective will move the camera to preserve the size of the 3D material. This setting is visible when you set the **Projection Method** to **Perspective Projection**.

- **Projection Scale**: adjusts the field of view of the camera. This setting is visible when you set the **Projection Method** to **Parallel Projection**.

- **Roll**: rotates the camera by twisting, without changes in position or direction.

- **Camera position**: you can use a slider or set numerical values for the **X**, **Y**, and **Z** axes, ensuring the camera angle will match your vision precisely.

- **Focal point Position**: sets the focal point of the camera. You can use sliders or numerical values to change the **X**, **Y**, and **Z** axes.

- **Adapt view to object**: toggle this on to change the focal point position depending on the selected 3D object.

You can also set the camera angle with preset camera angles. There are two ways to load these presets:

- Tap **Specify camera angle**, which is available from the preset icon for the Object Launcher.

- Alternatively, in the **Sub Tool Detail** palette, choose **Camera | Angle | Preset**.

For both options, a list of presets will load. You can choose whichever you want:

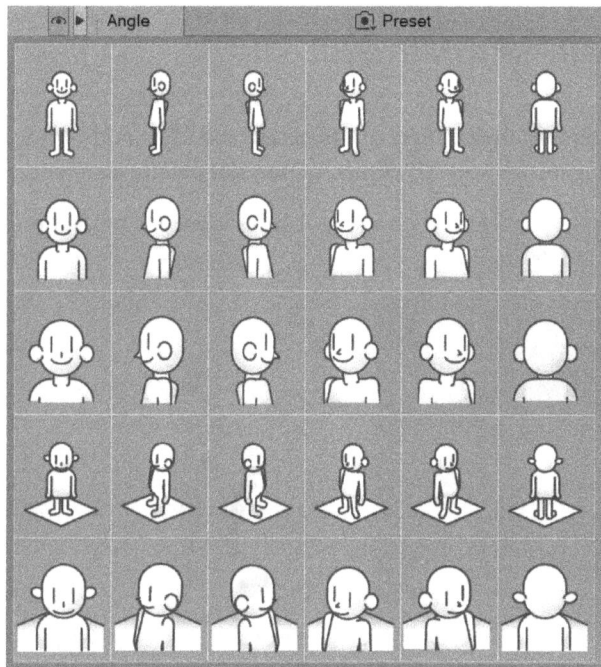

Figure 13.33 – Preset camera angles

Click on any of the presets to load it onto the 3D scene. You can also save specific camera angles. To save a camera angle, follow these steps:

1. Navigate to the **Tool Property** palette.

2. Go to **Switch camera | Current camera**.

3. On the right-hand side, there will be a **Camera** drop-down menu. Click the squared button next to **Camera**; a lock symbol will appear. This locks and saves the camera angle.

4. The new camera angle will be created with a generic name, such as Camera. To rename it, follow these steps:

    I. Open the drop-down menu next to **Camera**. A list of camera angles will appear.

    II. Unlock the camera angle by tapping on the squared button next to **Camera** so that you can make changes to it.

    III. Double-tap the name and type your desired choice.

    IV. Press *Enter* on your keyboard to make the change.

5. If you need to adjust the angle, tap the squared button next to **Camera** again to unlock it.

> **Important note**
>
> You cannot save a camera angle as a preset for all 3D materials. They are only saved for the projects in which they have been created.

To permanently save a camera angle in a material, you must register the 3D material as a new 3D material by clicking on the **Save 3D object to Material palette** icon on the Object Launcher.

Lastly, it's important you know there's an **All sides view** palette (EX only) where you can see 3D materials from multiple angles:

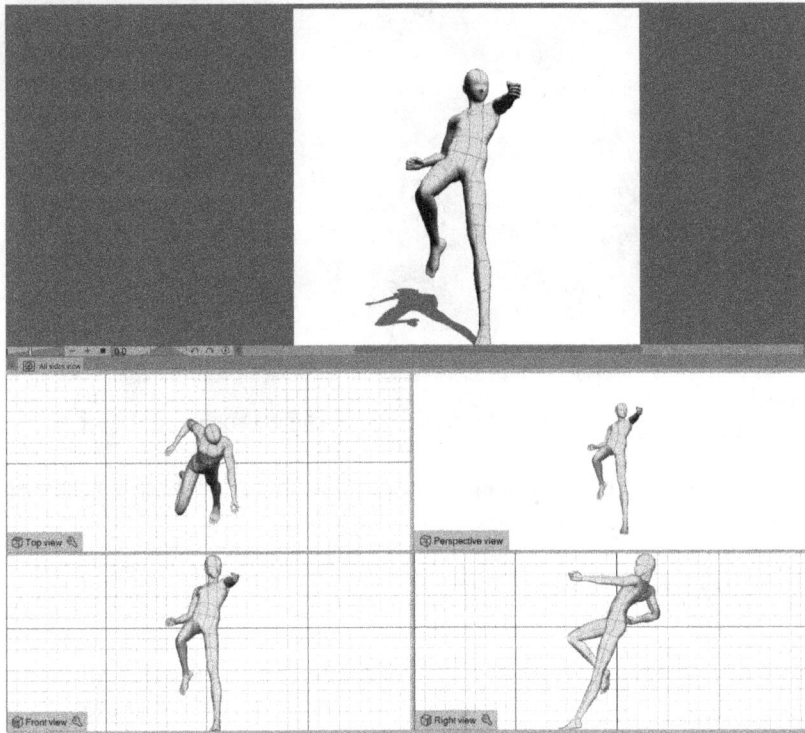

Figure 13.34 – The All sides view palette (EX only)

To locate the **All sides view** palette, go to **Window | All sides view(M)**. From here, you can see the 3D material from different angles simultaneously.

By now, you should have a clear understanding of how to position your 3D objects and adjust the camera to capture your desired view. These manipulations are key to creating a scene that feels balanced and visually appealing. As your 3D composition becomes more complex, managing multiple objects efficiently becomes crucial. The next step is to learn how to use the 3D material hierarchy, which will allow you to organize and manipulate objects more easily, especially when you need to adjust parts of a larger scene. Let's dive into maximizing this hierarchy for a smoother workflow and enhanced control.

Maximizing the 3D material hierarchy for easier manipulation

Managing complex 3D scenes or characters can sometimes feel overwhelming, especially when multiple elements need to be manipulated. The **3D material hierarchy** is a powerful organizational tool that allows you to streamline this process by linking parts of a 3D object together in a structured way. By understanding how to use this hierarchy effectively, you can manipulate multiple parts simultaneously, maintain control over your scene, and improve your workflow.

The 3D material hierarchy refers to the way 3D objects and their components are organized in a parent-child relationship:

- A *parent* object is the main 3D material (such as a character).
- *Child* objects are parts of that material, such as accessories and props.

Using hierarchy, you can control multiple elements simultaneously. For example, adjusting a character's body position will also adjust its glasses, hat, and sword, without you needing to select and move each piece individually. This significantly speeds up the process of arranging complex scenes or characters.

> **Important note**
>
> Changes that are made to the parent object (such as moving, rotating, or scaling) will automatically affect the child objects attached to it, but changes made to the child material will not affect the parent material.

Figure 13.35 shows an example of a 3D material hierarchy. The character is the parent and the sword is the child, so when we move the character, the sword will move as well:

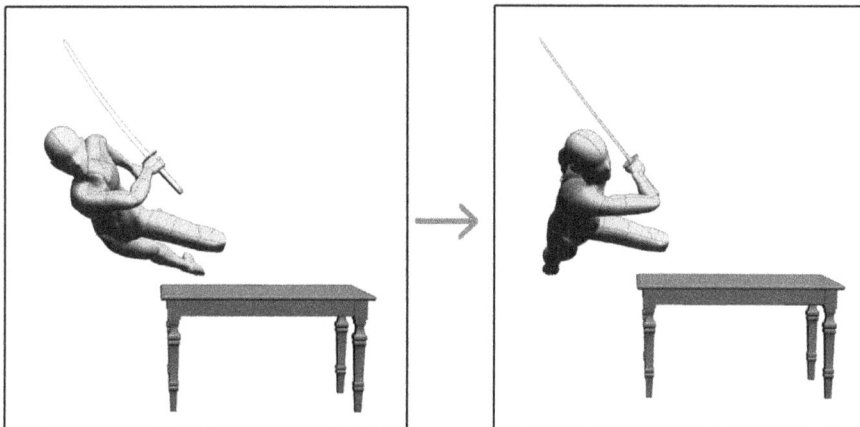

Figure 13.35 – 3D material hierarchy example

This setup allows for more efficient manipulation of complex 3D materials without the need to adjust each component. To set up a parent-child hierarchy, follow these steps:

1. Select a 3D material on your canvas with the **Object** sub tool (**Operation** tool).

2. Go to the **Sub Tool Detail** palette and select **Object list**. A list containing all of the 3D materials in a scene will appear, as we covered extensively earlier in the section *Mastering 3D manipulators for precise adjustments,* under Object Launcher:

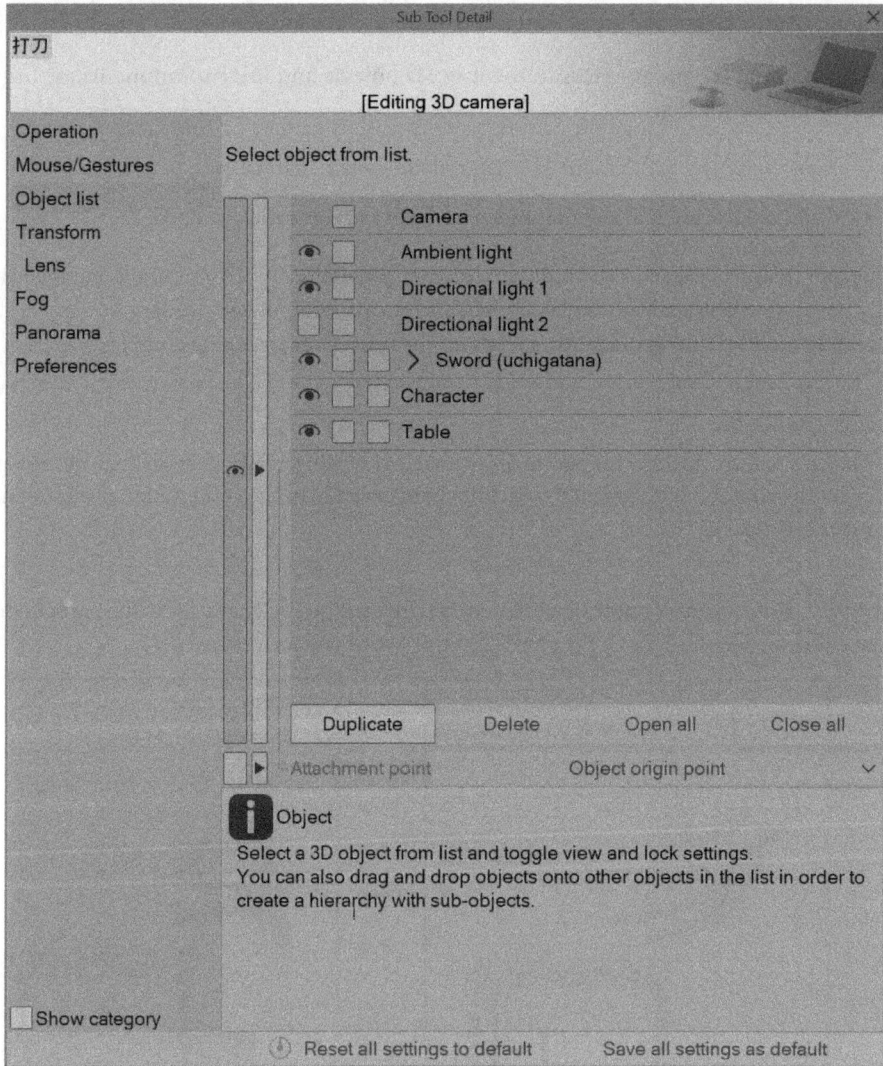

Figure 13.36 – The Sub Tool Detail palette | Object list

3. Drag and drop the child 3D material onto the parent 3D material. *Figure 13.37* shows the appearance of linked materials on the list - **Character** is the parent and **Sword (uchigatana)** is the child:

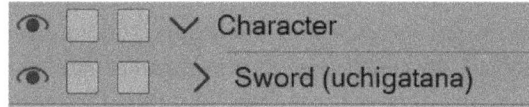

Figure 13.37 – Hierarchy on the Object list

4. You can set another level of connection with a grandchild material by placing 3D materials under a child material.

5. To unlink 3D materials, drag the child material outside of the **Object list** area until a red outline appears around the edges of the palette, then release it.

Models with joints, such as 3D drawing figures or characters, can have materials attached as child items to specific body parts, such as the hands or head. For example, attaching glasses to a figure's head will cause the glasses to move along with the head's motion. To attach items to specific body parts, follow these steps:

1. Set the hierarchy by following the preceding steps.

2. Select the child material from the **Object list** area.

3. Below the list, you'll find the **Attachment point** function and a drop-down menu that lets you select joints such as **Head**, **Hips**, and **Left hand**.

4. Select the joint to which you wish to attach the child material.

5. Adjust the child material's position. Now, when you modify the parent material, the child material will follow.

By understanding and utilizing the 3D material hierarchy, you can create more complex and flexible scenes while keeping the process organized and manageable. This hierarchical structure gives you greater control over your materials and enhances your ability to work quickly and efficiently.

Summary

Mastering 3D object manipulation is key to creating dynamic and polished scenes that feel natural and visually compelling. Beginning with the basics of introducing 3D materials onto the canvas, you can access and import various 3D assets to lay the groundwork for your designs. Once placed on the canvas, you can modify each 3D material's position by rotating, translating, and moving them using the on-screen manipulators. You can also use the **Sub Tool Detail** palette, ensuring the 3D composition will represent exactly the scene you envisioned.

Now that you have a solid understanding of camera adjustments, you've gained even more control over your scenes as you can utilize a range of 3D manipulators and functions. To further streamline scene building, the 3D material hierarchy helps organize and connect objects, allowing logical, responsive groupings where changes to one item can influence related parts.

You now have a comprehensive set of techniques for confidently handling 3D objects and creating well-integrated scenes. The next chapter focuses on helping you achieve greater precision by showing you how to freely position your 3D figures, offering a powerful way to ensure your characters align seamlessly with your vision.

Altering and Posing 3D Figures

Creating convincing and expressive 3D figures requires more than technical skill; you must understand how to convey emotion, movement, and personality through poses and proportions. Whether you're looking to bring a subtle, natural stance to a character or craft an exaggerated, dynamic posture, these techniques can make your scenes far more engaging. With 3D posing in **Clip Studio Paint** (**CSP**), every slight adjustment contributes to the overall impact, turning static figures into characters that feel alive.

In this chapter, we're going to cover the following topics:

- Changing the proportions of your 3D figure
- Posing your 3D figure
- Posing 3D hands

We'll explore how to customize and pose 3D figures to suit your artistic vision as well as how to adjust the proportions of 3D models, making them more stylized or realistic based on your needs. Additionally, we'll delve into the finer details of posing 3D hands, giving your characters natural and nuanced gestures. By the end of this chapter, you'll be equipped with skills to create characters that look unique and natural, with poses and proportions tailored to your scene's needs. These tools and techniques will allow you to add depth and personality to every 3D model you create.

Changing the proportions of your 3D figure

Adjusting the proportions of your 3D character is a powerful way to add individuality and depth to your creations. Whether you're designing a strongly built hero, a cute and tiny companion, or a character with exaggerated, cartoon-like features, manipulating body and facial proportions lets you fine-tune their appearance to suit your artistic vision. This flexibility opens the door to a wide range of storytelling possibilities, ensuring your characters stand out and align perfectly with your narrative.

You can change the entire body of the 3D figure, specific parts of the body, and the head. Let's start by covering how to change the body shape of your 3D model.

Altering the 3D body shape

Adjusting the overall body shape of your 3D figure is the foundation for creating diverse and unique designs. Altering height, weight, and muscle mass lets you quickly define a character's silhouette, which helps convey their personality, role, or background immediately.

To adjust the body shape of a figure, follow these steps:

1. Select the 3D figure with the **Object** sub tool (**Operation** tool).
2. Tap the **Change body shape** icon on the extreme right side of **Object Launcher**. We've covered the **Object Launcher** and other 3D manipulators extensively in *Chapter 13, Manipulating 3D Objects on the Canvas.*

    Alternatively, go to the **Sub Tool Detail** palette and tap on the **3D drawing figure** category.

When you follow these steps, you'll see these settings:

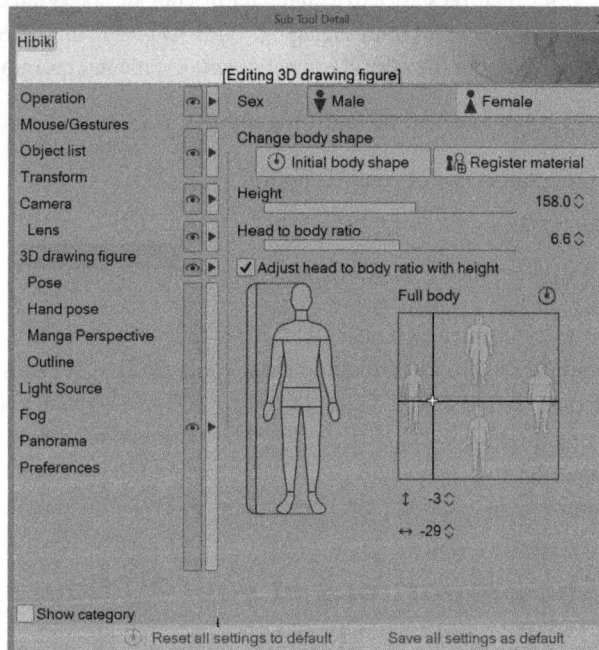

Figure 14.1 – 3D drawing figure settings

Let's cover how each part works.

First, you can choose the sex of the figure: **Male** or **Female**. Changing the sex will modify body proportions automatically, such as the hip-to-waist ratio. In the following figure, you can see that changing from **Male** to **Female** also modifies the height of the 3D figures:

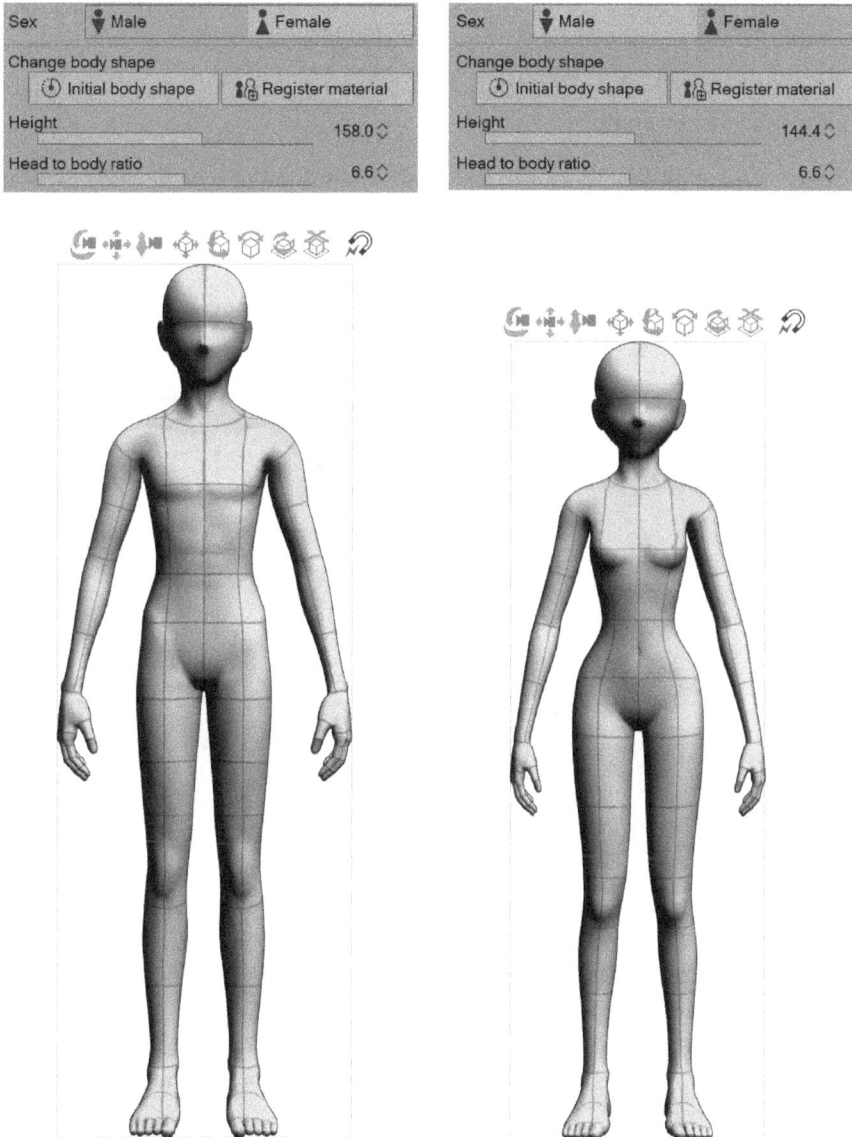

Figure 14.2 – How changing the sex affects the 3D figure

You can reset the body shape by clicking **Initial body shape** and save your current body shape as a preset by clicking **Register material**.

You can change the height and head-to-body ratio of your 3D figure with the following settings:

- **Height**: Determines the height of your character in centimeters.

- **Head to body ratio**: Determines the proportion of head and body. The bigger the head-to-body ratio, the more your character will appear childlike.

- **Adjust head to body ratio with height**: When toggled on, changing the height will modify the head-to-body ratio.

You can determine the length, width, and muscle definition of specific body parts and the entire body. Go to the **Sub Tool Detail** palette and find the full-body figure on the left side with a diagram on the right side:

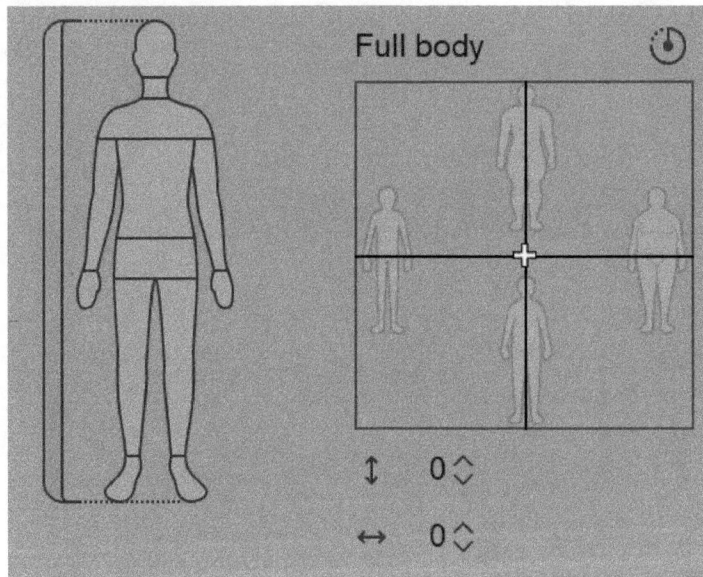

Figure 14.3 – Settings to adjust body proportions

Let's analyze this setting. First, you can select which body part will be affected: **Full body**, **Head**, **Neck**, **Shoulders**, **Torso**, **Hips**, **Arms**, **Hands**, **Legs**, or **Feet**. To select a body part, tap on it within the figure shown in *Figure 14.3* (left). For example, if you want to modify the shape of the arms, click on the figure's arms. For the full body, select the tall bar on the left side of the character, which is highlighted in blue in *Figure 14.3*.

Having selected which body part you wish to change, you can use the diagram to the right to modify the body part's shape. The diagram works as follows:

- **Up and down**: Dragging the cross in the slider up will increase muscle definition in the **Full body** category, and down will decrease it. You can see a **Full body** example here:

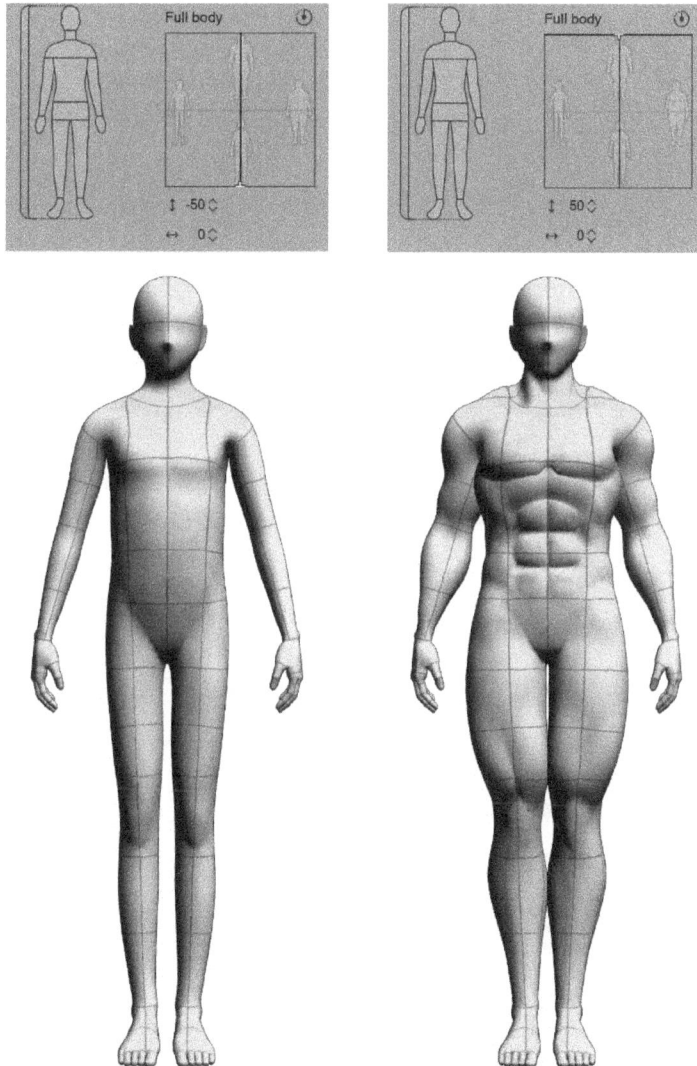

Figure 14.4 – Adjusting the full body with the diagram

In other body parts, dragging the cross up will make the limb longer, while dragging it down will make it shorter.

- **Left and right**: Dragging the cross to the left will result in a leaner body, and to the right will make it fuller. Here is an example of changes made to the legs in both height and fullness:

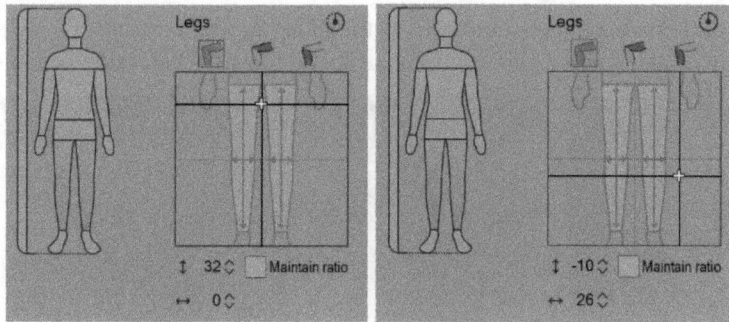

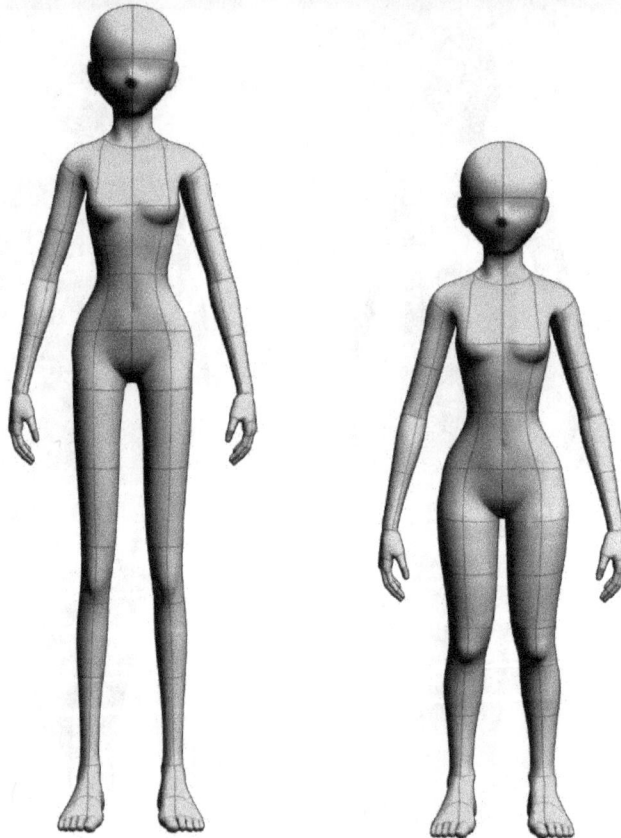

Figure 14.5 – Adjusting the legs with the diagram

- You can also set numerical values below the diagram for precise adjustments.

- Tap the *reset* button in the upper-right corner of the diagram to reset the slider to its default shape. This changes only the selected body part, not the entire figure.

When modifying the arms, legs, and torso, you can modify sub-sections, such as **Upper arm** and **Forearm**. These sub-sections are visible above the diagram and below the body part's name:

Figure 14.6 – Sub-sections you can change when Arms is selected

Tap on **Maintain ratio** (visible in *Figure 14.5*) to keep the original proportions.

If you wish to reset a 3D figure to its original body shape, follow the next steps:

1. Select the 3D figure with the **Object** sub tool (**Operation** tool).
2. Navigate to the **Sub Tool Detail** palette.
3. Under the **3D drawing figure** category, go to **Change body shape**.
4. Tap **Initial body shape** to reset all sliders related to body shape.
5. Alternatively, go to **Tool Property** | **Change body shape** | **Initial body shape**.

You can register a body shape as a material, which is convenient when creating sequential work and maintaining character's proportions. To register a body shape, follow the next steps:

1. Select the 3D figure with the **Object** sub tool (**Operation** tool).
2. Go to **Object Launcher** and tap **Save body shape as material**.

   Alternatively, go to **Tool Property** | **Change body shape** | **Register material**.

   Another option is to go to the **Sub Tool Detail** palette | **3D drawing figure** | **Change body shape** | **Register material**.
3. The **Material property** dialog will open.
4. Specify the name, add tags, and select the saving location.
5. Hit **OK** to register the body shape.

When you want to use a saved 3D body shape, go to the **Material** palette and locate your desired 3D body shape, then click and drag it to the canvas. Alternatively, select the 3D body shape material in the **Material** palette and tap the **Paste selected material to canvas** icon at the bottom of the palette. We've covered the **Material** palette extensively in *Chapter 3*, *Setting Up Materials for Consistency and Speed*.

> **Important note**
>
> You can drag and drop a 3D body shape on top of a 3D pose, and the 3D figure will have the selected pose. The opposite is also possible—first, put the 3D body shape on the canvas and then the pose on top of it.

Refining the entire body shape lets you establish a character's presence and overall aesthetic. Once you set the base shape, you can move on to more detailed modifications, focusing on specific body parts to perfect the design. Tweaking individual body parts allows you to add fine details and enhance realism or stylization in your characters. Whether you're adjusting arm length, torso width, or leg proportions, these targeted changes enable precise control over your character's anatomy.

Customizing body shape is essential for fine-tuning your character's design, ensuring each detail supports the overall vision. After shaping the body, the next step is to focus on the head, where even minor adjustments can impact individuality.

Modifying a 3D head

The head is one of the most critical elements of character design, as it's often the focal point for storytelling and emotional connection. By modifying facial proportions and features, you can create a dynamic and memorable character.

To find the 3D head models, go to the **Material** palette | **3D** | **Head**. Drag a 3D head model to the canvas to use and edit it. There are nine preset models you can choose from:

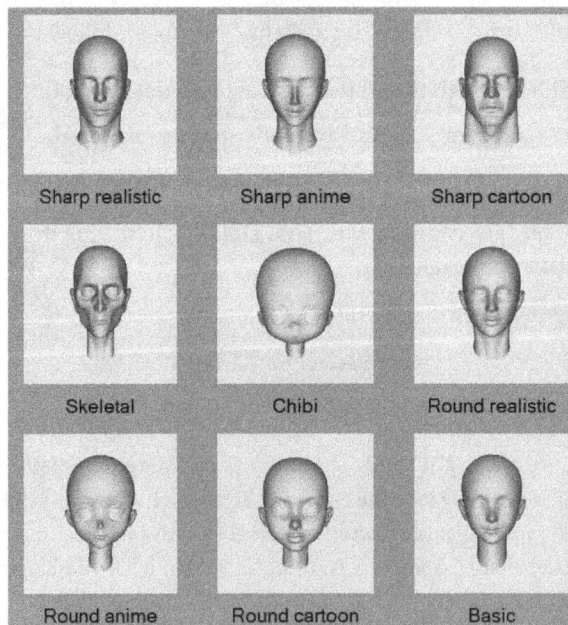

Figure 14.7 – 3D head model presets

If you want to modify one of the presets, there are two different methods. The first is to click on the 3D head model on the canvas and use the scale manipulators (the colored squares on the root manipulator) to make the head longer or broader:

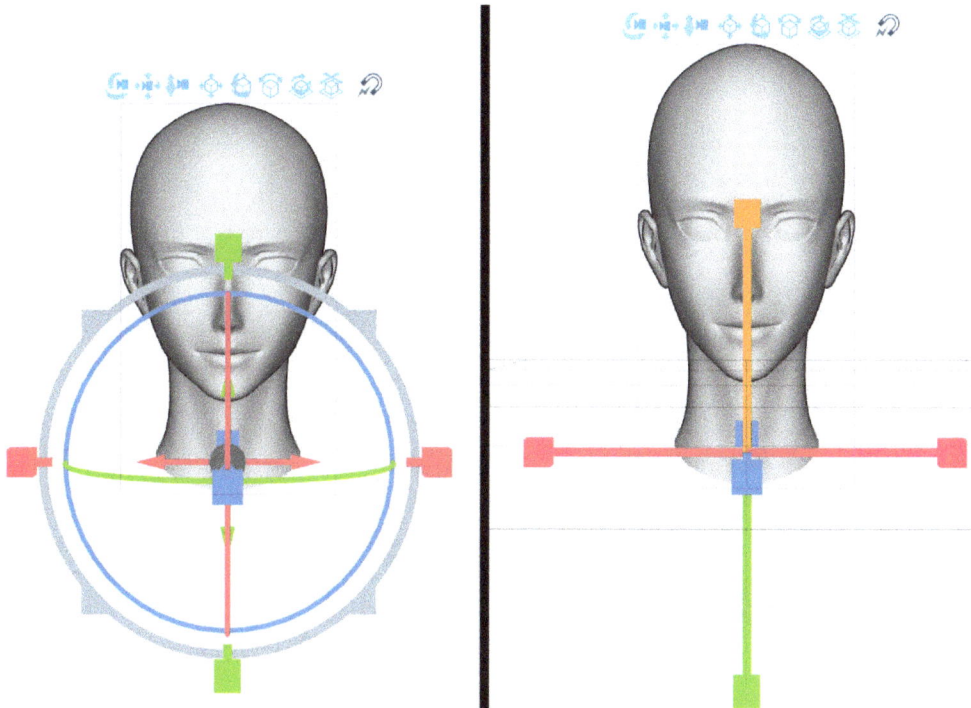

Figure 14.8 – Modifying a 3D head model with the scale manipulator

> **Important note**
>
> Changes made to the head proportion with the scale manipulators will not be registered in the **Material** palette once you register the 3D head model. If you wish to apply changes permanently and save them, you must use the **Sub Tool Detail** palette method covered next.

For more precise adjustments, alter the settings inside the **Sub Tool Detail** palette. To edit a 3D head model in detail, follow these steps:

1. Navigate to the **Sub Tool Detail** palette.
2. Select the **Head model** category.

Inside the **Head model** category, you can modify proportions using the **Face Mixer** or the **Facial features** sub-category. Let's start by covering **Face Mixer**.

Face Mixer

Face Mixer, shown in *Figure 14.9*, applies parts of preset proportions to the 3D head model.

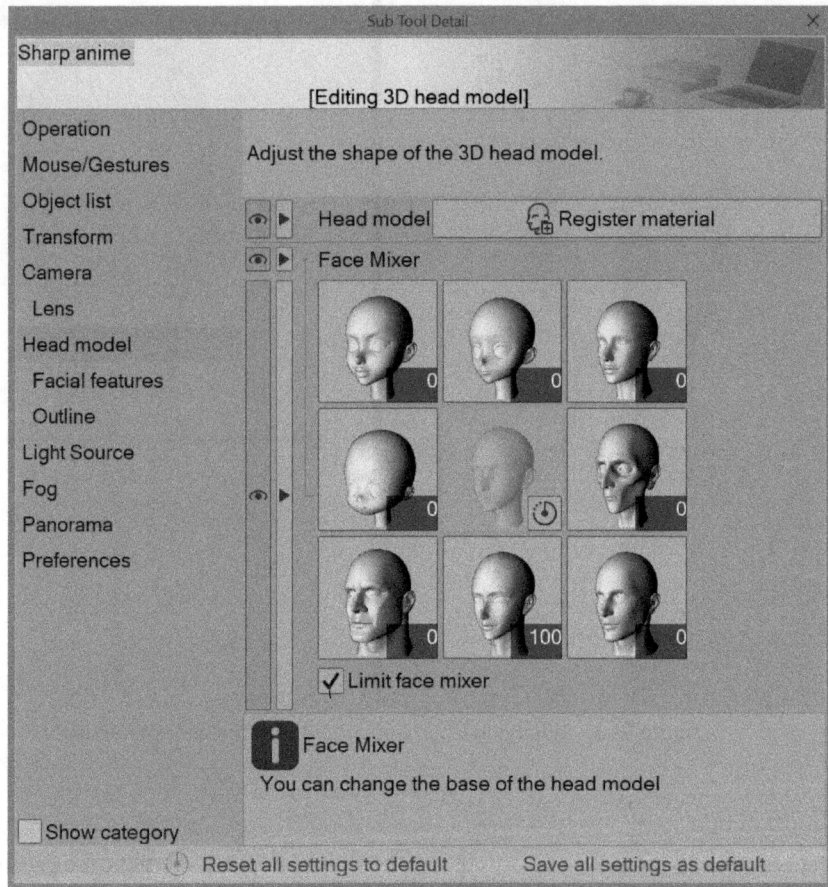

Figure 14.9 – Face Mixer

Face Mixer shows nine face dimensions, with the center tile being the default base face. At the bottom of each dimension, you can find a numbered value. The higher the number, the more that dimension will show on the 3D head model, with **100** being the highest value.

Figure 14.10 shows examples of different head proportions using some of the nine dimensions:

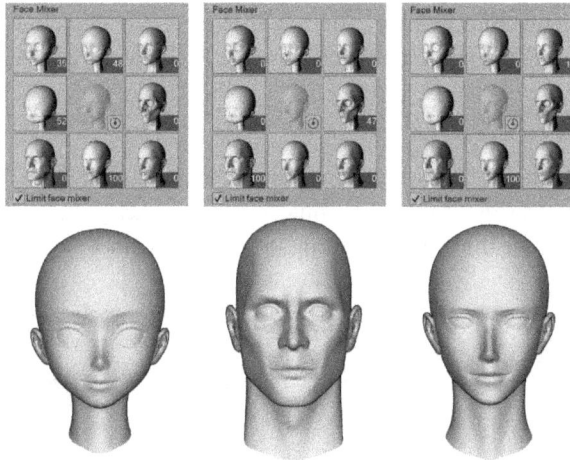

Figure 14.10 – Examples of 3D heads modified with Face Mixer

Important note
When you set several dimensions to a high level, it might distort the head.

To avoid facial distortion, you can toggle **Limit face mixer** on:

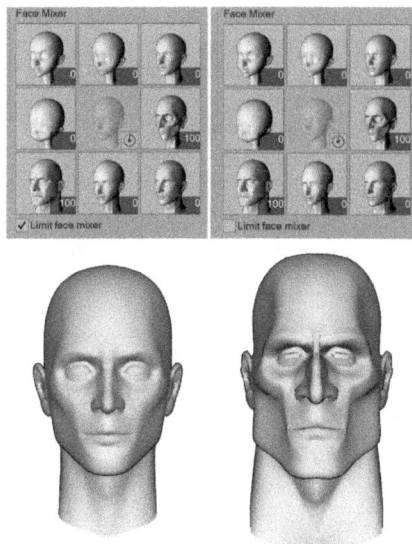

Figure 14.11 – The same 3D head with Limit face mixer toggled on (left) and off (right)

If you want an exaggerated or unrealistic appearance, you may leave it toggled off.

Face Mixer is convenient for quickly assigning specific proportions to your characters. However, it has limited precision. To fine-tune it further, use the **Facial features** category.

Facial features

In the **Head model** category in the **Sub Tool Detail** palette, you'll find the **Facial features** sub-category. It shows an image of a side profile, and you can click on each facial feature you want to adjust. In *Figure 14.12*, you can see the available settings for **Eyes** and **Nose**:

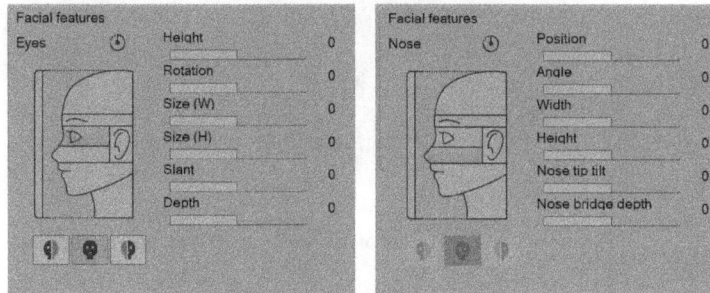

Figure 14.12 – Possible changes for Eyes and Nose inside Facial features

As you can see in the preceding figure, the settings will change depending on the facial feature you choose.

When you narrow down the palette size, the side profile picture disappears, and a drop-down menu shows up instead:

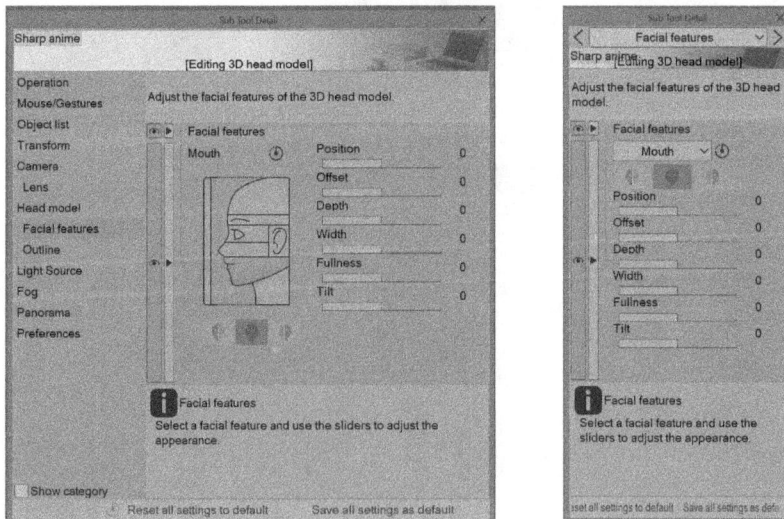

Figure 14.13 – The Facial features settings in full width (left) and collapsed (right)

If you wish to restore any facial feature to its default setting, tap the *reset* icon next to the facial feature name (**1** in *Figure 14.14*):

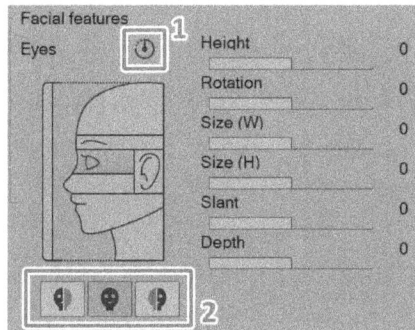

Figure 14.14 – The reset icon (1) and symmetry icons (2)

Following this procedure will reset only the selected facial feature.

Below the side profile image, you can select whether the changes will be only on the left side, symmetrical, or only on the right side by tapping on the bottom icons (**2** in *Figure 14.14*).

You can change the direction of the 3D head model by clicking on the tall bar on the left side of the side profile image (highlighted in blue in *Figure 14.15*). The default angle is **0**, keeping the chin level with the floor and the head facing straight ahead. You can change the **Tilt**, **Angle**, and **Side tilt** values to modify how the 3D head model appears:

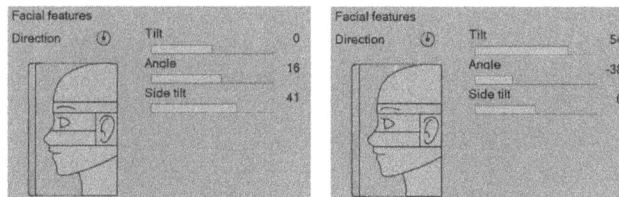

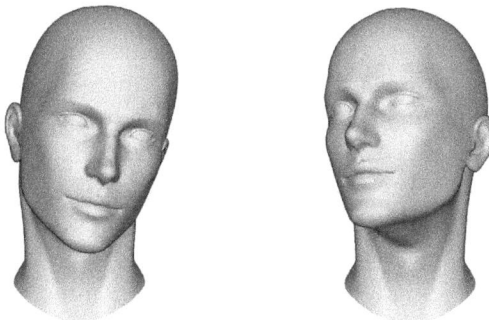

Figure 14.15 – Example settings for the 3D head direction

After you have set your character's facial proportions, you can use this 3D model to draw it at any angle you wish. This function is incredibly convenient for comics, where you draw the same character from many angles. To make your 3D head available in any project, save the 3D head model to the **Material** palette. Follow these instructions:

1. Go to the **Sub Tool Detail** palette | **Head model** | **Register material**.

    Alternatively, in **Object Launcher** below the 3D head model, tap the **Save the 3D head model to the Material palette** icon.

2. The **Material property** dialog will appear.

3. Place a name, select a saving location, add tags if you wish, and then hit **OK** to finish the registration.

4. Now, you can drag and drop this modified 3D head on any project you want.

> **Important note**
>
> When you place the 3D head on a layer, the head will float in space. To make it part of an existing 3D figure, you must set a hierarchy between the 3D figure and the 3D head model, as we covered in *Chapter 13, Manipulating 3D Objects on the Canvas.*

Pairing a custom 3D head model with specific body shapes creates customized characters that can significantly speed up your drawing process. By mastering the ability to adjust body proportions, facial features, and overall dimensions, you gain valuable tools for creating characters that resonate visually and emotionally. From subtle tweaks to bold transformations, these adjustments enable you to craft distinct and memorable figures easily.

With your character's proportions set, it's time to bring them to life by focusing on their pose. In the next section, we'll explore how to pose your 3D character, ensuring their stance and movement align seamlessly with their personality and purpose.

Posing your 3D figure

Posing your 3D figure is vital in bringing a character to life. A well-crafted pose conveys mood, attitude, and movement, turning static models into expressive figures that resonate with viewers. With a clear understanding of joint manipulation and pose dynamics, you can create scenes that feel real and characters that feel genuine. From understanding which joints to adjust to learning how to fine-tune poses for a natural effect, these skills will help you craft characters that move, stand, and interact believably.

You can import poses and create your own poses in CSP. We'll cover both of these processes, starting with importing.

Importing 3D poses into CSP

There are many ways you can pose your characters. The easiest one is to import a pose from the **Material** palette. CSP comes with some preset poses you can use, such as running and walking. To apply a preset pose on your 3D figure, follow these steps:

1. Go to the **Material** palette | **3D** | **Pose** folder and choose a pose.

2. Once you have selected your desired pose, drag and drop it onto the canvas. A figure with the chosen pose will appear.

3. If you already have a 3D figure on the canvas and its layer is selected, dropping the pose on the canvas will apply it to the 3D figure.

You can also import poses from *CLIP STUDIO ASSETS,* follow these steps:

1. Download a **3D Pose Material** asset at `https://assets.clip-studio.com`.

2. Inside CSP, go to **Window** | **Material** to open the **Material** palette.

3. Navigate to the **Downloads** folder.

4. Select your downloaded pose and drag and drop it onto the canvas. A figure with the selected pose will appear. If you already have a figure on the canvas, the pose will be applied to it.

You can also import poses from the Posemaniacs website or use the **Photo Scanner** feature to import poses. Let's cover first the Posemaniacs integration, which offers hundreds of poses from which you can choose.

Setting up poses with Posemaniacs

Browsing the Posemaniacs pose library opens a world of possibilities for creating lifelike and dynamic poses. With Posemaniacs, you can access a wide range of pre-made poses that serve as excellent starting points or inspiration for your characters. From simple standing positions to complex action stances, the library provides countless options to fit any scene.

There are four methods to apply a Posemaniacs pose on your CSP 3D figure. The first one is through the **File** menu inside CSP:

1. Go to **File** | **Import**.

2. Select **3D pose (Posemaniacs)....**

3. The Posemaniacs website will open, and you can browse and select a pose.

Another method is through the **Sub Tool Detail** palette:

1. Place a **3D Figure** or **3D Character** material on the canvas.

2. Select it with the **Object** sub tool (**Operation** tool).

3. Go to **Tool Property** or click the *wrench* icon in **Object Launcher** to open the **Sub Tool Detail** palette.

4. Select the **Pose** category and the **Pose** sub-section.

5. Click on the middle-bottom icon (the *P* with a circle and an arrow, which you can see in *Figure 14.16*):

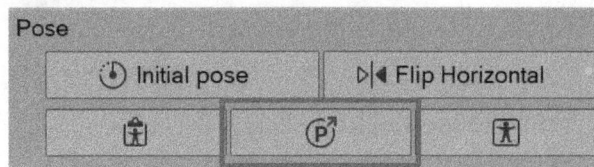

Figure 14.16 – The Posemaniacs button within the Sub Tool Detail palette

6. The Posemaniacs website will open, and you can browse and select a pose.

You can also use **Object Launcher**:

1. Place a **3D Figure** or **3D Character** material on the canvas.

2. Select it with the **Object** sub tool (**Operation** tool).

3. On **Object Launcher**, select **3D pose (Posemaniacs)**:

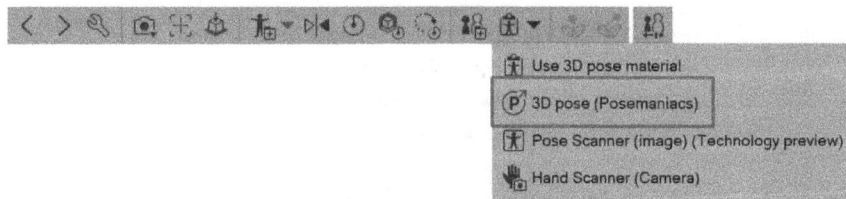

Figure 14.17 – The Posemaniacs button within Object Launcher

4. The Posemaniacs website will open, and you can browse and select a pose.

Lastly, you can open a Posemaniacs pose from your browser:

1. Open the Posemaniacs website: `https://www.posemaniacs.com/`.

2. On the top bar, click **Search** to view the poses library.

3. Select a pose.

In any of these methods, follow these steps once you have selected the pose:

1. On the Posemaniacs website, navigate to the section below the 3D model.

2. On the left side, you can find a button with the *CSP* icon and the text **Open**. Click on this icon.

3. A dialog will open to confirm. Click the **Open** button, and the pose will load on your CSP canvas.

> **Important note**
>
> If CSP is open but no canvas is open, it will not load the 3D pose in CSP. Make sure you have an open canvas, then launch the pose. If there are no 3D figures or characters on your canvas, a dialog will appear for selecting the drawing figure. If there are multiple 3D figures on a scene, it applies the pose to the selected figure.

Setting up poses with Posemaniacs provides a powerful way to explore and customize a vast library of dynamic and natural poses. Next, let's explore how the Pose Scanner feature can bring even more flexibility by allowing you to create custom poses directly from real-life references.

Using Pose Scanner

With **Pose Scanner**, you can scan a photo and import its pose into CSP. It reads a picture, uses **artificial intelligence** to analyze the pose, and applies it to your 3D model.

> **Important note**
>
> Pose Scanner does not consider hand and finger positions.

To open **Pose Scanner** and apply it to your 3D figure, follow these steps:

1. Select your 3D model with the **Object** sub tool (**Operation** tool).

2. There are three ways you can open **Pose Scanner**:

   • On **Object Launcher**, tap the downward-pointing arrow on the right side of **Apply pose to model**. Select **Pose Scanner (image) (Technology preview)**, as shown here:

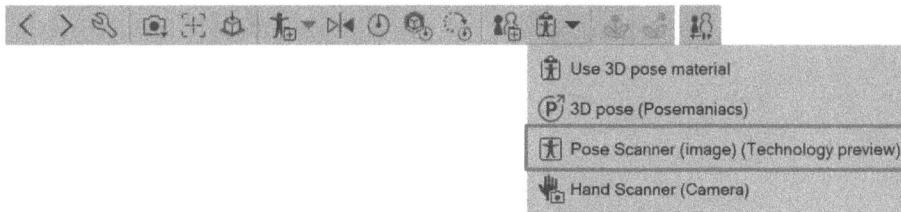

Figure 14.18 – The Pose Scanner button within Object Launcher

- Alternatively, navigate to the **Tool Property** palette or the **Sub Tool Detail** palette | **Pose**. Click on the bottom-right icon:

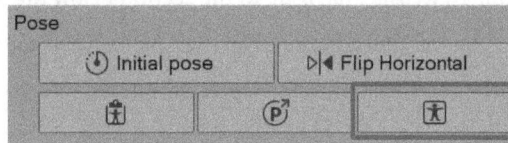

Figure 14.19 – The Pose Scanner button within the Sub Tool Detail palette

- Another method is to go to **File** | **Import**. Select **Pose Scanner (image) (Technology preview)(B)**.

3. If this is the first time you're using **Pose Scanner**, the following dialog will appear:

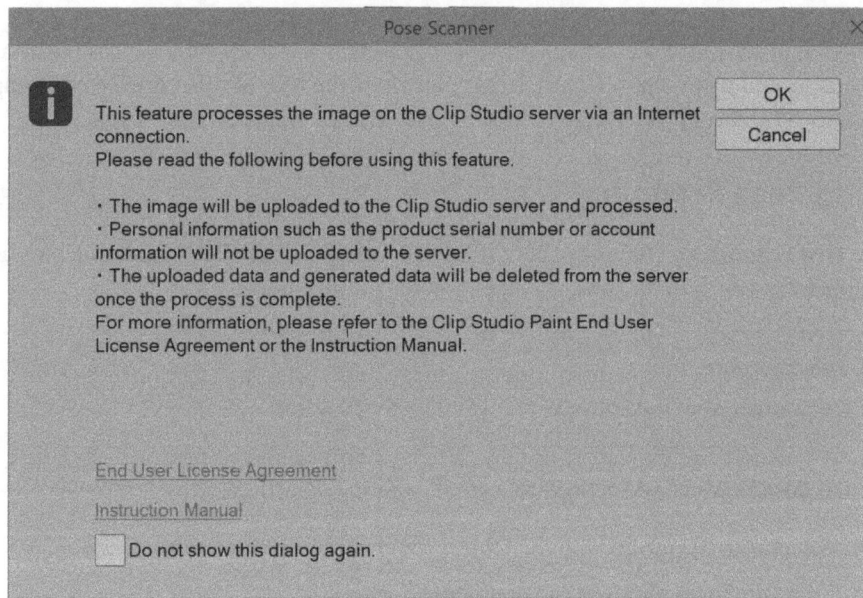

Figure 14.20 – Pose Scanner dialog

Press **OK** to continue.

4. A dialog will appear where you can select the reference photo from your device.

5. Once you have selected the reference photo, hit **OK**, and the reference pose will be applied to the 3D model:

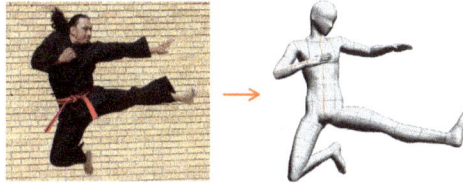

Figure 14.21 – Example use of Pose Scanner

Important note

If you select a photo with multiple figures, Pose Scanner will analyze the most prominent figure in the image. If the pose is unclear, Pose Scanner might not work correctly.

After applying the selected pose to your 3D figure in CSP, you can modify specific joints to fine-tune it further. This way, your selected pose from *CLIP STUDIO ASSETS*, Posemaniacs, or Pose Scanner can become a base for the pose. Let's see how to alter poses and create them from scratch next.

Modifying 3D character poses

Whether you want to start from scratch or modify an existing pose, manipulating character joints is invaluable for your 3D workflow. 3D figures and characters have connection points, or joints, that allow you to move body parts. You can only move body parts from their joints, and everything else cannot be bent or moved—just like a human body, with its movable joints and unbendable bones.

You can move a 3D body part by clicking on it with the **Object** sub tool and dragging it in the direction you want to move it, as shown in *Figure 14.22*:

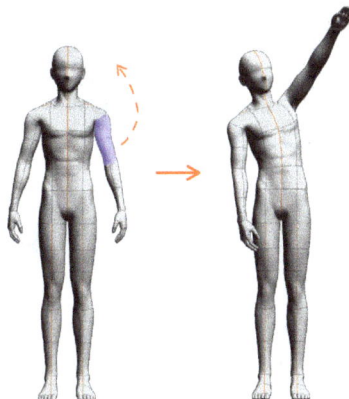

Figure 14.22 – Example of moving one body part

Other joints and body parts will also move when you proceed this way. You can lock those joints or use manipulators to prevent body parts from interlocking. To lock or unlock a 3D joint, follow the next steps:

1. Select the body part you wish to lock with the **Object** sub tool (**Operation** tool).
2. Navigate to **Object Launcher** below the 3D model.
3. Tap **Lock/release selected joints**, and the joint will be locked or unlocked.
4. Alternatively, you can go to the **Sub Tool Detail** palette | **Pose** | **Lock/release joint**.

When a body part is locked, it becomes the center of movement, which changes how the 3D model behaves when moving another body part. In the following figure, you can see the same action with and without locked joints. In the top part, no joint is locked, and when you pull the shoulder to the right, the arm, neck, and torso move along:

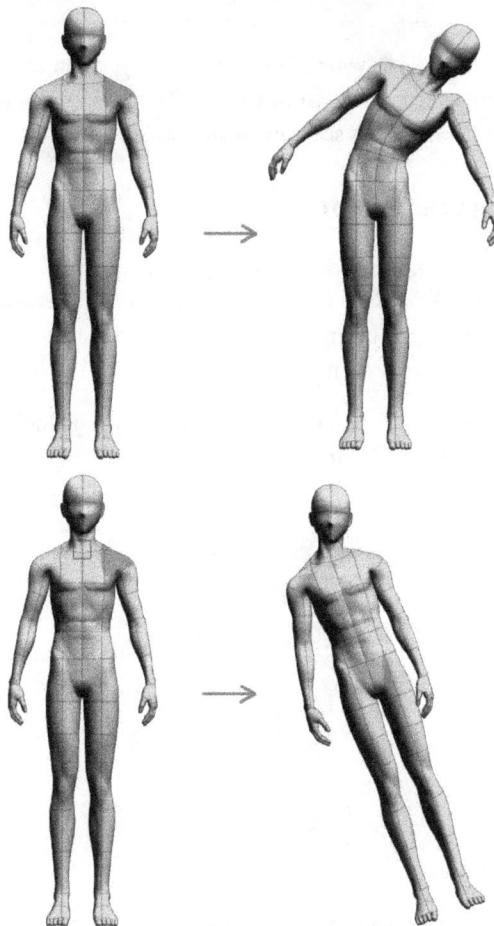

Figure 14.23 – The same action performed without (top) and with (bottom) a locked joint

In the bottom part of *Figure 14.23*, the torso is locked (represented by the blue square near the collarbone). When performing the same action (pulling the shoulder to the right side), the locked torso does not allow the upper body to move freely.

5. You can lock multiple joints, and to release them all, go to **Object Launcher** | **Release all locked joints**. Alternatively, go to the **Sub Tool Detail** palette | **Pose** | **Release all joints**.

Another great feature of CSP is the **Joint angle limit** feature, which you can find by going to the **Sub Tool Detail** palette | **Pose** | **Joint angle limit**. When toggled on, a joint can only move as much as it would in a natural human body. When toggled off, the angle of each body part can be modified freely, even in unnatural ways:

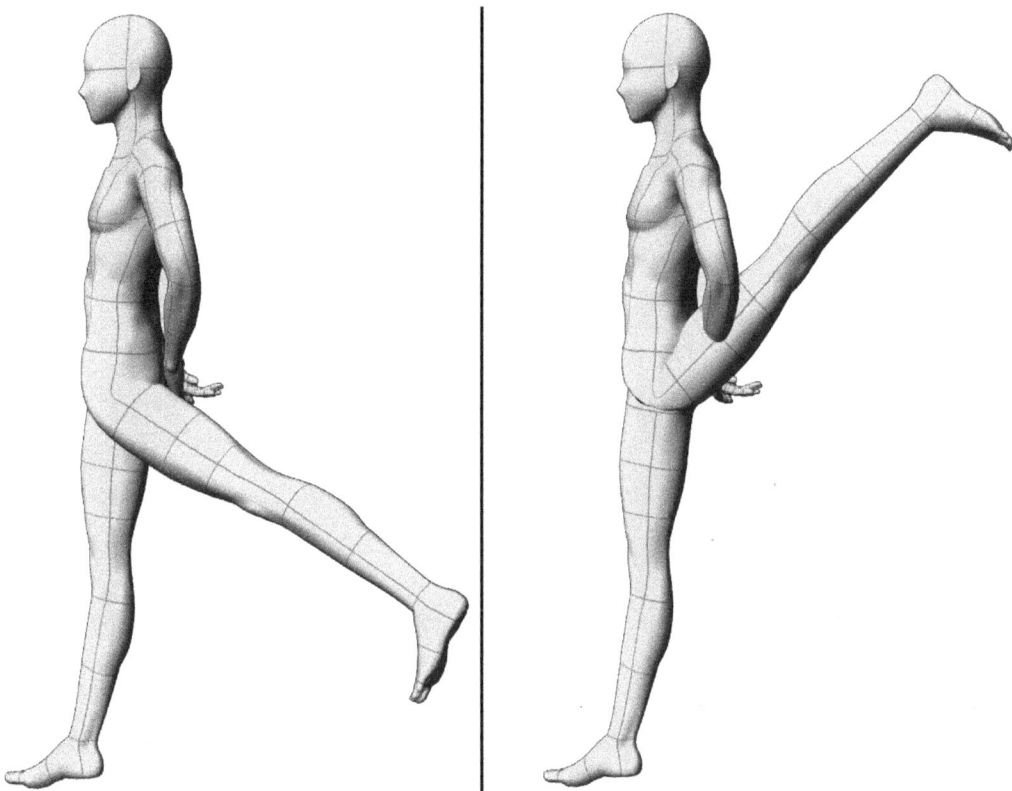

Figure 14.24 – Joint angle limit toggled on (left) and off (right)

On top of selecting and dragging the body part to a certain position, you can make finer adjustments with rotations, for which you'll use one of the 3D manipulators. There are two manipulators that change a 3D character's pose: pose controllers and local manipulators.

The **pose controller** is a manipulator that allows broad modifications of the pose, such as lowering the hips and bending the legs simultaneously. The pose controllers appear simultaneously with the **root manipulator** we covered in *Chapter 13, Manipulating 3D Objects on the Canvas*. You can see the pose controllers, represented as blue spheres, in *Figure 14.25*:

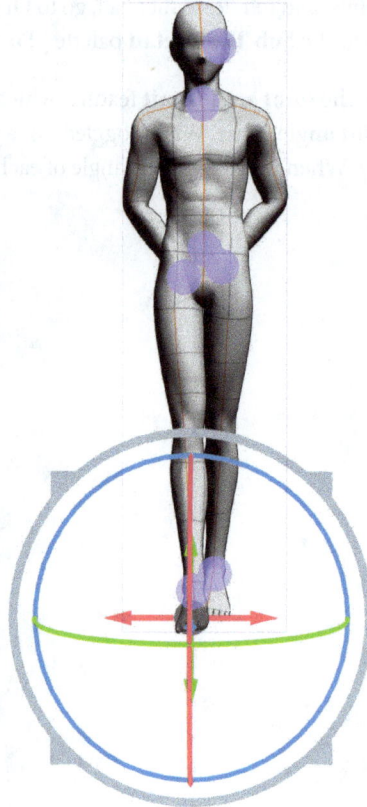

Figure 14.25 – The pose controllers are blue spheres on essential points such as torso and pelvis

Each sphere represents critical areas such as the wrists, torso, head, pelvis, and feet.

When you select a pose controller, colored arrows and rotation rings will appear on the selected area. These allow you to rotate and reposition the connected body parts. Follow these steps to use a pose controller effectively:

1. Select one of the pose controllers (the blue spheres) around the 3D figure.

2. Move the selected controller in the desired direction to position the corresponding body part.

    As you adjust the controller, the entire body will shift accordingly, ensuring smooth and coordinated movements.

This feature provides a comprehensive way to move multiple body parts simultaneously. In *Figure 14.26*, I dragged the hip controller (orange sphere on the left) down, which bent the legs accordingly:

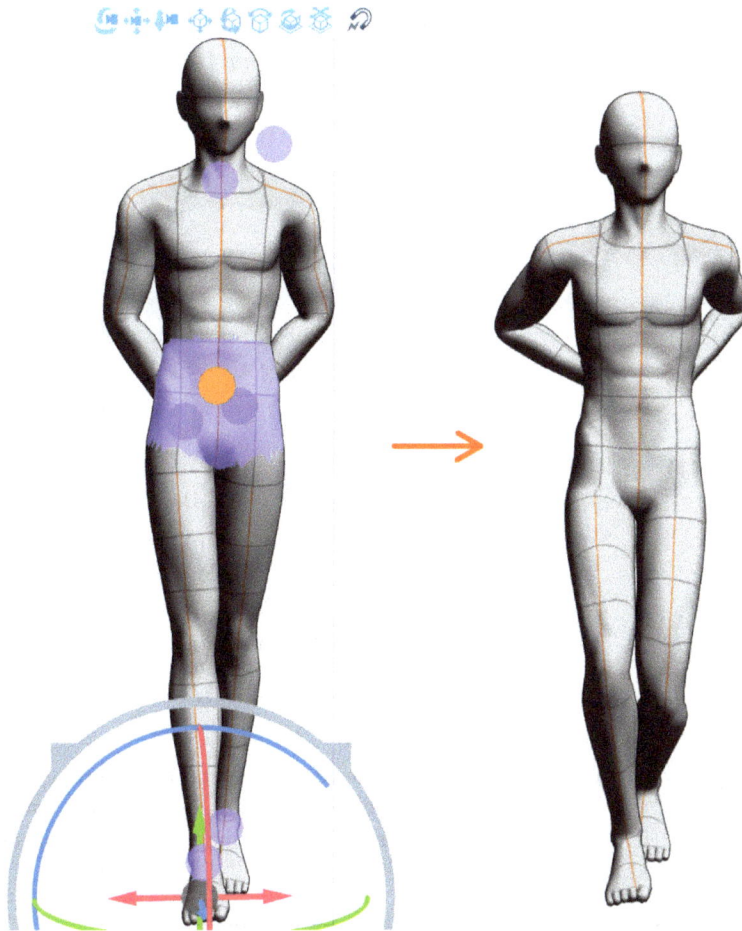

Figure 14.26 – Example use of a pose controller

Important note

The pose controllers ignore locked joint settings, so locked joints will move along.

Now that we have covered the pose controllers, which are great for broad changes, let's see how to move individual body parts. When you click on a body part with the **Object** sub tool, a **local manipulator** appears, much like the root manipulator. The local manipulators allow only rotation, and its appearance changes depending on the selected body part, as shown in *Figure 14.27*:

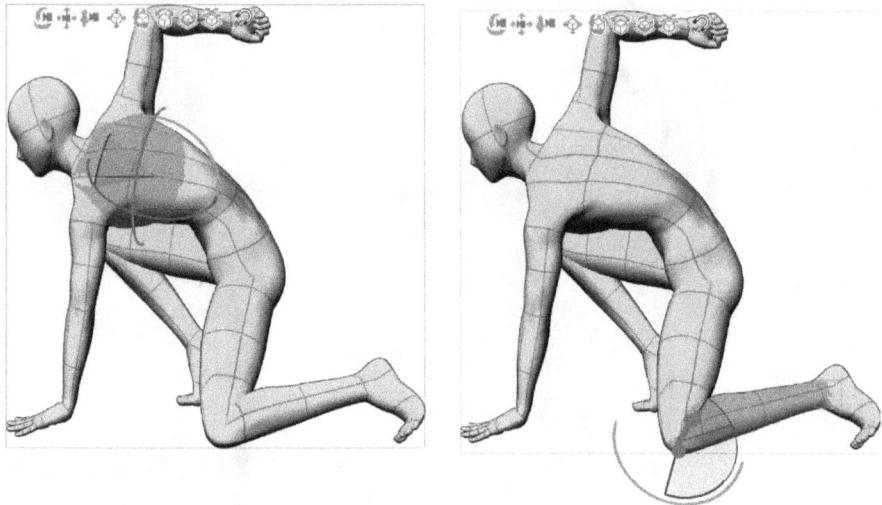

Figure 14.27 – The local manipulator on the upper back (left) and knee (right)

> **Important note**
>
> Clicking on a body part will switch between the local manipulator and the pose controllers. If you tap a body part and the local manipulator does not appear, it's because it switched to the pose controller. Click on the body part again, and the local manipulator will appear.

The local manipulators let you rotate body parts in four directions:

- **Twist (pink)**: Drag this pink ring to twist in the direction of the ring.
- **Bending rotation (Y) (green)**: Drag this green ring to bend in the Y axis.
- **Bending rotation (Z) (blue)**: Drag this green ring to bend in the Z axis.

- **Movable range**: Similar to a real human body, certain 3D body parts can only move within a defined range. This range is visually represented by a dark green diagram, showing the boundaries of movement, as shown here (left side):

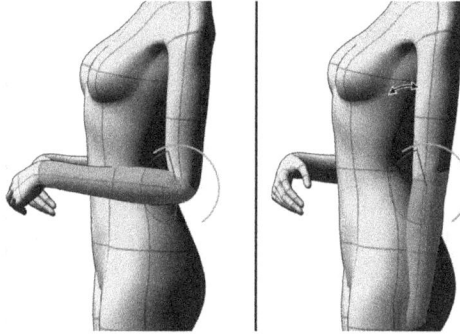

Figure 14.28 – The local manipulator's movable range

When you select a colored ring and adjust the body part, a magenta line will appear near the movable range to indicate that the limit has been reached (*Figure 14.28*, right side).

There are two extra manipulators exclusive to the elbow and the back of the knee. Let's discuss how these manipulators work:

- Dragging the elbow manipulator rotates only the elbow while fixing the shoulder and wrist positions and the elbow angle

- Dragging the knee manipulator rotates only the knee while maintaining the hips and feet positions and fixing the knee angle

Figure 14.29 shows an example of the knee manipulator in action, rotating the knee outward:

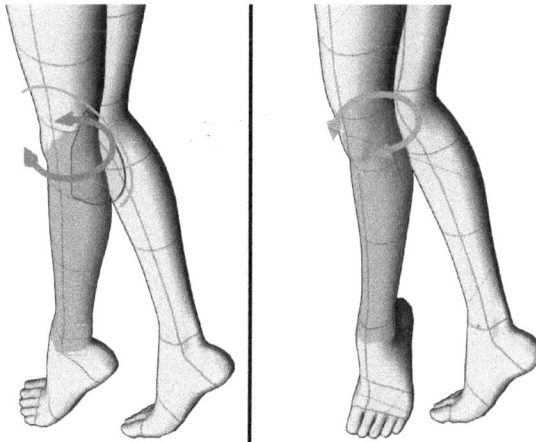

Figure 14.29 – Example use of the knee manipulator

While the manipulators are great for moving and rotating, there is yet another precise method to adjust the pose: with the **Sub Tool Detail** palette. Follow these steps:

1. Select the body part you wish to move with the **Object** sub tool (**Operation** tool).

2. Navigate to the **Sub Tool Detail** palette | **Transform**.

3. Under **Partial rotation**, move the sliders for the **X**, **Y**, and **Z** axes or set numbered values.

> **Important note**
>
> Although the three axes are visible in the **Partial rotation** setting, the selected body part will only move within possible bending and twisting motions. For example, when you select the forearm, it can only rotate on the *Y* axis.

You've now understood how to move, lock, and rotate body parts and joints. You can make more adjustments to any pose, such as making it symmetrical or straightening body parts.

To make a pose symmetrical, follow these steps:

1. Select your 3D model with the **Object** sub tool (**Operation** tool).

2. Go to the **Sub Tool Detail** palette.

3. In the **Pose** category, go to the **Mirror pose** setting.

4. Select which parts of the pose you want to mirror. You can choose **Arms**, **Hands**, and **Legs**.

5. Tap which side of the pose you want to mirror: copy the left side of the pose to the right side, or vice versa. Tapping this setting will apply the symmetry immediately. In *Figure 14.30*, I mirrored the arms from the left side to the right:

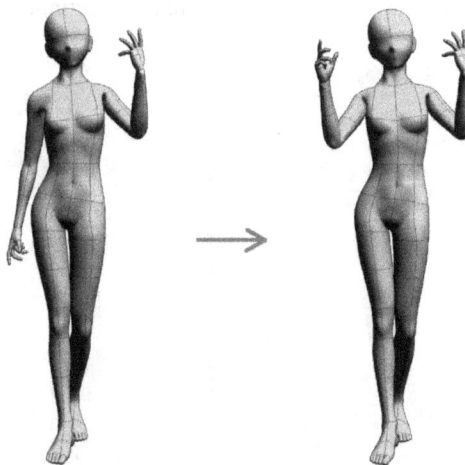

Figure 14.30 – Example use of the Mirror pose setting on the arms

You can also straighten the neck and torso of your 3D model. Follow these steps:

1. Select your 3D model with the **Object** sub tool (**Operation** tool).

2. Go to the **Sub Tool Detail** palette.

3. In the **Pose** category, go to the **Straighten pose** setting.

4. Select **Torso** or **Neck**. You can see an example of this feature in action in *Figure 14.31*:

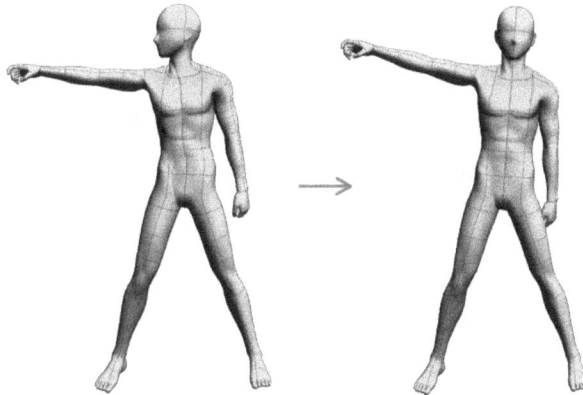

Figure 14.31 – Example use of the Straighten pose setting

When you have the perfect pose you've envisioned, you can save it as a material for later use in other projects. To save a pose, follow these steps:

1. Go to **Sub Tool Detail** palette | **Pose** | **Register Material** and click on the first icon, **Register full body pose as material**.

    Alternatively, tap the **Register full body pose** icon in **Object Launcher** below the 3D figure.

2. The **Material property** dialog will appear.

3. Enter a name, select a saving location, add tags, and then hit **OK** to finish the registration.

4. Now, you can drag and drop this 3D pose on any project you want.

Now that you know how to pose your characters, you can use this function to create any pose you envision. Whether your characters are fighting, walking, or chatting, you can import or create poses to aid in your storytelling process. Mastering the art of posing your 3D character allows you to precisely convey emotion, movement, and storytelling.

With your character's overall pose in place, it's time to focus on one of the most expressive parts of the body: the hands. In the next section, we'll dive into posing 3D hands, exploring how to capture subtle gestures and detailed movements that elevate your character's impact.

Posing 3D hands

Hands are a subtle yet powerful aspect of character design, conveying emotion, action, and personality. Whether your character is gripping a weapon, gesturing during a conversation, or striking a dramatic pose, correctly posed hands elevate the scene's realism and impact. Posing 3D hands gives you flexibility and precision to craft the perfect look.

We can import hand poses through the **Material** palette as we did with the body. To import a 3D hand, follow these steps:

1. Select the arm or the hand of the 3D figure with the **Object** sub tool (**Operation** tool).

2. Drag and drop a **Hand Pose** material from the **Material** palette onto the 3D figure.

3. The hand pose will be applied to the selected hand or arm.

> **Important note**
> If a central body part is selected, such as the waist, or if a body part is not selected, the hand pose will be applied to both hands.

You can also use **Hand Scanner** to set up hand poses. This feature scans your hand with your device's camera and applies it to your 3D figure, much like the Pose Scanner feature we covered in the previous section, *Posing your 3D figure*. To use **Hand Scanner**, follow these steps:

1. Select the 3D figure with the **Object** sub tool (**Operation** tool).

2. Go to **Object Launcher** and tap the **Pose Scanner (image) (technology preview)** icon.

    Alternatively, go to the **Sub Tool Detail** palette | **Pose** | **Hand pose** and click on the **Hand Scanner (Camera)** button.

3. If it's the first time you're opening **Hand Scanner**, the following dialog will appear:

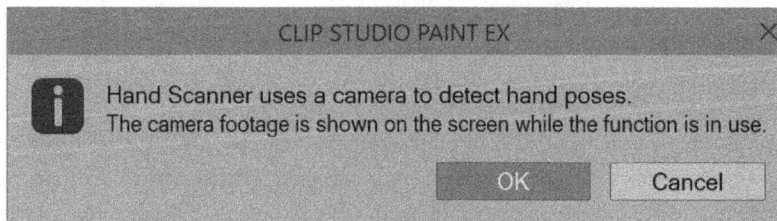

Figure 14.32 – Dialog that appears when first using Hand Scanner

4. Press **OK** to continue. The **Hand Scanner** dialog will open:

Figure 14.33 – The Hand Scanner dialog (top) and an example of use (bottom)

5. In the large area on the left side, you will see the hand your camera is capturing. As you move your fingers, the 3D hand of your figure will apply changes in real time.

6. Once you have the pose you desire, hit the **Pause/Resume** button to freeze the image. Tap again to restart the camera.

7. Below the **Pause/Resume** button, a drop-down menu shows which cameras are available and lets you choose one to capture the hand pose.

8. Select on which hand of the 3D figure this pose will be applied using **Apply to right/left hand**. If you wish to use the same pose on both hands, follow these steps:

   - Apply symmetry to the hand pose by going to the **Sub Tool Detail** palette | **Pose** | **Mirror pose**, as we covered in the *Modifying 3D character poses* section.

   - Alternatively, you can apply the pose to one hand, and then use **Hand Scanner** again for the other side.

9. Tap **OK** to set the hand pose.

> **Important note**
>
> The Hand Scanner feature only imports the position of the fingers. It does not change the position of the palm or wrist.

Even after importing a hand pose, you can adjust it to fit your desired action. You can move each finger one by one like any other body part, as we covered in the *Posing your 3D figure* section. Alternatively, you can use specific settings for the hand and fingers by following these steps:

1. Select the hand you wish to modify. If a central part of the body is selected, changes will affect both hands.

2. Go to the **Tool Property** palette | **Hand pose**.

    Alternatively, go to the **Sub Tool Detail** palette | **Pose** | **Hand pose**.

3. The following diagram will appear:

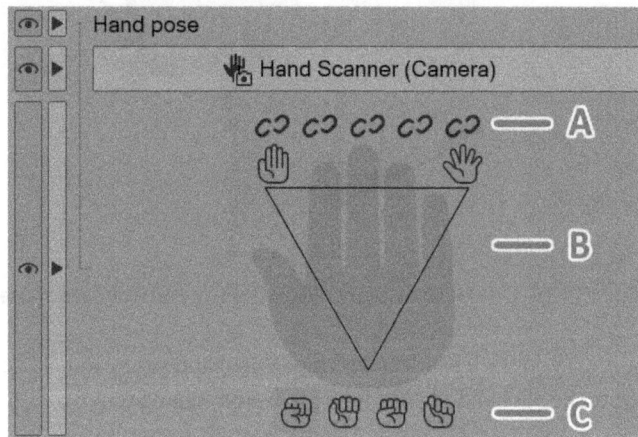

Figure 14.34 – The Hand pose diagram

These are its parts:

A. *Lock fingers*: There is one link icon for each of the fingers. Locking one or more of the fingers will ensure the locked ones do not move when you use the hand controller and the fist preset.

B. *Hand controller*: Drag the center cross to the left and right to narrow or widen the distance between fingers, and drag it up or down to open and close the fingers:

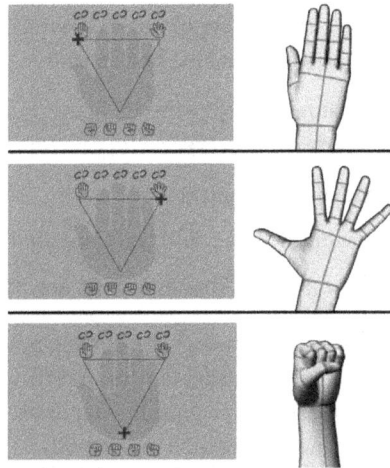

Figure 14.35 – The hand controller

C.   *Fist preset*: Choose one of the four presets to determine how the hand closes into a fist:

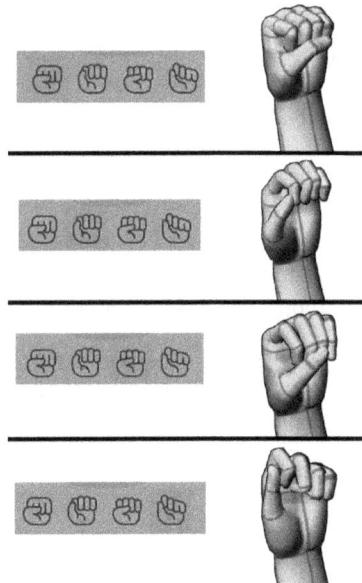

Figure 14.36 – Fist presets

When you have the perfect hand pose you've envisioned, you can save it as a material for later use in other projects. To save a 3D hand pose, follow these steps:

1.   Go to **Sub Tool Detail** palette | **Pose** | **Register material**.

2. Click the second icon, **Register left hand pose as material for both hands**, or the third icon, **Register right hand pose as material for both hands**.

   Alternatively, in **Object Launcher** below the 3D figure, tap **Register left hand pose as material** or **Register right hand pose as material**.

3. The **Material property** dialog will appear.

4. Enter a name, select a saving location, add tags, and then hit **OK** to finish the registration.

5. Now, you can drag and drop this 3D hand pose on any project you want.

Mastering hand poses enhances your character's storytelling potential, adding depth and emotion to your designs. By combining manual adjustments with the efficiency of Pose Scanner, you gain both creative freedom and time-saving precision. Once the hands are set, you're ready to take full control of your character's proportions, fine-tuning their entire body to align with your artistic vision.

Summary

Altering and posing 3D figures is essential for personalizing and refining your scenes with characters. Through thoughtful adjustments, characters can convey personality, emotion, and action, making your work more dynamic and engaging. You first understood how to craft the body shape of your character, ensuring they look exactly as you envisioned. You can make broad modifications to the whole body or modify individual body parts to suit your needs.

Next, you mastered full-body posing, how 3D joints move, and how to use tools such as the Posemaniacs integration and Pose Scanner for pre-made positions. Now, your characters can jump, fight, play, and do whatever your story requires. From there, hand posing took the spotlight, allowing intricate gestures and grips that add a sense of realism to your story. Using traditional 3D techniques and innovative tools such as the Hand Scanner tool, CSP helps you fine-tune the poses you create.

By mastering these techniques, you've built a solid foundation for working with 3D models, ensuring your characters look lifelike and tell your story. Next, we'll focus on a critical aspect of scene creation: illuminating your artwork with 3D lighting and Shading Assist, where you'll discover how to manipulate light and shadow to enhance the mood, depth, and storytelling of your artwork.

15

Illuminating Your Artwork with 3D Lighting and Shading Assist

Lighting is a powerful tool capable of transforming a simple scene into a compelling masterpiece. Proper illumination enhances the depth and realism of your work, sets the mood, highlights focal points, and guides the viewer's eye through the composition. Understanding how to manipulate lighting and shadow effectively in **Clip Studio Paint** (**CSP**) can enhance your artwork and make the painting process easier, ensuring accuracy in light and shadow placement.

In this chapter, we're going to cover the following topics:

- Setting up light in 3D space
- Using the Shading Assist function for quick light experiments

This chapter will teach you how to set up and control lighting in 3D space within CSP, as well as how to use the Shading Assist feature to quickly experiment with light and shadow. By mastering these techniques, you'll learn how to enhance your artwork with dynamic illumination and realistic shading effortlessly.

By the end of this chapter, you'll have the skills and confidence to use lighting creatively and effectively, ensuring your artworks leave a lasting impression on your audience. Let's dive into the tools and functions that will speed up your lighting process and improve your workflow!

Setting up light in 3D space

3D tools are some of the quickest and most useful tools to set up light systems precisely. In CSP, 3D lighting tools offer control over light direction, intensity, and color. Whether you're setting up natural daylight or an evocative spotlight, understanding how to manipulate these settings is essential for creating impactful and dynamic scenes.

When you place a 3D material on the canvas, it is automatically lit with a standard light setup. What many don't know is that you can change this light system to fit the mood and story of your scene. Let's start by covering how to modify the main light source of a 3D scene.

Changing the main light source of a 3D scene

The main light source determines the shadow placement of the 3D models. To modify the main light source, follow these steps:

1. Select the 3D object with the **Object** sub tool (**Operation** tool).

2. Go to the **Sub Tool Detail** palette and click on the **Light Source** tab.

3. Inside the **Light Source** category, you can see the following settings:

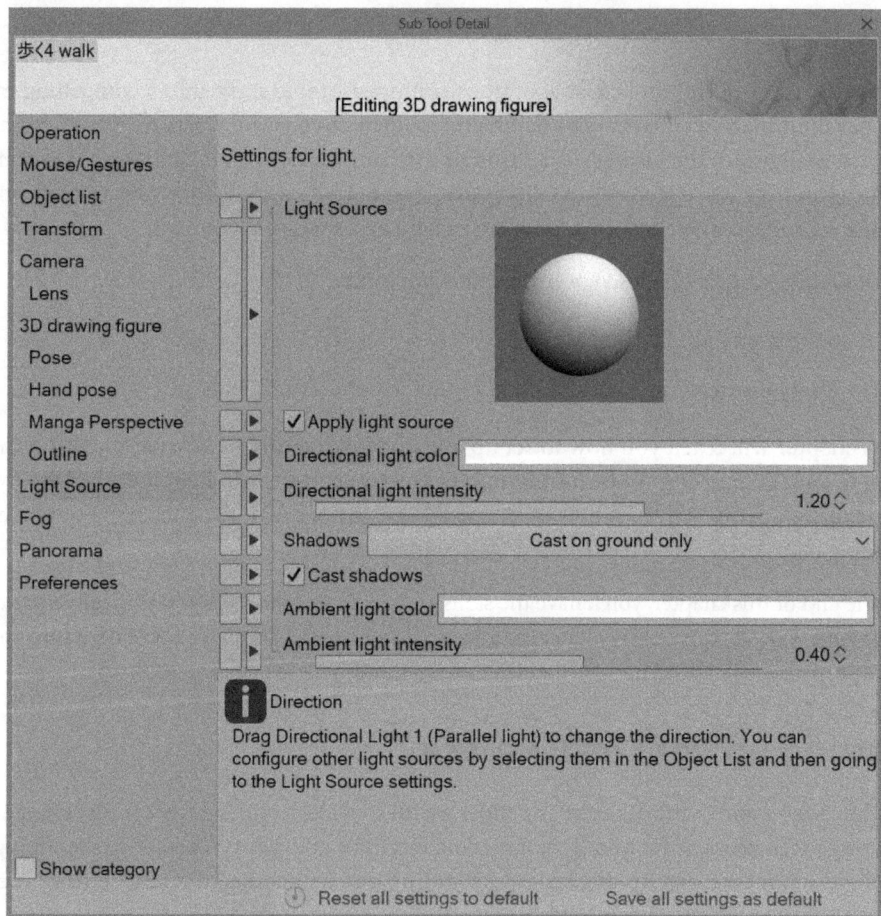

Figure 15.1 – Light Source settings

4. You can choose whether the scene will have a light source or not by tapping the **Apply light source** function. When toggled off, there is no visible light source on the 3D scene. Toggle it on to adjust light and shadows in your 3D scene.

5. Once you have **Apply light source** toggled on, you can adjust the direction of the direct light. To change the light angle, you'll use the diagram with a sphere—the *Light Source ball*. Tap and drag to move the light source and determine how it illuminates the entire 3D layer:

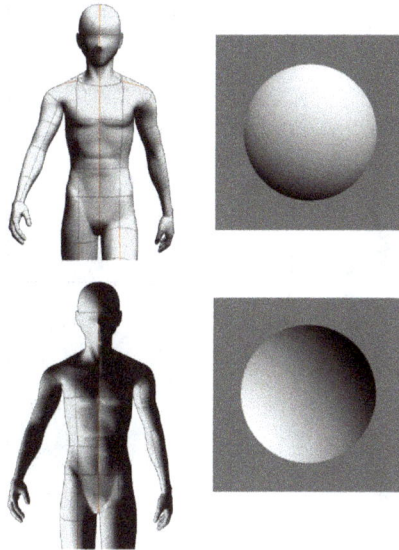

Figure 15.2 – Example settings of the Light Source ball

This is arguably the most useful 3D lighting feature since it allows you to determine the light source angle precisely.

6. Use **Directional light color** to decide the color of the directional light. Click on the colored rectangle, and a **Color settings** popup will let you choose what color to apply to the object. Here you can see an example of the same 3D head lit with different colors:

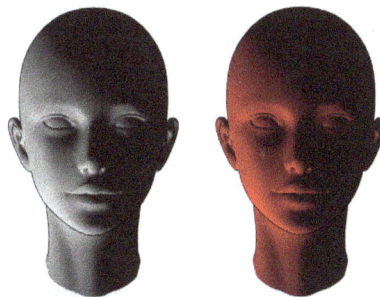

Figure 15.3 – Examples of different Directional light colors

7. You can also change **Directional light intensity** by dragging a slider or setting a numerical value. The higher the number, the stronger the light.

8. You can choose to cast shadows or not by toggling the **Cast shadows** function on and off. Casting shadows can be extremely useful in making your scene more realistic and ground your characters in the scene.

    When casting shadows, sometimes the shadow might disappear when it should be cast on top of another 3D object, as shown on the left side of *Figure 15.4*:

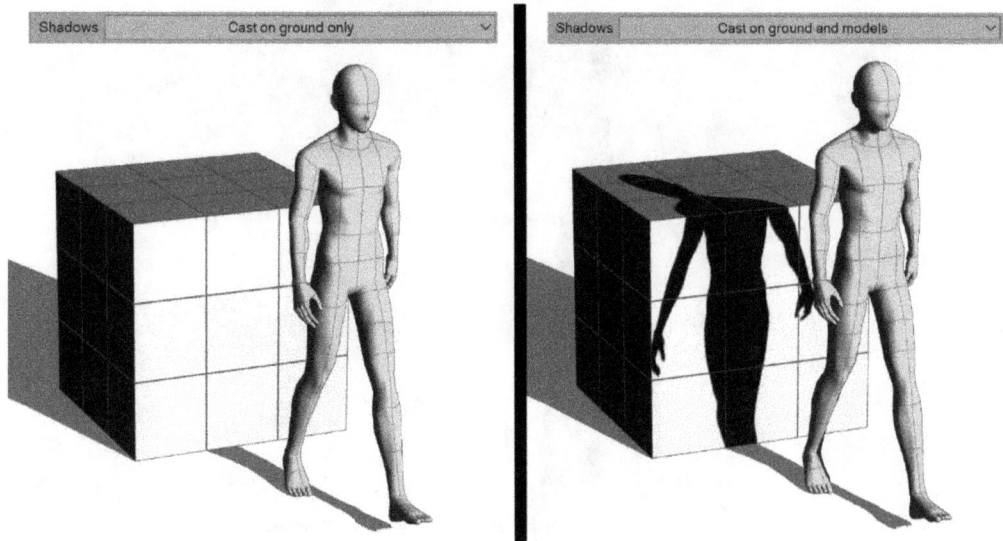

Figure 15.4 – Shadows | Cast on ground only (left) and Cast on ground and models (right)

To fix that, follow the next steps:

I. Select the 3D model with the **Object** sub tool (**Operation** tool).

II. Go to the **Sub Tool Detail** palette and select the **Light Source** category.

III. Under **Shadows**, select **Cast on ground and models**. Now, the shadows of that object will be cast on top of other 3D objects, as you can see on the right side of *Figure 15.4*. If it fits your scene, you can choose **Cast on ground only** or **Cast on 3D models only**.

9. If the shadows appear blurry, you can make them sharper by changing the **Shadow resolution** setting. Follow the next steps:

I. Go to the **Sub Tool Detail** palette and select the **Preferences** category.

II. Under **Shadow resolution**, you can pick from three options: **High**, **Medium**, and **Low**.

High means sharper shadows, and **Low** makes them blurrier. Although it might seem like it's best to always leave it on **High**, this might slow down your device and hinder your process.

Therefore, it's best to leave it at **Medium** or **Low** while you're manipulating the lights and the 3D materials and only select the **High** shadow resolution once the scene is set and you need to see the details.

After you have set the directional light source, you can experiment with ambient light and a secondary directional light. These are great for adding depth and realism and increasing the complexity of your light system. Let's see how to add ambient light and a secondary light source next.

Adding ambient light and a secondary light source

Ambient light is great for harmonizing your 3D objects with the environment around them. To set an ambient light, follow the next steps:

1. In the **Sub Tool Detail** palette, select the **Light Source** category.

2. Use the **Ambient light color** setting to alter the color of the ambient light. Click on the colored rectangle to change the ambient light color.

3. Use **Ambient light intensity** to modify the ambient light strength. Drag the slider or insert a number to change its intensity. Here you can see examples of different ambient light settings:

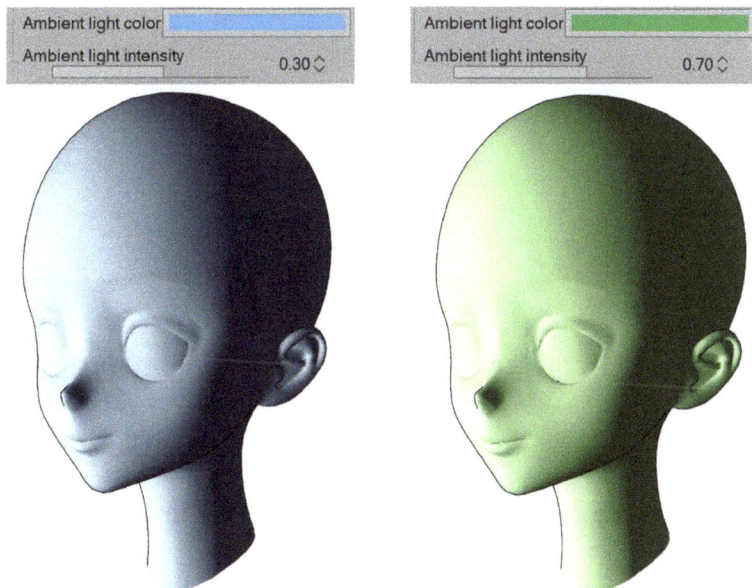

Figure 15.5 – Example settings of ambient light

> **Important note**
> Changes made to the ambient light are applied to the entire 3D layer, including the background.

After changing the ambient light, you can use **Directional light 2** to add a secondary light source if it fits your scene. This light is hidden by default, so to toggle it on, you must add it to the 3D object list by following these steps:

1. Go to the **Sub Tool Detail** palette and select **Object list**.

2. On the list, find **Directional light 2** and toggle visibility on by clicking on the left-side box:

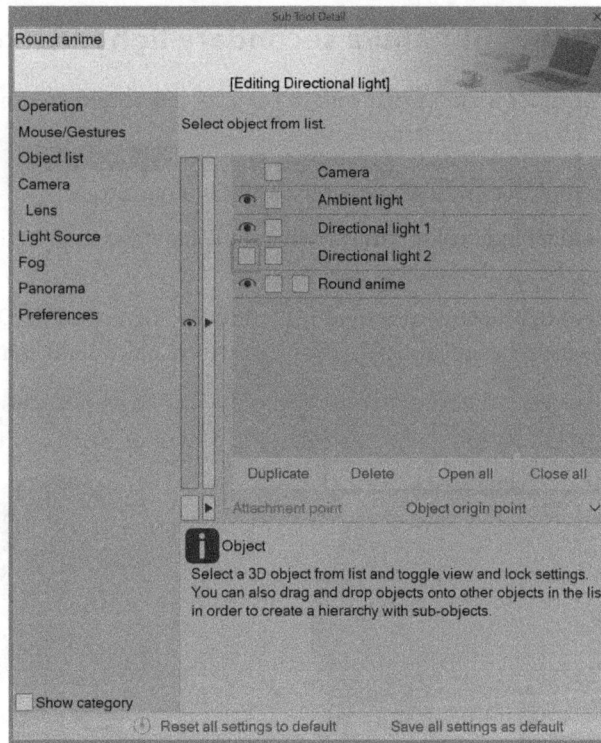

Figure 15.6 – Object list | Directional light 2

3. When this light source is visible, an eye icon will appear next to it.

4. To change the appearance of the secondary light, select **Directional light 2** in the object list, then go to **Sub Tool Detail | Light Source**:

    I.   You can modify the angle of **Directional light 2** like you did with the main light source: by dragging the light on the *Light Source ball*.

    II.   Change the secondary light color by clicking on the **Directional light color** colored box.

    III.   Modify the secondary light intensity with the **Directional light intensity** slider and the numerical value. Here is an example of a 3D head with two light sources—a white light on the left and a red light on the right:

Figure 15.7 – Example of the 3D head with two light sources

> **Important note**
> **Directional light 2** does not change the shape of shadows in 3D material, regardless of its position.

Now that you know how to set up lights in a 3D scene, let's apply this knowledge to a portrait. We'll start with a female 3D head and apply two light sources to it: one magenta and one cyan. First, place the **3D Head** model on the canvas and change the direction and color of the directional light source:

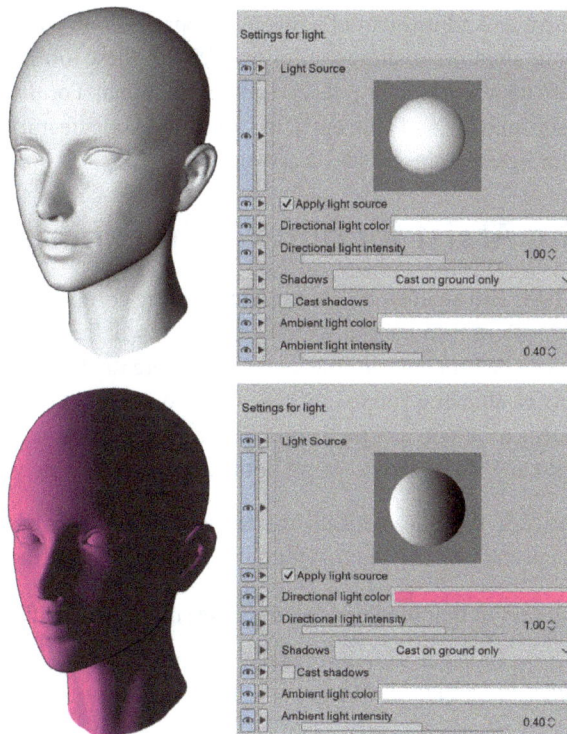

Figure 15.8 – A 3D head model with the default light source (top) and
after changing the Directional light 1 settings (bottom)

Then, on the object list, turn on the visibility for **Directional light 2** and change its color and angle:

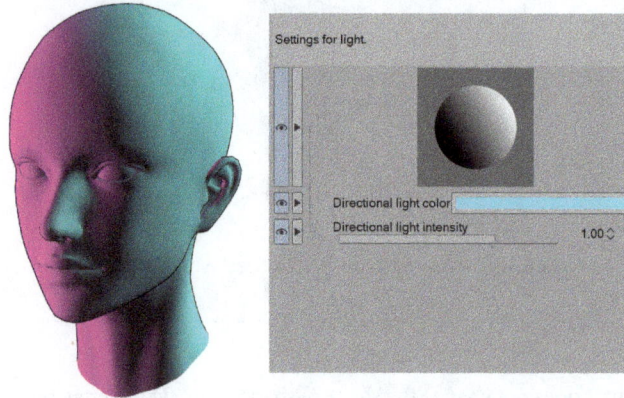

Figure 15.9 – Settings for Directional light 2

And voilà! We have a 3D head model with the exact light system we want, so we can easily visualize the light and shadow placement when it's time to paint the portrait.

Mastering the placement and adjustment of lights in 3D space allows you to control how your scene is perceived, from subtle shadows to dramatic contrasts. With these tools, you can create the desired atmosphere and ensure your work looks polished and professional. For those looking to experiment further with light setups quickly and efficiently, the **Shading Assist** feature offers a powerful way to test and refine different lighting options in 2D artworks.

Using Shading Assist for quick light experiments

Experimenting with light and shadow is essential for creating compelling artwork, and sometimes you don't have a clear idea in mind about which light angle will best convey your story. Manually testing various setups can be time-consuming, and that's where the **Shading Assist** feature comes in: it streamlines the process, allowing you to quickly explore different lighting scenarios with minimal effort. By leveraging this tool, you can focus on refining your composition and storytelling while ensuring that your light and shadow choices are both efficient and visually striking.

Shading Assist is a function that automatically creates light and shadow based on your line and color layers. There are some prerequisites you must follow to make sure **Shading Assist** works correctly:

1.   Separate your layers so that the lines and the base colors are in different layers.

2.   The line layer must be set as **Reference layer**. We covered this process in detail in *Chapter 8, Maximizing Efficiency and Organization with Layers*.

3.   The color layer or layers should be flat colors with little to no variation. Do not apply gradients of other forms of soft color transition in the color layers.

> **Important note**
>
> The selection of lines and colors combined must not surpass the limit of 250 colors, or else Shading Assist will not work.

After making sure you've followed the prerequisites, you can apply **Shading Assist**. Follow these steps:

1. Select all of the line and color layers in the **Layer** palette.

2. Go to the **Edit** menu | **Shading Assist(F)**....

3. The **Shading Assist** dialog will open. Here, you can see the **Shading Assist** dialog on the right side of the figure:

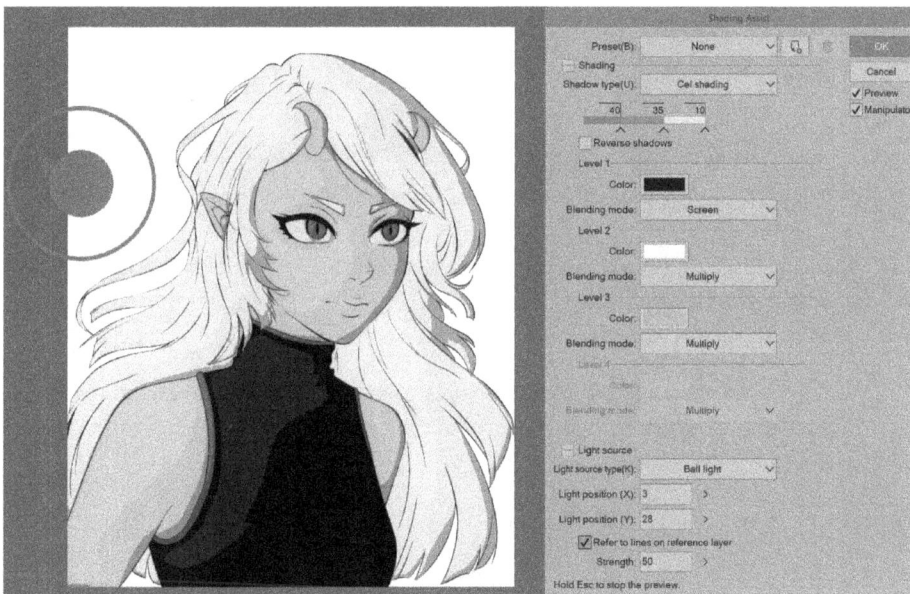

Figure 15.10 – The light source manipulator (left) and the Shading Assist dialog (right)

4. Toggle **Manipulator** on to show the *light source manipulator* on the screen. The light source manipulator is the blue sphere and ring you can see next to the painting on the left side of *Figure 15.10*.

    Use the light source manipulator to move the light on the canvas. We'll cover this manipulator in detail later in this section.

5. Make sure **Refer to lines on reference layer** is toggled on. This way, **Shading Assist** will consider the lines on the reference layer. If **Refer to lines on reference layer** is toggled off, **Shading Assist** will consider only color information.

When **Refer to lines on reference layer** is toggled on, the **Strength** setting determines the strength at which lines will affect the shading. Experiment with this function to find your desired visual.

6.   Make sure **Preview** is toggled on, so you can see changes in real time.

7.   Having followed the preceding steps, you can choose a **Preset(B)** light source or create your own light source. There are 10 presets available, and you can see some of them here:

Figure 15.11 – Examples of presets – Standard (left), Evening (middle), and Night (right)

8.   You can choose a preset and apply it by hitting **OK** or use the preset as a base and modify it to match your desired mood. To modify a preset or create a lighting scenario from scratch, follow these steps:

- Start by selecting a **Shadow type(U)** option. You can choose between **Cel shading** (hard edges) and **Smooth shading**. See the difference between these two types of shading in *Figure 15.12*:

Figure 15.12 – Shadow type: Cel shading (left) and Smooth shading (right)

You can fine-tune the lights and shadows further with specific settings that adjust based on the shadow type you select.

When **Shadow type(U)** is set to **Cel shading**, the following settings appear:

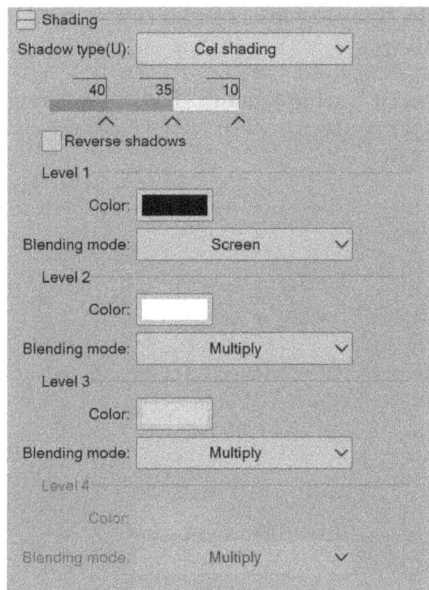

Figure 15.13 – Available settings for Cel shading

They work as follows:

- You can define shadows and highlights with a *shading scale* that offers precise control of light and shadow. Drag arrows left to reduce the proportion of a certain level and drag them right to increase their proportion. Clicking on the slider will create a new level, while dragging an arrow vertically will remove it.

- After distributing light and shadow with the levels slider, you can toggle **Reverse shadows** on to invert shadows and highlights:

Figure 15.14 – Reverse shadows

- You can set a **Color** and **Blending mode** option for each level, up to four levels. Paired with the shading scale, choosing colors and blending modes lets you experiment greatly with light colors and values.

When **Shadow type(U)** is set to **Smooth shading**, different settings appear:

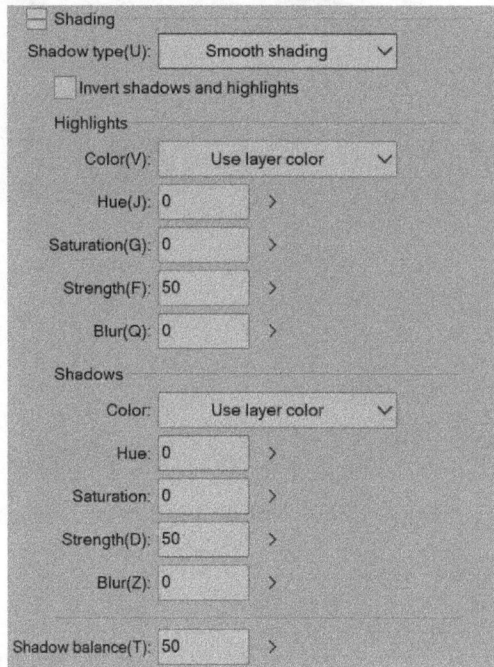

Figure 15.15 – Available settings for Smooth shading

Here you can see each function:

- First, you can toggle **Invert shadows and highlights** on to reverse the shadows and highlights.

- Then, you can modify **Highlights** and **Shadows**. Both have the same settings:

  - **Color(V)**: You can select the color of highlights and shadows. Choose between **Use layer color**, which will consider the original layer color, or **Use base color**, which lets you select a customized color.

  - **Hue/Saturation**: These let you tweak the hue and saturation to refine the shading. These settings are only available when **Color(V)** is set to **Use layer color**.

  - **Strength(D)**: Adjusts the intensity of the applied colors.

  - **Blur(Z)**: Controls the softness of the shadows and highlights by setting the blur radius.

- Use **Shadow balance(T)** to modify the ratio of shadows.

After deciding the type of shadows, you can select a **Light source type(K)** option:

- **Ball light**: The light source can be moved anywhere on the canvas and produces more easily recognizable shadows. With this light source, you can adjust the X and Y axes' position to move the light on the canvas.

- **Directional light**: This applies light to the whole canvas at the same angle and strength. Instead of adjusting the X and Y axes, you can determine the light angle from which the light shines.

Figure 15.16 shows examples of these light source types:

Figure 15.16 – Light source type: Ball light (left) and Directional light (right)

You might have noticed in *Figure 15.16* that the light source manipulator changes depending on the light source type selected. Let's analyze how this manipulator works.

Use the light source manipulator to adjust the position of the light source. The light source manipulator's appearance changes depending on the shadow type and light source type:

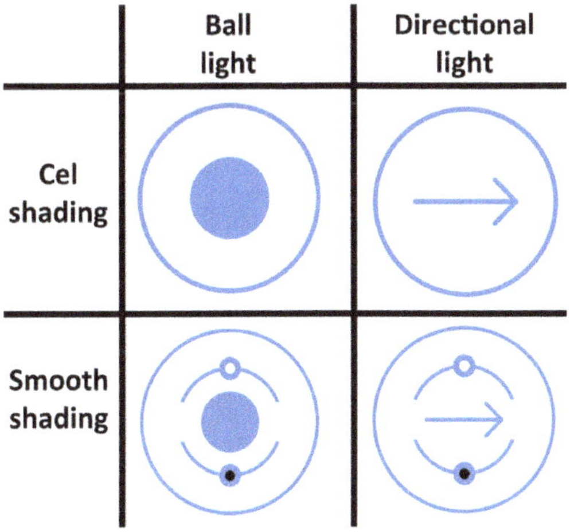

Figure 15.17 – Light source manipulator in different Shadow and Light types

This is how the light source manipulator works:

- The outer ring determines the intensity of light. Dragging it out will make it stronger and dragging it in will make it weaker.

- When **Directional light** is selected, an arrow at the center of the light source manipulator points the direction of light.

- When **Ball light** is selected, the center of the light source manipulator is a sphere you can drag to move the light source position.

- When **Smooth shading** is selected, there's one extra ring in the middle. The center ring controls the intensity of light and shadow. The top section, marked with a white circle, represents the light, while the bottom section, marked with a black circle, represents the shadows. Moving these circles adjusts their balance: dragging the white circle to the right increases the strength of highlights while dragging it to the left decreases the strength of highlights. The same happens with the black circle: dragging it to the right increases the strength of shadows while dragging it to the left decreases the strength of shadows.

With this, you've completely understood how to adjust lights and shadows in the **Shading Assist** dialog and you can create your own lights. If you wish to save a light setup as a preset, click on the icon on the right side of the **Preset** list:

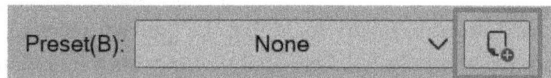

Figure 15.18 – Saving a light setup as a preset

> **Important note**
>
> Presets save information on shadow types, colors, and blending modes, but they do not include the angle of the light.

Once you are satisfied with the result, tap **OK** in the **Shading Assist** dialog to apply the light source. In the **Layer** palette, you'll notice new layers will be created above the color layers to apply the light system.

When using Shading Assist, the result might not be 100% how you want it to look. That's completely normal. This feature provides a solid foundation, and you can refine the outcome to better suit your artistic style. Simply adjust the layer masks of the generated layers—erasing or painting over them as needed—to fine-tune the shading and achieve the desired look. After all, Shading Assist is not meant to do the work for you, but to aid you in this process.

Shading Assist simplifies the creative process, giving you the flexibility to test and refine various lighting configurations. This tool provides a great foundation for exploring dynamic light setups quickly and efficiently.

Summary

Lighting is a fundamental aspect of any artistic composition, shaping not just the mood but also the narrative impact of a scene. You've now discovered the essential tools and techniques for mastering illumination in CSP, empowering you to control light and shadow with precision and creativity.

First, we explored setting up light in 3D space, a feature that allows realistic and dynamic lighting adjustments. By manipulating light sources and their properties such as intensity, direction, and color, you can transform a 3D scene into an environment that helps bring your image to life. Next, we introduced Shading Assist, a powerful feature designed for quick experimentation with light and shadow. This tool simplifies the process of testing different lighting setups, letting you focus on finding the perfect balance to enhance the depth and storytelling of your artwork. Its intuitive interface and adjustable parameters make it an invaluable asset for both beginner and advanced artists.

Together, these techniques help refine your ability to work with light, making your compositions more dynamic and engaging. Whether you're setting up a complex 3D scene or experimenting with quick lighting ideas, you now have the skills to create impactful illumination that supports your narrative.

With a solid understanding of lighting functions in CSP, it's time to dive deeper into advanced techniques. Next, you'll dive into the exciting possibilities of creating 3D backgrounds, where you'll learn how to construct 3D environments that enhance your art and storytelling.

16

Creating 3D Backgrounds

Creating compelling 3D backgrounds in **Clip Studio Paint** (**CSP**) can provide depth, perspective, and context that ground your characters and storytelling. When crafting a cityscape, a natural environment, or the interior of a room, understanding how to build and manipulate 3D environments can significantly speed up your process. Mastering 3D backgrounds ensures accurate proportions and perspective while saving time on complex scenes.

In this chapter, we're going to cover the following topics:

- Crafting background representations with primitive shapes
- Making complex backgrounds with multiple 3D objects
- Using 3D Panorama materials for 360-degree backgrounds

This chapter will teach you how to create 3D backgrounds in CSP using primitive shapes, multiple 3D objects, and Panorama materials. You'll gain the skills to construct detailed and accurate environments, enhancing the depth and realism of your artwork. By the end of this chapter, you'll be equipped to design any background with precision, whether it's a quick setup for reference or a fully rendered scene. Let's dive into the best practices to build 3D backgrounds and unlock the tools to bring your environments to life!

Crafting background representations with primitive shapes

Creating complex background art often requires a solid foundation, and primitive shapes like cubes, spheres, and cylinders offer clarity and simplicity during the planning stages of a scene. When sketching or working with 3D tools, finding the exact objects you want to place in your scene might take a long time. In this case, primitive shapes provide a clean, manageable framework. They help you visualize how objects relate to each other in space and guide you in maintaining proper perspective throughout the scene.

For example, a cube can represent a building or a room, a cylinder can outline a column or a tree trunk, and a sphere might stand in for a dome or hill. These forms can later be refined or replaced with detailed models, but their simplicity ensures that the foundational structure remains strong. We've covered 3D Primitives briefly in *Chapter 13, Manipulating 3D Objects on the Canvas*. Now, let's see how they can aid your 3D backgrounds.

Start by sketching the background you'll craft. Experimenting with composition during the sketch phase is much quicker and easier than with actual 3D models: when sketching, you can change the composition completely in just a few seconds with a handful of strokes, while 3D objects usually take longer to assemble. Then, once the basic layout is set on the sketch, you can place the 3D Primitives to aid your drawing. To place a 3D Primitive on the canvas:

1. Go to **Window | Material** palette.
2. Find the **3D** folder | **Primitives** to locate the Primitives.
3. You can choose between **Pyramid, Prism, Sphere, Cube, Plane, Billboard**, and **Polygon**. Select one of these shapes and drag and drop it onto the canvas. Alternatively, use the **Paste selected material to canvas icon** at the bottom of the **Material** palette.

Once you place the primitive on canvas, you can manipulate some of its characteristics, such as shape and color. Let's start by covering how to alter a primitive's shape.

Modifying a 3D Primitive's shape

Changing the shape of the primitive helps finetune it to tell your story. To find the available settings for altering the primitive's shape, go to the **Sub Tool Detail** palette and click on the **Primitive** category. You'll find the following settings:

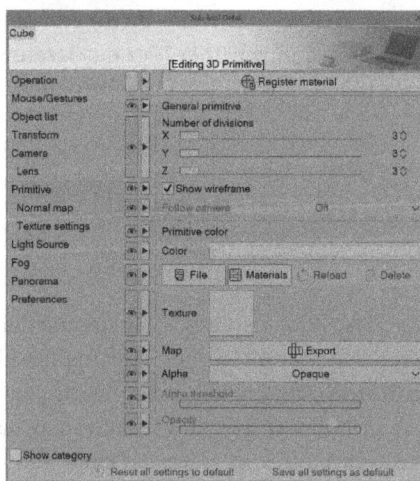

Figure 16.1 – Sub Tool Detail | Primitive settings

Under **Number of divisions**, you can determine precisely how many divisions the Primitive has in its *X*, *Y*, and *Z* axes. Setting up the number of divisions allows excellent customization: you can turn a pyramid into a cone, for example, as shown in *Figure 16.2*:

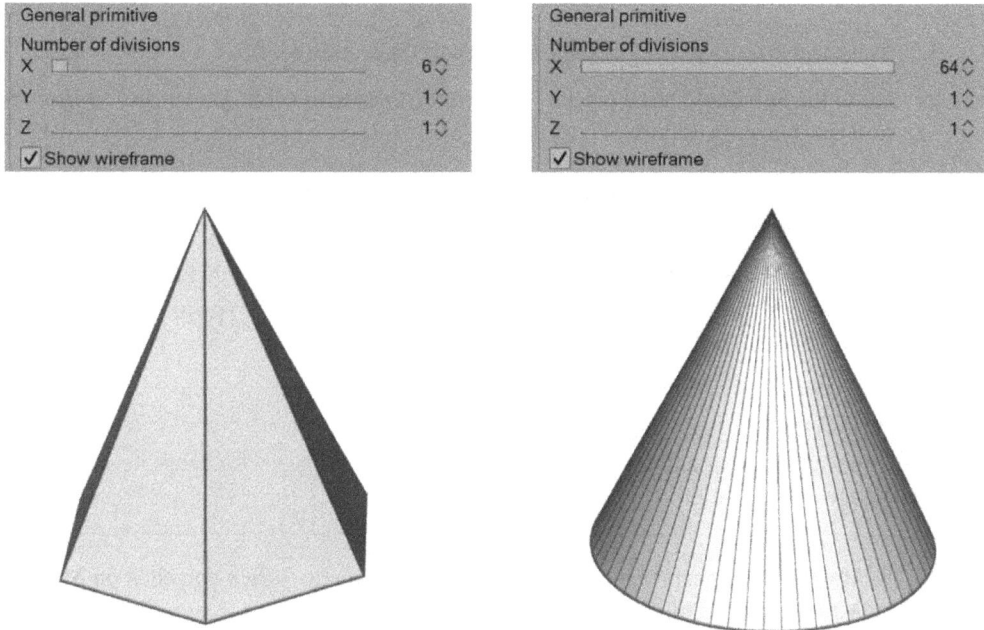

Figure 16.2 – The same Primitive with different Number of divisions

Changing the number of divisions lets you quickly change the primitive's shape to fit your desired scene better.

Use the **Sub Tool Detail** palette and the 3D manipulators to control dimensions and angles, ensuring your objects adhere to the intended scale and perspective. *Chapter 13, Manipulating 3D Objects on the Canvas*, covered how to move, rotate, and resize 3D objects.

After ensuring the primitive's shape fits your vision, you can change its color and add texture. We'll analyze these changes next.

Altering the color and texture of a 3D Primitive

Changing the color and texture of a 3D Primitive can aid construct the scene you envision. To modify these settings:

1. Select the Primitive with the **Object** sub tool (**Operation** tool).

2. Go to the **Sub Tool Detail** palette | **Primitive** | **Primitive color**. Under this category, you can find the following options:

   - **Color**: Click on the colored rectangle on the right side to open the **Color settings** dialog and choose a color for the 3D Primitive.

   - **File**: Launches the **Open** dialog to import an image file as texture for the primitive. You can import any file with the following formats: `.clip`, `.bmp`, `.jpeg`, `.tga`, `.png`, `.tiff`, `.psd`, and `.psb`.

> **Important note**
>
> When the primitive is a Plane or a Polygon, importing an image will change its scale to match the image's aspect ratio.

   - **Materials**: Imports textures from the Material palette. When you click on **Materials**, the **Add a texture** dialog opens. Select the material you wish to apply and hit **OK** to use it on the 3D Primitive.

   - **Reload**: Reloads the primitive texture when you are changing it in real-time.

   - **Delete**: Tap on this button if you want to remove the 3D texture.

   - **Texture**: This setting shows the texture applied to the 3D Primitive. Clicking on the texture image launches the **Open** dialog, and you can select a file from your computer.

   - **Map**: Use this setting to export the primitive as a **UV Map**, which is a flattened version of the shape. When you export a UV Map, you can edit the file and add texture and colors to it. In the following image you can see a Prism primitive (top left), its UV Map (top right), and how the primitive looks after adding colors to the UV Map (bottom left and bottom right):

Figure 16.3 – A 3D Prism (left) and its UV Map (right)

Exporting the edited file in `.clip` format will reflect the colors and texture of the 3D Primitive on the UV Map. If you save the edited file as `.png` or `.jpg`, you'll need to apply the new texture on the Primitive. To do so, go to the **Sub Too Detail** palette | **Primitive** | **Primitive color** | **Texture** and upload the edited file to it.

The exported *UV Map* file has three separate raster layers: *Texture*, which contains the image or material used for the texture; *Background Color*, filled with a solid color; and UV Map, which displays the UV lines as grid guidelines. The *UV Map* file can be customized and edited directly. Once you've modified the *UV Map* file, you can apply the updated texture to the 3D Primitive by importing it through the **Sub Tool Detail** palette | **Primitive** | **File** setting.

- **Alpha**: Use this setting to alter the opacity of the semi-transparent parts of the texture. There are three options:

  - **Opaque**: Semi-transparent parts of the texture will show the primitive's shape and color below the texture.

  - **Remove with threshold**: You can set a threshold that delimits which parts become opaque and which are transparent. The edges are hard around the transparent area.

  - **Semi-transparent**: Semi-transparent areas on the texture are transparent on the primitive. Depending on the texture material, the edges can be soft.

You can see examples of the Alpha settings in the image below:

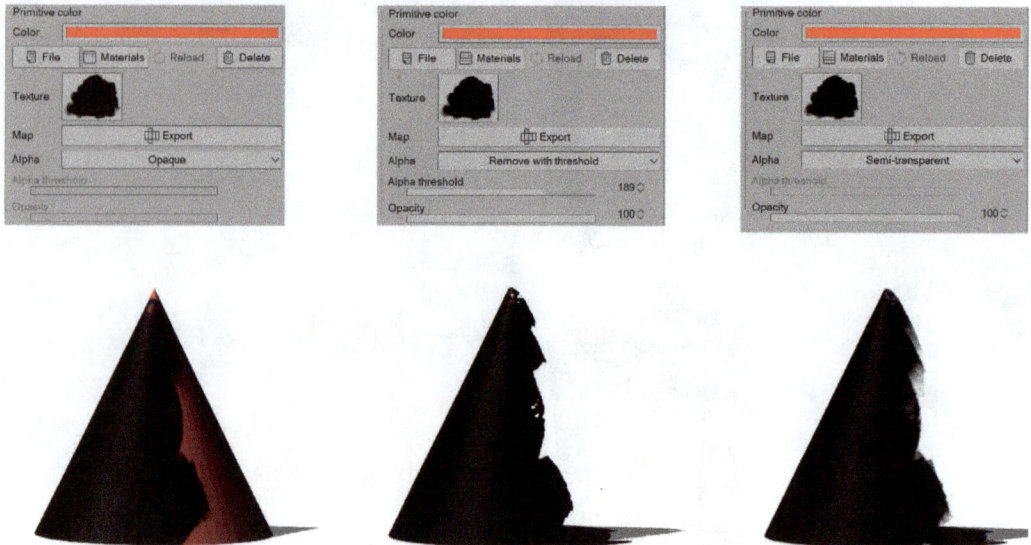

Figure 16.4 – Alpha settings for a primitive

- **Opacity**: Sets the visibility of the texture. This option is only available when you select **Remove with threshold** or **Semi-transparent** under **Alpha**.

The **Primitive** category of the **Sub Tool Detail** palette includes the basic settings for color and texture. You can dive deeper if you go to **Sub Tool Detail | Normal map** and **Sub Tool Detail | Texture** settings. Below is an explanation of each category and their functions:

1. **Normal map**: You can use this category of settings to add a **3D Normal map**, which adds texture to 3D materials. The settings within the Normal map category are similar to the ones we've covered above: **File**, **Materials**, **Reload**, **Delete**, and **Texture**. They work the same as the homonymous settings under **Sub Tool Detail | Primitive | Color**.

2. **Texture settings**: Use the following settings to modify the tiling, scale, and texture position.

   - **Tiling**: Changes the texture repetition method. When set to **Repeat**, the texture repeats in its original orientation. When set to **Reverse**, the texture alternates by flipping horizontally and vertically with each repetition:

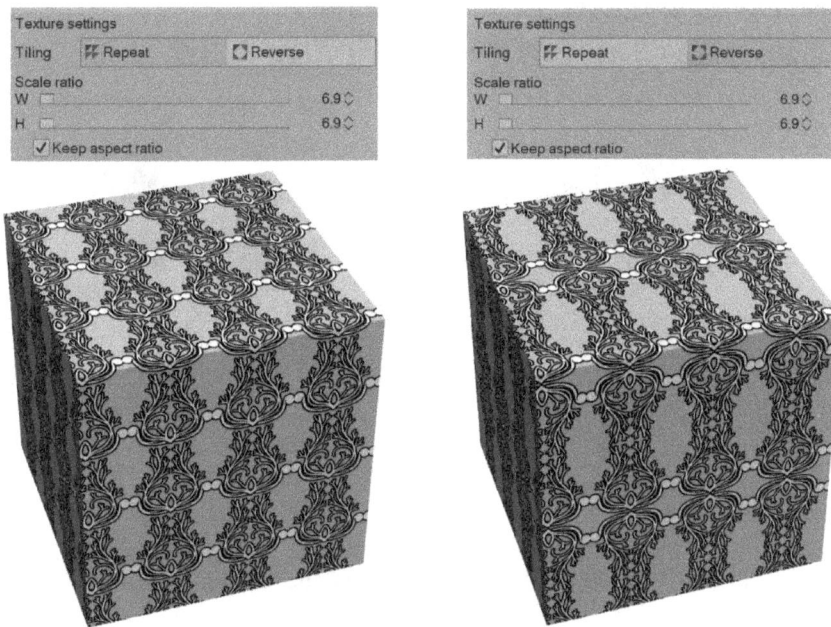

Figure 16.5 – The same texture with different Tiling settings

- **Scale ratio**: Changes the texture ratio in relation to the 3D Primitive, increasing or decreasing its size. When the texture is small, it becomes a repeating pattern, and the **Tiling** setting comes into place.

- **Position**: Changes the position of the texture on the 3D Primitive.

You now understand how to change the shape, color and texture of 3D primitives. There's a special primitive that you can use to represent complex images, such as trees: the **Billboard** primitive. Let's cover how it works next.

The Billboard primitive

The **Billboard** is a 3D Plane with a drawing or painting set as texture. You can draw your own trees, lamps, or whatever object you want to place as a Billboard. Then, follow the next steps:

1. Go to **Window | Material** palette.
2. Find the **3D** folder, then locate the **Primitives** folder.
3. Select the **Billboard** and place it on the canvas by dragging and dropping or pressing the **Paste selected material to canvas** icon at the bottom of the **Material** palette.
4. In the **Sub Tool Detail** palette, navigate to **Primitive | Texture**.
5. Use the **File** or **Materials** settings to select the image you want to place on the Billboard.

The image will be applied to the Billboard material:

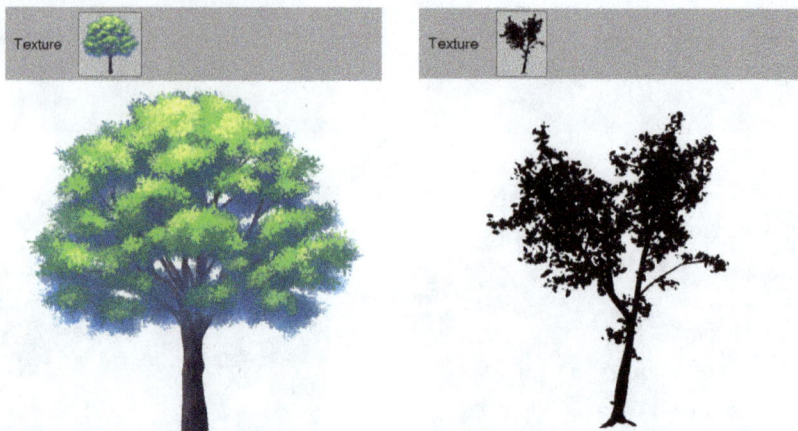

Figure 16.6 – The Billboard material with different images as Texture

You can set 3D Primitive Planes and Polygons, including the Billboard, to always face the camera as the camera moves around the object. Follow the steps below:

1. Select the 3D Primitive with the **Object** sub tool.

2. Go to the **Sub Tool Detail** palette | **Primitive**.

3. Enable **Follow camera**. When you select **On**, the 3D Primitive adjusts to always face the camera directly. When this option is **Off**, the material behaves like a standard 3D object, rotating naturally with the camera's position. If you select **Only horizontal**, the primitive will rotate to face the camera only when the camera moves horizontally.

    You can see an example of how this might be useful in *Figure 16.7*, in which letting the Billboard rotate created a distortion (left) and adjusting it to **Follow camera** fixes the issue (right).

Figure 16.7 – Follow camera off (left) and on (right)

After you've customized a primitive, you can save it as a material. To register a 3D Primitive:

1. Select the 3D Primitive with the **Object** sub tool (**Operation** tool).

2. Click the **Save 3D primitive to Material palette** icon in the **Object Launcher**.

3. Alternatively, go to the **Sub Tool Detail** palette | **Primitive** category and select **Register material**.

4. The **Material property** dialog will open. You can specify a name, save location, and tags for the material. Once you've set these details, click **OK** to add the **3D Primitive** to the **Material** palette.

Using primitive shapes effectively transforms the daunting task of creating backgrounds into manageable steps. Building a scene's structure with these simple forms gives you the confidence and clarity to tackle more complex designs. Now that we've covered how primitive shapes can serve as a foundation, let's explore how to improve your backgrounds further by integrating multiple objects into intricate 3D scenes.

Making complex backgrounds with multiple 3D objects

Creating backgrounds using multiple 3D objects is essential for artists who want to add depth, detail, and realism to their compositions. By combining various 3D materials, you can construct dynamic environments, whether it's for illustrations, comics, or concept art. This process lets you organize and manipulate objects efficiently, ensuring your scene is visually compelling, cohesive, and well-structured.

When crafting a 3D scene, it might be necessary to align materials - especially in artificial environments, such as a classroom or a kitchen. The **Snap to 3D models** feature is incredibly useful in such moments. This tool aligns objects precisely, allowing you to build structures or align items seamlessly with existing 3D models. For instance, when creating a building, snapping ensures that walls, doors, and windows are perfectly positioned without gaps or misalignment.

To toggle **Snap to 3D models** on, go to **Sub Tool Detail** | **Operation** and toggle this setting on. When snapping is toggled on, an orange box appears around objects to align them:

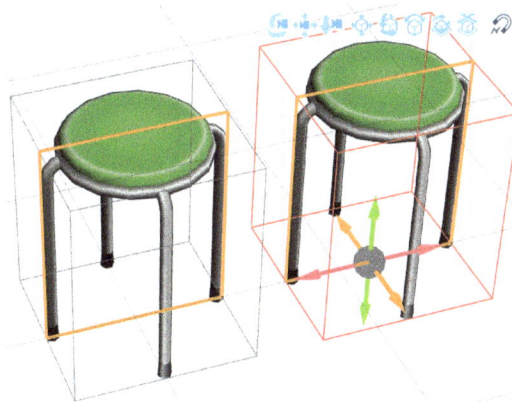

Figure 16.8 – Snap to 3D models setting

This orange box also appears when rotating and scaling objects, ensuring all objects are aligned correctly in position, angle, and size.

On top of aligning 3D models, when working with multiple 3D objects, one of the most important features you must master is the **Object list** in the **Sub Tool Detail** palette.

The Object list lets you manage visibility, a key aspect of working with multiple 3D objects—especially when fine-tuning specific areas of your background without distraction. You can also use the Object list to set material hierarchies and create groups of materials linked to one another. We've extensively covered the Object list and material hierarchies in *Chapter 13, Manipulating 3D Objects on the Canvas*, under the sections *Introducing 3D Materials onto your canvas* and *Maximizing 3D Material hierarchy for easier manipulation.*

Within the Object list you can find the **Duplicate** option, which is excellent for organizing complex scenes. It streamlines your workflow by enabling you to copy and reuse materials in an environment. To duplicate a material:

1. Navigate to **Sub Tool Detail | Object list**.
2. Select the material you wish to duplicate on the **Object list**.
3. Click on **Duplicate**.
4. Alternatively, you can go to the **Edit** menu | **Copy** or press *Ctrl/command + C* on your keyboard, then go to the **Edit** menu | **Paste** or press *Ctrl/command + V* on your keyboard.

The Duplicate feature is great for repetitive elements such as furniture and streetlights, saving time while maintaining uniformity. You can create evenly spaced copies of objects and design symmetrical layouts or repetitive patterns, like rows of trees, columns, or fences. To create equally spaced duplicates:

1. Select the 3D material you wish to duplicate with the **Object** sub tool, as shown in *Figure 16.9* (top.)
2. Go to the **Edit** menu | **Copy** or press *Ctrl/command + C* on your keyboard.
3. Go to the **Edit** menu | **Paste** or press *Ctrl/command + V* on your keyboard. The duplicated material will be placed exactly on top of the original material.
4. Select the copy and move it to the desired location as shown in *Figure 16.9* (middle.) Use the *Root manipulator* or the **Sub Tool Detail** palette to move the duplicate, as we covered in *Chapter 13, Manipulating 3D Objects on the Canvas*, under the section *Mastering 3D manipulators for precise adjustments.*

5. Go to the **Edit** menu | **Paste** or press *Ctrl/command + V* on your keyboard. The duplicated material will be placed according to the spacing arranged in the previous step, as shown in *Figure 16.9* (bottom):

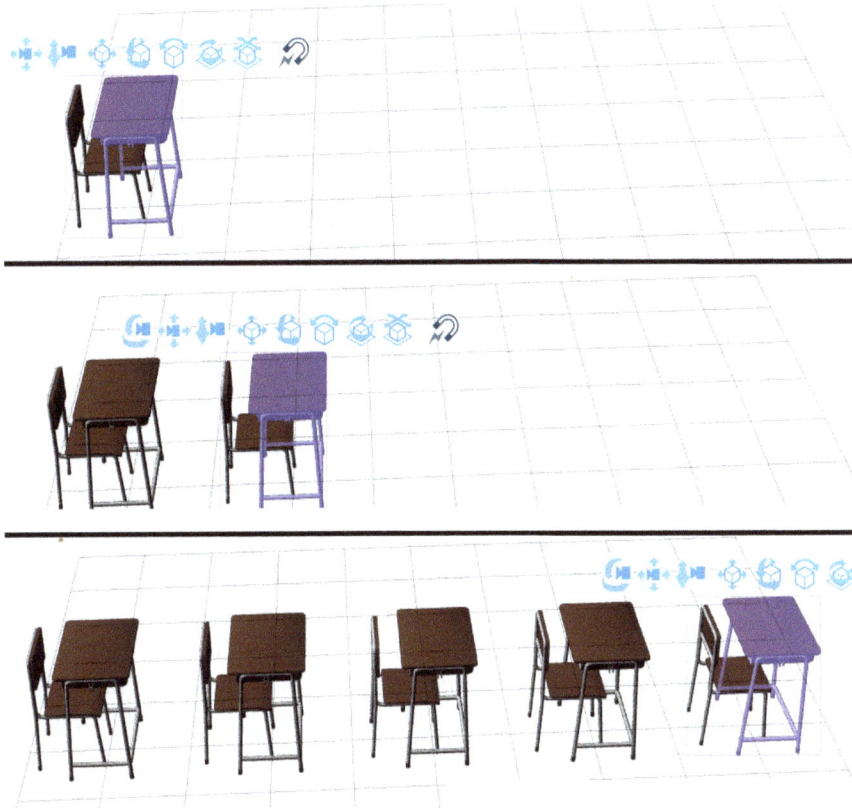

Figure 16.9 – Creating equally spaced duplicates

Following the steps above, you can quickly populate your background with consistent and well-organized elements, such as chairs, lamps, and bookshelves.

When working with multiple selected 3D materials, you can adjust the reference point for rotation or scaling. Setting a pivot point allows you to move, rotate, or scale a group of objects around a designated point. To change the pivot point:

1. Go to the **Sub Tool Detail** palette | **Operation**.

2. Set a pivot point under the **Pivot point for multiple objects** setting. Below are the possible options:

- **First selected object**: The *Root manipulator* appears at the position of the first selected 3D material. Rotation and scaling are applied relative to this material's pivot point. In the figure below, the first selected object was the second chair from left to right:

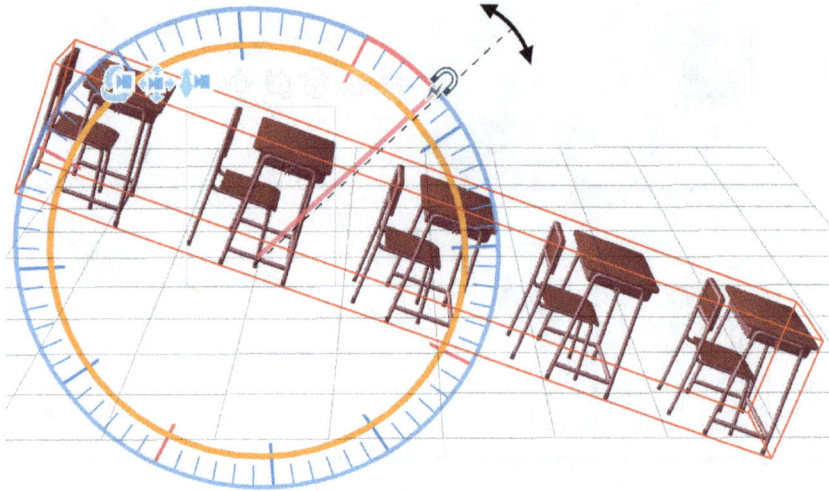

Figure 16.10 – Pivot point: First selected object

- **Local pivot points**: The *Root manipulator* appears around the first selected 3D material, but each material rotates and scales individually based on its pivot point. In the figure below, the first selected object was the second chair from left to right:

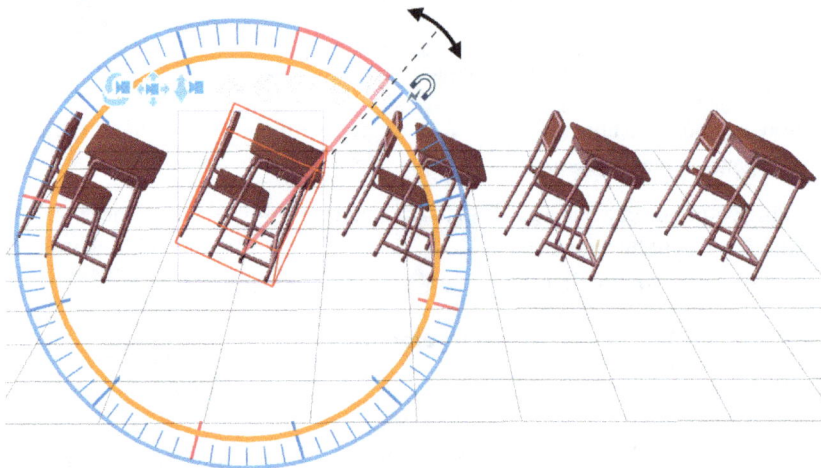

Figure 16.11 – Pivot point: Local pivot points

- **Midpoint of multiple objects**: This setting positions the *Root manipulator* at the center of all selected 3D materials, allowing you to rotate and scale the materials relative to the collective midpoint while maintaining their relative positions to one another. In the figure below, the first selected object was the second chair from left to right:

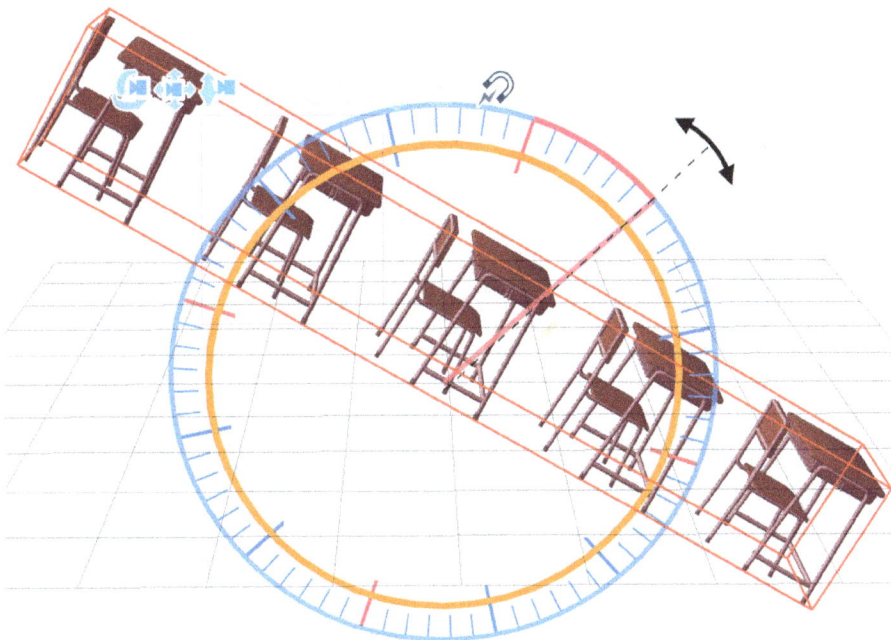

Figure 16.12 – Pivot point: Midpoint of multiple objects

3. On **Movement axis** and **Rotation axis**, you can choose whether the 3D materials follow the axis of the ground or the object when being moved and rotated.

Combining these features allows you to build intricate and realistic environments that suit your project's needs. The ability to manipulate and manage 3D objects effectively ensures a smoother creative process and more polished results.

When searching for the best 3D models, use *CLIP STUDIO ASSETS* to download the perfect model that fits your needs. There, you can find everything from individual objects to complete environments. For details on using *CLIP STUDIO ASSETS*, refer to *Chapter 3, Setting Up Materials for Consistency and Speed*, under the section *Downloading and uploading materials inside CLIP STUDIO ASSETS*.

Now that you know how to create complex backgrounds with multiple 3D materials, it's time to integrate immersive and panoramic settings. The next section delves into using panorama 3D models for 360-degree backgrounds, a tool that will significantly speed up your background painting process.

Using 3D Panorama materials for 360-degree backgrounds

Creating immersive environments is an essential part of digital art, especially for storytelling and establishing the mood in a scene. 3D Panorama materials offer a powerful solution, allowing you to work with expansive 360-degree backgrounds that envelop your entire workspace. These materials create a fully immersive environment for characters and objects, eliminating the need for intricate manual background creation while ensuring proper perspective and scale.

A **3D Panorama** is a 360-degree background image set on a **3D layer**, offering immersive and realistic environments for illustrations and comics. Panoramas can include photos from 360-degree cameras or equirectangular images exported from 3D software. Once applied, the panorama wraps around the scene as a spherical or cylindrical background, offering a seamless 360-degree view. In the figure below, you can see two different camera angles of the same 3D Panorama:

Figure 16.13 – Different camera angles of the same 3D Panorama

To rotate the camera of a Panorama, click and drag around the canvas. You can also change the zoom and the camera lens by using the following settings:

1.   **Sub Tool Detail | Panorama | Fish-eye perspective**: When you increase the value of the fish-eye perspective, the visible area expands. However, edges will be distorted as if in a fish-eye lens.

2.   **Sub Tool Detail | Camera | Perspective**: Like the previous setting, the Perspective setting lets you change the type of camera lens—whether it will be wider or narrower. The wider the lens, the more distortion appears.

You can see examples of the Fish-eye perspective and the Perspective settings below:

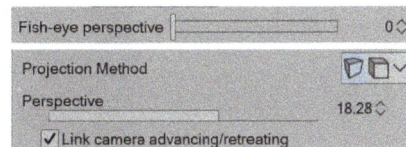

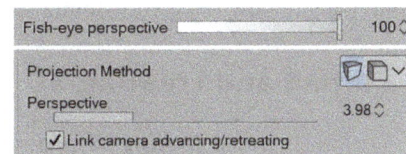

Figure 16.14 – Different perspective settings for a 3D Panorama

3. When operating a panorama, going to the **Sub Tool Detail** palette | **Preferences** | **Display settings for editing** option lets you switch between **Fast** and **Normal** modes. This setting changes how the Panorama appears during adjustments. When set to **Normal**, the Panorama is invisible outside of the canvas, while **Fast** shows the entire Panorama in the working area:

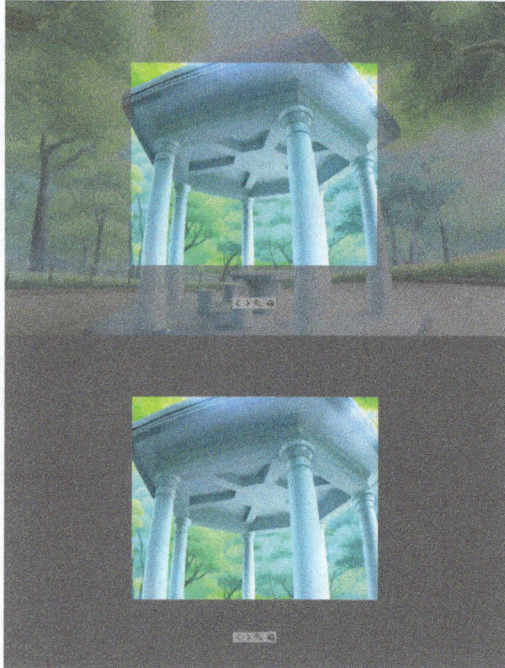

Figure 16.15 – Display settings for editing: Fast (top) and Normal (bottom)

Understanding the basics of 3D panoramas is a gateway to crafting immersive and dynamic backgrounds. Now that you've explored the foundational aspects of 3D panoramas, let's take it a step further by diving into how you can customize or even create your own panoramas.

Editing and creating 3D Panoramas

Customizing and creating 3D panoramas allows you to tailor every aspect of your scene, ensuring it aligns perfectly with your artistic vision and storytelling needs. There are four ways to import and create 3D Panorama materials.

You can import 3D Panorama materials from the *CLIP STUDIO ASSETS* library by following the next steps:

1. Download a **3D Panorama** material on the website `https://assets.clip-studio.com`.

2. Inside CSP, locate the 3D Panorama in the **Material** palette.

3. Paste the 3D Panorama on the canvas by dragging and dropping or pressing the **Paste selected material to canvas** icon at the bottom of the **Material** palette.

Another alternative is to apply a new 360-degree image on an existing 3D Panorama. Follow the steps below:

1. Find or create the panorama image that suits your artistic vision. There are three options:

    *   Look for panorama images on the internet by searching **High Dynamic Range Image** (HDRI).

    *   Capture your own 360-degree photographs.

    *   Transform a 3D scene into a 3D Panorama. Follow the steps below:

        i.   Create your 3D scene with all its objects.

        ii. When the 3D scene is complete, go to **Sub Tool Detail** and select the **Panorama** category.

        iii. Click on **Export as panorama image**. Below you can see an example of a 3D classroom (top) and its Panorama (bottom):

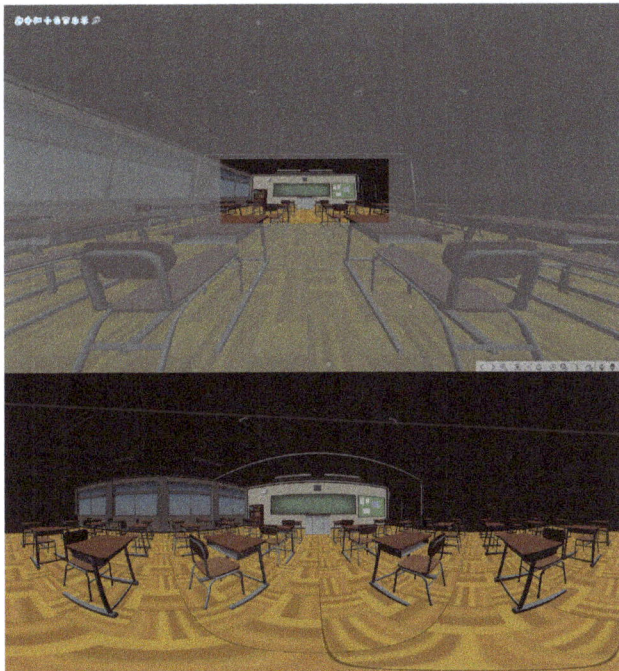

Figure 16.16 – A 3D scene (top) and its Panorama (bottom)

        iv. This process saves a 360-degree view of the 3D layer centered around the active camera. Note that the camera roll and tilt are reset, and any empty areas will appear transparent in the exported file.

> **Important note**
>
> When you save a 3D scene as a 3D Panorama, you can no longer edit 3D objects and models. Make sure you save a `.clip` file of your 3D scene in case there's anything you need to change later.

2.   After following one of the methods described above for finding or creating 360-view images, you'll have an image file such as `.png` or `.jpg`.

3.   Your next step is to transform this image file into a 3D Panorama. Follow the steps below to load it as a 3D Panorama material:

    i.   Start with an existing Panorama material. Navigate to the **Material** palette | **3D** | **Panorama**.

    ii.   Select a 3D Panorama material and load it into your workspace by dragging it onto the canvas.

    iii.   In the **Sub Tool Detail** palette, go to **Panorama** | **Texture** and select your desired panorama image. Below you can see a default park Panorama (top) and how it looks after changing the texture to a classroom 360-view image (bottom):

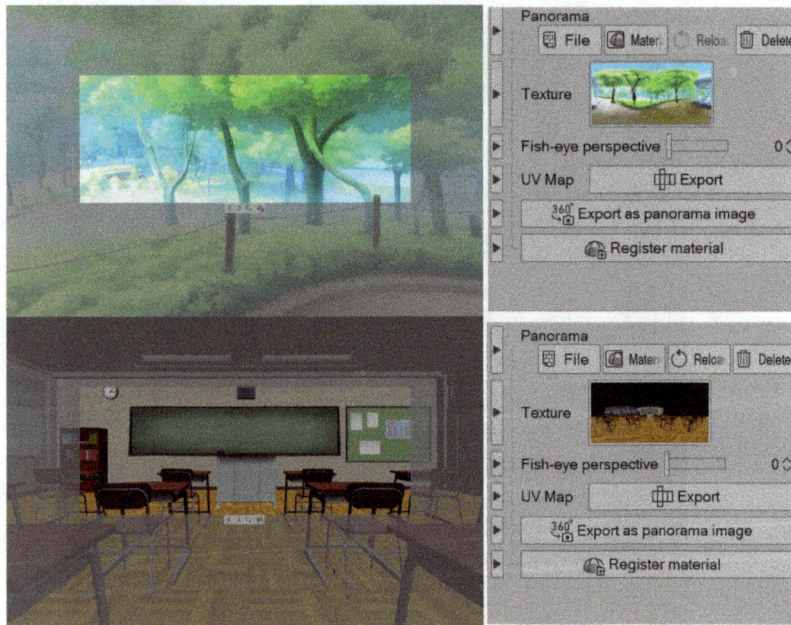

Figure 16.17 – Changing the Texture of a Panorama

4.   You can export 3D Panorama images for additional editing or direct use. To save the texture of an existing panorama:

    i.   Go to **Sub Tool Detail** and select the **UV Map** category.

ii.   Click on **Export**. Exporting the UV Map creates a `.clip` file containing the panorama *Texture* layer, a *Background color* layer, and a *UV Map* layer with gridlines for precise editing:

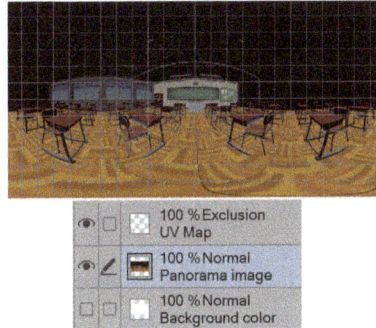

Figure 16.18 – Panorama UV Map

The exported `.clip` file has a canvas size of 8192 x 4320 pixels (*8K*), ensuring high resolution.

iii. You can draw and paint on this image or make color adjustments. Anything you paint and edit on the UV Map will become part of the Panorama Texture. Below you can see an example of changes in color and how they affect a Panorama—I selected the floor and used a **Hue/Saturation/Luminosity Correction Layer** (covered in *Chapter 12, Enhancing Your Art with Post-Processing Adjustments*) to make the floor green:

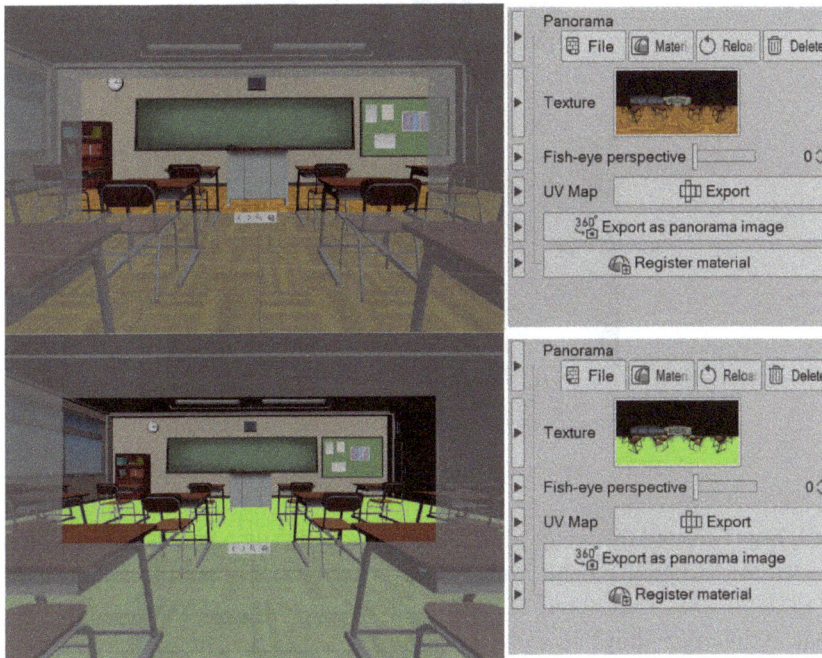

Figure 16.19 – How changes in a UV Map can transform a Panorama

      iv.   When satisfied with the result, save the *UV Map* file by going to **File | Save** or pressing *Ctrl/command + S* on your keyboard.

      v.   Load the *UV Map* file onto the **Sub Tool Detail | Panorama | Texture** setting of an existing Panorama.

      vi.   To preview and adjust your custom panorama while editing it, use the **Reload** button to see updates in real-time. This iterative process is ideal for refining details and ensuring proper alignment.

5.   Once satisfied with the Panorama material, you can save it as a 3D Material:

      i.   Go to the **Object Launcher** and click on **Save panorama to Material palette**.

      ii.   Alternatively, go to **Sub Tool Detail | Panorama | Register material**.

You can use Panoramas to quickly add a background to your scene. Below you can see how an image can look complete once you add a Panorama and tweak the character and background to become harmonious:

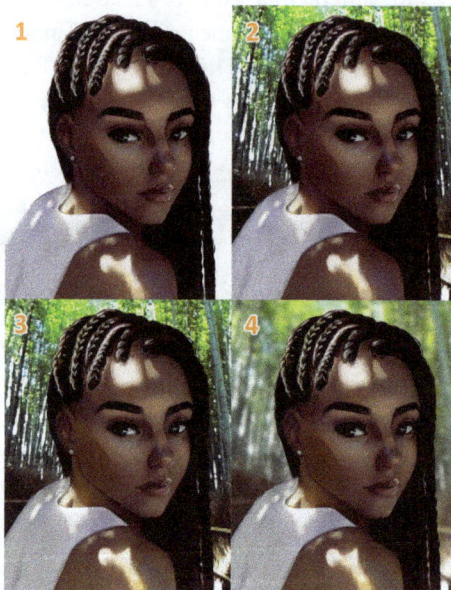

Figure 16.20 – Adding a Panorama background to a character painting

I'll explain how I created the image above. In step 1 (top left), I had the character already painted and there was no background behind her. In step 2 (top right), I added a Panorama material I found in *CLIP STUDIO ASSETS* (Content ID: 1931657). At this point, the character and the background didn't match: the colors didn't fit, and because the Panorama is a photo, it looks out of place when compared to the painted character.

In step 3 (bottom left), I added some greens to the character to represent how the surrounding forest affects her – that fixed the problem with the colors. Lastly, in step 4 (bottom right), I did three things: first, I blurred the background to fix the disconnection between the painting and the panorama photo. Then, I created a **Hue/Saturation/Luminosity Correction Layer** (covered in detail in *Chapter 12, Enhancing Your Art with Post-Processing Adjustments*) to shift hue, reduce saturation, and increase brightness to make the background fit the image. To finish it, I used an **Add Glow** layer (covered in *Chapter 9, Mastering Layer Blending Modes for Stunning Colors*) to make the bottom of the background lighter and make the character stand out more because of the value difference.

By leveraging 3D Panorama materials, you can maintain a professional level of depth and realism in your backgrounds, speeding up your process and elevating your art.

Summary

Mastering the creation of 3D backgrounds opens new possibilities for crafting immersive scenes in your artwork. Using primitive shapes, you can build simple yet effective representations of background elements, simplifying the process of sketching ideas and laying out compositions. For more intricate designs, combining multiple 3D objects allows for creating complex settings with precision and flexibility. Techniques such as snapping objects, duplicating materials, and aligning them using pivot points enable efficient customization and fine-tuning.

The use of 3D Panoramas adds a dynamic layer to your workflow, providing 360-degree environments that can transform how you approach background design. Whether drawing from panoramic photographs or constructing a custom stage, these tools offer unparalleled perspective control and environmental context.

By integrating these techniques, you can create detailed, interactive backgrounds that enhance the visual depth of your projects and streamline your creative process. The tools and methods discussed equip you to push the boundaries of what is possible with 3D elements in CSP, bringing your artistic visions to life.

Congratulations on reaching the end of this book! You've taken a significant step in mastering advanced techniques and tools that will elevate your digital art, unlocking new possibilities to bring your creative visions to life. The more you apply the knowledge you've acquired, the more natural each process will become. Your dedication and effort reflect your passion for improving your craft, and that commitment will undoubtedly shine through in your artwork. Remember, every great artist continues to learn, experiment, and refine their skills—this is just one milestone in your artistic journey. Now, take what you've learned, unleash your creativity, and keep inspiring the world with your art!

Get This Book's PDF Version and Exclusive Extras

UNLOCK NOW

Scan the QR code (or go to `packtpub.com/unlock`). Search for this book by name, confirm the edition, and then follow the steps on the page.

Note: Keep your invoice handly. Purchase made directly from packt don't require one.

17
Unlock Your Exclusive Benefits

Your copy of this book includes the following exclusive benefit:

- Next-gen Packt Reader
- DRM-free PDF/ePub downloads

Follow the guide below to unlock them. The process takes only a few minutes and needs to be completed once.

Unlock this Book's Free Benefits in 3 Easy Steps

Step 1

Keep your purchase invoice ready for *Step 3*. If you have a physical copy, scan it using your phone and save it as a PDF, JPG, or PNG.

For more help on finding your invoice, visit `https://www.packtpub.com/unlock-benefits/help`.

> **Note**
> If you bought this book directly from Packt, no invoice is required. After *Step 2*, you can access your exclusive content right away.

Step 2

Scan the QR code or go to `packtpub.com/unlock`.

On the page that opens (similar to *Figure 17.1* on desktop), search for this book by name and select the correct edition.

Figure 17.1: Packt unlock landing page on desktop

Step 3

After selecting your book, sign in to your Packt account or create one for free. Then upload your invoice (PDF, PNG, or JPG, up to 10 MB). Follow the on-screen instructions to finish the process.

Need help?

If you get stuck and need help, visit
`https://www.packtpub.com/unlock-benefits/help`
for a detailed FAQ on how to find your invoices and more. This QR code will take you to the help page.

Note

If you are still facing issues, reach out to `customercare@packt.com`.

Index

Symbols

3D Background 317

3D Body type 314

3D character 316

  body shape, altering 344-349

  head, modifying 350, 351

  materials, setting 328, 329

  poses, modifying 361-369

  proportions, adjusting 343

3D figure

  posing 356

3D hands

  posing 370-374

3D Head 315

3D manipulators 320

  Movement Manipulator 321

  Object Launcher 326

  Root Manipulator 329, 330

3D material hierarchy 339

  child object 339

  maximizing 339-341

  parent object 339

3D materials 313

  placing, onto canvas 314, 319

  selecting, for canvas 320

3D materials types

  3D Background 317

  3D Body type 314

  3D Character 316

  3D Head 315

  3D Object 316

  3D Pose 314

  3D Primitive 318

  Panorama 317

3D Object 316

3D Object materials

  functions 329

3D Panorama 404

  creating 406-411

  editing 406-411

  materials, using for 360-degree

    backgrounds 405, 406

3D Pose 314

  importing, into CSP 357

3D Primitive 318

  color and texture, altering 394-397

  shape, modifying 392, 393

3D scene

  ambient light, adding 379

  camera angle, modifying 334-338

  main light source, modifying 376-379

  secondary light source, adding 380-382

3D space

  light, setting up 375, 376

A

Add blending mode 211
Add (Glow) blending mode 211, 212
Airbrush 255
Angle Dynamics 83, 84
anti-aliasing 94
Anti-overflow feature 113, 114
artificial intelligence 359
auto actions 31
  creating 35, 36
  examples 31, 32
  modifying 34, 35
  palette 33
  pre-made auto actions, downloading 37
  using 33, 34
Auto select tool 244
  customizing 244-247

B

background representations
  crafting, with primitive shapes 391, 392
Billboard primitive 397-399
Binarization 291
blending modes 198-201
  Add 211
  Add (Glow) 211, 212
  applying, to real painting 227-233
  Brightness 225
  Color 224
  Color burn 204
  Color dodge 209
  Darken 202
  Darker color 206
  Difference 217, 218
  Divide 212, 213
  Exclusion 222, 223
  Glow dodge 210
  Hard light 216
  Hard mix 221, 222
  Hue 223
  Lighten 208
  Lighter color 213
  Linear burn 204
  Linear light 219, 220
  Multiply 203, 204
  Overlay 215
  Pin light 220, 221
  Saturation 224
  Screen 208, 209
  Soft light 216
  Subtract 205
  Vivid light 218, 219
Blur filters 292-296
Brightness blending mode 225
Brightness/Contrast correction
    layer 279, 280
brush dynamics 77
  Angle Dynamics 83, 84
  Direction of particle Dynamics 84, 85
  Pen pressure 78-80
  Random 82, 83
  Tilt 81
  Velocity 82
brush properties 86, 87
Brush shape settings 95, 96
  Brush tip 96-98
  Spraying effect 98-100
  Stroke section 100, 101
  Texture section 101-103
Brush Size setting 87, 88
Brush tip 96-98
Brush tool 77

C

camera angle
  modifying, of 3D scene 334-338
cell 299
CLIP STUDIO ASSETS 58
  materials, downloading 58-60
  materials, uploading 58-60
Clip Studio Paint (CSP) 3, 25, 39, 61, 77, 121, 235, 277, 343
  Command Bar, configuring 12-15
  Tool Property palette 15, 17
  workspace configuration 3, 18-22
Clip Studio Paint EX 66
Color balance 288-290
Color blending mode 224
Color burn blending mode 204
Color dodge blending mode 209
Color Jitter 92, 93
Color Match 266, 273
  applying, to artwork 266-270
color-related palettes 7
  color history 8
  color mixing 8
  color set 8
  color slider 8
  color wheel 8
  intermediate color 8
Color Set palette
  functions 274, 275
color sets 273
  creating 275
  saving 273
Command Bar 8, 12
  configuring 12-15
complex backgrounds
  making, with multiple 3D objects 399-403
consistent file structure
  maintaining 69

control points 122
Correction filters 296, 297
correction layers 278
  Binarization 291
  Brightness/Contrast 279, 280
  Color balance 288-290
  Gradient map 292
  Hue/Saturation/Luminosity 280, 281
  Level Correction 284-286
  Posterization 282, 283
  Reverse Gradient 283
  Tone Curve 286-288
  utilizing, for final touches 278, 279
Correction setting 109-111
Correct line tool 129
  Adjust line width sub tool 134, 135
  Connect vector line sub tool 133, 134
  Control point sub tool 129, 130
  Pinch vector line sub tool 130, 131
  Redraw vector line sub tool 135
  Redraw vector line width sub tool 136
  Simplify vector line sub tool 131, 132
CSP guide tools
  Grid tool 142, 143
  guide lines 142
  guide lines, creating 142
  Ruler bar 140, 141
  Ruler tool 144-147
Curve ruler 148-150
custom brushes
  creating 115-119

D

Darken blending mode 202
Darker color blending mode 206
depth-of-field (DoF) effects 293
Difference blending mode 217, 218

Direction of particle Dynamics feature 84, 85
Distort filters 297, 298
Divide blending mode 212, 213
Dual brush feature 103-106

E

Effect filters 299-301
Ellipse sub tool 236-238
Erase function 108, 109
Erase selection sub tool 242, 243
Exclusion blending mode 222, 223

F

Face Mixer 352, 353
Facial features 354-356
Figure ruler 150, 151
files
  clear naming conventions, using for 70
Fill tool 260
  for fast painting 261-265
filters
  Blur filters 292-296
  correction filters 296, 297
  Distort filters 297, 298
  Effect filters 299-301
  Render filter 302
  Sharpen filters 302
  using, for creative enhancements 292
floating palette 12

G

Glow dodge blending mode 210
gradient maps 266-273, 292
  applying, to flat image 270-272

Grid tool 142
  customizing 143
  toggling 143
Guide lines 142
  creating 142
guides 140

H

Hard light blending mode 216
Hard mix blending mode 221, 222
High Dynamic Range Image (HDRI) 407
Hue blending mode 223
Hue/Saturation/Luminosity correction layer 280, 281

I

image materials
  creating 43-46
Ink settings 88
  Blending Mode 89
  Color mixing 89-91
  Opacity 89

J

Joint angle limit feature 363

K

knee manipulator 367

L

Lasso fill sub tool 258-260
Lasso sub tool 238
  using 239

layer comps 66
  example 67, 69
  settings 67
layer list 177
  functions 177, 178
Layer palette 170
  command bar 175-177
  menu 171, 172
  property bar 172-175
Layer Property palette 179
  Border effect 181, 182
  Color mode 193, 194
  Display decrease color 191
  Expression color 190, 191
  Extract lines 183-186
  functions 179, 180
  Layer color 189
  Mask expression 192
  Overlay texture 193
  Tone 186-189
  Tool navigation 192
layer-related palettes 11
layers 169
  color-coding 63
  grouping 64, 65
  naming 62, 63
  optimizing, with pro techniques 194-196
  organizing 61, 62
Level Correction 284, 285
light
  setting up, in 3D space 375, 376
Lighten blending mode 208
Lighter color blending mode 213
lighting 375
Linear burn blending mode 204
Linear light blending mode 219, 220
Linear ruler 144-148

Liquify tool
  maximizing 303-306
local manipulator 366, 367

M

Magnetic lasso sub tool 240
main light source
  modifying, of 3D scene 376-379
Material palette 39
  navigating 40-42
materials 39
  downloading, in CLIP STUDIO
    ASSETS 58-60
  registering 57
  uploading, in CLIP STUDIO ASSETS 58-60
modifier keys 28
  tool, modifying temporarily 28-30
Movement Manipulator 320, 321
  functions 321-325
multiple 3D objects
  complex backgrounds, making 399-403
Multiply blending mode 203, 204

N

non-destructive editing 66

O

Object Launcher 320, 326
  functions 326-328
Object list 326
  settings 327
Overlay blending mode 215

P

Panorama 317
patterns
  applying efficiently 52-54
  creating 47, 48
  seamless patterns, creating 48-51
Pencil tool 77
Pen pressure dynamics 78-80
Pen tool 77
personalized shortcuts
  creating 25-28
Perspective ruler 144, 155, 319
  applying, for dynamic images 155
  creating 155-158
  implementing 162, 163
  parts 158-161
  settings, customizing 156, 157
Pin light blending mode 220, 221
Polyline sub tool 241
  using 241
pose controller 364
Posemaniacs
  poses, setting up 357-359
  reference link 328
Pose Scanner
  using 359, 360
Posterization 282, 283
primitive shapes
  background representations,
    crafting 391, 392
proportions
  adjusting, of 3D character 343
Puppet warp transformation 307
  using 307, 308

Q

Quick Mask 247, 248
  creating 248, 249

R

Random slider 82, 83
Rectangle sub tool 236-238
reference palettes
  Information 10
  Item bank 10
  Navigator 10
  Sub View 10
Render filter 302
Reverse Gradient 283
**Root Manipulator 320, 321,
    329, 330-334, 364**
  functions 332, 333
Ruler bar 140, 141
  toggling ways 141
Ruler pen 152, 153
rulers 140
Ruler tool 144
  types 144
  using 144-147

S

Saturation blending mode 224
**Scalable Vector Graphics (SVG)
    file formats 123**
Scaling mode 246
Screen blending mode 208, 209
Selection area tool 235
  Ellipse sub tool 236
  Erase selection sub tool 242, 243

Lasso sub tool 238, 239
Magnetic lasso sub tool 240
Polyline sub tool 241, 242
Rectangle sub tool 236
Selection pen sub tool 242, 243
Shrink selection sub tool 243, 244
using 236
Selection Launcher 252
customizing 253, 254
functions 254
Selection Layer 247-250
example 251
Selection pen sub tool 242, 243
selection tools
practical uses 255, 256
usage, optimizing 252-254
Shading Assist
using 382-388
shadows 201
Sharpen filters 302
Shrink selection sub tool 243
snapping
enabling 140
Soft light blending mode 216
Special ruler 153-155
Spraying effect 98-100
Starting and ending settings 111-113
Stroke section 100, 101
Sub Tool Detail palette 86, 87
Ink section 88
Sub Tool palette 6
Subtract blending mode 205
Symmetrical ruler
usage, optimizing 164, 165

T

templates
setting up 55-57
Texture settings 101-103
Tilt setting 81
Tone Curve 286-288
Tool palette 5, 6
Tool Property palette 7, 15
settings 16, 17

V

vector layers 121
creating, from scratch 122, 123
raster layers, converting into 124, 125
SVG files, importing from other
    software 123, 124
vector lines
editing 125, 126
editing, with Correct line tool 129
erasing 136-138
transforming 125, 126
transforming, with Object sub tool 126-128
Velocity setting 82
Vivid light blending mode 218, 219

W

Watercolor edge feature 107, 108
work
backing up 70-72
saving 70-72
workflow
reflecting 72
reviewing 72
streamlining 69

workspace configuration, CSP 3, 18-22

    color-related palettes 7, 8

    Command Bar 8

    default workspace 4

    floating palette 12

    layer-related palettes 11

    main canvas area 4, 5

    reference palettes 9, 10

    tool-related palettes 5-7

‹packt›

packtpub.com

Subscribe to our online digital library for full access to over 7,000 books and videos, as well as industry leading tools to help you plan your personal development and advance your career. For more information, please visit our website.

Why subscribe?

- Spend less time learning and more time coding with practical eBooks and Videos from over 4,000 industry professionals

- Improve your learning with Skill Plans built especially for you

- Get a free eBook or video every month

- Fully searchable for easy access to vital information

- Copy and paste, print, and bookmark content

At www.packtpub.com, you can also read a collection of free technical articles, sign up for a range of free newsletters, and receive exclusive discounts and offers on Packt books and eBooks.

Other Books You May Enjoy

If you enjoyed this book, you may be interested in these other books by Packt:

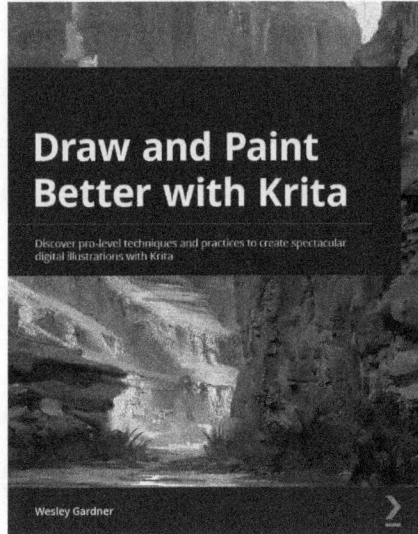

Draw and Paint Better with Krita

None Gardner

ISBN: 978-1-80107-176-5

- Use layers, layer management, and layer blending modes to make images pop
- Understand Krita's default workspace and customize it
- Understand the terminology of digital visual communication (dots per inch, resolution, and more)
- Explore color in a digital space, such as RGB profiles and Look-Up-Tables (LUTS)
- Discover the color wheel for painting and learn how digital color (light and alpha channels) works as opposed to traditional painting materials
- Focus on proper layer management for easy, non-destructive manipulation of art pieces quickly

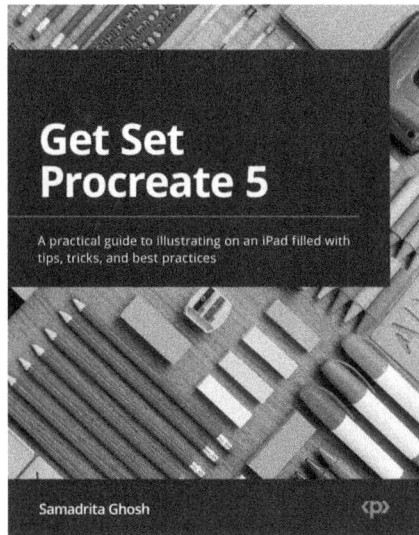

Get Set Procreate 5

Samadrita Ghosh

ISBN: 978-1-80056-300-1

- Become well-versed with the fundamentals of Procreate
- Personalize the Procreate application to suit your workflow
- Gain preliminary knowledge of the tool to further explore it for your artwork
- Speed up your workflow with gestures and shortcuts
- Explore, edit, and create a wide range of brushes with the help of Brush Library and Brush Studio
- Use assisted drawing tools to enhance your accuracy
- Learn animation using Procreate s Animation Assist tools
- Get up-to-date with the new features of Procreate 5.2 like Page Assist and 3D painting.

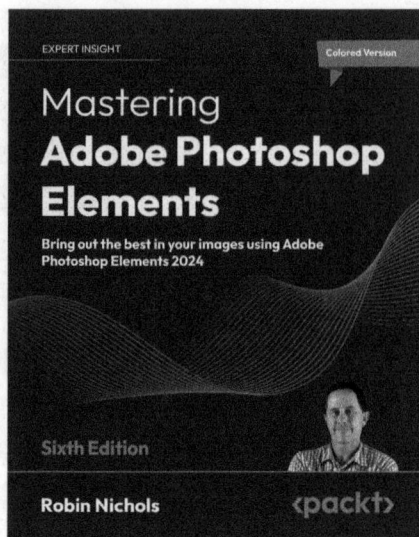

Mastering Adobe Photoshop Elements

Robin Nichols

ISBN: 978-1-83546-938-5

- Master new features in Photoshop Elements 2024, including AI-powered tools and one-click fixes on mobile
- Create captivating photo collages, digital paintings, and graphic designs
- Efficiently organize your photo collections for easy access and management
- Enhance your social media presence with professionally edited photos and artworks
- Employ advanced layer techniques for more powerful and immersive illustrations
- Gain comprehensive knowledge to become a proficient Photoshop Elements user

Packt is searching for authors like you

If you're interested in becoming an author for Packt, please visit `authors.packtpub.com` and apply today. We have worked with thousands of developers and tech professionals, just like you, to help them share their insight with the global tech community. You can make a general application, apply for a specific hot topic that we are recruiting an author for, or submit your own idea.

Share Your Thoughts

Now you've finished *Mastering Clip Studio Paint*, we'd love to hear your thoughts! Scan the QR code below to go straight to the Amazon review page for this book and share your feedback or leave a review on the site that you purchased it from.

`https://packt.link/r/1-805-12403-X`

Your review is important to us and the tech community and will help us make sure we're delivering excellent quality content.